CHALLENGE OR CRISIS?

CHALLENGE OR CRISIS?

Texts by
Pope John Paul II

Edited and arranged by
Seamus O'Byrne

with a Foreword by
✠ Brendan Comiskey

VERITAS

First published 1987 by
Veritas Publications
7-8 Lower Abbey Street
Dublin 1

Copyright © Seamus O'Byrne, 1987

ISBN 0 86217 238 1

Cover design: Eddie McManus
Typesetting by Printset & Design Ltd, Dublin
Printed in the Republic of Ireland by
Mount Salus Press Ltd, Dublin

LIST OF CONTENTS

	Editor's Note	1
	Foreword by ✠ Brendan Comiskey	2
1.	Address to the Women Religious of Rome — 10 November 1978.	3
2.	Address to the Union of Mothers General — 16 November 1978.	6
3.	Address to Superiors General of Men Religious — 24 November 1978.	9
4.	Address to the Sisters of Mexico — 27 January 1979.	13
5.	Address to Enclosed Nuns, Guadalajara — 30 January 1979.	15
6.	Address to General Chapter, O.F.M. — 21 June 1979.	18
7.	Address to Religious, Maynooth — 1 October 1979.	20
8.	Address to Brothers, Chicago — 4 October 1979.	22
9.	Address to Sisters, Washington — 7 October 1979.	25
10.	Apostolic Exhortation *Catechesi Tradendae* — 16 October 1979.	29
11.	Address to Religious of St Pius V Parish, Rome — 28 October 1979.	29
12.	Homily: Union of Women Superiors General — 14 November 1979.	32
13.	Address: Union of Men Superiors General — 26 November 1979.	36
14.	Address: Chapter Members of Daughters of Charity — 11 January 1980.	39
15.	Address to Brothers — 12 January 1980.	41
16.	Homily: Mass for Religious — 2 February 1980.	45
17.	Message to Congregation for Religious and for Secular Institutes — 7 March 1980.	47
18.	Address to Sisters, Kinshasa — 3 May 1980.	52
19.	Address: Carmelite Convent, Nairobi — 7 May 1980.	56
20.	Letter to Superior General of the De La Salle Brothers — 13 May 1980.	59
21.	Address to Italian Benedictine Abbesses — 22 May 1980.	62
22.	Address to Sisters, Rue du Bac, Paris — 31 May 1980.	65

23. Address to Contemplative Nuns, Lisieux — 2 June 1980. 68
24. Address to the Union of Major Superiors of France — 2 June 1980. 71
25. Address to Sisters, Sao Paulo — 3 July 1980. 72
26. Address to Men Religious, Sao Paulo — 3 July 1980. 79
27. Address to Benedictines, Monte Cassino — 20 September 1980. 83
28. Address to Union of Women Major Superiors of Italy — 11 October 1980. 87
29. Homily: Mass for Religious, Altötting — 18 November 1980. 90
30. Homily: Mass for Religious — 2 February 1981. 96
31. Address to Sisters, Baclaran — 17 February 1981. 98
32. Homily: Mass for Religious, Manila — 17 February 1981. 103
33. Address to Sisters, Nagasaki — 26 February 1981. 107
34. Address to Episcopal Vicars for Religious, U.S.A. — 20 March 1981. 109
35. Address to Participants in Congress on *Mutuae Relationes* — 30 April 1981. 112
36. Letter to the Superior General of the Vincentians — 12 May 1981. 115
37. Letter to the Superior General of the Discalced Carmelites — 14 October 1981. 119
38. Address: S. Cong. for Religious and Secular Institutes — 20 November 1981. 122
39. Address to the De La Salle Brothers — 21 November 1981. 126
40. Apostolic Constitution *Familiaris Consortio* — 22 November 1981. 128
41. Address to Men Superiors General — 28 November 1981. 129
42. Address to the Salesian Sisters — 12 November 1982. 132
43. Address to Religious, Ibadan, Nigeria — 15 February 1982. 135
44. Address to Jesuit Major Superiors — 27 February 1982. 138
45. Address to Priests and Religious, Montenero — 12 March 1982. 148

46.	Address to Clergy and Religious, Fatima — 13 May 1982.	151
47.	Address to Religious, London — 29 May 1982.	160
48.	Address to Priests and Religious, Edinburgh — 31 May 1982.	163
49.	Letter to the Discalced Carmelite Nuns — 31 May 1982.	165
50.	Address to Chapter Members, Capuchins — 5 July 1982.	169
51.	Address to Cloistered Nuns, Avila — 1 November 1982.	172
52.	Address to Men Religious, Madrid — 2 November 1982.	176
53.	Address to Sisters, Palermo Cathedral — 21 November 1982.	183
54.	Address to Chapter Members, St John of God Brothers — 17 December 1982.	186
55.	Address to Cloistered Nuns, Greccio — 2 January 1983.	188
56.	Address to Women Religious, Costa Rica — 3 March 1983.	190
57.	Address to Men Religious, Guatemala — 7 March 1983.	194
58.	Letter to the Bishops of the U.S.A. — 3 April 1983.	198
59.	Address to the Union of Mothers General — 13 May 1983.	203
60.	Address to Religious, Milan — 20 May 1983.	208
61.	Address to Chapter Members, O.F.M. Conv. — 9 July 1983.	211
62.	Address to Women Religious, Lourdes — 15 August 1983.	214
63.	Address to Chapter Members, Augustinians — 25 August 1983.	216
64.	Address to the General Congregation of the Jesuits — 2 September 1983.	220
65.	Address to Chapter Members, Dominicans — 5 September 1983.	227
66.	Homily at Mariazell — 13 September 1983.	234
67.	Address to Group of U.S. Bishops — 19 September 1983.	239
68.	Address to the Major Superiors of Europe — 17 November 1983.	244
69.	Homily to Religious — 2 February 1984.	248

70. Apostolic Exhortation *Redemptionis Donum* —
    25 March 1984. ... 252
71. Address to Chapter Members of Salesians — 3 April
    1984. ... 275
72. Address to the Religious of Switzerland, Fribourg —
    13 June 1984. ... 278
73. Homily: Mass for Contemplative Nuns, Hull, Canada
    — 19 September 1984. ... 282
74. Address to the Chapter Members of the
    Redemptorists — 18 November 1985. ... 287
75. Address to the Congregation for Religious and for
    Secular Institutes – 24 January 1986. ... 289
76. Address to the Society of St Paul – 22 March 1986. ... 293
78. Address to Chapter Members of the Passionists –
    14 October 1988. ... 300
Index ... 304

EDITOR'S NOTE

Since his election, Pope John Paul II has spoken and written much on religious life. This book contains a selection of these talks and writings — some destined for religious in general and others addressed specifically to members of the larger, more representative religious families.

The text has been taken from the English language edition of the *Osservatore Romano*, with the permission of the Libreria Editrice Vaticana. The material is arranged in chronological order and is presented here as an aid to meditations and talks on religious life. Thanks are due to all who helped in its publication.

It is hoped that the repetition and overlap, inevitable in a collection of this kind, will serve to highlight key points of the Holy Father's teaching.

Seamus O'Byrne

FOREWORD

What Pope Paul VI said of the Second Vatican Council could well be said about religious life and especially about any religious community's engagement in renewal. Any religious community on a path of renewal has three questions to answer:
- from what point are we to set out?
- what road do we intend to travel?
- what goal do we propose to reach?

The history of religious life shows the life cycle of any religious community as having five major parts or eras. In the first place there is the era of institutional origin in which a Founder intuits the unspoken needs in a society and responds to these in the light of the Gospel. Next comes the period of expansion which in turn is followed by a period of stabilisation. Fourthly there is a period of breakdown during which morale drops, productivity deteriorates and membership starts to decline. Fewer people are attracted to the group and lifelong members begin to question its value. Some even leave.

This period of breakdown may signal the 'death' of a religious community — more than two-thirds of all religious orders founded before 1800 are no longer in existence — or it may usher in a time of transition. The Vatican Council described this period of transition as one of returning to the standards of the Gospel, the spirit of the Founder, the needs of the members and the circumstances of the age.

No one would claim that the task of reading the signs of the times, of seeing through the filter of the Gospel the new needs of the world around them, is an easy task for any religious family. All who are concerned about the renewal of religious life will welcome, therefore, this invaluable resource booklet containing as it does no fewer than seventy-three addresses of Pope John Paul II on religious life. What more authentic guide and interpreter could be brought along the path of renewal?

Father Seamus O'Byrne has placed us all in his debt: religious men and women and their communities; retreat masters, chapter and assembly facilitators; priests, bishops and laity and all who look upon religious life as a gift given by God to his people, the Church.

✠Brendan Comiskey
Bishop of Ferns

Address to the Women Religious of Rome
10 November 1978

Dear Sisters, I welcome all of you gathered here today. I wish to greet you in the first place as the new Bishop of Rome and I wish to specify your place in this local church, in this actual diocese, of which I am preparing to take possession solemnly on Sunday next. Judging by the living centuries-old tradition of the Church, by the recent doctrine of the Second Vatican Council and also by my previous experience as a bishop, I come here with the deep conviction that this is a special place.

This is seen from the vision of man and of his vocation which Christ himself expressed to us. *"Qui potest capere, capiat"* (Mt 19:12) ("He who is able to receive this, let him receive it"); thus he spoke to his disciples who were asking him insistent questions on the legislation of the Old Testament and especially on the legislation regarding marriage. In these questions, as also in the tradition of the Old Testament , there was included a certain limitation of that freedom of the children of God which Christ brought us, and which St Paul, subsequently, confirmed so forcefully. The religious vocation is precisely the fruit of this freedom of spirit, reawakened by Christ, from which there springs the availability of complete giving to God himself. The religious vocation lies in the acceptance of a severe discipline, which does not come from an order, but from an evangelical counsel; the counsel of chastity, the counsel of poverty, the counsel of obedience. And all that, embraced consciously and rooted in love for the Divine Bridegroom, is, in fact, the particular revelation of the depth of the freedom of the human spirit. Freedom of the children of God: sons and daughters.

This vocation is derived from a living faith, consistent with the ultimate consequences, which opens up to a man the final perspective, that is, the perspective of the meeting with God himself, who alone is worthy of a love above everything, an exclusive and nuptial love. This love consists of the giving of our whole human being, body and soul, to him who gave himself completely to us men by means of the Incarnation, the Cross and abasement, by means of poverty, chastity, obedience. He became poor for us ...so that we might become rich (cf. 2 Co 8:9). In this way, therefore, the religious vocation takes life from these riches of living faith. This vocation is, as it were, the spark which lights a bright flame of love in the soul, as St John of the Cross wrote. This vocation, once accepted, once solemnly confirmed by means of the vows, must continually be nourished by the riches of faith; not only when it brings with it inner joy, but also when it is accompanied by difficulties, aridity, and inner suffering, which is called the "night" of the soul.

This vocation is a special treasure of the Church, which can never cease to pray that the Spirit of Jesus Christ will bring forth religious vocations in souls. They are, in fact, both for the community of the people of God, and for the world, a living sign of the future life: a sign which, at the same time, is rooted (also by means of your religious habit) in the everyday life of the Church and of society, and permeates its most delicate tissues. The persons who have loved God unreservedly are particularly capable of loving man, and of giving themselves to him without personal interests and without limits. Do we need proofs? We can find them in every age of the Church's life; we find them also in our times. During my preceding episcopal ministry, I met such testimonies at every step. I remember the institutes and hospitals for the seriously ill and for the handicapped. Everywhere, where no one could render service as a good Samaritan any longer, there was always still a Sister to be found.

This is certainly only one of the fields of activity, and therefore only an example. These fields are certainly far more numerous, in actual fact. Well, meeting you here today for the first time, dear Sisters, I wish to tell you, in the first place, that your presence is indispensable in the whole Church, and especially here in Rome, in this diocese. It must be a visible sign of the Gospel for all. It must also be the source of a particular apostolate. This apostolate is so varied and rich that it is even difficult for me to list here all its forms, its fields, its orientations. It is united with the specific charism of every congregation, with its apostolic spirit, which the Church and the Holy See approve with joy, seeing in it the expression of the vitality of the Mystical Body of Christ! This apostolate is usually discreet, hidden, near to the human being, and so is more suited to a woman's soul, sensitive to her neighbour, and hence called to the task of a sister and mother. It is precisely this vocation which is at the very heart of your religious being. As Bishop of Rome I beg you: be spiritually mothers and sisters for all the people of this Church which Jesus, in his ineffable mercy and grace, has wished to entrust to me. Be such for everyone, without exception, but especially for the sick, the suffering, the abandoned, the children, the young, families in difficult situations... Go out towards them!

Do not wait for them to come to you! Look for them yourselves! Love drives us to do so. Love must seek! *"Caritas Christi urget nos* — the love of Christ drives us!" *(2 Co 5:14).*

And I entrust to you another request at the beginning of this pastoral ministry of mine: commit yourselves generously to collaborating with the grace of God, in order that many young souls may accept the Lord's call and new forces come to swell your ranks, to meet the growing requirements that are emerging in the vast fields of the modern apostolate. The first form of collaboration is certainly assiduous invocation to the Lord of the harvest to enlighten and guide the hearts of the many girls "in quest" who certainly exist, today too, in this diocese, as in every part of the world. May they understand that there is no greater ideal to which to dedicate their lives, than that of the complete gift of themselves to Christ for the service of the kingdom. But there is a second way, no less important, of assisting God's call, and it is that of the witness that emanates from your lives:

— the witness, in the first place, of sincere consistency with Gospel values and with the specific charism of your institute: any surrender to compromise is a disappointment for those who approach you, do not forget!

— the witness, moreover, of a harmonious and mature personality, which is able to establish relations with others without unjustified prejudices or ingenuous imprudence, but cordial openness and serene balance;

— the witness, finally, of your joy, a joy that can be read in your eyes and in your attitude as well as in your words; a joy which clearly manifests, to those who look at you, awareness of possessing that "hidden treasure", that "pearl of great value", the purchase of which takes away all regret at having renounced everything in accordance with the evangelical counsel (cf. *Mt 13:44-45*).

And now, before concluding, I wish to address a special word to the dear enclosed Sisters, to those present at this meeting and to those who are in their austere enclosure, chosen for a special love of the Divine Bridegroom. I greet you all with particular intensity of sentiments, and in spirit I visit your convents, apparently closed, but actually so deeply open to the presence of God living in our human world, and therefore so necessary for the world. I commend to you the Church and Rome; I commend to you men and the world! To you, to your prayers, to your "holocaust" I commend also myself, the Bishop of Rome. Be with me, close to me, you are "in the heart of the Church"! May there be fulfilled in each of you that which was the programme of life for St Therese of the Child Jesus: "I will be love in the heart of the Church!"

In this way I end my first meeting with the Sisters of Rome. In you continues the extraordinary sowing of the Gospel, the extraordinary expression of that call to holiness which the Council recently recalled to us in the Constitution on the Church. I expect a great deal from you. I place great hopes in you. I wish to enclose and express all this in the blessing which I willingly impart to you.

I commend you to Mary, the Bride of the Holy Spirit, the Mother of the noblest love!

O.R. 556   23 November 1978

Address to the Union of Mothers General
16 November 1978

Dear Sisters, *"Ecce quam bonum et jucundum habitare fratres in unum..."* You love this psalm and you are living it at this moment. The time when religious congregations met but little, for geographical reasons and others perhaps, is practically over. God be praised! And congratulations to you, too, my Sisters: you bear witness, in various ways, to one treasure entrusted by Christ himself to his Church, the incomparable treasure of the evangelical counsels!

Certainly, your International Union of Mothers General is just emerging from infancy. It is only thirteen years old! But it has already yielded good fruit. The new Pope, like his very deserving predecessor Paul VI, who received you so many times, would like it to yield even more. The famous parable of the vine and the vinedresser must often be present to my spirit and yours.

Your meeting had as its subject "Religious life and new mankind". It is a fundamental subject, a very old one and very relevant today. Though the whole people of God is called to become a new mankind in Christ through Christ (cf. *Lumen Gentium,* 5), the ways of access to this new mankind, in other words to holiness, are different and must remain so. Precisely chapter six of *Lumen Gentium,* without making the least discrimination among members of the people of God which would contradict the redeeming plan of Christ Jesus —

a plan of holiness and unity for the world — always illumines your way.

Since the Council, the religious congregations have in fact multiplied the times and the means of deepening essential religious values. They have rightly put them back into the wake of the primary, ontological, ineffaceable consecration which is baptism. And all Sisters have, as it were, conveyed to one another a password: "Let us first be Christians!", a certain number preferring or adding the following: "Let us first be women!". It is evident that the two do not exclude each other. These striking formulae have found a favourable echo in a large part of the people of God. But the positive side of this awareness cannot dispense with continuous and prudent vigilance. The treasure of the evangelical counsels and the commitment — taken after mature reflection and irrevocable — to make them the charter of a Christian existence cannot be relativised by public opinion, even if it were ecclesial. The Church and, let us say, the world itself need, more than ever, men and women who sacrifice everything to follow Christ in the way of the apostles. And to such an extent that the sacrifice of conjugal love, of material possessions, of the completely autonomous exercise of freedom, becomes incomprehensible without love of Christ.

This radicalism is necessary to proclaim prophetically, but always very humbly, this new mankind according to Christ, completely available for God and completely available for other men. Every woman religious must bear witness to the primacy of God and must dedicate a sufficiently long period of time every day to stand before the Lord, to tell him her love, and above all to let herself be loved by him. Every woman religious must signify every day, by her way of life, that she chooses simplicity and poor means for everything that concerns her personal and community life. Every woman religious must do God's will and not her own every day, to signify that human plans, hers and those of society, are not the only plans in history, but that there exists a plan of God which calls for the sacrifice of one's own freedom. This real prophetic element of the evangelical counsels, lived day after day, and altogether possible with the grace of God, is not a proud lesson given to the Christian people. It is a light absolutely indispensable for the life of the Church — which is sometimes tempted to have recourse to the means of power — and even indispensable for mankind wandering along the alluring and disappointing paths of materialism and atheism.

And if your consecration to God is really such a deep reality, it is not unimportant to bear permanently its exterior sign which a simple and suitable religious habit constitutes: it is the means to remind yourselves constantly of your commitment which contrasts strongly with the spirit of the world; it is a silent but eloquent testimony; it is a sign that our secularised world needs to find on its way, as many Christians, moreover, desire. I ask you to turn this over carefully in your minds.

That is, my Sisters, the price of your realistic participation in the proclamation and the building up of this new mankind. For man cannot be fully satisfied — beyond earthly goods, necessary for his life and, alas! so badly shared out — except by knowledge and love of God, inseparable from acceptance and love of all men, especially the poorest on the human and moral plane. All the efforts, all the transformations of your congregations, must be carried out in this perspective, otherwise you are working in vain!

All that, my Sisters, is the ideal towards which you are striving personally, and towards which you draw along your companions of the evangelical way in a motherly and firm manner. In practice, you know it better than others, from time to time you come up against unavoidable contingencies: either the rapid social changes in a country, or the small number and aging of your subjects, or again the wind of interminable researches and experiments, the requests of the young, etc... Accept all these realities. Take them seriously, never tragically. Seek calmly for progressive, clear, and courageous solutions. While remaining yourselves, seek with others. Above all, be daughters of the Church, not only in words but in deeds! In ever-renewed faithfulness to the charism of their founders, the congregations must, in fact, endeavour to meet the expectations of the Church and the commitments which the Church, with her pastors, considers most urgent today in order to face up to a mission which needs skilled workers so much. A guarantee of this exemplary love of the Church — inseparable from love of Christ Jesus — is your dialogue with those in charge of your local Churches, with a resolution of faithfulness and devotion to these Churches; also guarantees are your trustful relations with our Congregation for Religious and for Secular Institutes. Dear Sisters, the capital of generosity of your congregations is immense. Use these forces responsibly. Do not allow them to be scattered thoughtlessly.

I ask you to express to each of your Sisters, whatever her place may be in the congregation for which you are responsible, the Pope's affection but also the hope that he sets in her for the renewal of an exacting practice of the evangelical counsels, for the significant witness of all religious communities whose ardent faith, apostolic inspiration and, of course, interpersonal relations would make those who are seeking new ways in our society harassed by materialism, violence and fear, say: "we have found a model to imitate..." Yes, my Sisters, in the Church herself, in the footsteps of St Catherine of Siena and of St Teresa of Avila, among so many others, you can show the place that is due to woman.

May the Holy Spirit act powerfully in you! With Mary, who was perfectly docile to him, live listening to God's word and put it into practice, unto the cross. May your complete gift to Christ always be a source of joy, dynamism and peace! To all of you, to all those whom you represent, our Apostolic blessing.

O.R. 557   30 November 1978

Address to Superiors General of Religious Orders of Men
24 November 1978

Beloved Sons, this is my first opportunity to meet the Superiors General of the male Orders, a meeting to which I attach particular importance. When I see you gathered here, there appear before my eyes magnificent figures of saints, the great saints who gave rise to your religious families: Basil, Augustine, Benedict, Dominic, Francis, Ignatius of Loyola, Francis de Sales, Vincent de Paul, John Baptist de La Salle, Paul of the Cross, Alphonsus Liguori. And then nearer to us, there are Joseph Benedict Cottolengo, John Bosco, Vincent Pallotti; not to speak of the most recent ones, whose holiness still awaits the definitive judgment of the Church, but whose beneficial influence is testified by the host of generous souls who have chosen to follow their example.

All these names — and I have mentioned only some — bear witness that the ways to holiness, to which the members of the people of God are called, passed and still pass, to a great extent, through the religious life. This should not surprise us, since religious life is based on the most precise recipe for holiness, which is constituted by love realised according to the evangelical counsels.

Furthermore, each of your Founders, under the inspiration of the

Holy Spirit promised by Christ to the Church, was a man who possessed a particular charism. Christ had in him an exceptional instrument for his work of salvation, which especially in this way is perpetuated in the history of the human family. The Church has gradually assumed these charisms, evaluated them and, when she found them authentic, thanked the Lord for them and tried to put them in a safe place in the life of the community, so that they could always yield fruit.

This was recalled by the Second Vatican Council, which stressed how the ecclesiastical hierarchy, on which there falls the task of feeding the people of God and leading them to good pastures, "in docile response to the promptings of the Holy Spirit accepts rules of religious life which are presented for its approval by outstanding men and women, improves them further and then officially authorises them. It uses its supervisory and protective authority, too, to ensure that religious institutes established all over the world for building up the Body of Christ may develop and flourish in accordance with the spirit of their founders." *(Lumen Gentium, 45, 1).*

This is what I desire first of all to recognise and express during our first meeting. I do not intend here to make reference to the past, understood as a historical period that is concluded in itself; I intend to refer to the life of the Church in her deepest dynamics. To her life, as it is presented before us, **today,** bringing with it the riches of the traditions of the past, to offer us the possibility of taking advantage of them **today.**

The religious vocation is a great problem of the Church of our time. For this very reason it is necessary in the first place to reaffirm forcefully that it belongs to that spiritual fullness which the Spirit himself — the Spirit of Christ — brings forth and moulds in the people of God. Without religious orders, without consecrated life, by means of vows of chastity, poverty and obedience, the Church would not be fully herself. Religious, in fact "at the deepest level of their being are caught up in the dynamism of the Church's life, which is thirsty for the divine Absolute and called to holiness. It is to this holiness that they bear witness. They embody the Church in her desire to give herself completely to the radical demands of the beatitudes. By their lives they are a sign of total availability to God, the Church and the brethren" (Paul VI: Apostolic Exhortation *Evangelii Nuntiandi, 69).*

Accepting this axiom, we must examine with all perspicacity how the religious vocation must be helped today to become aware of itself and mature, and how religious life must function in the life of the

contemporary Church as a whole. To this question we are still seeking an answer — and rightly so. We can find it:
a) in the teaching of the Second Vatican Council;
b) in the Exhortation *Evangelii Nuntiandi*;
c) in the many statements of the Pontiffs, the Synods and the Episcopal conferences.

This answer is a fundamental and multiform one. One postulate, however, seems to stand out particularly therein: if the whole life of the Church has two dimensions, the vertical and the horizontal, the religious orders must take the vertical dimension into account above all!

It is well known that the religious orders have always set great store by the vertical dimension, entering life with the Gospel and bearing witness to it with their own example. With the gospel re-read authentically: that is, on the basis of the teaching of the Church and in faithfulness to her magisterium. It must be so today also. *Testificatio — sic, contestatio — non!*

On every community, on every religious there weighs a particular co-responsibility for the real presence of Christ, who is meek and humble of heart, in the world of today — of the Crucified and Risen Christ — Christ among brothers: the spirit of evangelical maximalism, which is differentiated from any socio-political radicalism. "At the same time as being a challenge to the world and to the Church herself, this silent witness of poverty and abnegation, of purity and sincerity, of self-sacrifice in obedience", which religious are called to bear, "can become an eloquent witness capable of touching also non-Christians who have good will and are sensitive to certain values" *(Evangelii Nuntiandi, 69, 2).*

The joint document of the Sacred Congregation for Religious and Secular Institutes and of the Sacred Congregation of Bishops indicates what the relationship of the orders and religious congregations must be with the episcopal college, the bishops of individual dioceses and the episcopal conferences. It is a document of great importance, to which special attention should be devoted in the next few years, in the attempt to assume the interior attitude of maximum availability, in harmony, moreover, with that humble and ready docility, which must be a distinctive note of the true religious.

Wherever you are in the world, you are, with your vocation, "for the universal Church", through your mission "in a given local Church". Therefore your vocation for the universal Church is realised in the structures of the local Church. Every effort must be made that consecrated life may develop in the individual local Churches, in order that it may contribute to their spiritual building up, in order that it may constitute their particular strength. Unity with the universal Church, through the local Church: that is your way.

Before concluding, allow me to return to a point which I consider a fundamental one in the life of every religious, whatever may be the family to which he belongs: I mean the contemplative dimension, the commitment to prayer. The religious is a man consecrated to God, by means of Christ, in the charity of the Spirit. This is an ontological datum which demands to emerge to consciousness and to orientate life, not only for the benefit of the individual person, but also for the advantage of the whole community, which, in consecrated souls, experiences and enjoys in a quite special way the life-bringing presence of the divine Bridegroom.

You must not be afraid, therefore, beloved sons, to remind your confreres frequently that a pause for true worship has greater value and spiritual fruit than the most intense activity, were it apostolic activity itself. This is the most urgent "contestation" that religious must oppose to a society in which efficiency has become an idol, on the altar of which human dignity itself is not infrequently sacrificed.

Your houses must be, above all, centres of prayer, meditation and dialogue — personal and of the whole community — with him who is and must remain the first and principal interlocutor in the industrious succession of your days. If you are able to nourish this climate of intense and loving communion with God, it will be possible for you to carry forward, without traumatic tensions or dangerous confusion, that renewal of life and discipline, to which the Second Vatican Ecumenical Council committed you.

The soul that lives in habitual contact with God and moves within the warm range of his love, can easily protect itself from the temptation of particularisms and oppositions, which created the risk of painful divisions. It can interpret in the right evangelical light the option for the poorest and for every victim of human selfishness, without surrendering to socio-political radicalisations, which in the long run turn out to be inopportune, self-defeating and often causes of new forms of tyranny. It can approach people and take its place in the midst of the people, without questioning its own religious identity, or dimming that specific originality of its own vocation, which derives from the pecular following of Christ, poor, chaste and obedient.

These, beloved sons, are the reflections which I was anxious to submit to your consideration in this first meeting of ours. I am certain that you will not fail to undertake to transmit them to your confreres, enriching them with the contribution of your experience and your wisdom. May you be assisted in your delicate task by the Blessed Virgin! She, whom my predecessor Paul VI of venerable memory indicated in his Apostolic Exhortation *Marialis Cultus* as the Virgin listening, the Virgin in prayer, the Virgin who begets Christ and offers him for the salvation of the world, remains the unsurpassable model of every consecrated life. May it be she who acts as your guide in the laborious but fascinating ascent towards the ideal of full assimilation with Christ the Lord.

I accompany the wish with my Apostolic Blessing.

O.R. 558.　　　　　　　　　　　　　　　　　　　　7 December 1978

Address to the Sisters of Mexico

27 January 1979

Beloved Religious Daughters of Mexico, this meeting of the Pope with Mexican Sisters, which was to have been celebrated in the Basilica of Our Mother of Guadalupe, takes place here in her spiritual presence; before her, the perfect model of woman, the best example of a life dedicated entirely to her Son the Saviour, in a constant inner attitude of faith, hope, and loving dedication to a supernatural mission.

In this privileged place and before this figure of the Virgin, the Pope wishes to pass some moments with you, the many Sisters present here, who represent the more than 20,000 scattered all over Mexico and outside their homeland.

You are a very important force within the Church and within society itself, spread in innumerable sectors such as the schools and colleges, the clinics and hospitals, the field of charity and welfare, parish work, catechesis, the groups for apostolate, and so many others. You belong to different religious families, but with the same ideal within different charisms: to follow Christ, to be living witnesses to his everlasting message.

Yours is a vocation which deserves the highest esteem on the part of the Pope and the Church, yesterday and today. For this reason

I wish to express to you my joyful confidence in you, and encourage you not to be discouraged along the way that you have undertaken, which is worth continuing with renewed spirit and enthusiasm. Be assured that the Pope accompanies you with his prayer, and that he delights in your faithfulness to your vocation, to Christ and to the Church.

At the same time, however, allow me to add some reflections which I propose for your consideration.

It is certain that a praiseworthy spirit of faithfulness to their own ecclesial commitment prevails in a good many Sisters, and that aspects of great vitality can be seen in religious life with a return to a more evangelical view, growing solidarity among religious families, greater closeness to the poor, who are given rightful priority of attention. These are reasons for joy and optimism.

But there are not lacking, either, examples of confusion with regard to the very essence of consecrated life and one's own charism. Sometimes prayer is abandoned and it is replaced by action; the vows are interpreted according to the secularising mentality which dulls the religious motivations of one's own state; community life is abandoned with a certain irresponsibility; socio-political attitudes are adopted as the real aim to pursue, even with well-defined ideological radicalisations.

And when the certainties of faith are sometimes dimmed, motives are put forward such as the seeking of new horizons and experiences, perhaps with the pretext of being closer to men, maybe concrete groups, chosen with criteria that are not always evangelical.

Beloved Sisters: never forget that to maintain a clear concept of the value of your consecrated life you need a deep vision of faith, which is nourished and preserved with prayer (cf. *Perfectae Caritatis*, 6). This faith will enable you to overcome all uncertainty with regard to your own identity, and will keep you faithful to that vertical dimension which is essential for you in order to identify you with Christ from the Beatitudes, and in order to be true witnesses to the kingdom of God for men of the modern world.

Only with this concern for the interests of Christ (cf. *1 Co 7:32*) will you be capable of giving to the charism of prophecy its suitable dimension of witness to the Lord: without options for the poor and needy which do not spring from the criteria of the Gospel, but are inspired by socio-political motivations which — as I said recently to the Mothers Superiors General in Rome — turn out in the long run to be inopportune and self-defeating.

You have chosen as your way of life the pursuit of some values which are not merely human ones, although you must also esteem the latter in their rightful measure. You have opted for service of others for love of God. Never forget that the human being is not exhausted in the earthly dimension only. You as professionals of faith and experts in the sublime knowledge of Christ (cf. *Ph 3:8*), open them to the call and dimension of eternity in which you yourselves must live.

I would have many other things to tell you. Take as said to you what I indicated to the Mothers Superiors General in my address of 16 November last. How much you can do today for the Church and for mankind! They are waiting for your generous commitment, the dedication of your free heart, expanding in an unsuspected way its potentialities of love in a world that is losing the capacity of altruism, self-sacrificing and disinterested love. Remember, in fact, that you are mystical brides of Christ and of Christ crucified (cf. *2 Co 4:5*).

The Church repeats to you today her trust: be living witnesses to this new civilisation of love, which my predecessor Paul VI rightly proclaimed.

In order that strength from above may support you in this magnificent and hopeful enterprise, that it will keep you in renewed spiritual youth faithful to these resolutions, I accompany you with a special Blessing, which I extend to all the Sisters in Mexico.

O.R. 568   12 February 1979

Address to Enclosed Nuns at Guadalajara

30 January 1979

Beloved Enclosed Sisters, in the Cathedral of Guadalajara, I wish to greet you with the beautiful and expressive words that we frequently repeat in the liturgical assembly: "May the Lord be with you" *(Roman Missal)*. Yes, may the Lord, to whom you have dedicated your whole life, always be with you.

How could a meeting of the Pope with contemplative Sisters fail to take place during the visit to Mexico? If I would like to see so many persons, you have a special place because of your particular consecration to the Lord and to the Church. For this reason, the Pope too, wishes to be close to you.

This meeting wishes to be the continuation of the one I had with other Mexican Sisters. I said many things to them which are also for you, but now I wish to refer to what is more specifically yours.

How often the Magisterium of the Church has shown its great esteem for, and appreciation of, your life dedicated to prayer, silence and to an exceptional way of dedication to God! In these moments when everything is changing so much, does this type of life continue to have a meaning or is it something that is already outdated?

The Pope tells you: Yes, your life is more important than ever, your complete consecration is fully relevant today. In a world that is losing the sense of the divine, in the light of the over-estimation of material things, you, beloved Sisters, committed from your cloisters to be witnesses of certain values for which you live, be witnesses to the Lord for the world of today, and instil with your prayer a new breath of life into the Church and into modern man.

Especially in contemplative life, it is a question of realising a difficult unity: to manifest to the world the mystery of the Church in this world and to enjoy here already, teaching them to men, as St Paul says, "the things that are above" *(Col 3:1)*.

Being a contemplative does not mean breaking radically with the world, with the apostolate. The contemplative has to find her specific way of extending the kingdom of God, of collaborating in the building up of the earthly city, not only with her prayers and sacrifices, but also with her testimony, silent, it is true, yet which can be understood by the men of good will with whom she is in contact.

For this reason you have to find your own style which, within a contemplative vision, will let you share with your brothers the gratuitous gift of God.

Your consecrated life comes from baptismal consecration and expresses it with greater fullness. With a free response to the call of the Holy Spirit, you decided to follow Christ, consecrating yourselves to him completely. "The more stable and firm this bond (the unbreakable bond of union that exists between Christ and his Church) is," — the Council says — "the more perfect will the Christian's religious consecration be" *(Lumen Gentium, 4)*.

You contemplative religious women feel an attraction that brings you to the Lord. Relying on God, you abandon yourselves to his fatherly action which raises you to him and transforms you into him, while he prepares you for eternal contemplation which is the ultimate goal for us all. How could you advance along this path and be faithful to the grace that animates you, if you did not respond with your whole being, by means of a dynamism the impulse of which is love, to this call that directs you permanently to God? So, consider any other activity as a testimony, offered to the Lord, of your deep communion with him, so that he may grant you that purity of intention which is so necessary in order to meet him in prayer itself. In this way you will contribute to the extension of the kingdom of God, with the testimony of your life and with a "hidden apostolic fruitfulness" *(Perfectae Caritatis, 7)*.

Gathered in Christ's name, your communities have as their centre the Eucharist, "a sacrament of love, a sign of unity, a bond of charity" *(Sacrosanctum Concilium, 47)*.

Through the Eucharist, the world also is present at the centre of your life of prayer and offering, as the Council explained: "Let no one think that their consecrated way of life alienates religious from other men or makes them useless for human society. Though in some cases they have no direct relations with their contemporaries, still in a deeper way they have their fellow men present with them in the heart of Christ and cooperate with them spiritually, so that the building up of human society may always have its foundation in the Lord and have him as its goal: otherwise those who build it may have laboured in vain" *(Lumen Gentium, 46)*.

Contemplating you with the tenderness of the Lord when he called his disciples "little flock" (cf. *Lk* 12:32) and announced to them that his Father had been pleased to give them the Kingdom, I beg you: keep the simplicity of the "little ones" of the Gospel. Know how to find it in intimate and deep relations with Christ and in contact with your brothers. You will then know "overflowing joy through the action of the Holy Spirit", the joy of those who are introduced into the secrets of the Kingdom (cf. *Apostolic Exhortation on the Renewal of Religious Life, 54)*.

May the beloved Mother of the Lord, whom you invoke in Mexico with the sweet name of Our Lady of Guadalupe, and following whose example you have dedicated your life to God, obtain for you, on your daily path, that unfailing joy that only Jesus can give.

Receive my warm Apostolic Blessing as a great greeting of peace which is not exhausted in you present here, but which extends invisibly to all your contemplative Sisters in Mexico.

O.R. 568.   12 February 1979

Address to Chapter Members of the Friars Minor
21 June 1979

Dear sons, members of the General Chapter of Friars Minor, it gives us great pleasure to grant you this special audience and we greet you wholeheartedly...

We ask you to let sink deeply into your minds and hearts the words with which our first encyclical letter begins: "The Redeemer of man, Jesus Christ, is the centre of the universe and of history". The implication of these words must be made known to you; namely your Order must regain the vitality it had at the beginning to make it suitable to make Christ known to the world, and following the example of your Seraphic Father to give that witness of love for the Church which he gave in an outstanding way.

To discover that former vitality you are led, we think rightly, to the very place where the General Chapter is being held. We are speaking of the convent of Saint Mary of the Angels, where, as Saint Bonaventure relates, your illustrious father "began in a humble way, made progress in virtue, and died happily". For it was there that he carried out in a remarkable way that penance he had planned for himself from the beginning of his life of dedication to God. But to achieve any kind of spiritual renewal it is necessary to begin with penance, which is the same as *metanoia*, that is, a change of heart. Certainly on this condition the sons of St Francis will fulfil their vocation.

On this fidelity to your original way of life depends also the effectiveness of the role you will play in the salvific work of the Church in so far as you devote yourselves and your works to the ministry of the Gospel whilst adhering strictly to the magisterium of the Church.

Therefore accept the fatherly exhortation which the Roman Pontiff gives you today. Love the Church as St Francis loved it. Love it more than yourselves. Give up, if necessary, the ways of thinking and living, which, if suited to the past, are now less appropriate to promote the vitality of the Church and to extend the horizons of its charity.

Whilst renewing this ecclesial vocation of yours you must comply with the will of the Seraphic Father who sent his brethren to all parts of the world to preach peace and penance to men for the remission of sins. Make contact with men in the very conditions of their daily lives. Assist and cultivate that divine seed which is in them (cf. *1*

Jn 3:9), so that they may come to know the incarnate Son of God and accept him and become children of God.

No one, as is well known, understood the sacredness of creation as did St Francis, who — to use the words of our venerated predecessor Paul VI -"after he had left all things for Christ, through'lady poverty' experienced, so to say, something of that initial joy when the whole world came forth from the hands of the Creator. In this complete renunciation of things, when he was already almost blind, he was able to sing the immortal Canticle of Creatures, and likewise the praises of our brother Sun; the praises of the things in the whole of nature which had become for him a clear and pure reflection of the divine glory" (Apostolic Exhortation *Gaudete in Domino, 4*).

Therefore it is also part of your vocation to teach men to relate the things of this world to the work of salvation, and while they dwell upon these things, to lead them at the same time to a hope which transcends all created things.

Dear Franciscans, since you have been constituted as religious in the very depth of your Christian conscience, as it were, we have addressed these words to you to strengthen you, to stimulate you, and to invite you to a daily greater keenness such as is proper that you may be co-operators of the successor of blessed Peter "upon whom was imposed in a special way the great duty of spreading the Christian name" *(Lumen Gentium, 23)*.

May the holy Mother of God guard and protect you! For she has a special place in your theological tradition, especially regarding the mystery of the Immaculate Conception. Through this mystery she became the most perfect human type of the Church, which Christ, its founder, wanted to be "having no spot or wrinkle, but holy and without blemish" (cf *Ep 5:27*). Imitate Mary, who was entirely devoted to the will of God. Listen to her who gives you this exhortation concerning her Son: "Whatsoever he shall say to you, do it" *(Jn 2:5)*.

Finally to strengthen you always to respond zealously to your noble Franciscan vocation, with the loving sentiments of a father we impart to you here present and to your entire religious family the Apostolic Blessing.

O.R. 591   23 July 1979

Address to Religious at Maynooth

1 October 1979

......I wish to speak a special word to religious Brothers. The past decade has brought great changes, and with them problems and trials unprecedented in all your previous experience. I ask you not to be discouraged. Be men of great truth, of great and unbounded hope. "May the God of hope bring you such joy and peace in your faith that the power of the Holy Spirit will remove all bounds to hope" *(Rm 15:13)*. The past decade has also brought a great renewal in your understanding of your holy vocation, a great deepening of your liturgical lives and your prayer, a great extension of the field of your apostolic influence. I ask God to bless you with renewed fidelity in vocation among your members, and with increased vocations to your Institutes. The Church in Ireland and on the missions owes much to all the Institutes of Brothers. Your call to holiness is a precious adornment of the Church. Believe in your vocation. Be faithful to it. "God has called you and he will not fail you" *(1 Th 5:23)*.

The Sisters too have known years of searching, sometimes perhaps of uncertainty or of unrest. These have also been years of purification. I pray that we are now entering a period of consolidation and of construction. Many of you are engaged in the apostolate of education and the pastoral care of youth. Do not doubt the continuing relevance of that apostolate, particularly in modern Ireland, where youth are such a large and important part of the population. The Church has repeatedly, in many solemn recent documents, reminded religious of the primary importance of education, and has invited congregations of men and women with the tradition and the charism of education to persevere in that vocation and to redouble their commitment to it. The same is true of the traditional apostolates of care of the sick, nursing, care of the aged, the handicapped, the poor. These must not be neglected while new apostolates are being undertaken. In the words of the Gospel, you must "bring out from (your) storeroom things both new and old" (cf. *Mt 13:52*). You must be courageous in your apostolic undertakings, not letting difficulties, shortage of personnel, insecurity for the future, deter or depress you.

But remember always that your field of apostolate is your own personal lives. Here is where the message of the Gospel has first to be preached and lived. Your first apostolic duty is your own sanctification. No change in religious life has any importance unless it be also conversion of yourselves to Christ. No movement in religious life has any importance unless it be also movement inwards to the "still centre" of your existence, where Christ is. It is not what you do that matters most; but what you are, as women consecrated to God. For you, Christ has consecrated himself, so that you too "may be consecrated in truth" (cf. *Jn 17:19*).

To you and to priests, diocesan and religious, I say: Rejoice to be witnesses to Christ in the modern world. Do not hesitate to be recognisable, identifiable, in the streets as men and women who have consecrated their lives to God and who have given up everything worldly to follow Christ. Believe that contemporary men and women set value on the visible signs of the consecration of your lives. People need signs and reminders of God in the modern secular city, which has few reminders of God left. Do not help the trend towards "taking God off the streets" by adopting secular modes of dress and behaviour yourselves!

My special blessing and greeting goes to the cloistered Sisters and contemplatives, men as well as women. I express to you my gratitude for what you have done for me by your lives of prayer and sacrifice since my papal ministry began. I express the Pope's need for you, the Church's need for you. You are foremost in that "great, intense and growing prayer" for which I called in *Redemptor Hominis*. Never was the contemplative vocation more precious or more relevant than in our modern restless world. May there be many Irish boys and girls called to the contemplative life at this time when the future of the Church and the future of humanity depends on prayer.

Gladly do I repeat to all contemplatives, on this feast of Saint Therese of Lisieux, the words I used in addressing the Sisters of Rome: "I commend to you the Church; I commend mankind and the world to you. To you, to your prayers, to your 'holocaust' I commend also myself, Bishop of Rome. Be with me, close to me, you who are the heart of the Church! May there be fulfilled in each of you that which was the programme of life for Saint Therese of the Child Jesus: "I will be love in the heart of the Church'!......

To all of you I say: this is a wonderful time in the history of the Church. This is a wonderful time to be a priest, to be a religious, to be a misionary for Christ. Rejoice in the Lord always. Rejoice in your vocation. I repeat to you the words of Saint Paul: "I want you to be happy, always happy in the Lord; I repeat, what I want is your happiness. There is no need to worry; but if there is anything you need, pray for it, asking God for it with prayer and thanksgiving and that peace of God which is so much greater than we can understand, will guard your hearts and your thoughts, in Christ Jesus" *(Ph 4:4-7)*.

Mary, Mother of Christ, the Eternal Priest, Mother of priests and of religious, will keep you from all anxiety, as you "wait in joyful hope for the coming of our Lord and Saviour, Jesus Christ". Entrust yourselves to her, as I commend you to her, to Mary, Mother of Jesus and Mother of his Church.

O.R. 603.   15 October 1979

Address to Brothers at Chicago

4 October 1979

Brothers in Christ, "I thank my God whenever I think of you; and every time I pray for you I pray with joy, remembering how you have helped to spread the Good News for the day you first heard it right up to the present" *(Ph 1:3-5)*. These words of St Paul express my feelings this evening. It is good to be with you. And I am grateful to God for your presence in the Church and for your collaboration in proclaiming the Good News.

Brothers, Christ is the purpose and the measure of our lives. In the knowledge of Christ, your vocation took its origin; and in his love, your life is sustained. For he has called you to follow him more closely in a life consecrated through the gift of the evangelical counsels. You follow him in sacrifice and willing generosity. You follow him in joy "singing gratefully to God from your hearts in psalms, hymns, and inspired songs" *(Col 3:16)*. And you follow him in fidelity, even considering it an honour to suffer humiliation for the sake of his name (cf *Acts 5:41*).

Your religious consecration is essentially an act of love. it is an imitation of Christ who gave himself to his Father for the salvation of the world. In Christ, the love of his Father and his love for mankind are united. And so it is with you. Your religious consecration has not only deepened your Baptismal gift of union with the Trinity, but it has also called you to greater service of the people of God. You are united more closely to the person of Christ, and you share more fully in his mission for the salvation of the world.

It is about your share in the mission of Christ that I wish to speak this evening.

Let me begin by reminding you of the personal qualities needed to share effectively with Christ in his mission. In the first place, you must be interiorly free, spiritually free. The freedom of which I speak is a paradox to many; it is even misunderstood by some who are members of the Church. Nevertheless it is the fundamental human freedom, and it was won for us by Christ on the Cross. As St Paul said: "We were still helpless when at his appointed moment Christ died for sinful men" *(Rm 5:6)*.

This spiritual freedom which you received in Baptism you have sought to increase and strengthen through your willing acceptance of the call to follow Jesus more closely in poverty, chastity and obedience. No matter what others may contend or the world may believe, your promises to observe the evangelical counsels have not shackled your freedom: you are not less free because you are obedient; and you are not less loving because of your celibacy. On the contrary. The faithful practice of the evangelical counsels accentuates your human dignity, liberates the human heart and causes your spirit to burn with undivided love for Christ and for his brothers and sisters in the world (cf. *Perfectae Caritatis, 1, 12*).

But this freedom of an undivided heart (cf. *1 Co 7:32-35*) must be maintained by continual vigilance and fervent prayer. If you unite yourself continually to Christ in prayer, you shall always be free and ever more eager to share in his mission.

Secondly, you must centre your life around the Eucharist. While you share in many ways in the passion, death and Resurrection of Christ, it is especially in the Eucharist where this is celebrated and made effective. At the Eucharist, your spirit is renewed, your mind and heart are refreshed and you will find the strength to live day by day for him who is the Redeemer of the world.

Thirdly, be dedicated to God's word. Remember the words of Jesus: "My mother and my brothers are those who hear the word of God and put it into practice" *(Lk 8:21)*. If you sincerely listen to God's word, and humbly but persistently try to put it into practice, like the seed sown in fertile soil his word will bear fruit in your life.

The fourth and final element which makes effective your sharing in Christ's mission is fraternal life. Your life lived in religious community is the first concrete expression of love of neighbour. It is there that the first demands of self-sacrifice and generous service are exercised in order to build up the fraternal community. This love which unites you as brothers in community becomes in turn the force which supports you in your mission for the Church.

Brothers in Christ, today the universal Church honours St Francis of Assisi. As I think of this great saint, I am reminded of his delight in God's creation, his childlike simplicity, his poetic marriage to "Lady Poverty", his missionary zeal and his desire to share fully in the Cross of Christ. What a splendid heritage he has handed on to those among you who are Franciscans, and to all of us.

Similarly, God has raised up many other men and women outstanding in holiness. These too he destined to found religious families which, each in a distinctive way, would play an important role in the mission of the Church. The key to the effectiveness of every one of these religious institutes has been their faithfulness to the original charism God had begun in their founder or foundress for the enrichment of the Church. For this reason, I repeat the words of Paul VI: "Be faithful to the spirit of your founders, to their evangelical intentions and to the example of their holiness... It is precisely here that the dynamism proper to each religious family finds its origin" *(Evangelica Testificatio, 11-12)*. And this remains a secure basis for judging what specific ecclesial activities each institute, and every individual member, should undertake in order to fulfil the mission of Christ.

Never forget the specific and ultimate aim of all apostolic service: to lead the men and women of our day to communion with the Most Holy Trinity. In the present age, mankind is increasingly tempted to seek security in possessions, knowledge and power. By the witness of your life consecrated to Christ in poverty, chastity and obedience, you challenge this false security. You are a living reminder that Christ alone is "the way, the truth and the life" *(Jn 14:6)*.

Religious brothers today are involved in a wide range of activities: teaching in Catholic schools, spreading God's word in missionary activity, responding to a variety of human needs by both your witness and your actions, and serving by prayer and sacrifice. As you go forward in your particular service, keep in mind the advice of St Paul: "Whatever you do, work at it with your whole being. Do it for the Lord rather than for men" *(Col 3:23)*. For the measure of your effectiveness will be the degree of your love for Jesus Christ.

Finally, every form of apostolic service, of either an individual or a community, must be in accord with the Gospel as it is put forward by the magisterium. For all Christian service is aimed at spreading the Gospel; and all Christian service incorporates Gospel values. Therefore be men of God's word: men whose hearts burn within them when they hear the word proclaimed (cf. *Lk 24:32*); who shape every action according to its demands; and who desire to see the Good News proclaimed to the ends of the earth.

Brothers, your presence in the Church and your collaboration in promoting the Gospel are an encouragement and joy to me in my role as Pastor of the whole Church. May God give each of you long life. May he call many others to follow Christ in the religious life. And may the Virgin Mary, Mother of the Church and model of consecrated life, obtain for you the joy and consolation of Christ, her Son.

O.R. 605   29 October 1979

Address to Sisters at Washington

7 October 1979

Dear sisters, may the grace, love and peace of God our Father and our Lord Jesus Christ be with you.

I welcome this opportunity to speak with you today. I am happy for this occasion because of my esteem for religious life, and my gratitude to women religious for their invaluable contribution to the mission and very life of the Church.

I am especially pleased that we are gathered here in the National Shrine of the Immaculate Conception, for the Virgin Mary is the model of the Church, the Mother of the faithful and the perfect example of consecrated life.

On the day of our Baptism, we received the greatest gift God can bestow on any man or woman. No other honour, no other distinction will equal its value. For we were freed from sin and incorporated in Christ Jesus and his Body, the Church. That day and every day after, we were chosen "to live through love in his presence" *(Ep 1:4)*.

In the years that followed our Baptism, we grew in awareness — even wonder — of the mystery of Christ. By listening to the Beatitudes, by meditating on the Cross, conversing with Christ in prayer and receiving him in the Eucharist, we progressed towards the day, when we solemnly ratified with full awareness and freedom our Baptismal consecration. We affirmed our determination to live always in union with Christ, and to be, according to the gifts given us by the Holy Spirit, a generous and loving member of the people of God.

Your religious consecration builds on this common foundation which all Christians share in the Body of Christ. Desiring to perfect and intensify what God had begun in your life by Baptism, and discerning that God was indeed offering you the gift of the evangelical counsels, you willed to follow Christ more closely, to conform your life more completely to that of Jesus Christ, in and through a distinctive religious community. This is the essence of religious consecration: to profess within and for the benefit of the Church, poverty, chastity and obedience in response to God's special invitation, in order to praise and serve God in greater freedom of heart (cf. *1 Co 7:34-35*) and to have one's life more closely conformed to Christ in the manner of life chosen by him and his blessed Mother (cf. *Perfectae Caritatis,* 1; *Lumen Gentium,* 46).

Religious consecration not only deepens your personal commitment to Christ, but it also strengthens your relationship to his spouse, the Church. Religious consecration is a distinctive manner of living in the Church, a particular way of fulfilling the life of faith and service begun in Baptism.

On her part, the Church assists you in your discernment of God's will. Having accepted and authenticated the charisms of your various institutes, she then unites your religious profession to the celebration of Christ's Paschal Mystery.

You are called by Jesus himself to verify and manifest in your lives and in your activities your deepened relationship with his Church. This bond of union with the Church must also be shown in the spirit and apostolic endeavours of every religious institute. For faithfulness to Christ, especially in religious life, can never be separated from faithfulness to the Church. This ecclesial dimension of the vocation of religious consecration has many important practical consequences for institutes themselves and for each individual member. It implies, for example, a greater public witness to the Gospel, since you represent, in a special way as women religious, the spousal relationship of the Church to Christ. The ecclesial dimension also requires, on the part of individual members as well as entire institutes, a faithfulness to the original charisms which God has given to his Church, through your founders and foundresses. It means that institutes are called to continue to foster, in dynamic faithfulness, those corporate commitments which were related to the original charism, which were authenticated by the Church, and which still fulfil important needs of the people of God. A good example in this regard would be the Catholic school system which has been invaluable for the Church in the United States, an excellent means not only for communicating the Gospel of Christ to the students, but also for permeating the entire community with Christ's truth and his love. It is one of the apostolates in which women religious have made and are still making an incomparable contribution.

Dear sisters in Christ: Jesus must always be first in your lives. His person must be at the centre of your activities — the activities of every day. No other person and no activity can take precedence over him. For your whole life has been consecrated to him. With St Paul you have to say: "All I want is to know Christ and the power of his Resurrection and to share his sufferings by reproducing the pattern of his death" *(Ph 3:10).*

Christ remains primary in your life only when he enjoys the first place in your mind and heart. Thus you must continuously unite yourself to him in prayer. Without prayer, religious life has no meaning. It has lost contact with its source, it has emptied itself of substance, and it no longer can fulfil its goal. Without prayer there can be no joy, no hope, no peace. For prayer is what keeps us in touch with Christ. The incisive words written in *Evangelica Testificatio* cause us all to reflect: "Do not forget the witness of history: faithfulness to prayer or its abandonment is the test of the vitality or decadence of religious life". *(no. 42).*

Two dynamic forces are operative in religious life: your love for Jesus — and, in Jesus, for all who belong to him — and his love for you.

We cannot live without love. If we do not encounter love, if we do not experience it and make it our own, and if we do not participate intimately in it, our life is meaningless. Without love we remain incomprehensible to ourselves (cf. *Redemptor Hominis,* 10).

Thus every one of you needs a vibrant relationship of love to the Lord, a profound loving union with Christ, your spouse, a love like that expressed in the psalm: "God, you are my God whom I seek, for you my flesh pines and my soul thirsts: like the earth, parched, lifeless and without water. Thus have I gazed towards you in the sanctuary to see your power and your glory" *(Ps 63:1-2).*

Yet far more important than your love for Christ is Christ's love for you. You have been called by him, made a member of his Body, consecrated in a life of the evangelical counsels and destined by him to have a share in the mission that Christ has entrusted to the Church: his own mission of salvation. For this reason, you centre your life in the Eucharist. In the Eucharist, you celebrate his death and Resurrection and receive from him the Bread of eternal life. And it is in the Eucharist especially that you are united to the One who is the object of all your love. Here, with him, you find ever greater reasons to love and serve his brothers and sisters. Here, with him — with Christ — you find greater understanding and compassion for God's people. And here you find the strength to persevere in your commitment to selfless service.

Your service in the Church is then an extension of Christ to whom you have dedicated your life. For it is not yourself that you put forward, but Christ Jesus as Lord. Like John the Baptist, you know that for Christ to increase, you must decrease. And so your life must be characterised by a complete availability: a readiness to serve as the needs of the Church require, a readiness to give a public witness to Christ whom you love.

The need for this public witness becomes a constant call to inner conversion, to justice and holiness of life on the part of each religious. It also becomes an invitation to each institute to reflect on the purity of its corporate ecclesial witness. And it is for this reason that in my address last November to the International Union of Superiors General I mentioned that it is not unimportant that your consecration to God should be manifested in the permanent sign of a simple and suitable religious garb. This is not only my personal conviction, but also the desire of the Church, often expressed by so many of the faithful.

As daughters of the Church — a title cherished by so many of your great saints — you are called to a generous and loving adherence to the authentic magisterium of the Church, which is a solid guarantee of the fruitfulness of all your apostolates and an indispensable condition for the proper interpretation of the signs of the times.

The contemplative life occupies today and for ever a place of great honour in the Church. The prayer of contemplation was found in the life of Jesus himself, and has been a part of religious life in every age. I take this opportunity therefore — as I did in Rome, in Mexico and in Poland — to encourage again all who are members of contemplative communities. Know that you shall always fulfil an important place in the Church, in her mission of salvation, in her service to the whole community of the people of God. Continue faithfully, confidently and prayerfully, in the rich tradition that has been handed down to you.

In closing, I remind you, with sentiments of admiration and love, that the aim of religious life is to render praise and glory to the Most Holy Trinity, and, through your consecration, to help humanity enter into fullness of life in the Father, and in the Son and in the Holy Spirit. In all your planning and in all your activities, try also to keep this aim before you. There is no greater service you can give; there is no greater fulfilment you can receive. Dear sisters; today and forever: Praised be Jesus Christ!

O.R. 606. 5 November 1979

Apostolic Exhortation ''Catechesi Tradendae''
16 October 1979

.....Many religious institutes for men and women came into being for the purpose of giving Christian education to children and young people, especially the most abandoned. Throughout history, men and women religious have been deeply committed to the Church's catechetical activity, doing particularly apposite and effective work. At a time when it is desired that the links between religious and pastors should be accentuated and consequently the active presence of religious communities and their members in the pastoral projects of the local Churches, I wholeheartedly exhort you, whose religious consecration should make you even more readily available for the Church's service, to prepare as well as possible for the task of catechesis according to the differing vocations of your institutes and the missions entrusted to you, and to carry this concern everywhere. Let the communities dedicate as much as possible of what ability and means they have to the specific work of catechesis.....

O.R. 607. 12 November 1979

Address to Religious Communities of St Pius V Parish, Rome   28 October 1979

Beloved brothers and sisters in the Lord, in this pastoral visit of mine, it was essential to have a special meeting with all of you, priests and men and women religious, who are numerous in this parish.

Therefore I happily find myself here with you, and express my joy to you all as a father, a brother and a friend: and at this short meeting I would like to suggest to you some thoughts that rise from the demands of our time.

What is the general characteristic of the time in which Providence has called upon us to live? It seems that we can answer that it is a great spiritual crisis: of intelligence, of religious faith and, consequently, of moral life.

We are called to live in this age of ours and therefore to love it in order to save it. What, then, does it require us to do?

Our time calls in the first place for deep philosophical and theological convictions.

Many failures in faith and in consecrated life, past and recent, and many present situations of distress and perplexity, have their origin in a crisis of a philosophical nature. It is necessary to dedicate serious efforts to one's own cultural formation. The Second Vatican Council stressed the necessity of always keeping St Thomas Aquinas as both teacher and doctor, because it is only in the light and on the basis of "perennial philosophy" that the edifice of Christian doctrine, both logical and demanding, can be founded. Leo XIII, of venerated memory, in his famous Encyclical *Aeterni Patris*, which still is relevant today, the centenary of which falls this year, stressed and illustrated in an admirable way the validity of the rational foundation for Christian faith.

Today, therefore, our first concern must be with truth, both for our interior needs and for our ministry. We cannot sow error or leave people in the shadow of doubt! Christian faith of the hereditary and sociological type becomes more and more demanding, and this is certainly a good thing, but we must have in order to be able to give! Let us remember what St Paul wrote to his disciple Timothy: "Guard what has been entrusted to you. Avoid the godless chatter and contradictions of what is falsely called knowledge, for by professing it some have missed the mark as regards the faith" *(1 Tm 6:20).*

It is a valid exhortation especially for our time, which is so thirsty for certainty and clarity and so deeply threatened and tormented.

Our time calls for mature and well-balanced personalities.

Ideological confusion gives rise to personalities that are immature and inadequate psychologically; pedagogy itself is seen to be uncertain and sometimes deviated. For this very reason the modern world is in painful pursuit of ideals, and as often as not is left disappointed, defeated and humiliated. Therefore we must be mature personalities, who are able to control our sensitivity, assume our own roles of responsibility and guidance, and try to reach fulfilment in the place and work in which we find ourselves.

Our time calls for serenity and courage to accept reality as it is, without depressing criticisms and without utopias, in order to love it and save it.

Endeavour, therefore, all of you, to reach these ideals of maturity, through love of duty, meditation, spiritual reading, examination of conscience, the methodical use of the Sacrament of Penance, and spiritual direction. The Church and modern society need mature personalities: we must be so, with God's help!

Finally, our time calls for a serious commitment with regard to our own sanctification.

The spiritual necessities of the present-day world are immense! If we look at the boundless forests of buildings in modern metropolises, invaded by numberless multitudes, we cannot but be frightened. How can we reach these persons and bring them to Christ?

We are helped by the certainty of being only instruments of grace: it is God himself who acts in the individual soul, with his love and his mercy.

Our real and constant goal must be that of personal sanctification, to be suitable and effective instruments of grace.

The truest and most sincere wish I can form for you is just this: "Make yourselves saints and do so quickly!", while I repeat to you the words of St Paul to the Thessalonians: "May the God of peace himself sanctify you wholly; and may your spirit and soul and body be kept sound and blameless at the coming of our Lord Jesus Christ" *(1 Th 5:23).*

Beloved in Christ, let us be happy to live in these times of ours and let us commit ourselves courageously to the plan that Providence carries out mysteriously, also through us.

St Pius V, "whose outstanding figure — John XXIII said — is united with the great ordeals that the Church had to go through in times far more difficult than our own", teaches us, too, to have recourse in our difficulties to Holy Mary, our heavenly Mother, who overcomes all errors and all heresies. Let us pray to her always, let us pray to her especially with the Holy Rosary, in order that our one supreme ideal may always be the salvation of souls.

I willingly impart to you my special Apostolic Blessing.

O.R. 610. 3 December 1979

Homily during Mass for the Union of Women Superiors General
14 November 1979

Dear sisters in the Lord, it is a great joy for me to meet you today, you who are particularly authorised representatives of the great riches that religious life constitutes in the Church. By means of it, in fact, a particularly evident testimony is offered of what complete donation to love and service of God means. I am happy at the same time to see and greet in you, as it were, the image of the universality of the Church. You represent here all the continents and the various cultures, and you manifest together the multiform realisation of the response to the Lord's call.

Through you I wish to affirm again to all Sisters the appreciation and trust that the Church has in them, not only on account of their intelligent, constant and generous apostolate, but even more because of the life of consecration, of dedication that is very often concealed, and of joyful and courageous acceptance of the inevitable trials and difficulties. I ask you to transmit my very special blessing to all Sisters sorely tried or exhausted in body and in spirit, to the old and the sick, whose lives of abnegation and sacrifice are an extremely precious, unique value, not to be renounced, for the Church, the Pope and the people of God.

I wish further that this Eucharistic celebration together with the Pope will be for each of you a salutary moment of encouragement and comfort in the accomplishment of a commitment that is always demanding, often accompanied by the sign of the Cross and by painful solitude, and which calls on your side for a deep sense of responsibility, a generosity without weakness or confusion, and constant forgetfulness of yourselves. You, in fact, must sustain and guide your fellow Sisters in this post-conciliar period, which is certainly rich in new experiences, but also so exposed to errors and deviations, which you try to avoid and correct. We all know the positive evolution of the last few years in religious life, which is interpreted with a more evangelical, more ecclesial and more apostolic spirit. However, it cannot be ignored that certain practical choices, even if prompted by good, but not always enlightened intentions, have not offered the world the true image of Christ, whom the Religious Sister should make present among men.

Finding yourselves gathered round the altar to renew Christ's offering to the Father, you feel yourselves intimately invited to repeat, also on behalf of your fellow Sisters, the consecration of yourselves which, already begun with Baptism, was made definitive and perfect by means of the religious vows.

Take to heart, therefore, my first exhortation to fervent and persevering prayer, in order that the importance of the religious vocation and the necessity of examining thoroughly its essential value, in the life of the Church and of society, may be more and more evident. The life-story of every woman religious, in fact, is centred on the nuptial love for Christ, as a result of which she, modelled by his spirit, gives him her whole life, adopting his sentiments, his ideals and his mission of charity and salvation. As I said already to the Sisters in Ireland: "No movement in religious life has any importance unless it be also movement inwards to the 'still centre' of your existence, where Christ is. It is not what you **do** that matters most; but what you **are,** as women consecrated to God" (1 October 1979).

— Pray that every Sister, living joyfully her unique and faithful relationship with Christ, may find in her consecration the highest fulfilment of her own characteristic reality as a woman, which seeks expression in self-giving.
— Pray confidently that every Institute may easily overcome its difficulties of growth and perseverance and that your annual meeting may contribute to an ever greater perfecting of the individual Congregations to which you belong.
— Finally, pray uninterruptedly for religious vocations: may the ideal of consecrated life, an immense and gratuitous gift from God, exert an ever greater attraction on numerous young women, straining towards the highest and most noble achievements.

May the subject chosen by the S. Congregation for Religious and for Secular Institutes for the next Plenary meeting, "the contemplative dimension of religious life", be a very special opportunity to become more deeply aware of the fundamental value of prayer. In this connection, I intend to address a fervent thought and a blessing to Sisters of contemplative life, whom I thank warmly for their intense and constant prayer, which is an irreplaceable help in the Church's mission of evangelisation.

My second exhortation, now, is a call to commit yourselves to religious witness in keeping with our time.

After the years of experience, aimed at updating religious life, according to the spirit of the Institute, the time has come to evaluate objectively and humbly the attempts made, to recognise their positive elements, and many deviations, and finally to prepare a

Rule of stable life, approved by the Church, which should constitute for all the Sisters a stimulus to deeper knowledge of their commitments and to joyful faithfulness in living them.

Let the first witness be that of filial adherence and unfailing faithfulness to the Church, Christ's bride. This link with the Church must be manifested in the spirit of your Institute and in its tasks of apostolate, because faithfulness to Christ can never be separated from faithfulness to the Church. "You are called to a generous and loving adherence to the authentic magisterium of the Church, which is a solid guarantee of the fruitfulness of all your apostolates and an indispensable condition for the proper interpretation of the signs of the times" *(Address to Sisters of the United States, 7 October 1979)*.

In imitation of Mary, the Virgin whose heart was always open to God's word, you must find your inner serenity, your joy, in availability for the word of the Church and of him whom Christ has placed as his Vicar on earth.

Let a second witness be that of community life.

The latter, in fact, is an important element of religious life. It has been a characteristic of the lives of religious persons from the beginning, because spiritual bonds cannot be created, developed and perpetuated unless through daily and prolonged relations. This community life, in evangelical charity, is closely linked with the mystery of the Church, which is a mystery of communion and participation, and gives proof of your consecration to Christ. Make every effort that this community life may be facilitated and loved, becoming in this way a precious means of mutual help and personal fulfilment. Special witness is also that of a religious garb. It constitutes, in fact, an evident sign of complete consecration to the ideals of the Kingdom of Heaven, always considering all due circumstances, such as, for example, tradition, the various fields of apostolic commitment, the environment, etc. It is also a sign of definitive detachment from merely human and earthly interests; it is a sign, furthermore, of poverty lived joyfully and loved in confident abandonment to God's providential action.

Beloved Superiors General, you must assume the delicate and sometimes difficult, but also precious task of promoting among religious women everything that can contribute to the union of mind and hearts. A sisterly, fervent and authentic life is indispensable in order that women religious may cope in a lasting way with the obligations, toil and difficulties that a life of consecration and apostolate entails in the world of today.

Your task in the happy realisation of such a life, deeply rooted in evangelical values, is of the utmost importance. The exercise of authority, is a spirit of service and love for all fellow Sisters, is a vital task, even though a difficult one, which calls for no little courage and dedication. The Superior has the duty to help the Sister to realise her vocation more and more perfectly. She cannot shirk this obligation, which is certainly an arduous one; but indispensable.

To carry out this duty calls for constant prayer, reflection, consultation, but also courageous decisions, in awareness of your responsibility before God, the Church and the Sisters themselves who expect this service. Weakness, like authoritarianism, are deviations that are equally harmful for the good of souls and the proclamation of the Kingdom.

In conclusion, I exhort you affectionately: have confidence. Always be courageous in your religious dedication; do not become disheartened by possible difficulties, by the reduction of personnel and by uncertainties as regards the future. Do not doubt the validity of tested forms of apostolate in the field of education of the young, for the sick, children, the old and all those who are suffering.

Be certain that if your Institutes strive sincerely to promote among the Sisters constant, generous and dynamic faithfulness to the requirements of their consecrated life, the Lord, who does not let himself be outdone in generosity, will send you the desired vocations you await for the advent of his Kingdom.

Attentive to the suggestions and to the words of Wisdom, as is fitting for persons called to carry out a high responsibility of government, and grateful to God, together with all your fellow Sisters, for the special vocation you have received, walk with serene confidence along the path of your commitment of total consecration to Christ and to souls. May the Most Holy Mary, the Mother and model of all consecrated persons, strengthen you and sustain you, and may my Apostolic Blessing accompany you with special benevolence.

O.R. 609.   26 November 1979

Address to Union of Men Superiors General
26 November 1979

Beloved brothers and sons, allow me to tell you openly my joy at receiving you today, in this house, as qualified members of the Council of the Union of Superiors General and therefore representatives of vast hosts of Religious scattered all over the world. I thank you for having desired this meeting, which enables me to address my cordial word to you.

The organism of which you are the expression, and which you represent, fosters not only greater fellowship among the various religious families, but also more compact action on their part within, and for the building up of, the holy Church. I hope it will always be so in actual fact.

My intention, here and now, is just to recall together with you some great aspects of religious life, which, by their nature, also inspire actual behaviour. The Conciliar Decree *"Perfectae Caritatis"*, on the renewal of religious life, contains the following already in the Introduction:, "All those who are called by God to the practice of the evangelical counsels, and who make faithful profession of them....live more for Christ and for his Body, the church (cf. *Col 1:24*). The more fervently, therefore, they join themselves to Christ by this gift of their whole life, the fuller does the Church's life become and the more vigorous and fruitful its apostolate" (no. 1).

Beloved in Christ, you represent in the Church a state of life that goes back to the first centuries of her history and which has always expressed in turn within the various religious families, abundant and savoury fruit of holiness, incisive Christian witness, efficacious apostolate, and even a considerable contribution to the formation of a rich heritage of culture and civilisation. Well, all this has been, and still is, possible precisely on the basis of that total and faithful union with Christ, of which the Council speaks, and which is not only asked of you but can also be favourably realised owing to the special status of religious consecrated to the Lord.

The charism peculiar to each of the Institutes represented by you is an eloquent sign of participation in the multiform riches of Christ, the "breadth and length and height and depth" *(Ep 3:18)* of which always far surpasses what we can realise when drawing upon their fullness. The Church, which is the visible face of Christ in time, receives, and nourishes within her, Orders and Institutes of such different style, because all together they contribute to revealing the variegated nature and the multiple dynamism of the incarnate Word of God and of the community of believers in him.

But there is another reason above all which justifies and demands the religious state. In an age and a world in which there is a proximate danger of constructing man with one dimension only, which inevitably ends up by being the historicist and immanentist one, religious are called to keep high the value and the sense of worshipping prayer, not separated from, but united with, the living commitment of generous service to men, which draws possibilities and impetus precisely from his prayer.

It is a question of a programme of life which it is particularly appropriate for religious, even more than for the secular clergy, to carry out and incarnate, by means of faithful and joyful observance of the evangelical counsels and with special emphasis on the immediate communion with him "who dwells in unapproachable light, whom no man has ever seen or can see:" *(1 Tm 6:16)*. Men must learn from you to pay him "honour and eternal dominion" *(ibid.)*, without thereby creating sterile conflicts with their temporal commitments, so that, in fact, they may thus find a salutary way of bringing things into perspective and a fruitful direction of elevation towards Christ, in whom all things are united, "things in heaven and things on earth" *(Ep 1:10)*.

Today's society wishes to see in your Families how much harmony exists between the human and the divine, between "things that are seen" and "things that are unseen" *(1 Co 4:18)*, and how much the latter surpass the former, never making them trivial or humiliating them, but giving them new life and raising them in accordance with the eternal plan of salvation. Prayer and work, action and contemplation: they are dual concepts which, in Christ, never deteriorate into antithetical opposition, but mature, complementing and integrating each other fruitfully. Well, the task of the witness of religious is precisely this: to show the world of today how much humanity there is in the mystery of Christ (cf. *Tt 3:4*) and at the same time how much commitment among men calls for the transcendental and the supernatural (cf. *Ps 127:1*).

This harmonious synthesis is, after all, also the real reason for your impact and the attraction you exert on the men and especially the young of today. And it is also on the basis of a healthy balance between human and Christian values that religious life can be renewed and purified and shine forth more and more, as everyone desires. Of course, there will be no lack of difficulties, risks and tensions, which you well know. But we must not labour under the illusion of solving the inevitable problems for a purely wordly standpoint or, on the contrary, a disembodied one. The most adequate yardstick of behaviour cannot but be the example of Jesus and our pure faith in him. It is from the Gospel, in fact, that there comes our sense of unshakeable adherence to the Father's will and at the same time a boldness which, however, is not rash, in our decisions, the sense of a courageous projection towards the future as well as prudent preservation of the rich spiritual heritage acquired in the past.

No step forward is possible, in any direction, unless starting from those already taken; but, vice versa, to stop at the latter is a sign of sterile stagnation. Furthermore, progress in an evangelical direction is certainly made at the level of individual holiness, but also at that of public witness to Christ. Now, he is the Lord of the whole of human history, not only the past but also the present and what still stretches out in front of us, and therefore requires an adherence that is always total but always adapted. The Apostle Paul, reminding the Galatians that "in Christ Jesus neither circumcision nor uncircumcision is of any avail, but faith working through love" *(Ga 5:6)*, has given all Christians a fundamental hermeneutical principle for their existence in the world, a principle which must hold good all the more clearly for religious. When one "holds fast to the Head", which is Christ *(Col 2:19)*, then one does not fear any changing historical conditioning, inculturation or obstacle, since everything, on the contrary, becomes valid material for inner progress, open witness and apostolic efficacy; provided that everything "may increase thanksgiving, to the glory of God" *(2 Co 4:15)*.

It is from here that we must all draw courage and confidence. From you, in particular, the Church expects a great deal by way of an impelling example of radical communion with Christ, which will naturally produce a generous commitment among men.

I propose these thoughts to you and to all those you worthily represent, urging you to meditate on them and keep them always in mind, not only in specific moments of prayer, but also and particularly in carrying out, even in small matters, the various educative, welfare, cultural, missionary and promotional activities in general, which are such a distinctive mark of yours. Precisely in consecrated persons, more than in other baptised persons, there must shine forth, as in Jesus, perfect symbiosis between moments of transfiguration (cf. *Lk 9:28-36*) and those of deep integration among the demanding multitude, which waits at the foot of the mountain (cf. *ibid., 9:37-43*).

If this task is not an easy one, if it requires a great ascetic effort and, even more, the abundant and indispensable grace of God, be certain that you do not lack my fatherly closeness and the comfort of my poor but constant prayer, in order that "the Lord make his face to shine upon you" *(Nb 6:25)* and that in you, men may see "the light of the gospel of the glory of Christ" *(2 Co 4:4)*.

To these good wishes I am happy to add my special Apostolic Blessing, in propitiation, and I extend it with equal benevolence to all your dear and well-deserving confreres.

O.R. 613.   24 December 1979

Address to Chapter Members of the Daughters of Charity of St Vincent de Paul

11 January 1980

Reverend Mother, Sisters, imagine with me that St Vincent de Paul and St Louise de Marillac, your two founders, so united in their evangelical passion to serve the poor, and who returned to the Lord within a few months of each other over three centuries ago, are present at this family meeting; and yet they are with us mysteriously. Allow me to leave it to them to speak, becoming their interpreter.

While you are pursuing the work of the General Assembly of the Company, those whom you venerated as your father and your mother wish in the first place to strengthen you in the relevance of your vocation today. The warmth of charity is what human beings need most of all today as always. Certainly, the social miseries of the seventeenth century and of the period of the Fronde are far away. But "the poor are always with us"! Who can give us precise statistics on real poverty in each country and on the world scale? Figures are often published which concern trade, agriculture, industry, banks, armaments, etc. But, in the age of computers, do we know the exact number of illiterates, abandoned children, undernourished, blind and infirm people, broken homes, prisoners, outcasts, prostitutes, unemployed, people living in the shanty towns of the whole world!... Dear Sisters, have eyes and hearts only for the poor, like St Vincent and St Louise! And to stimulate you more — if it were necessary — they say to you: Contemplate Our Lord Jesus Christ, listen to him as he recalls to you the meaning of his mission: "The Spirit of the Lord is upon me...he has anointed me to preach good news to the poor, he has sent me to proclaim release to the captives and recovering of sight to the blind, to set at liberty those who are oppressed..." *(Lk 4:18)*. It is true, the Gospel nearly always presents Christ to us among the poor. It is his sphere of life.

It seems to me also that these two great saints of charity entreat you tenderly and firmly to defend and develop your radical belonging to Jesus Christ, according to the promises that you renew every year on 25 March. Chastity, because of Christ and the Gospel, is their deepest sign. And far from being an alienation of the person, it is an astonishing promotion of every woman's capacities and needs of motherhood! You are mothers. You collaborate in the protection, the guidance, the blossoming, the cure, the peaceful end of so many lives, on the physical, moral and religious plane! Always see your consecrated celibacy as a way of life for others, and reveal this secret to the young who hesitate to undertake the way that you have followed. Not only love the poor, but love to be poor yourselves, in spirit and in acts. St Vincent de Paul and St Louise de Marillac said more with their concrete service of the poor — night and day — than with long treatises on poverty. Likewise St Francis of Assisi was more eloquent when he stripped off his clothes than if he had published a periodical review on detachment from earthly goods. And Charles de Foucauld brought more with his smile and his kindness in the midst of the poor than by publishing his autobiography as a converted young officer, having chosen to be in the position of humility and among the poor. It could also be recalled that my venerated predecessor Paul VI, in abandoning his tiara, carried out an act that is still bearing fruit in the Church.

Finally, you hear your two models of life urge you not to let the spirit of dependence disappear, whereas the tendency today is to keep a free space in which one does not depend on anyone, in order to indulge better one's imagination and flights of fancy. Religious obedience, as you know, is certainly the sharpest of the three gold nails which attach the imitators to the will of Jesus Christ. Is it possible to look at the cross of the Lord Jesus, without conforming to his mystery of obedience to the Father? That religious superiors should be human and understanding, is their duty! But let the subjects themselves be more and more adult and responsible, to the extent of deepening and living the value of obedience as oblation!

In a word, your founders tell you and all your companions: "Be in the world, without ever letting yourselves be contaminated by the spirit of the world, of which St John speaks". You know that salt, if diluted, becomes insipid. What shines forth is the purity of crystal!

To you, Reverend Mother, who have just been re-elected, I am particularly happy to address my good wishes for fruitful service of the Company. I give my affectionate Apostolic Blessing to the members of the Chapter, whom I thank for their visit, and to all the Daughters of Charity who serve Christ in his poor all over the world — without forgetting their highly appreciated service in the Vatican.

O.R. 618.   4 February 1980

Address to Brothers of Clerical and Lay Institutes
12 January 1980

Beloved sons, I am really happy to meet you this morning in the familiarity of this audience. I attach a special significance and affection to this talk. Today it is actually entirely for you, Brothers of the various Congregations, whose contribution is so important for the life and activity of the respective religious families, and, more in general, for the life of life of the whole Church. Receiving you, it is my intention to stress the appreciation that the Church has for your function, and to give space to some reflections which will highlight the specific aspects of your choice of life.

Opening to you, therefore, the doors of my house, beloved Brothers, I also open my heart and address to you an affectionate greeting which, through your persons, is intended to reach all lay religious Brothers scattered over the world, and to bring them the testimony of my sincere esteem and high appreciation.

You are called to walk towards perfection along the way of the evangelical counsels, professed with generous totality of commitment. You are, in fact, fully "religious". The Second Vatican Council, as you know, solemnly confirmed the principle according to which your choice of life "is a state for the profession of the evangelical counsels which is complete in itself" *(Perfectae Caritatis, 10)* and it had a special word to confirm you in your vocation (cf. *ibid.*), in order that, from renewed certainty about the validity of your commitment, there might be derived a strengthening of resolutions and a more generous impetus of creative dynamism.

Renew in yourselves, therefore, the awareness and joy of your state as consecrated persons; Christ must be the purpose and the measure of your lives. Your vocation had its origin in the meeting with him: faith in him determined the "yes" of your commitment, the hope of his help now supports its persevering fulfilment, the love that he has lit in your hearts nourishes the enthusiasm necessary for overcoming inevitable difficulties and for the daily renewal of your offer.

In Christ, who "came down from heaven for us men and for our salvation", you have also discovered the deep reason for your gift to brothers. This is a point that deserves a stop for reflection. Your religious consecration not only strengthened the baptismal gift of union with the Trinity, but also called you to greater service of the people of God.

You must live your service, whatever it may be, with your spirit open to the whole Church: you contribute to her life with your activity and with your witness (cf. *Lumen Gentium. 44*). Here it is opportune to come down to concrete matters, in the attempt to shed light on some characteristic aspects of the riches which your life as lay religious Brothers represents for the Church.

Your religious profession is set, in the first place, in the line of baptismal consecration, and expresses the bipolarity of the universal priesthood, which is based on this consecration. In life as lay religious, in fact, there takes place the offering of the spiritual sacrifice, the exercise of worship in spirit and truth, to which every Christian is called; at the same time, there rings out in it before the world a very clear proclamation of the marvels of salvation. A double direction, therefore, towards God and towards men, characterises your life; and at the basis of both there is the same one baptismal priesthood, in both there is expressed the same love spread in the heart by the Spirit (cf. *Rm 5:5*), in both there is lived in fullness the identical charism of the laity, conferred by the grace of the sacraments of Christian initiation.

There is more. The text of the Decree *Perfectae Caritatis* points out a particular form of ecclesial service which lay religious are called to carry out. They take part in a very useful way "in the exercise of its (the Church's) pastoral duty of educating the young, caring for the sick, and in its other ministries" *(no. 10)*, which are not further specified, but which each of you can well exemplify, thinking of the activity you carry out. Well, it is important that each of you should be fully aware of the essentially ecclesial character of your work, whatever it may be.

This is true above all since according to the interior dynamics of grace, your religious consecration, by its nature, directs to the life of the Mystical Body every form of activity to which you are called in virtue of obedience. The believer is well aware that the importance of his own contribution to the life of the Church does not depend so much on the type of activity he carries out, as rather on the amount of faith and love that he puts into the carrying out of his service, however humble it may seem.

I am anxious, furthermore, to stress the complementariness that exists between your witness and that of the secular laity. In fact, the witness of laymen, who live in the world, may be useful to you to remind you that your consecration must not make you indifferent to the salvation of men or to earthly progress, which is also desired by God. On the other hand, the laymen engaged in the world may be beneficially reminded by your witness that earthly progress is not an end in itself.

This puts you, if you permit the expression, at the point at which human realities and ecclesial, the kingdom of man and the Kingdom of God, are welded: with your material tasks on which the smooth operation of the whole community depends, with your apostolic service alongside your priest confreres, with your presence in the world of the school, work, and technology, you are called to carry out a function of connection both within your respective religious families in view of a better organic unity, and in the external world of professions and work, where you can play an extremely important role in helping to bring those environments closer to the Church.

It is clear that the delicacy of such a position also brings risks with it: there is, in fact, always the temptation of losing sight of eternal things, of becoming laicised, letting one's vital relations with God cool off and thus losing contact with the Source from which the nourishment and support of every activity is derived.

Your work, in fact, is seen to be a living expression of consecration to the Lord only if referred explicitly to him with a consciously renewed resolution of consecrated life. This presupposes, in the first place, a daily revision of life with regard to faithfulness to the commitments undertaken by religious profession. Be generous, beloved sons, in responding to the voice of Christ, who calls you to follow him closely by means of the practice of poverty, chastity and obedience.

Be able, furthermore, to preserve that "primacy of spiritual life" of which the Decree *Perfectae Caritatis* speaks (cf *No. 6*). Interior life is nourished — it is recalled there — by means of assiduous recourse to the genuine sources of Christian spirituality, which are Holy Scripture and the Liturgy.

In connection with the latter, always remember that conscious participation in liturgical prayer will help you to understand yourselves and the meaning of your presence in the Church more thoroughly. It is necessary to add, however, that such participation would not be possible, in the absence of the habit of personal prayer. Each one must learn to pray also within himself and by himself. Personal devotion, meditation cultivated in the intimacy of one's own spirit, filial and spontaneous conversation with God One and Three, dwelling in the depths of the soul, constitute the premise of truly liturgical prayer.

I wish to indicate another condition for the authenticity of your witness and for its full apostolic efficacy: to offer your cordial and responsible adherence to community life. Living in a religious community is a concrete expression of love for others, and it is a secret of serene and harmonious personal maturation. Acceptance of one's brother, with his qualities and his limitations, the effort to coordinate one's own initiatives with decisions matured together, the self-criticism imposed by continuous confrontation with the evaluations and points of view of others, become not only a very effective training ground of human and Christian virtues, but also a precious opportunity for constant verification of the earnestness with which one endeavours to put into practice in life the obligations assumed in the religious profession.

Beloved sons, who spend the best energies of your minds and hearts in the education of youth; and you who care for the sick with brotherly and patient dedication, seeing in them the suffering Christ (cf. *Mt* 25:36); and you again who offer your services, as precious as they are humble, alongside your priest confreres, be aware of the special mission entrusted to you, by the Lord, in the life of his Church.

Learn to cultivate a spirituality which, opening to perception of God's action in the world, will responsibly undertake the task of cooperating in carrying out his plans of salvation. You must endeavour with all the resources of your discernment to grasp the requirements of man, your contemporaries, and then try to meet them with all the riches of your heart. It is up to you to strive to use to advantage all the gifts of your intelligence, in order that your service may be more and more qualified and therefore more worthy of that Jesus, whom you are aware of meeting in every brother, towards whom you go, driven by love.

And be joyful in the daily exercise of your tasks, because it is written that "God loves a cheerful giver" *(2 Co 9:7)*. With this good wish, I entrust the generous resolutions you cherish in your hearts to the motherly intercession of the Blessed Virgin, your special Patroness and continual model in the hidden life at Nazareth; and, while I invoke on you and on your work the abundance of heavenly gifts and comforts, I grant to all my Apostolic Blessing, as a token of my special benevolence.

O.R. 618. 4 February 1980

Homily to Men and Women Religious

2 February 1980

.....You have gathered to take part in today's liturgy, you, dear Brothers and Sisters, who, by means of religious profession, have dedicated your life completely to God.

This consecration of yours to God, which is complete, definitive and exclusive, is, as it were, a continual growth and a splendid blossoming of that initial consecration, which took place in the Sacrament of Baptism; it has its deep roots in it and is a more perfect expression of it (cf. *Perfectae Caritatis, 5*).

By means of religious profession — as the dogmatic Constitution *Lumen Gentium* affirms — the Christian "consecrates himself wholly to God, his supreme love. In a new and special way he makes himself over to God, to serve and honour him. True, as a baptised Christian he is dead to sin and dedicated to God; but he desires to derive still more abundant fruit from the grace of his baptism. For this purpose he makes profession in the Church of the evangelical counsels. He does so for two reasons: first, in order to be set free from hindrances that could hold him back from loving God ardently and worshipping him perfectly, and secondly, in order to consecrate himself in a more thorough-going way to the service of God" *(44)*.

For this reason the feast of the Presentation of the Lord is a special feast for you, consecrated souls, since you participate to an exceptional extent in Christ's donation to the Father, which was announced at the Presentation at the Temple. The offering of your life, which you made joyfully by means of the three vows, finds its constant model, its prize, its encouragement, in the offering of himself, that the Word of God makes to the Father and in his Mother's arms.

Simeon utters the words about light before Jesus, at the moment of the Presentation.

Also your lives, beloved Brothers and Sisters, must be a "light", such as to illuminate the world and temporal reality. In the midst of everything that passes, vanishes and disappears, you, consecrated souls, real sons and daughters of light (cf. *Ep 5:8; 1 Th 5:5*), must bear truthful witness to future light, to eternal light, to undying light. The Second Vatican Council recalled this to you forcefully: "All the members of the Church should unflaggingly fulfil the duties of their Christian calling. The profession of the evangelical counsels shines before them as a sign which can and should effectively inspire them to do so. For the people of God has here no lasting city but seeks the city which is to come. The religious state of life, in bestowing greater freedom from the cares of earthly existence on those who follow it, simultaneously reveals more clearly to all believers the heavenly goods which are already present in this age, witnessing to the new and eternal life which we have acquired through the redemptive work of Christ preluding our future resurrection and the glory of the heavenly kingdom" *(Lumen Gentium, 44).*

The words of Jesus apply to you in a very special way: "Let your light so shine before men, that they may see your good works and give glory to your Father who is in heaven" *(Mt 5:14-16; cf. 1 P 2:12).* Yes, Brothers and Sisters! Let it shine forth, the light of your strong faith; the light of your active charity; the light of your joyful chastity; the light of your generous poverty!

How much the Church and the world need this light, this witness!

What an effort we must make in order that its full splendour and its intact eloquence be realised!

How necessary it is that we should reproduce in ourselves, mortal beings, the mystery of Christ's dedication to the Father for the salvation of the world; the dedication which started marvellously with this Presentation at the Temple, the memory of which the whole Church is celebrating today.

How necessary it is that we, too, should fix our eyes on Mary's soul, this soul which, in the words of Simeon, was pierced by a sword that thoughts out of many hearts may be revealed (cf. *Lk 2:35).*

Today, dear Brothers and Sisters, as a sign of that great mystery of the liturgy, and simultaneously of the mystery of your hearts, you present to me the lighted candles. The consecration of the

Temple is multiplied, in a way, through the dedication of so many consecrated hearts in the world...
May the thoughts of all these hearts be revealed before the Mother, who knows your consecration and surrounds it with special love.
This Mother is Mary.
This Mother is also the Church.
Amen.

O.R. 620. 18 February 1980

Address to the Congregation for Religious and for Secular Institutes 7 March 1980

.....You have wished to send me the testimony not only of the sincere affection — so willingly returned — that binds you to the Vicar of Christ, but also of the will that has sustained your work in these days, with the aim of bringing it about that men and women religious in the world, by means of faithful adherence to the teachings of the Gospel, may live in deeper communion with the Church.

Expressing to you my gratitude for this commitment, I am happy to confirm to you, in the first place, my convinced appreciation for what the specific charism of religious life represents in the structure of the Mystical Body. It is a great treasure in the Church; without religious Orders, without consecrated life, the Church would not be fully herself.

In fact the profession of the evangelical counsels makes it possible for those who have received this special gift to conform more deeply to that life of chastity, poverty and obedience, which Christ chose for himself and which Mary, his Mother and Mother of the Church embraced (cf. Apostolic Exhortation *Evangelica Testificatio no. 2*), as a typological model for the Church herself. At the same time, this profession is a very special testimony of the constant search for God and absolute dedication to the growth of the kingdom, to which Christ invites those who believe in him (cf. *Mt 6:33*). Without this concrete sign, the "salt" of faith would run the risk of being diluted in a world that is being secularised, such as the present one (cf. *Evangelica Testificatio, 3*).

It is clear that, to remain faithful to their consecration to the Lord and to be able to offer a visible testimony of it, religious must perfect their charity, in the dialogue of prayer with God. To keep perception of the value of consecrated life quite clear, a deep vision of faith is necessary, and this is sustained and nourished by means of prayer.

The subject chosen for this Plenary Meeting must, therefore, be considered of prime importance and I am certain that from this meeting of yours there will derive for all religious a precious encouragement to persevere in the commitment of bearing witness before the world to the primacy of man's relationship with God. Strengthened by the indications which will spring from your meeting in Rome, they will not fail to dedicate, with renewed conviction, a sufficiently long time to pauses of prayer before the Lord, to tell him their love and, above all, to feel loved by him.

Without prayer, religious life loses its meaning and does not reach its purpose. The incisive words of *Evangelica Testificatio* make us reflect: "Do not forget the witness of history: faithfulness to prayer or its abandonment are the model of the vitality or decadence of religious life" *(n. 42)*.

During these days, you have made an effort to study deeply the value of contemplation on the one hand, and, on the other, the opportune ways to immerse the religious life more and more into it. In the case of religious of apostolic life, it will be a question of promoting integration between interiority and activity. Their first duty, in fact, is that of being with Christ. A constant danger for apostolic workers is to become so much involved in their own work for the Lord, as to forget the Lord of all work.

It will be necessary, therefore, for them to become increasingly aware of the importance of prayer in their lives and to learn to dedicate themselves to it generously (cf. *Evangelica Testificatio 45*). To arrive at this, they need the silence of their whole being, and this calls for areas of actual silence and personal discipline, to facilitate contact with God.

Participation in the Liturgy of the Church *(Divine Office, sacramental life)* is a very special means of contemplation, especially at the climax of the Eucharistic Sacrifice, in which inner prayer mingles with exterior worship. The commitment to take part in it daily will help religious renew daily the offering of themselves to the Lord.

Gathered in the Lord's name, religious communities have the Eucharist as their natural centre; it is natural, therefore, that they should be visibly assembled round an oratory, in which the presence of the Blessed Sacrament expresses and realises what must be the principal mission of every religious family (cf. *Evangelica Testificatio,* 48).

Religious houses must, therefore, be above all oases of prayer and meditation, places of personal and community dialogue with him who is and must remain the first and principal interlocutor of their days, so full of work. Superiors must not be afraid, therefore, of reminding their confreres often that a pause of real worship is more fruitful and rich than any other activity, even if intense, and of an apostolic character. In fact, "no movement in religious life has any importance unless it be also movement inwards to the 'still centre' of your existence, where Christ is. It is not what you do that matters most; but what you are..." *(Address to Priests and Religious at Maynooth, 1 October 1979).*

The contemplative life of religious would be incomplete if it were not directed to filial love towards her who is the Mother of the Church and of consecrated souls. This love for the Virgin will be manifested with the celebration of her feasts, and in particular with daily prayers in her honour, particularly the Rosary. The daily recitation of the Rosary is a centuries-old tradition for religious and so it is not useless to recall the opportuneness, fragrance and efficacy of this prayer, which proposes to our meditation the mysteries of the Lord's life.

I know that in the context of your work you have devoted special attention to souls consecrated to contemplative life, recognising in them one of the most precious treasures of the Church. Docile to the invitation of the divine Master, they have chosen the good portion (cf. *Lk 10:42*), that is, prayer, silence, contemplation, exclusive love of God and complete dedication to his service. They must know that the Church relies a great deal on their spiritual contribution.

In the Decree *Perfectae Caritatis* the Second Vatican Council did not confine itself to affirming that the contemplative Institutes keep, today too, a fully valid meaning and function; it said that the place they occupy in the Mystical Body is an "honoured" one *(praeclara pars).* For contemplatives "offer to God an exceptional sacrifice of praise", they lend lustre to God's people with "abundant fruits of holiness", they "sway them by their example", and they "enlarge the Church by their hidden apostolic fruitfulness" (cf. *n. 7*).

Certainly, the requirements raised for the Church by evangelisation today, are multiple and urgent. It would be a mistake, however, to consider, on the basis of the necessities, also urgent ones, of the apostolate today, a form of life dedicated exclusively to contemplation as a thing of the past. The Council Fathers, tackling in the Decree *Ad Gentes* the problem of the proclamation of the Good News to all men, wished on the contrary to stress the effective contribution of contemplatives to apostolic work (cf. *n. 40*). They expressed the hope that, in the young Churches, among the various forms of religious life, there will also be the constitution of communities of contemplative life, to guarantee "the fullness of the Church's presence" (cf. *n. 18*).

Is it not significant, moreover, to point out, looking back on the history of the Church, that it is precisely in the centuries in which the necessities of evangelisation were greatest, that contemplative life had an almost miraculous blossoming and expansion? Should we not see in that an indication of the Spirit, who reminds us all, often tempted by the promptings of efficiency, of the supremacy of supernatural means over purely human ones?

So I turn my eyes confidently towards these souls dedicated with totality of commitment to contemplation, and I entrust to the ardour of their charity the harassing cares of the universal ministry, which has been entrusted to me. I know how attached they are to this special vocation, how joyfully they accept its requirements of daily sacrifice, how they are able to give a place in their prayer to the work, the sorrows and the hopes of their contemporaries. My hope is that they will study more and more deeply, in order to live it more and more intensely, the spirituality of their founders, without letting themselves be tempted by more fashionable methods or techniques, the inspiration of which has often little to do with the Gospel. The contemplative and mystical heritage of the Church is exceptionally vast and deep: it is necessary, therefore, to take care that all monasteries will undertake to get to know it, cultivate it and teach it.

It will be very helpful in order to attain these purposes for enclosure to be observed with rightful rigour, in accordance with the Second Vatican Council which spoke out in favour of its maintenance (cf. *Perfectae Caritatis, 16*). In fact, the abandonment of enclosure would mean loss of what is specific in one of the forms of religious life, with which the Church manifests to the world the pre-eminence of contemplation over action, of what is eternal over what is temporal. Enclosure does not "isolate" contemplative souls from the communion of the Mystical Body. It puts them, on the contrary, at the heart of the Church, as my predecessor, Pope Paul VI, rightly affirmed, adding that these souls "nourish the spiritual riches of the Church, exalt her prayer, sustain her charity, share her sufferings, toils, her apostolate, her hopes, and increase her merits"

(*Address: 2 February 1966*). There is, furthermore, a particular problem, the importance of which deserves to be mentioned today: that of the close relations between religious institutes and the clergy with regard to the contemplative dimension that every life dedicated to the Lord must have as its fundamental element.

Secular priests need to draw from contemplation the strength and support of their apostolate. As in the past, they must normally find backing, in this connection, in experienced religious and in contact with monasteries, ready to receive them for spiritual exercises and for periods of meditation and renewal.

On their side, religious must be able to find in the clergy, confessors and spiritual directors, capable of giving them help to understand and put into practice their consecration in a better way. The influence of priests is, moreover, very often a determinant in encouraging the discovery and subsequent development of the religious vocation.

It is necessary, therefore, that the clergy and religious, and in particular the bishops and superiors, should endeavour to find, for the important problem of the interdependence of the two states, a solution adapted to the time in which we live.

I would also like to add a reference to the new forms of contemplative life which are emerging here and there in the Church and in which one or other element of spiritual life is stressed. They are all interesting experiments and the Church follows them benevolently and attentively.

What I am anxious to recall is that these experiments must not weaken, however, in any way attachment and faithfulness to the forms of contemplative life, tested by centuries of history: they remain true sources of prayer and reliable schools of holiness, the fruitfulness of which has never been belied.

Beloved brothers, religious life does not have a definitive goal in this life: it is a gift in continual development and a progress towards more and more noble aims. In this sense, St Benedict affirmed that the monk's life is a continual apprenticeship for the Lord's service: "*dominici schola servitii*" (*Rule, prol.*). A school, in which the interior Teacher is the Spirit.

In the course of these days, you have sought to listen to this silent and sweet Teacher, to gather his suggestions faithfully and express their interior light in concrete norms. May your work produce abundant fruit, offering all religious opportune help to carry out what the Lord expects of them, to the advantage of the whole Christian community.

With this hope and invoking the motherly protection of the Blessed Virgin, the peerless model of complete consecration, I willingly send you my special Blessing, which I am happy to extend to all souls that, in chastity, poverty and obedience, are endeavouring to follow already in this life "the lamb, wherever he goes" (cf. *Rv. 14:4*).

Address to Sisters at Kinshasa   3 May 1980

Dear Sisters, let us give thanks to God our Father, through his Son Jesus, our Lord, in the spirit who dwells in our hearts, for the great happiness of this meeting and for the fruits that will spring from it in your respective communities and in the life in the Church in Africa!

At these very special moments, forget your legitimate particular characteristics in order to feel deeply your unique belonging to the same God and Father, recalled in a striking way by the Apostle Paul in his letter to the Ephesians: "one Lord, one faith, one baptism, one God and Father of us all" *(Ep 4:5-6)*. Let me encourage you to celebrate deeply and fervently the anniversary of your birth to divine life by the grace of baptism, as the most important event of your existence, and the most significant one of your Christian vocation is brotherhood.

Having come to religious life from very different social environments, countries and even continents, you live in communities to bear witness — contrary to nationalistic feelings, prejudices, sometimes hatred — to the possibility and the reality of this universal brotherhood, to which all peoples aspire vaguely. You are Sisters also because you have heard the same evangelical call: "If you would be perfect, go, sell what you possess and give to the poor, and you will have treasure in heaven; and come, follow me" (cf. *Mt 19:21*). This unique call in its divine source is another requirement — whether you are dedicated to contemplation or engaged in the direct tasks of evangelisation — to be on extremely fraternal terms among yourselves and among congregations, and to help one another better and better on three planes which seem to me essential: to see your consecration in the right way and carry it out courageously, to be eager to take part in the mission of the

Church, to pursue a solid spiritual formation and judicious openness to the realities of your age and your environments.

In a few words, the Second Vatican Council describes consecrated life as ''a gift of God which the Church has received from her Lord and which by his grace she always safeguards'' *(Lumen Gentium, 43)*. Without ignoring the shadows of the bimillenary history of the people of God, it can be stated that woman — on her side — has responded magnificently to Christ's calls to the evangelical fullness of the gift of oneself.

There is, it seems, in a woman's body and heart, an extraordinary disposition to make her life a royal offering to Christ as the one Bridegroom. This femininity — often considered by a certain public opinion as sacrificed in a crazy way in religious life — is, as a matter of fact, refound and expanded on a higher plane: that of the Kingdom of God. For example, physical fecundity, which has such a great place in African tradition, as well as attachment to the family, are values that can be lived by the African Sister within a far wider and ever renewed community, and to the benefit of an absolutely astonishing spiritual fecundity. It is in this perspective that religious chastity, very faithfully observed, stands out clearly as preferential love of the Lord and complete availability for others.

In the same way many African women who have entered religion are trying to give the vow of poverty a new face, more in keeping with the environments from which they have come. They are anxious to live on the fruit of their work and to share this fruit constantly with others.

While remaining strictly faithful to the authentic conception of religious obedience — which is always the sacrifice of one's own will — many Sisters are endeavouring to live it in trusting dialogue with their leaders in whom they see a presence of Christ. This new aspect is in keeping with the dignity and the advancement of woman in our time.

Speaking to you in this way, dear Sisters, I would like to help you to grasp, again, the essential characteristic of your religious state: the complete consecration, for ever, of your innermost self and your feminine capacities to Christ and his Kingdom. We have reached here the very heart of the mystery of your life, which is difficult to understand outside of the faith. A mystery which goes beyond all the rest: the acquisition of qualifications and diplomas, the distribution of duties and responsibilities, cares of administration or implantation, problems of structures and observances. In a word, your consecration, lived radically, is the essential feature of your religious state, the permanent rock, which enables congregations and their subjects to cope with the adaptation required by circumstances without running the risk of weakening or betraying the charism with which Christ endowed his Church.

Solidly rooted in the prior requirements of your complete gift, authenticated by the Church, your life cannot but be consumed in the service of this Church for which Christ gave himself up (cf. *Ep 5:25*).

The mission of the Church is in the first place prophetic. She proclaims Christ to all nations (cf. *Mt 28:19-20*) and transmits to them his message of salvation. This involves your personal and community lifestyle in the first place (cf. *Evangelii Nuntiandi, 14*). Is it really luminous (cf. *Mt 5:16*), prophetic? The present-day world is awaiting everywhere, perhaps vaguely, consecrated lives which tell, in acts more than words, of Christ and the Gospel. The Epiphany of the Lord which you like to celebrate in Africa, depends on you! The prophetic Church also relies on you, here as in other continents, to take part eagerly in her immense catechetical work.

Sisters who are catechists and Sisters devoted to the formation of lay catechists, are awaited everywhere. Are women religious who — for reasons of personal fulfilment — abandon too easily this important ecclesial task, always certain that they are faithful to their consecration? I know that the effects and the results of catechetical teaching in Africa are remarkable. But they must be continued and expanded. Christians of all ages and from all walks of life need to be accompanied in order to cope with the social and cultural changes of our times. I ask you, my Sisters, to contribute even more to the prophetic mission of the Church.

Evangelisation, of oneself and of others, leads to divine worship. The Church has also a priestly vocation with which you are closely associated. Following in the steps of St Benedict or St Bernard, St Clare of Assisi or St Teresa of Avila, enclosed nuns assume full time, on behalf of the Church, this service of divine praise and intercession. This form of life is also an apostolate of very great ecclesial and redeeming value, which St Therese of the Child Jesus illustrated magnificently in the Carmelite convent at Lisieux. Let us not forget that Pope Pius XI proclaimed her patron saint of the missions. So I express my deepest encouragement to contemplatives on African soil and I ask God that their convents may be filled with seriously motivated vocations.

How could I forget sick Sisters, infirm and old? Throughout the day and often at night, when sleep is difficult, they present to the

Lord the silent offering of their almost uninterrupted prayers, their physical or moral sufferings, their "fiat" to divine will. They, too, are the priestly people that Christ won with his blood on the Cross. With him, they save the world.

As for Sisters who exercise a direct apostolate in towns and villages, the Church, in the person of bishops and priests, expects a great deal of their talents and their zeal for the animation of Christian assemblies. Initiation to the deep meaning of the liturgy, to the celebration of the sacraments, especially the Holy Eucharist, as well as the formation of children and adults to personal prayer, to the generous offering of their daily life, in union with that of Christ, is an extremely important field in which you are capable of excelling, owing to your pedagogical qualities, your innate sense of the mystery of God, and your own generosity in prayer. The fervour of the people of God, honouring their Lord, depends a great deal on you.

Finally the mission of the Church is a royal one. It is in the first place the bishop who must watch over the growth and unity of faith, as well as the brotherhood of love, in his diocese. It is he who directs and stimulates apostolic activities. But in the people of God, who are all urged to devote their forces and their specific talents in the various pastoral sectors of the life of dioceses and parishes, Sisters certainly have their place (cf. *Evangelii Nuntiandi, 69*). I leave it to African bishops to discern with wisdom the signs of the times in their own dioceses and to see concretely, with the various congregations, how Sisters can be more effectively integrated in the pastoral activities of the diocesan Church today. Allow me, however, to stress here that your feminine gifts predispose you to exercise among African girls and women the very precious role of counsellors, in a similar way to the service carried out by "village mothers".

Dear Sisters, I do not want to conclude this fatherly talk without encouraging you warmly to remain always in search of spiritual deepening and human formation, in order to be, to an increasing extent, more a woman and more a Sister.

Help one another, among religious houses, among congregations, to organise times and places of silence and meditation, in order to benefit from sessions of spirituality, theology and apostolate. Encourage one another to take part in them. Contribute by mutual aid to cover the expenses caused by these retreats and sessions. With your diocesan leaders, take care always to appeal to reliable and competent guides. Jesus himself used the proverb "a tree is judged by its fruits"! With calmness and common sense, always see where these retreats and sessions are taking you. To more intimacy with the Lord? To more courage and evangelical transparency? To more brotherly love? To more personal and community poverty? To more sharing of what you are and what you have with the underprivileged? To more zeal for the mission of the Church? If so, the means chosen were reliable and have been utilised seriously. If not, it is important to change them before it is too late.

Because you are Sisters today, it is indispensable, even if you are contemplatives, to watch over your human formation, to know sufficiently the life and the problems of people today, especially if you have the mission of proclaiming the Gospel to them. Young people and adults are sensitive to the humanity of those who have "lost everything and gained everything" to follow Christ! On this plane of the obligation to seek formation and information, take stock fairly of how far you have got: the golden rule is the constant subordination of your human acquisitions to the very special mission that Christ has entrusted to you in his Church, for the salvation of your human brothers.

Dear Sisters, I know that you pray for me a lot, and I thank you with all my heart. In exchange, I wish to assure you that Sisters of the whole world have a very great place in my everyday life and prayer. You are, all of you, my concern and my joy, my support and my hope! May the Lord strengthen you in your consecration and your mission, for his glory and for the greater good of your African dioceses and the whole Church!

O.R. 633   19 May 1980

Address at the Carmelite Convent, Nairobi
7 May 1980.

Dear Sisters in our Lord Jesus Christ, being your neighbour for two days, I could not fail to come and visit your Carmel. It gives me great joy to know that, near the house of the Pope's representative, there is a house of prayer where God's praises are constantly sung and where the sacrifice of your cloistered life is offered in joyful generosity to the Father. The fact that other contemplative communities in Kenya have gathered here with you gives me added joy. My dear Sisters, I bring you the greetings and love of the whole Church, and I thank you for your contribution to evangelisation and for the inspiration of your lives. Yes, it is a great tribute to the grace of God and to the power of the death and Resurrection of the Lord that many years ago the contemplative religious life took root in African soil, bringing forth abundant fruits of justice and holiness of life. You are indeed the recipients of a particular gift from God: the contemplative vocation in the Church. The introduction of the contemplative life in a local Church is an important indication of the dynamic implantation of the Gospel in the heart of a people. This is a sign which, together with missionary activity, shows the maturity of the local Church. To live the holiness of Christ and to share the ardent desire of his heart — "I must preach the Good News of the kingdom of God to the other cities also; for I was sent for this purpose" *(Lk 4:43)* — these are the hallmarks of Christ's Church.

Here in the heart of Kenya you are called to fulfil your exalted mission in the Body of Christ: to perpetuate Christ's life of prayer and loving immolation. The Church has learned from her Founder — and centuries of experience have confirmed her profound conviction — that union with God is vitally necessary for fruitful activity. Jesus has told us: "I am the vine, you are the branches...apart from me you can do nothing" *(Jn 15:5)*. The Church is deeply aware, and without hesitation she forcefully proclaims, that there is an intimate connection between prayer and the spreading of the Kingdom of God, between prayer and the conversion of hearts, between prayer and the fruitful reception of the saving and uplifting Gospel message. This alone is enough to assure you all contemplative religious throughout the world just how necessary your role is in the Church, just how important your service is to your people, just how great your contribution is to the evangelisation of Kenya and all Africa.

In your lives of prayer, moreover, Christ's praise of his Eternal Father goes on. The totality of his love for his Father and of his obedience to the Father's will is reflected in your own radical consecration of love. His selfless immolation for his Body, the Church, finds expression in the offering of your lives in union with his sacrifice. The renunciation involved in your vocation shows the primacy of Christ's love in your lives. In you the Church gives witness to her fundamental function, which is, as I said in my Encylical: "to point the awareness and experience of the whole of humanity towards the mystery of God..." *(Redemptor Hominis, 10)*.

Your lives and your activities are very much a part of the whole Church; they are in the Church and for the Church. You live in the very heart of the Church as did Saint Therese of the Child Jesus and so many other contemplative nuns throughout the Church's past. And as you pursue your vocation in fidelity to the Christ who called you, you remain spiritually very close to your families and the communities from which you come. As you live out your lives totally for Jesus Christ, your Spouse, and for all who have been called to life in him — the entire Christian family — you can rightly feel near to all your brothers and sisters as they strive for salvation and the fullness of human dignity. In your lives of material detachment and in the earnest work that you perform each day, you show your solidarity with the whole working community to whose service you are called. And through your prayers and the fruitfulness of your spiritual activities you are in a position to contribute effectively to the great cause of justice and peace and to the human advancement of countless men and women. Through your cloistered lives children are brought to Christ, the sick are comforted, the needy assisted, human hearts reconciled and the poor have the Gospel preached to them.

In certain places in Africa, a monastery of contemplative religious has been established in the vicinity of the major seminary. Is it not especially meaningful that those who saw the necessity of promoting vocations to the priesthood, so as to enable the young Churches to become fully implanted in the native soil, also professed their conviction that only the grace of God, humbly sought in constant prayer, could sustain the fervour of the priesthood? I ask you, therefore, as a special request on this occasion, to make it one of the primary intentions of your prayers, to beseech the Lord of the harvest to send out labourers into his harvest (cf. *Mt 9:38)*, and to bless his Church in Africa with many good, generous and committed priests, whose example of a holy and truly pastoral life constitutes the best guarantee for the life of the Church and the propagation of the faith.

Yours is then a truly important life of faith in Jesus Christ. In the words of Saint Peter: "Without having seen him, you love him; though you do not now see him, you believe in him and rejoice with unutterable and exalted joy" (*1 Pt 1:8*). And precisely because of this, your lives become lives of great service to the Church. With Mary you are called to meditate on the word of God, and to cooperate in bringing forth to spiritual life those who believe in Christ. For you, therefore, the future is clear. You are on the right path — of total joyful consecration to Jesus Christ and of loving service to all your brothers and sisters in Africa and throughout the Church.

Dear Sisters: in all your efforts to walk with Mary and to ascend the mountain that is Christ by loving more deeply and serving more generously, remember that "your life is hid with Christ in God" (*Col* 3:3) for the glory of the Most Holy Trinity: the Father, and the Son, and the Holy Spirit.

Amen.

O.R. 643. 26 May 1980

Letter to the Superior General of the De La Salle Brothers
13 May 1980

You were so kind as to inform me that, in these days, the Brothers of the Christian Schools are going to celebrate the opening of the third centenary of the foundation of their Institute and that they also desire to reaffirm their fervent faithfulness to Peter's successor, in conformity with the teaching of their Father, St John-Baptist De La Salle. Did he not ask God, in his "Testament", that the Society founded by him should always be sincerely obedient to the Pope and to the Roman Church?

The Pope wishes himself to participate in the very legitimate joy of all the Brothers scattered all over the world; with you he contemplates the past, rich in precious indications for the present and encouragement for the future.

Your Institute, throughout these three centuries, has spread, in the midst of hard trials and great difficulties, all over the world, with a progression which nothing was able to stop, because it was animated, fecundated and sustained by the grace of God, to which thousands and thousands of Brothers have responded with exemplary dedication and generosity. The 101 Brothers who composed your religious congregation in 1719, the year of the death of your holy Founder, have become about 11,000 today, and the twenty-three houses of that time have risen to over 1,300. These figures, so significant and eloquent, are the proof of the interior dynamism and fruitful vitality of an institution that was really providential for the period in which it came into being and that maintains all its value in the context of the contemporary Church and society.

The figure and personality of St John-Baptist De La Salle have aroused the respect and admiration of historians of all trends. There is no one today who can question the exceptional merits of his work on the historical, social and civil planes. In a period in which popular education did not, in fact, exist, John-Baptist De La Salle was the real founder of the modern popular school: whether it is a question of the elementary school, the institute for the training of teachers, vocational secondary education, the creation of evening and Sunday classes for workers and apprentices, and the reformatory for those condemned by the courts.

But at the basis of these ingenious creations of a psychological and pedagogical character, there was in this Saint a Christian vision which gave a full and global meaning to the concepts of "culture" and "education". For him, who was animated by Christ's charity, a school could not be just a place where it was possible to transmit or impose ideas, however useful and interesting they might be; it must be a real community of love, in which the young pupil is considered, not as "a vessel to be filled, but a soul to be formed". For the school to be able to attain this noble aim, the Saint realised the necessity of lay religious, school teachers duly trained and prepared, whom he called "Brothers of the Christian Schools": Brothers, in the first place among themselves, for they are united by the same ideal of consecration to God and dedication to the young; Brothers with regard to their pupils, for they are all united by love, which is the reflection of their union with Christ and of the love they have for him; Brothers, finally, because everyone, teachers and pupils, must be disciples of the one Master, Jesus (cf. *Mt 2:8,10*).

In an age when the children of poor families were abandoned to themselves in the street, and therefore easy prey of evil, the Saint stated that "the main fruit that is to be expected from the institution of the Christian schools is to ward off these disorders and prevent their evil consequences" *(Common Rules, chap. 1, art. 6)*. In this perspective, the school, for John-Baptist, could not tolerate mediocre teachers, thinking only of their own interest, without a liking for their task, nor even those who were merely learned, but were not saints. "It is your duty to rise every day to God in prayer to learn from him all that you must teach them" — he would often repeat to his spiritual sons — "and then to descend to them, adapting yourselves to their understanding, to instruct them about what God has communicated to you for them: both in prayer and in the holy books" *(Meditation 198 for retreat time)*. Thanks to this conception of the Christian school, the pupil was stimulated and helped in the discovery of a centre of unity in the midst of the various scholastic subjects in proportion as he studied them. This centre was Christ, presented through a continuous and daily catechesis.

To realise this view of the school authentically and sincerely, the Brother, dedicating his life to the very noble and meritorious task of education and the formation of the young, will feel the need of prayer, vigilance and good example; he will be animated with a deep spirit of faith (cf. *Rules, chap. 11*). He will make his teaching a continual catechesis, that is, a way of faith which he will carry out, day after day, with his pupils, through his word and the example of his life. He will exercise his ministry in the Church, as St John-Baptist De La Salle said: "Consider your occupation as one of the most eminent and excellent in the Church since it is among those most capable of sustaining her by giving her a solid foundation" thanks to the Christian education of youth *(Meditation 155, 2nd point)*. A special vow will also distinguish the Brother of the Christian Schools, namely, the vow to teach the poor free of charge.

I hope, therefore, that the celebration of your third centenary will be for all of you, very dear Brothers of the Christian Schools, a special occasion to reflect on the requirements of your vocation. The first requirement remains that of faithfulness to the charism of the Founder, whose topical interest, modernity and value are seen even more clearly in this period in which the Catholic school must proclaim, reaffirm — and sometimes even defend — its freedom, its dignity, its purpose, its function and even its survival (cf. *Gravissimum Educationis 8; Gaudium et Spes, 61-62)*.

Faithfulness to the original charism means joyful faithfulness to the religious vocation, that is, to the unconditional and absolute consecration you have made of yourselves to God with the sacred vows of poverty, chastity and obedience. The Brother of the Christian Schools, who has responded with generous enthusiasm to the pressing call of Jesus: "Follow me" (cf. *Mt 8:22; 19:21; Lk 18:22*) follows, every day, the poor Christ who has nowhere to lay his head (cf. *Mt 8:20; Lk 9:58*); the Christ who is the model of complete consecration to the Kingdom of heaven and who invites others to it (cf. *Mt 19:12*); the obedient Christ who, from the first moment of the Incarnation, proclaims his complete adherence to the Father's will (cf. *Heb 10:9*). The Brother will imitate the holy Founder's life of continual union with God, his deep sense of the presence of God ("let us remember that we are in the holy presence of God"), his full availability with regard to God's action: may every religious of the Institute be able to repeat, day after day, what John-Baptist De La Salle murmured at the moment of his death: "I adore in everything God's will for me".

The whole Church, beloved Brothers, joins in your joy on the third centenary of your foundation; she thanks the Holy Trinity for having given her, for having given her the world, a family of lay religious who have worked so well; she asks you, and she beseeches God to permit you to do so, to continue, with renewed ardour and in full communion with the pastors whom Christ has put at the head of his flock, to carry out your meritorious mission as educators and formers of so many generations of young people who are seeking the truth and joy.

Expressing these wishes and repeating to your Institute my sentiments of esteem and affection, I invoke on it, through the intercession of the Blessed Virgin Mary and of St John-Baptist De La Salle, the abundance of the gifts of the Risen Christ, and, as a testimony of my continual benevolence, I willingly grant a special Apostolic Blessing to you and to all the Brothers of the Christian Schools, to their pupils and to their families.

O.R. 639.   30 June 1980

Address to Italian Benedictine Abbesses
22 May 1980

Beloved Benedictine Mother Abbesses of Italy, at the end of your study meeting on "monastic prayer considered in its development from the origins to Vatican II", you wished to meet the Pope, to manifest your faith and filial devotion, and to hear a word of encouragement and support. I thank you heartily, therefore, and, while extending my particularly affectionate greeting to you, I express to you and all your fellow Sisters my deep appreciation for your religious consecration and your constant commitment in *aggiornamento* and in deepening one's knowledge in the cultural and formative sphere.

I wish to repeat to you, too, what I said to enclosed nuns in the Carmelite convent of Nairobi: "The Church is deeply aware, and without hesitation she forcefully proclaims, that there is an intimate connection between prayer and the spreading of the Kingdom of God, between prayer and the conversion of hearts, between prayer and the fruitful reception of the saving and uplifting Gospel message" *(7 May 1980)*.

Therefore, the spiritual joy you feel at being completely consecrated to Jesus Christ and to the Church, is also my joy and deep consolation. There is, moreover, a particular motive that makes you dear to my heart: you are the daughters of St Benedict and you dedicate yourselves to perpetuating his glorious and universal message of Christian and religious formation, an austere message, and yet a sweet one, which for fifteen centuries has been spreading its perfume and its energy all over the world. You must feel very happy, in this year commemorating his birth, at all the initiatives that are being undertaken to recall your Holy Founder in a worthy way and to evaluate better and better the marvellous spiritual riches of his Rule.

I can imagine how many wise and useful reflections you have made in these days of study on the very interesting subject of monastic prayer. And, in conclusion, I wish to leave you a short exhortation, which may be of use to you and to all those called to monastic life, in this age of such importance in the development of history.

What is the value of monastic prayer in our time? It has certainly so many, and you know them. Some of these values are eminently relevant today and characteristic.

Today monastic prayer has in the first place an apologetic value, or, as is also said, prophetic. Today the most striking feature of the modern world is the crisis of faith. Well, monastic prayer, as St Benedict wished it to be and as it was subsequently practised by the various forms of spirituality, is, as it were, a luminous sign in the night, an oasis in the desert of disappointments and dissatisfaction, a stable and safe vessel amid the stormy waves of feelings and passions. With his prayer, which springs from a faith that has matured for a long time and is deeply lived, the monk, the woman religious of contemplative life, in the serene atmosphere of the *"lectio"* and the *"meditatio"* of Holy Scripture, seem to say to the whole world, with modesty but with firmness: "I know that God exists and is the almighty and provident Father, and I believe it firmly — I know that God manifested himself in Christ, the Lord Incarnate, and I love him tenderly — I know that Christ is present in his Church, and I follow her faithfully".

In this connection, I am happy to recall a passage of the Message of the Italian Bishops for the 15th centenary of the birth of St Benedict: "Our time needs to discover again the power of God who speaks, rouses, challenges, reveals himself, communicates himself, calls and attracts to communion with him. Yesterday everything seemed to lead to God; today it seems that nothing and no one helps to think of him. Surrounding God there is almost a tacit conspiracy of silence. But it is not so: every day each of us, and all together, can discover again the fascination of his presence and the need we have of him to breathe, to live. Today, perhaps, "theologies", "discourses about God", however important, are no longer sufficient. Lives that cry out silently the primacy of God are needed. Men and women are needed to treat the Lord as the Lord, who spend themselves in worshipping him, who sink into his mystery, under the sign of gratuitousness and without human compensation, to bear witness that he is the Absolute".

Monastic prayer has also a high value of propitiation and supplication.

St Benedict, meditating assiduously on Holy Scripture, knew very well that God is infinitely good and merciful, but is also infinitely just, and, knowing the situation of moral disorder of his time, he wished precisely to open his monastery mainly for the eternal salvation of so many persons.

What the Saint feared in that rough and violent age, we must fear even more, unfortunately, in this proud and sophisticated age of ours. Today many people risk their eternity terribly! We know, indeed, as the author of the Letter to the Hebrews says, that "it is appointed for men to die once, and after that comes judgement" *(Heb 9:27)*. But God's love is immense, and monastic prayer can save so many souls through the power of grace: *Parce, Domine, parce populo tuo!* (Spare, Lord, spare your people).

Now that I am about to go as a pilgrim to the Sanctuary of Lisieux, I recall what St Therese of the Child Jesus wrote, she who is still today the wise teacher and fearless friend on the path of our lives: "One Sunday, looking at a picture of Our Lord on the Cross, I was struck by the blood that was dripping from one of his divine hands; I felt great sorrow at the thought that that blood would drip to the ground without anyone troubling to gather it and I resolved to remain in spirit at the foot of the Cross to receive the divine dew which was falling from it and which — I understood — I should then sprinkle on souls...". Monastic prayer must be so: a prayer at the foot of the Cross for the salvation of the world.

Beloved Mother Abbesses, returning now to your convents, take to your fellow Sisters my greetings and my good wishes for peace and joy, in union with the Blessed Virgin, who lived her life in continual prayer, near her divine Son Jesus, and whom we remember in these days praying in the Upper Room, with the Apostles, while waiting for the Spirit. May she guide you in the asceticism of your lives consecrated to Christ and to the Church!

May my Blessing accompany you.

O.R. 639.   30 June 1980

Address to the Sisters at the Rue De Bac, Paris,
31 May 1980

My dear Sisters, in the course of my apostolic journeys, I feel a deep and ever new happiness on meeting Sisters, whose existence, consecrated by the three evangelical vows, "belongs undeniably to the life and holiness" of the Church *(Lumen Gentium, 44).* Let us bless together the Lord who has permitted this meeting! Let us bless him for the fruits it will yield in your personal lives, in your Congregations, in the people of God! Thank you for having come in such large numbers from all the districts of Paris and of the Parisian region, and even from the provinces. I am happy to express to you who are here, as to all women religious of France, my esteem, my affection and my encouragement.

This gathering, in an almost rustic setting, makes me think of those moments of pause and breathing space which Christ himself reserved for his first disciples on their return from certain apostolic tours. You too, my dear Sisters, arrive from your places and tasks of evangelisation: dispensaries or hospitals, day schools or boarding schools, catechetical centres or chaplaincies for the young, parish services or work in poor environments. I have pleasure in repeating to you the words of the Lord: "Come away by yourselves...and rest a while" (cf. *Mk 6:31).* Together, we will meditate on the mystery and the evangelical treasure of your vocation.

Religious life is not your property, no more than it is the property of an Institute. It is "a gift of God which the Church has received from her Lord and which by his grace she always safeguards"

(Lumen Gentium, 43). In a word, religious life is a heritage, a reality that has been lived in the Church for centuries, by a multitude of men and women. The deep experience they have made of it transcends the social and cultural differences that may exist between one country and another, surpasses also the descriptions they have left of it, and is set beyond the diversity of achievements and researches of today. It is important to listen to, and imitate, those men and women who have best embodied the ideal of evangelical perfection, and who sanctified and rendered illustrious the land of France in such large numbers.

Up to the evening of your life, remain in wonder and thanksgiving for the mysterious call that re-echoed in the depths of your heart one day: "Follow me" (cf. *Mt 9:9; Jn 1:43*), "Sell what you possess, and give it to the poor, and you will have treasure in heaven; and come, follow me" *(Mt 19:21).* To begin with, you kept this call like a secret, then you subjected it to the discernment of the Church. It is, in fact, a very great risk to leave everything to follow Christ. But already you felt — and you have experienced since — that he was able to fill your hearts. Religious life is a friendship, an intimacy of the mystical order with Christ. Your personal path must be, as it were, an original re-edition of the famous poem of the Song of Solomon. Dear Sisters, in the heart-to-heart relationship of prayer, absolutely vital for each of you, as on the occasion of your different apostolic commitments, listen to the Lord murmuring the same call to you: "Follow me". In this way you will go from faithfulness to faithfulness!

To follow Christ is something quite different from admiration of a model, even if you have a good knowledge of Scripture and of theology. To follow Christ is something existential. It is to want to imitate him to the extent of letting oneself be configured to him, assimilated to him, to the extent of being for him — according to the words of Sister Elizabeth of the Trinity — "an additional humanity". And that in his mystery of chastity, poverty and obedience. Such an ideal surpasses understanding and goes beyond human strength! It can be realised only thanks to special times of silent and ardent contemplation of the Lord Jesus. Active Sisters must be at certain hours contemplatives, following the example of the enclosed nuns whom I will address at Lisieux.

Religious chastity, my Sisters, is to want really to be like Christ; all the other reasons that can be brought forward disappear before this essential reason: Jesus was chaste. This state of Christ was not only a transcending of human sexuality, foreshadowing the future world, but also a manifestation, an ''epiphany'' of the universality of his redeeming oblation. The Gospel shows continually how Jesus lived chastity. In his human relations, which were extraordinarily wide as compared with the traditions of his environment and his age, he reaches perfectly the deep personality of the other. His simplicity, his respect, his goodness, his art of bringing out the best in the hearts of the persons he met, overwhelm the Samaritan woman, the adulterous woman and so many other people.

May your vow of consecrated virginity — deepened and lived in the mystery of Christ's chastity — and which already transfigures your persons, impel you to join in actual fact your brothers and sisters in humanity, in the concrete situations in which they find themselves! So many people in our world are, as it were, lost, crushed, desperate! In faithfulness to the rules of prudence, make them feel that you love them in the manner of Christ, drawing from his heart the human and divine tenderness that he bears them.

You have also promised Christ to be poor with him and like him. Certainly, the society of production and consumption raises complex problems for the practice of evangelical poverty. This is not the place or the time to discuss them. It seems to me that every Congregation must see in this economic phenomenon a providential invitation to give an answer, at once traditional and new, to Christ in his poverty. It is by contemplating him often and at length in his radically poor life, it is by frequenting assiduously the humble and the poor, who are also his face, that you will be capable of giving all that you are and all that you have. The Church needs to be borne along, as it were, by your witness. Judge your responsibility.

As for the obedience of Jesus, it has a central place in his work of redemption. You have often meditated on the pages in which St Paul speaks of the initial disobedience, which was, as it were, the gateway to sin and death in the world, and he speaks of the mystery of Christ's obedience which starts humanity's climb back again towards God. Dispossession of oneself, humility, are more difficult for our generation enamoured of autonomy and even of fantasy. It is impossible, however, to imagine religious life without obedience to superiors, who are guardians of faithfulness to the ideal of the Institute. St Paul stresses the bond of cause and effect between Christ's obedience unto death on the Cross *(Ph 2:6-11)* and his glory as the Risen Christ and Lord of the universe. Likewise the obedience of every Sister — which is always a sacrifice of the will, out of love — yields abundant fruits of salvation for the whole world.

You have agreed, therefore, to follow Christ and imitate him more closely, to manifest his true face to those who already know him as to those who do not know him. And that through all these apostolic activities to which I referred at the beginning of our meeting. On this plane of commitments, without detriment to the special spirituality of your Institutes, I exhort you earnestly to seek integration in the immense network of pastoral tasks of the universal Church and the dioceses (cf. *Perfectae Caritatis, 20*). I know that Congregations cannot — for lack of subjects — answer all the appeals that come from bishops and from their priests. Do your utmost, however, to carry out the vital services of parishes and dioceses. Let duly prepared Sisters collaborate in the apostolate of new situations, which are numerous. In a word, invest all your natural and supernatural talents as much as you can in contemporary evangelisation. Be present, always and everywhere, in the world without being of the world (cf. *Jn 17: 15-16*). Never be afraid to let your identity as women consecrated to the Lord be clearly recognised. Christians, and those who are not, have the right to know who you are. Christ, the Teacher of us all, made his life a courageous revealing of his identity (cf. *Lk 9:26*). Take heart and be confident, my dear Sisters! I know that for years you have reflected a great deal on the religious life, on your Constitutions. The time has come to live, in faithfulness to the Lord and to your apostolic tasks. I pray with all my heart that the witness of your consecrated lives and the aspect of your religious Congregations may awaken in the hearts of many young people the project of following Christ, like you. I bless you and all women religious of France working on the soil of their homeland or in other continents. And I bless all those who are in your hearts and in your prayers.

O.R. 636.   9 June 1980

Address to Contemplative Nuns at Lisieux
2 June 1980

My dear Sisters, peace and joy in Christ Jesus! To you who surround the humble successor of the Apostle Peter! And, through you, to all enclosed nuns in France.

I must tell you first of all my deep emotion at being able to pray near the shrine that contains the remains of St Therese. I have already expressed at length my thanksgiving and my attachment for the "spiritual way" that she adopted and offered to the whole Church. I now feel great joy at visiting this Carmelite convent which was the setting of her life and her death, of her sanctification, in the midst of her Sisters, and which must remain an important place of prayer and sanctification for the Carmelites and for all pilgrims. It is from there that I would like to strengthen you all, whatever your spiritual family may be, in your contemplative life, which is absolutely vital for the Church and for mankind.

While loving our age deeply, it has to be recognised that modern thought easily confines to subjectivism everything that concerns religious, the faith of believers, religious sentiments. And this view does not spare monastic life. To such an extent that public opinion, and, alas, sometimes some Christians who tend to appreciate only practical commitment, are tempted to consider your contemplative life as an escape from real life, an anachronistic and even useless activity. This incomprehension may make you suffer, and even humiliate you. I will tell you like Christ: "Fear not, little flock" *(Lk 12:32)*. In any case, a certain monastic revival, which is manifested throughout your country, must buoy up your hope.

But I must also add: take up the challenge of the modern world and of the world of always, by living more radically than ever the very mystery of your quite original state, which is folly in the eyes of the world and wisdom in the Holy Spirit: exclusive love of the Lord and of all your human brothers in him. Do not seek to justify yourselves! All love, provided it is authentic, pure and disinterested, bears in itself its own justification. To love gratuitously is an inalienable right of the person, even — and one should say, above all — when the Beloved is God himself. In the footsteps of contemplatives and mystics of all times, continue to bear witness with power and humility to the transcendent dimension of the human person, created in the likeness of God and called to a life of intimacy with him. St Augustine, at the end of meditations made as much with his heart as with his penetrating intelligence, assures us that man's bliss lies there: in loving contemplation of God! That is why the quality of your belonging lovingly to the Lord, on the personal plane as well as on the community plane, is of extreme importance. The fullness and radiation of your lives, hidden in God, must challenge the men and women of today, must question the young who are so often looking for the meaning of life. Meeting you or seeing you, every visitor, guest or retreatant in your monasteries should be able to say or at least feel that he has met God, that he has experienced a revelation of the Mystery of God who is Light and Love! The times in which we live need witnesses as much as apologists! Be, on your part, these very humble and always transparent witnesses!

Let me assure you further — in the name of the constant tradition of the Church — that not only can your life proclaim God's absoluteness, but that it possesses a marvellous and mysterious power of spiritual fruitfulness (cf. *Perfectae Caritatis, 7*). Why? Because your loving oblation is integrated by Christ himself in his work of universal Redemption, in m,uch the same way as the waves merge in the depths of the ocean. Seeing you, I think of the Mother of Christ, I think of the holy women of the Gospel, standing at the foot of the Lord's cross and communing in his salvific death, but also messengers of his resurrection. You have chosen to live, or rather Christ has chosen you to live his Paschal Mystery with him through time and space. All that you are, all that you do every day, whether it is the office intoned or sung, the celebration of the Eucharist, work in your cells or in fraternal teams, respect of enclosure and silence, mortifications chosen or imposed by the rule, everything is assumed, sanctified, used by Christ for the redemption of the world. In order that you may have no doubt on this matter, the Church — in Christ's own name — took possession one day of all your powers of living and loving. It was your monastic profession. Renew it often! Following the example of the saints, dedicate yourselves, sacrifice yourselves more and more, without even seeking to know how God uses your collaboration. Whereas at the basis of every action, there is a purpose and therefore a limitation, a finitude, the gratuitousness of your love is at the origin of contemplative fruitfulness. A very modern comparison comes into my mind: you kindle in the world the fire of revealed truth and love, in rather the same way as the masters of the atom light space rockets: from a distance.

Finally I would like to add two encouraging thoughts which seem to me opportune. The first concerns faithfulness to the charism of your founders or foundresses. The brotherhood and cooperation that exist more than before among monasteries must not lead to a certain levelling of contemplative institutes. Let every spiritual family watch over its particular identity in view of the good of the whole Church. What is done in one place is not necessarily to be imitated elsewhere.

My second encouragement is the following. In a civilisation that is more and more mobile, sonorous and vocal, areas of silence and rest become a vital necessity. Monasteries — in their original style — have therefore more than ever the vocation of remaining places of peace and interiority. Do not let pressure from within or without strike at your traditions and your means of mediation. Endeavour rather to educate your guests and your retreatants to the virtue of silence. You certainly know that I had occasion to recall to participants in the plenary session of the Congregation for Religious, on 7 March last, strict observance of monastic enclosure. I recalled in this connection the very strong words of my predecessor Paul VI: "Enclosure does not isolate contemplative souls from the communion of the Mystical Body. Far more, it puts them at the heart of the Church". Love your separation from the world, perfectly comparable to the biblical wilderness. It is there that the Lord speaks to your heart and closely associates you in his work of salvation.

These are the convictions that I was anxious to confide to you very simply, my dear Sisters. You will make the best use of them, I am convinced. You pray a great deal for the fruitfulness of my ministry. Receive my hearty thanks! Rest assured that the Pope also reaches — and very often — in heart and in prayer, the monasteries of France and of the whole world. I hope and I ask the Lord, through the intercession of the holy Carmelite of Lisieux, that strong and numerous vocations will come to increase and renew your various contemplative communities. I bless you from the bottom of my heart, in the name of the Father and of the Son and of the Holy Spirit.

O.R. 638. 22 June 1980

Address to the Union of Major Superiors of France
2 June 1980

The talks I had the privilege of having, on Saturday in Paris, with Sisters engaged in tasks of evangelisation, and just now in this Carmelite convent, with a large group of contemplatives, were intended by me for all monks and all enclosed nuns, for all men and women religious in France, who spend their lives consecrated to Christ in the ecclesial service of prayer or of the apostolate.

To you, dear brothers and sisters, who have been chosen to bear the responsibility for your Institutes, I wish to address a special and important encouragement.

The Council has very happily recalled that all authority in the Church was a service and must be lived in the very spirit of the Lord Jesus (cf. *Lk 22:27*). This evangelical and imperative norm must not lead you to renounce your own responsibilities. The formula "everyone responsible" which has met with great success for a good ten years now, is valid in a certain sense only. You are seriously responsible in the last resort for the religious spirit of your subjects, their apostolic output, the faithfulness of the members of your Institute to their specific ideal and the quality of their testimony in the Church and the world of today.

I know on the other hand all the work of research and experiments that your Congregations have carried out since the Council. The balance-sheet includes happy orientations. Take good care that religious life is an "epiphany" of Christ. The modern world needs signs. A starless night is a source of anguish. In a word, see to it that it is accepted everywhere in your religious families that the time has come for the serene and persevering observance of the revised and approved constitutions. Dear brothers and sisters, I trust in your wisdom and courage. I invoke the most abundant blessings of the Lord on yourselves and on your Institutes.

O.R. 638.   23 June 1980

Address to Sisters at Sao Paulo   3 July 1980

Dear Daughters in Christ, this meeting with you gives me great joy. As Sisters, you are the wealth and treasure of the Church and, at the same time, a solid basis for evangelisation and an important reference point for the Christian people, encouraged in its faith by the form in which you live yours. In you, I greet cordially all Sisters in Brazil.

My joy grows on contact with your infectious enthusiasm, characteristic of a nation of young people, and consistent with the characteristics of Brazilian optimism, lively and generous. I rejoice also to know that the history of the Church in Brazil is bound by very deep ties to the constant and manifold activity of a large number of Sisters. While I thank you for for your presence here, I invite you to express gratitude with me to "the God and Father of our Lord Jesus Christ, who has blessed us in Christ with every spiritual blessing in the heavenly places", and who "chose us...that we should be holy and blameless before him" (cf. *Ep 1:3-4*).

My greatest joy is that this meeting with the Pope should be for you and your religious families an incentive and a comfort for your sublime vocation and for your commitment in deepening its essential value of very special witness of charity in fidelity to God and to the requirements of his Kingdom. It is not necessary to tell you the great and sincere confidence that the Church places in you: in your state as religious, in your presence, and in your mission. You know the reasons for this confidence: because of your life of prayer you are the sign of God's Absolute Being and of the importance of contemplation; because of your availability, always prompt, you are the spearhead for missionary needs; and because of your life in community you are the affirmation of communion and participation as an appeal to live the community dimension of the Church. You are a particular expression of the mystery of the Church herself, in her insertion in time, vital, concrete and adapted, and in her universality.

You know that to maintain a clear perception of consecrated life, a deep vision of faith is necessary, supporting your generosity and illuminating your continual progress in charity. For this reason dialogue with God in prayer is necessary. Without prayer religious life loses its meaning and does not achieve its goals. It is important to pray always in order to bring to life God's gift.

As for that, it was the Lord himself who informed us. To instil this truth into us, he used two meaningful images: "I am the vine, you are the branches. He who abides in me, and I in him, he it is that bears much fruit, for apart from me you can do nothing" *(Jn 15:5)*. Another time, after having said that those who follow him must be "the salt of the earth", he concluded: "Salt is good; but if salt has lost its taste...it is fit neither for the land nor for the dunghill; men throw it away" *(Lk 14:35)*. We know that the best of ourselves, the enjoyment of God that we must spread in the sweetness of the witness of charity, passes through Christ and is prudently and continually strengthened in us by the presence and the action of the Holy Spirit, requested and supported consciously in constant prayer in all its forms: individual, communal and liturgical. This is very important, in order that we can be an efficacious "sign" of God.

It is opportune here, in view of the nature of the Body of Christ which is the Church (cf. *1 Co 12:12*), to highlight the role carried out in evangelisation by Sisters consecrated to prayer, silence, hidden sacrifice and penance. Their life has a marvellous and mysterious power of apostolic fruitfulness (cf. *Perfectae Caritatis*, 7). I am happy to repeat to you here today what I said a month ago in the Carmelite Convent at Lisieux, in France — and I repeat it thinking of all the contemplative sisters in Brazil: "Your loving oblation is integrated by Christ himself into his work of universal Redemption, in much the same way as the waves merge in the depths of the ocean". Live the missionary dimension of your consecration in the likeness of St Therese of the Child Jesus!

But all forms of religious life have room for contemplation, necessary so that members can deeply accept the appeals, the needs, and the difficulties of brothers, in the genuine charity of Christ.

While causing the light of the witness of this charity to shine forth before men, it must not be forgotten, however, that it is always invested with a special character; you are in the world without being of the world; and it is precisely your consecration which, far from impoverishing, rather characterises your Christian witness. Your commitment to live according to the evangelical counsels makes you more available for this witness. Actually, you are no less free to obey, nor less capable of loving, because of the fact that you have chosen consecrated virginity. In fact the contrary is true; and by virtue of the vow of poverty that obliges you to follow the poor Christ, you can understand better and share the painful tragedies of those who lack everything.

Poverty must, however, be genuinely evangelical in order to be able to recognise Christ in the humblest; it is necessary to be able to identify oneself with one's brother in need, being "poor in spirit" (cf. *Mt 5:3*); now this calls for simplicity and humility, love of peace, freedom from dissipative commitments or attachments, inclination towards complete abnegation, free and obedient, spontaneous and constant, sweet and strong, in the certainties of faith.

You are living your consecration bound to an institute and in a fraternal community. These are very important elements of your religious life in the mystery of the Church, which is always a mystery of communion and participation.

You have chosen "an existence regulated by freely accepted norms of life" in a world and a civilisation that tend to alienate persons from one another and to disperse them to such an extent that their spiritual unity, the condition for their union with God, is sometimes compromised.

God forbid that an excessive desire for flexibility and spontaneity should lead someone to regard as obsolete rigidity or — what would be even worse — to abandon that minimum of regularity in customs and fraternal society, which is normally required by life in community and by progress in personal growth. (cf. Apostolic Exhortation *Evangelica Testificatio, 32*). Fidelity to this minimum provides the criterion of personal identification with consecration out of love.

Thus it is the duty of everyone to remain faithful to community life and to contribute to its being a fraternal meeting place, an environment of mutual help and spiritual comfort, an environment that each one desires and seeks, in order to make, as a spiritual author said, a "pilgrimage" to her own heart (cf. *Is 48:8*) and to gain new strength in God.

Even outside the community, all the activities and contacts of Sisters always have a community and public dimension: religious life is always a visible sign of the Church. For this reason I exhort you to be personally, always and everywhere, visible witnesses to the Church and to her Lord, in a world which, with the pretext of being modern, advances more and more towards desecration: may all persons be able to see in your behaviour, in your appearance, and in your dress, a sign with which God summons them.

At the present time, in this so beautiful country, as also in others, there are many incentives for sisters to embrace new activities and to launch new ways of involvement in the life and activity of the Church, or even in temporal activities in different areas.

It may happen that the works and activities to which your religious families traditionally dedicate themselves are neglected. I do not want to pass over in silence a very simple thing which you all know: these works and activities need to be updated in order to correspond better to the reality of Brazil today. However, neither must it be forgotten that the schools, the hospitals, the welfare centres and many other initiatives that have already existed for a long time for the service of brothers, particularly the poorest, or for the cultural and spiritual development of the populations, should keep all their validity.

What is more, if duly and timely renewed with sound principles, these works and activities continue to prove to be very special places of evangelisation, and of witness to real charity and human advancement. It is obvious that the fundamental prudent criterion to be followed in adaptations to new requirements is always that of the Gospel: in the light of the signs of the times, focussed on the proper perspective, to be able to draw out "things old and new" from the rich treasure of a past built on experiences.

It sometimes becomes necessary, however, to abandon works or activities in order to engage in others, even of a more pastoral character; and for this reason smaller communities are created, which need to adopt new forms of presence in the world of men. I know the care you take in seeking and implementing these new forms of presence and I have nothing but appreciation to express for all this commitment of yours. However, I would like to recall with you some conditions to be observed always in these new experiments of religious life.

a) These experiments must always be carried out in a climate of prayer. The soul that lives in the habitual presence of, and in contact with, God and lets itself be permeated by the warmth of his love, will easily know how:
— to shun the temptation of specialisation and oppositions which in themselves carry the risk of leading to painful divisions;
— to interpret, in the light of the Gospel, the stand for the poor and for all the victims of human selfishness, without giving in to sociopolitical radicalism which, sooner or later, proves to be inopportune, produces effects contrary to the ones desired, and brings forth new forms of oppression;
— to approach persons and become integrated in the environment without jeopardising one's own religious identity, without hiding or disguising the specific originality of one's own vocation: to follow Christ, poor, chaste and obedient.

b) In addition to the climate of prayer in which they must be carried out, these experiments of new involvements must be prepared by thorough study, in close collaboration with the responsible superiors and in constant dialogue with the bishops concerned. In this way it will be possible to find correct solutions. It is also necessary to proceed with the preparation of plans and programmes adapted to the choices made, and with the implementation of initiatives, "exercising judgment" and "taking counsel" beforehand, as the Lord says (cf. *Lk 14:28 ff.*), with regard to the possibilities of success, and this without fearing the risks, as the parables of the kingdom of heaven teach us (cf. *Mt 13*), and always acting in conformity with the most urgent requirements and according to the character of the institute.

c) Finally, in all these new foundations it is important to act always in agreement with the norms and guidelines given by the hierarchy, evaluating objectively and in a well-balanced way, and applying oneself humbly and courageously, when necessary, to correct, suspend, or direct in a more opportune way the experiments that are being carried out.

In everything and always in religious life, for sound judgement it is necessary to behave as daughters who love the Church, following her principles and directives, by means of generous and faithful adherence to the true magisterium. Here lies the guarantee of the fruitfulness of life and activity in consecration. Here is a prerequisite for an adequate interpretation of the signs of the times. On touching this point there comes to my mind what my predecessor Paul VI said: the universal Church must be present in every ecclesial community which always needs the breath of universality in order not to die of spiritual asphyxia. The fidelity promised to Christ can never be separated from fidelity to the Church: "He who hears you hears me" *(Lk 10:16)*.

In this area there is ample room for action open to the superiors and directors of institutes and communities. Their function will lead them to procure the best means to promote what certainly guarantees the union of spirits and hearts. Nothing of all this can be done without praying and acting in such a way that all sisters will find in consecration the highest fulfilment of their status as a person and as a woman, in order that institutes and communities may overcome any difficulties of growth or perseverance, and that the ideal of consecrated life may exercise a real attraction on youth.

A final word to the beloved sisters who dedicate their life to contemplation and live their religious life in meditation and in cloister. Your form of life, dear daughters, sets you at the heart of the mystery of the Church. Your personal life has its centre in nuptial love of Christ. For this reason, moulded by his Spirit, you must give him your whole being, making your own his sentiments, his projects, and his mission of charity and salvation. Now all of that is not confined within the four walls of monasteries, but is connected with the great history of men, where justice is established, where communion and participation in material and spiritual goods is created, where the attempt is made to establish the civilisation of love, where, finally, God's salvation must arrive, with the good news of the Gospel.

For this reason your contemplative life is absolutely vital for the Church and for mankind, in spite of the lack of understanding or even opposition that sometimes appears in modern thought, in public opinion and perhaps even in certain poorly lit fringes of Christianity. With this certainty live in joy that basic principle of your state from its very beginning: exclusive love for the Lord and, in him, love for all your brothers in humanity. Applying your capacity for loving in worship and prayer, your very existence silently proclaims the primacy of God, bears witness to the transcendent dimension of the human person and leads men, women and the young to think and to question themselves about the meaning of life.

May your convents remain places of peace and interior life, without allowing outside pressure to destroy your wholesome traditions and wipe out your means of cultivating and promoting meditation. And pray, pray a great deal for those who also pray, for those who cannot pray, and for those who do not want to pray. And be confident! With this word the Pope wishes to stimulate the generosity of all contemplative sisters of Brazil, whatever their spiritual family may be.

Beloved Sisters, I have in my heart many other things that I would like to communicate to you, if it were not for the lack of time. I renew to all, therefore, my esteem and trust. My wish for you all is "that your love may abound more and more, with knowledge and all discernment, so that you may approve what is excellent, and may be pure and blameless" *(Ph 1:9-10)*.

This "greater knowledge" which is expected of you has already been indicated by the Holy Spirit in the words of the Apostle: "to know nothing...except Jesus Christ and him crucified" *(1 Co 2:2)*. Only he, Christ, is the stable principle and permanent centre of the mission that God has entrusted to you in the world of contrasts: to live and bear witness to his love, immersing yourselves in that mystery of the divine economy which has united salvation and grace with the Cross (cf. *Redemptor Hominis, 11*).

Blessing you all, I willingly bless your religious families and your life of generous sacrifice, entrusting you to the Blessed Virgin, the Mother of the Church and the model of your consecrated life. Rely on the Pope's prayers. Accompany him with your prayers too, especially in these days of his apostolic pilgrimage through your beloved Brazil.

O.R. 642. 21 July 1980

Address to Men Religious at Sao Paulo
3 July 1980

Beloved sons, called by God to a special consecration in religious life: he who feels, at this moment of his pilgrimge through Brazil, the sincere joy of meeting with you, is the same one who, as Archbishop of Krakow, sought every opportunity to meet the men and women religious of his diocese and, as Bishop of Rome, tries to be with them either receiving them at his home, or going to meet them in the pastoral visits to Roman parishes. I do so for two reasons: because I am convinced of the efficacy of religious in the life and pastoral action of the Church at all levels, and because I am deeply aware of the inestimable value of religious life in itself.

What shall I say to you, Brazilian religious — Brazilian by birth or adoption — of the presence of religious in the pastoral action of the Church? Preparing interiorly for this visit, I studied with affectionate attention the history of the Church in this country, and it was a revelation for me to discover how closely this history, throughout its entire course, is linked — it could sometimes be said identified — with the tireless missionary activity of innumerable religious of various institutes. The first apostles of the land, as soon it was discovered, are religious — and we can mention one of the greatest as a tribute to them all: that admirable Jose de Anchieta whom I proclaimed Blessed, with deep and particular satisfaction, less than two weeks ago. Religious, too, were the majority of the priests dedicated to the evangelisation of the Indians, to their education in full keeping with their identity and, whenever it was necessary, to their defence, even at the cost of personal sacrifice. Even today, religious form just over half of the Brazilian clergy. I do not know any other country which can point to 193 religious among their 343 bishops, and among them two cardinals of the Holy Church, according to statistics of 31 December 1979!

What more shall I say to you? Your presence is for the Church of Brazil not something superfluous which can be done without, but a vital necessity. Some points will make this presence become more and more efficacious:

— first, priest religious should prove capable of fitting in, in a loyal and disinterested way, with diocesan priests, whose tasks they are called to share, not by way of exception, but on a habitual basis:

— second, lay religious should learn more and more to integrate their activity in an overall project, which is that of the whole Church, both at the diocesan and at the national level;

— third, in the spirit of the Document *Mutuae Relationes*, religious superiors should seek, accept, and cultivate a frank and filial dialogue with the Pastors placed by the Spirit of God to govern his Church. In this sense it cannnot be stressed too much how important are the relations between the National Conference of Bishops, whose task it is to work out and establish pastoral plans for the country, and the Conference of Religious, which assumes the task of promoting the religious life, taking care that it should remain faithful to its deepest roots and to the charism that characterises it.

Here we touch upon the second aspect: the deep identity of religious life. It is not because it is useful to the apostolate that religious life has a well-defined place in the Church and an unquestionable value. The contrary is true: religious life carries out an efficacious service for the apostolate because, and to the extent that, it remains firmly faithful to the place it occupies in the Church and to the charisms that characterise this place.

It is impossible to try to make here even a summary of the theology of religious life. But it will not be useless — as a living souvenir, as it were, of this meeting with the Pope — to recall some aspects.

The first one, on which everyone is agreed and which is not even a subject of discussion, is that when we speak of religious life, we refer to something very precise in the experience of the Church, at least with regard to essential elements.

Every Christian enjoys the full and legitimate freedom, according to his conscience, of entering religious life or not. But it is not up to him to define or reorganise what is essential in religious life, disregarding the life, the history and, I repeat, the 2,000 years experience of the Church.

These essential elements were reaffirmed not long ago by the Council, and by some documents dedicated to its correct interpretation in this matter. You know very well what they are:

1) Religious life is a *Schola Dominici servitii*, according to the fine formula of St. Benedict *(Rule, Pr. 45)*, a diligent, loving, persevering apprenticeship of those who desire only one thing in life: to serve the Lord. All the other dimensions of religious life, as the Second Vatican Council stresses them, are arranged in view of this service.

2) Religious life, the Council teaches, does not take its place in the Church on the level of institutional structures (it is not a hierarchical grade, not is it added as a third element between pastors and lay people), but in the line of charisms, and more exactly in the dynamism of that holiness which is the primary vocation of the Church. The first reason for which a Christian becomes a religious is not to assume a post, a responsibility, or a task in the Church, but to sanctify himself. This is his task and his responsibility, "and all these things shall be his as well". This is his service for the Church: the Church needs this school of holiness, in order to realise concretely her own vocation of holiness.

3) If the testimony which is expected of the layman is that of secularity, action in temporal affairs, then the testimony connatural to religious life in general, and to every religious in particular, is that of the Beatitudes, lived in everyday life. It is that of God's Absolute Being before which all the rest, even the most important temporal commitments, become utterly relative. It is, therefore, the testimony of the invisible, and finally that of the *Parousia*, which must be lived in hope even in this life.

4) For all these reasons, the total consecration that every religious makes of himself to God by the vows, which put the evangelical counsels into practice in his life, is seen to be important. This total consecration will signify for him the deepest, truest, and fullest liberation, which will lead him to greater communion with God and with his brothers, and to greater participation in divine life and in the community of men, beginning with the community of those who seek with him the Face of God. This total consecration brings with it, as a consequence, complete availability. The Church has always experienced in the course of her history that she could rely on religious for the most delicate missions.

5) It follows from all this that the religious cannot be other than a man of prayer, one who prays a great deal. This applies to contemplatives, but it also applies to any religious whatsoever.

In the light of this essential feature, and applying concretely some of its aspects, I wish to say to you, dear brothers and sons, some words of admiration and encouragement.

In the first place, I recall that the Church, in various recent documents, has spoken of the renewal of religious life. I think it is unnecessary to stress that, to be wholesome and to correspond to the view of the Church, and therefore to God's plan, this renewal cannot make itself an absolute, becoming an end in itself and disregarding valid criteria. Two criteria, among others, seem to me most important: the first is that religious life (and concretely every religious community) is not truly renewed if the purpose of the renewal is in practice the pursuit of what is easiest and most convenient, but only if the purpose is the pursuit of what is most authentic and most consistent with the aims of religious life itself. The second criterion is that religious life is renewed in order to become even more a path of holiness. Here that statement of the Lord which says "You will know them by their fruits", is particularly applicable. As far as it depends on us, we must do everything lest it could be said that the renewal of religious has led to its relaxation and then to its dissolution.

In the light of these criteria, I should say to you: bring about with all humility the desired renewal of religious life. It deserves the most serious efforts of religious families and of the Conference of Religious at all levels.

In the second place I would like to point out the originality of the presence of the religious in the world. Already on other occasions this point has been diagrammed as follows: there are two forms of presence in the world: one physical, direct, material; the other, invisible and spiritual, but no less real for that reason. Lay people, due to the fact that they affirm their vocation of physical presence in the world, need that strong sap that comes to them precisely from the spiritual presence of religious, and they would feel the lack of it if, through the euphoria of "immersion in the world", religious ended up by denying the Church the contribution of what is specifically theirs. It is not a call to alienation; on the contrary, it is an invitation to think that in the Church, according to the concept of St Paul, the clear difference (and not confusion!) and the valid complementarity (and not isolation!) of charisms and vocations, continues to be important. The presence of religious in temporal struggles will never be fruitful in the long run (but will it even be useful immediately?), if it takes place at the cost of the essential values, even the humblest, of religious life.

The third reflection: in the pursuit of collaboration there is a fequent temptation to dilute as much as possible, almost to the point of extinction, that which characterises and identifies religious life and religious. It is clear that this is not helpful either for religious life or for collaboration. A religious priest, immersed in the apostolate alongside diocesan priests, should show clearly by his attitude that he is a religious. The community should be able to sense it. The same should be said of a religious who is not a priest, or of a sister, in their respective collaboration with lay people.

The last reflection, in the same line as the previous one: there is a temptation, not an unreal nor even a remote one, for men and women religious to abandon the characteristic features of their religious family in order to merge with others, and a temptation to abandon the works which they were carrying out in order to engage in what is conventionally called the "direct apostolate". It seems that the facts are already beginning to show that the spiritual richness of the Church, and of her service to men, lies in variety. There is an impoverishment whenever everyone, under the pretext of unity or impressed by a certain priority, begins to do the same thing. I hope that religious may help the Church to continue to be present in the most diverse fields of her pastoral activity: education, assistance, care of the sick, assistance for orphans, the exercise of charity, etc.

I am certain that the human community in general, as well as the ecclesial community, will be grateful to religious life for this.

There remains for me only to bless you in the Lord's name. Doing so I ask the Lord that you may be, in the midst of men for their good, witnesses and heralds of the *mirabilia Dei* and the *investigabiles divitias Christi*.

O.R. 642.   21 July 1980

Address to Benedictine Monks and Nuns at Monte Cassino   20 September 1980

In the splendid setting of this Basilica, resurrected miraculously from the ruins of war and consecrated again by my unforgettable predecessor, Paul VI, overflowing today with such an elect assembly of sons and daughters of St Benedict — unique, perhaps, in the history of Cassino for more than a millennium — before his glorious tomb, here round the altar where the Eucharistic Sacrifice is being celebrated today, almost as if we caught a glimpse of him alive again, there spontaneously rises to my lips the jubilant cry of Isaiah: O venerated Father, *leva in circuitu oculos tuos, et vide: omnes isti congregati sunt, venerunt tibi, filii tui de longe venerunt, et filiae tuae de latere surrescerunt.*

They have come from all over the world to celebrate your jubilee, joyful to tell you their filial faithfulness, to express their wishes to you, to ask for your fruitful blessing in visible and longed-for communion with Peter's successor. And the latter is happy to be with them, to manifest to you, Patriarch, after the passing of so many centuries and millions of monks, the esteem and love that the whole Church professes for you, the architect, by the plan and grace of God, of an immeasurable amount of civilisation, culture, and above all, holiness.

Your life, although it took place in the restricted radius of one region, was marvellous for its virtue and miracles; but the action of your life-giving message spread to the whole of Europe and to the whole world, until it reached our day, thanks to that little, yet so great, book of yours, destined to become *fermentum divinae justitiae*, a Christian leaven for the multitudes that God was preparing for you, as in the past for Abraham, as an incomparable heritage.

It is very joyful and moving for me, and for all those here present, to think that in this very monastery, in a tiny obscure corner that even war respected, that book, your Rule, was written: as that inscribed stone there recalls, *hic scripsit Regulam, et verbo et opere docuit.*

Venerable Abbots, beloved sons and daughters of such a great Father and Lawmaker: at this meeting which we can define exceptional, and at this climax of the centenary celebrations of his birth, we must refer to that august book and start out from it again for the moral and religious reconstruction which urgently concerns us and which we promptly owe to the world. My very recent Apostolic Letter *Sanctorum Altrix* set out to propose, in a panoramic view, as it were, all the vital and fertile elements that Benedict's teaching and institution can still offer, not only for the life of monastic perfection, but also for the revival and strengthening of the attitude and practice inspired by the Gospel.

I learn furthermore with immense pleasure that, in worthy memory of the centenary, you are celebrating in Rome, the heart of Christendom, an original symposium precisely on the Rule, for the noble purpose of ascertaining and discovering, as a result of many recent studies and on the basis of experiments already made or in progress, the valid and vivifying elements it still possesses, the supporting and firm structures that must endure, and the subsidiary ones which the evolution of the times has made and makes outdated, and the indispensable values to adhere to tenaciously in the monasteries so that they can recognise themselves as still being seriously integrated in the Benedictine family.

As happens in all present-day thought and practice, you especially who are the pastors of the communities rightly feel the need that your identity as sons and disciples of Benedict should be quite clear. *Scientibus loquor:* you who have read and meditated at length upon your Rule, know very well what the Patriarch wishes to construct and at the same time teach by means of it, from which not to *temere declinetur a quoquam (3,7)*.

He wishes to construct, as is well known, the *dominici schola servitii (Prol. 45),* Your identity is in this absolute and complete service of the Absolute Value that is God. The whole world is in God; but the monastery, as Benedict likes to define it, is *domus Dei (53, 22)* in particular: the monk is there to serve the Lord of this house, in humility, obedience, prayer, silence, work, and especially in charity. You know the special stress that your Lawmaker, following Christ, lays on this virtue, as informing the whole of monastic life. The chapter on instruments of good works *(Rule 4)* informs us that Benedictine ascetics and mystical theology are actually just evangelical, drawn from a Gospel accepted and practised in all its consequences.

When this identity is accepted, here we have the intention and love — also so widespread today — authenticity. This is what I want, this is what all of us in the Church and in the world want from the Benedictines: fully aware of what the monk of the *mens* of the Patriarch is, we are really monks who are *revera* (he himself says), seekers of God, happy to live secluded from the world, but in a communion of love with brothers in the world, in a family context of obedience and charity, from which peace and joy springs: *nemo perturbetur neque contristetur in domo Dei (31, 19)*.

A very long and uninterrupted tradition, nearest in length to that of the Church itself, has tested the nobility, the beauty, the fruitfulness of Benedictine spirituality. Be proud of it in a holy way, and continue, albeit with due and prudent adaptations to today's changed circumstances, along the way laid down by the ancient Father and by the fathers of your tradition, without letting yourselves be overtaken or tempted by tendencies to secularism, by unreasonable and unnecessary innovations, and by exaggerated theories of pluralism, which end up by causing you to deviate from the line of your Lawmaker. It has been pointed out that one of the outstanding qualities of the Rule is clarity: everyone can easily learn and know what the great Master prescribes and recommends; all that remains is to follow it humbly, docilely, and joyfully,

Continue, therefore, with God's blessing, with the motherly smile of Mary the Queen of Monks, with the patronage of your Lawmaker, with the message of his word interpreted by sound tradition and expressed in your faithful example, to repeat, today and tomorrow, the power of faith, the sweet duty of prayer, passionate love of the liturgy, the advantage of authority and obedience, the cult of *lectio divina* and of all sacred studies, the sweetness of your Gregorian chant, willing dedication to manual work, dignity in the same external composure of attitudes and in the religious habit, the joy of community life, and above all, sincere pursuit of peace and charity.

But in this extraordinary and consoling meeting with all Benedictine Abbots and Superiors, it is a pleasure, and it seems to me a duty, to refer to what I already recalled in the above-mentioned Apostolic Letter on the characteristic fatherly note that your Lawmaker imprints on abbey government. You are superiors, administrators, teachers, but above all, fathers. In this "world without fathers", as I recalled there, you must bear witness that St Benedict thought of setting up his monastery as a family society in which there is a father who provides, teaches, and above all, loves his monks, respects them, esteems their personal dignity, makes them jointly responsible for decisions, and follows them with an affection that has even the tenderness of a mother's heart.

For you the norm is *plus amari quam timeri (64,15)*, and the two chapters assigned to your government (2 and 64), and especially chapter 64, an admirable one, which really sprang from a heart rich in wisdom and love, are the *magna carta* on which your behaviour must be based and by which it must be inspired. But it is the whole Rule that speaks of you, to instil in you wisdom, prudence, inflexibility with regard to vices, the promotion of virtues, sympathy for the weak, and above all that Roman and Christian *discretio* which distinguishes the remarkable code and is perhaps the main reason for its diffusion and validity. The abbot's balance brings about and nourishes mutual love between abbot and sons, and among brothers. In our world, where lack of love empties hearts of energy and of joy, let people know and see, through your generous sacrifice, that the monastery is a society of true human and supernatural love.

Finally, I wish to address a special greeting to all the female branches, some of which are also officially represented here. Behind the wake of the light and the fragrant virtue of Scholastica, who lies here beside her brother, your pure and virginal presence, all you daughters of St Benedict, brings joy and edification to the people of God. In the silence of your cloister or in the humility of your works, you in particular reproduce, and you must make an effort to do so with conviction, the spiritual attitude of the Virgin Mother, content to be an *ancilla Domini,* completely available solely for the will of the heavenly Father. *Frondete, flores, quasi lilium et date odorem, et frondete in gratiam,* and for the joy and benefit of all brothers on earth sing to the Lord the most chaste praises, and to Christ your Bridegroom the exultation of your loving intimacy.

Fathers and brothers and all sisters, with immense joy therefore, *gaudeamus diem festum celebrantes in honorem beati Benedicti,* in whose glory the Angels and Saints exult, from whose example and patronage the Church and the whole world avails itself. His voice still rings out: *"Christo nihil omnino praeponere" (72,11).* It is his fundamental message, and if his most beautiful dream is that all members of the monastic family should be at peace, that dream will be a happy reality for the whole human family if Christ is at last inserted in its context.

O.R. 654. 20 October 1980

Address to the Union of Women Major Superiors of Italy
11 October 1980

Beloved Sisters in the Lord, at the end of your annual assembly you have desired this audience, reserved completely for you, Mothers General and Provincial of the many Congregations and religious houses scattered in all the regions of Italy. I greet you warmly and through you I wish to extend my affectionate greeting to all your fellow Sisters in Italy who, in the frantic metropolises as well as in remote mountain villages, are living with love and joy their consecration to Christ and to souls. Yes, beloved Sisters, take to all the Sisters entrusted to your responsibility the greeting of the Pope; tell them that he remembers them, follows them, esteems them, prays for them, suffers with them, is concerned about their human and spiritual experiences, and would like them to be always joyful and generous, even in inevitable tribulations.

I wish furthermore to express to you my satisfaction with this general assembly of yours, in which you have wanted to participate in such large numbers to study the subject: "Religious life and the family", which echoes the theme dealt with in the Synod of Bishops now in progress, and to talk about it among yourselves, exchanging your experiences.

It is an important subject because the relations of Sisters with family communities are frequent. Sisters, in fact, are in continual contact with children in nursery schools and are acquainted with the background of every home; they approach boys and girls in schools, oratories, Catholic associations, and in the various ecclesial groups; they take part in pastoral councils and in parish and diocesan catechesis. Above all, Sisters are present in orphanages, hospitals, homes for the aged, clinics, places of assistance and care for the handicapped, visits to the sick in the homes, and also to places of aid for drifters, those excluded from society, drug addicts, etc.

It can be said that the Sister, in a certain way, accompanies families on their existential way, and therefore her responsibility is great, but great also must be her consolation, being able in this way to make her concrete contribution of faith and charity to what is the masterpiece of love of God, the Creator and Redeemer.

Today, more than ever, many persons are tormented by the problem of existence and of their own identity. They feel the longing to go beyond the limits of history and time, they feverishly look for truth! So the first task and the first duty of the Sister in her relations with the family is to bear witness to truth, that is, to help the modern family rediscover the real meaning of life and history.

Dear Sisters, bring to families the truth as it was revealed by Christ and as it is taught by the Church! Do not let yourselves be disturbed by the sensation made by the many insistent ideologies which confuse and depress. Always sow the good seed of truth, following the teaching of the Church and the example of the saints.

Hence the necessity of a serious and authentic updating in the various fields of doctrine on the part of the Sister, overcoming the dangers of superficiality and emotion. It is necessary, therefore, to watch carefully over the various means of *aggiornamento* and guidance (books, newspapers, reviews, courses of study, etc.), in order not to be disconcerted by false ideas, and then misdirect the persons that have to be approached. Every family wants the truth from those who are consecrated to God: therefore be faithful and happy to be able to proclaim it and bear witness to it!

Then bring to the family peace! The spirit must be firm and the staunch in truth, but the heart must be full of understanding and compassion. The family needs above all spiritual help and encouragement, great support and affection. Never so much as now does the family need to feel the Divine Master close and consoling, willing to bestow his forgiveness, certainty, hope and love! Certainly, evil must be combatted and error condemned; but every person must be understood and loved; the oil of kindness and mercy must be spread on every wound, as was done by the Good Samaritan in the parable.

But to bring peace it is necessary to possess it! Therefore your houses must be oases of serenity, achieved through the school of patience and mutual charity.

Bring peace to families with your faith and your love! Bring it especially where suffering groans, where loneliness reigns, where division weighs, where the hope of a life after death is lacking! Bring peace, pointing to the Crucified Christ and our real country which is in heaven (cf. *Ph 4:20*).

Beloved Sisters, Sister Elizabeth of the Holy Trinity wrote: "Let us live with God as with a friend; let us make our faith alive in order to communicate with God through everything that makes saints. We bear in us our heaven, because he who satisfies the glorified in the light of vision gives himself to us in faith and in mystery. It is the same thing. It seems to me that I have found my heaven on earth, because heaven is God, and God is in my soul. The day when I understood this, everything was illuminated in me and I would like to whisper this secret to those I love, in order that they, too, through everything, may always adhere to God and that Christ's prayer: 'Father, let them be consummated in one', may be realized" (*Scritti, Roma, Post. gener. dei Carmelitani Scalzi, 1967*).

You, too, live this secret and proclaim it to families, with the help and assistance of the Blessed Virgin and St Joseph: it is the secret that illuminates, comforts and saves!

With these wishes, imploring from the Lord an abundance of heavenly favours, I warmly impart to you the conciliatory Apostolic Blessing, which I gladly extend to all your fellow Sisters.

O.R. 656.   3 November 1980

Homily: Mass for Religious at Altötting

18 November 1980

Dear brothers and sisters in the Lord, on the pilgrimage through your country we come together at the house of the Lord, at this sanctuary, to have a special meeting with Mary, our Blessed Lady. You, revered brothers and sisters, who as members of religious orders, secular institutes and other religious communities are living a special vocation, participate in this meeting most of all. You can say about yourselves that through your consecrated total offering of yourselves "your life is hidden with Christ in God" (*Col 3:3*).

.....Allow me to compare our common visit to Altötting with Mary's visit to Zachary and Elizabeth. I am confident that our visit will bear abundant fruit if we try to make it similar to Mary's. In this we want to be guided as much as possible by the light of the word of God which we bear in this liturgy.

Mary enters the house of her relative, she greets Elizabeth, and hears her words of greeting. These words are most familiar to us. We repeat them innumerable times, especially when we meditate on the mysteries of the Rosary: "Blessed are you among women, and blessed is the fruit of your womb" (*Lk 1:42*). That is how the wife of Zachary greets Mary. With these words she proclaims a first beatitude whose sound echoes in the history of the Church and of mankind, in the history of human hearts and thoughts. Has man ever been able to attain to anything more exalted? Has he ever been able to experience about himself anything more profound? Has man been able through any achievement of his being man, through his intellect, the greatness of his mind or through heroic deeds, to be lifted up to a higher state than has been given to him in this "fruit of the womb" of Mary in whom the Eternal Word, the Son who is of one being with the Father, became flesh; is the vastness of the human heart able to receive a greater fullness of truth and love than that in which God himself sets about to give his only Son to man? The Son of God becomes man, conceived by the Holy Spirit! Yes indeed, Mary, you are blessed more than all other women.

To her first beatitude Elizabeth adds a second one: "Blessed is she who believed that the promise made her by the Lord would be fulfilled" (*Lk 1:45*). Elizabeth extols and praises the faith of Mary. With this she entered in a profound way into the unique greatness of the moment when the Virgin from Nazareth had heard the words of the Annunciation. For this message had burst open all limits of human understanding in spite of the elevated tradition of the Old Testament. And behold, Mary did not only hear these words, she did not only receive them, she gave the answer which fully responded to them: "Behold, I am the handmaid of the Lord; be it done to me according to your word" (*Lk 1:38*). Such an answer demanded from Mary an unconditional faith, a faith after the example of Abraham and Moses, a faith even greater than that. It is precisely this faith of Mary which Elizabeth extols.

My dear brothers and sisters! With regard to the mystery of the personal call of each one of you we can repeat in a certain sense — keeping in mind the proportions, of course — : "Blessed are you because you have believed." The faith of Mary has shone also in you when you spoke your *"fiat"*, your "yes" to the call to the special fellowship of Christ. It was only in faith that you were able to take the first steps as people called by the Lord — just as once upon a time the disciples did at the Sea of Galilee; it was in faith that you perceived the word of the one who called you; in faith you left behind your previous life with all its possibilities; in faith you started to follow the Lord, ready from now on to expect the meaning and fruitfulness of your life only from your total union with him.

Believing in the faithfulness of the One who calls and in the power of his Spirit, you put yourselves at God's disposal through the vows of poverty, consecrated virginity, and obedience; and this not as an obligation which can be revoked, not as life in a monastery for a time, not as co-workers in a group which has come together for a specific task and which breaks up again at will. No, in faith you have spoken a "yes" which is all-inclusive and for ever and which finds its expression in your way of life and even in your religious garb. In our time where people shy away from binding ties, where many would like to turn to a "life of probation", it belongs to you to testify that one can dare to enter into a definitive bond and to take a decision for God which embraces the whole life.

Your "yes" given years or decades ago has to be ever reaffirmed to the Lord. This requires a daily listening and probing into the daily responding to his crucified — and crucifying — love. Only he is able to keep the gift of vocation alive in you. Only he is able through his Spirit to overcome the weakness experienced time and again.

Also Mary's "yes" which she spoke in a unique decision had to be redeemed by her over and over again, until she was standing beneath the cross where she offered her Son and became our Mother. He who wanted Mary's "yes" for the cooperation in salvation, also wants your "yes". You *did* say it! Say it every day anew! Then it will be true for you, too: "Blessed are you because you have believed!"

Faith makes the status of religious become a special witness of the coming kingdom of God. Christ speaks about this kingdom in connection with the mystery of the resurrection of the body: "In the resurrection they neither marry nor are given in marriage" *(Mt 22:30)*. In the liturgy we celebrate today at Our Blessed Lady's shrine at Altötting, this mystery is enunciated in the Letter of St Paul to the Corinthians: "When this perishable nature has put on imperishability, and when this mortal nature has put on immortality, then the words of scripture will come true: 'Death is swallowed up in victory'. Death, where is your victory? Death, where is your sting? Now the sting of death is sin, and sin gets its power from the Law. So let us thank God for giving us the victory through our Lord Jesus Christ." *(1 Co 15:54-57)*.

Today these impressive words of the Apostle of the Gentiles have been read in honour of Mary. For through her Assumption into heaven she has attained to the full participation in the resurrection of Christ.

The very same words, however, the Apostle addresses also to you, dear brothers and sisters; because by the great "yes" of your life you have chosen consecrated celibacy "for the sake of the kingdom" *(Mt 19:12)*. In this way you are a visible sign of the coming kingdom of God!

The heart of each one of you who has forgone fatherhood and motherhood of this earth, may be filled again and again by the inestimable richness of spiritual fatherhood and motherhood which so many of your fellow-creatures are in urgent need of! You do not love less; you love more! The fact that in a very profound way you know how to care, to help, to heal, to educate, to guide, and to console is shown, last but not least, by the many and often moving letters by which the Pope is being implored not to allow sisters, priests or brothers to be withdrawn from a certain kindergarten, a school, an old folks' home or hospital, from a station for social work, or a parish.

Why is your service valued so much? It is not only because of your professional proficiency; not only because you are able, due to your choice of life, to give more time; it is in the first place because people feel that through you someone else is at work. Because to the extent you live your full surrender to the Lord, you communicate something from him; and it is he for whom the human heart is longing in the last end.

It is he whom you love in all those who are entrusted to your manifold care, your prayer of intercession, your hidden sacrifices, him you serve "in the sick and the old, the handicapped and the underprivileged whom no one else cares for ... in the children, the young adults, in school, catechesis and pastoral work. Him you serve in the most humble things as well as in the performances of tasks which sometimes require a high education" (cf. *Allocution in Czestochowa, 5 June 1979*). For his sake many from your communities leave their native country in order to serve the kingdom of God in the young Churches with an untiring engagement. Him you seek and find everywhere, similar to the Bride of the Song of Songs: "... I found him whom my heart loves" *(Sg 3:4)*. This fulfilment of life — the fact that in everything you find him and in him everything — is at the same time the best encouragement for young Christians to respond within the Church to the call of Jesus — also to the call to a life according to the evangelical counsels. In you they can come to understand that whosoever gives himself up has found the meaning of his life (cf. *Mk 8:35)*.

Mary to whom we have come today as pilgrims to Altötting carries the features of that woman whom the Apocalypse describes: "A woman adorned with the sun, standing on the moon, and with twelve stars on her head for a crown *(Apoc 12:1)*. The woman, who stands at the end of the history of creation and salvation, corresponds evidently to the one about whom it is said in the first pages of the Bible that she "is going to crush the head of the serpent".

Between this promising beginning and the apocalyptic end Mary has brought to light a Son "who is to rule all nations with an iron sceptre" *(Apoc 12:5)*.

Her heel it is which is being persecuted by that first "serpent". She it is with whom the apocalyptic dragon makes war, for being the Mother of the Redeemed, she is the image of the Church whom we likewise call mother *(Lumen Gentium, 68)*.

Dear brothers and sisters! You are called in a special way to take part in this spiritual battle! You are called into this permanent conflict which our Mother Church endures and which forms in her the image of the Woman, the Mother of the Messiah. you who find the very centre of your vocation in the adoration of the Holy God, you are also exposed to the temptation of the evil one in a special way — as it can be seen in an exemplary way in the temptation of the Lord. The war is raging between the Word of God and the device of the evil one. Between "Tell these stones to turn into loaves!" and "Man does not live on bread alone" *(Mt 4:3 f)*. God wants to conquer the earth (cf. *Gn 1:28*) by bringing it — and ourselves — to perfection. The temptation of the evil one wants us to disfigure it and ourselves; to become enslaved by work and spoiled by our leisure time; to make endless sacrifices for our outside and wither away inside; to adorn our home and be homeless; to value having and forget being; that possessions become our "god". Through your inner battle for the spirit of poverty and through this poverty which can be seen and serves as a sign, dear sisters and brothers, you help all members of the Church and of mankind to be careful stewards of this world, to possess things in such a way that they do not possess us, not to allow the sustenance of life to become the meaning of life.

"Throw yourself down", says the second temptation of Jesus (cf. *Mt 4:6*). Throw yourself into the adventure, dare to jump into the realm of dreams, is the allurement of today; get drunk from life's horn of plenty — in the drunkenness of speed, the drunkenness of sensuality, the drunkenness of delusions, and the drunkenness of violence. God has given us a heart to experience (and enjoy) things, and much which can fill us — above all the "thou". But without him all is too little. We either seek our happiness in him or we miss it — being chased by our pursuit of happiness, from disappointment to disappointment, up to disgust and aversion. Through your renouncement of the "thou" which brings fulfilment in marriage and through your special cultivation of loving openness for God, dear brothers and sisters, you help all in the Church; to give themselves without losing themselves; to turn towards each other and so to grow into God; to enjoy the things that pass in such a way that one keeps united with the eternal things at the same time, as it is said in a liturgical prayer (seventeenth Sunday during the year).

Even more glorious and more dangerous than "world" and "thou", than wealth and happiness, is the "I" and its claims to self-realisation. God wants man "in his own image and likeness" (cf. *Gn 1:6 f.*); Lucifer wants him as an anti-god — who refuses to worship God (cf. *Jr 2:20*) and in return falls a prey to idols: "He showed him all the kingdoms of the world...: I will give you all these, if you fall at my feet and worship me" *(Mt 4:8 f.)*. All creative exertion and any self-realisation — in politics, in economics, in the intellectual life, and even in the Church — carries with itself the danger of vanity, of pride and even of ruthlessness. My dear religious, by your faithful struggle for the spirit of obedience and for its visible sign, obedience towards your superior, you help all the faithful and the Church herself to understand and to overcome the temptation of power; you help them to come to the perfection of freedom in the surrender of self.

Today, maybe more than ever before, the kingdom of God which "suffers violence" (cf. *Mt 11:12*) needs new "warriors" in response to the temptations and demands of our time. It wants to find them in your monasteries and communities, moulded and supported by the regular life. Be convinced that such generous men and women will attract new generations who follow Christ and "renew the face of the earth" *(Ps 104:30)* also today as well as tomorrow!

During these days of my pilgrimage with you the Church commemorates three saints of your country. To them, in conclusion, I would like to recommend your way and service in the Church. May St Albert help you to perceive from the signs of the time the call of God and to respond to it in the spirit of your founders. May St Gertrude implore for you the zeal and the fruit of finding God in your meditation and liturgy. May St Elizabeth help you to have a delicate sense and unlimited openness as you turn to all who need you. Albert, Gertrude, Elizabeth — they are joined here in Altötting by the humble and cheerful porter of St Anne's Monastery, St Brother Konrad. We see him kneeling in his cell — before the small window which had been made especially for him so that he could always look at the altar of the church. May we, too, in our daily lives break through the walls of the visible world in order to keep our eyes always and everywhere fixed upon the Lord! Together with Mary let us now continue our visit to the sanctuary she loves so much. Let us enter together with her and let us repeat:

"My soul proclaims the greatness of the Lord, and my spirit exults in God my saviour; because he has looked upon his lowly handmaid. Yes, from this day forward all generations will call me blessed, for the Almighty has done great things for me. Holy is his name, and his mercy reaches from age to age for those who fear him" *(Lk 1:46-50)*.

Indeed, my dear brothers and sisters! The Almighty has done "great things" for each one of you! Great things! For each one of you! Do not cease praising him! Do not cease thanking him! Do not cease living your total surrender, your vocation each single day anew under the protection of the Immaculate Virgin, Our Blessed Lady of Altötting!

And so the kingdom of God will be alive in you!

O.R. 662.　　　　　　　　　　　　　　　　　　15 December 1980

Homily: Mass for Religious
2 February 1981

.....Today, forty days after the solemnity of the mystery of Christ's Nativity, with the feast of the Presentation of the Lord, the liturgy now intends to illuminate before us the perspective of the Paschal Vigil, in which the candle, the symbol of the Risen Christ, the conqueror of sin and death, will be blessed.

Today, too, the Church has us bless the candles which you, beloved brothers and sisters, have brought with you in a gesture of offering, replete with a deep interior meaning. The candle which you hold in your hands is in the first place the symbol of Christ, "the glory of Israel and the light of peoples", and also the symbol of his Messianic power and mission. For this reason we share this light with others and we intend to transfer it to all the attitudes of our lives.

This candle also represents the gift of faith, infused into you in holy Baptism, in which you are offered and consecrated to the Blessed Trinity. But this candle, in your hands as men and women religious, is intended to signify in particular that unconditional choice which you have made of Christ, the light of your lives, in the definitive and complete gift of yourselves, by dedicating yourselves to religious life, which is a more perfect form of baptismal consecration: "The members of each institute should recall, first of all, that when they made profession of the evangelical counsels they were responding to a divine call, to the end that, not merely being dead to sin but renouncing the world also, they might live for God alone. This constitutes a special baptismal consecration, and is a fuller expression of it" *(Perfectae Caritatis, 5).*

You are therefore called to a special imitation of Jesus and to vigorous witness of the spiritual requirements of the Gospel in modern society. And if the candle which you hold in your hands is also the symbol of your life, offered to God, this life must be consumed entirely for his glory.

Be strengthened, helped and spurred on to this imitation and this witness by the exemplary interior disposition of the persons of whom the Gospel speaks to us today: by the silent and tender love of St Joseph; the strong and constant faith of old Simeon; the continual and prayerful fidelity of the aged prophetess Anna; but above all, by the absolute and complete availability of the Blessed Virgin, the protagonist, together with her Son, of this mystery of salvation, which directs the episode of the presentation in the Temple towards the salvific event of the Cross. The Church herself — Paul VI wrote — "has recognised in the heart of the Virgin, who takes her Son to Jerusalem to present him to the Lord, a will for oblation, which went beyond the ordinary meaning of the rite" *(Marialis Cultus, 20)*.

You, too, beloved brothers and sisters, must always keep intact that "will for oblation", with which you generously responded to the invitation of Jesus to follow him more closely along the way to Calvary, through the sacred bonds which unite you with him in an extraordinary way in chastity, poverty and obedience: these vows constitute a synthesis, in which Christ wishes to express himself, undertaking — through your response — a decisive struggle against the spirit of this world. Chastity, embraced for the kingdom of heaven, makes the person's heart free in a special way, so as to set it on fire more and more with charity for God and for brothers; poverty, accepted voluntarily in order to follow Christ, makes people participate in that poverty of Christ, who though he was rich, became poor for our sake, so that by his poverty we might become rich; obedience, by which the complete consecration of our own will offered to God as a sacrifice of ourselves, unites us with God's salvific will (Cf. *Perfectae Caritatis, 12-14*).

But precisely through this choice, such a radical one, you have become, like Christ and Mary, a "sign that is contradicted", that is a sign of division, rupture and conflict with regard to the spirit of the world, which sets man's finality and happiness in riches, in pleasure and in self-assertion of one's own individuality.

Today, as we mutually communicate and share the "light" which shines from the candles, let us think of all the men and women religious, scattered all over the world; let us pray intensely for them so that, wherever they may be and function, they may really shine with that light which is Christ, and always be a real sign of his Gospel and his Spirit!

May all men and women religious be able to offer themselves together with Christ, like a flame that is consumed in love! May they live in him and for him, in the Church and for the Church! And may the Blessed Virgin bring them to this ever deeper intimacy with her Son, leading them along the way to oblation and donation. May Mary always be your example, your model, your strength, beloved brothers and sisters. This woman becomes also — as I said on another occasion — the sign of contradiction to the world, and at the same time the sign of hope... This woman who conceived spiritually before she conceived physically, this woman who... was inserted intimately and irrevocably into the mystery of the Church,

exercising a spiritual motherhood with regard to all peoples. This woman...is the great expression of total consecration of Jesus Christ" (*Address to Women Religious, Washington, 7 October 1979*).
This is my wish and my blessing.
Amen. Amen.

O.R. 670.   9 February 1981

Address to Women Religious at Baclaran

17 February 1981

Dearly beloved sisters, I bless the providence of God that has brought me back to Manila, back to this Sanctuary of Our Lady of Perpetual Help, where I once celebrated Mass. I bless the providence of God that has brought me to you, and you to me. It always brings me happiness to be with sisters during my apostolic journeys, but today there is the special joy of knowing that your country is one of those where vocations to the consecrated life are flourishing, and that this generous response to grace is itself a gift of God to you.

And as I thank the Lord for the many people whom he has called to the religious life, I wish to express to you my esteem and affection in Christ Jesus, and I wish to offer you my encouragement. In the first place, I would like to help you preserve and increase in your hearts the reverence and love for your sublime vocation. I pray that every day you will respond to that vocation more generously, so that you will grow steadily in the likeness of Christ your Ideal and your Teacher; for your religious consecration is essentially an act of love for Jesus Christ.

The more intensely you live this love and unite yourselves more closely to Jesus, the greater witness you will bear to the Gospel. It has often been noted that there is a close connection between the fervour of the religious life of a country and the condition of the Church in that country: fervent religious life means a living and apostolic Church; where that fervour grows cold, the vitality of the local Church is reduced. If, by a mischance, tepidity and mediocrity were to set in, they would soon be reflected among the Christian people. On the other hand, throughout the history of the Church, when she has been assailed by crises, it has always been the religious life that has given the signal for a reawakening and a renewed fidelity to the Gospel.

And your own responsibility in this regard is increased by the fact of the special situation prevailing in the Philippines. Yours is a land profoundly marked by Catholicism, in an immense part of the world that needs the witness of a fervent and vital Church, so that the Gospel may be more widely known and embraced.

You have perfectly understood this, and all your activity shows that your generous consecration to the love of God makes you particularly capable of loving all your brothers and sisters, ready to spend yourselves for them with no thought of self and without reserve. I know how hard you work for children, for the sick and the aged, for families, for the poor and for the many refugees who have come to this region. I know that your devotion also reaches out to the mission lands; I know that you share in catechetical work, and I assure you that this work is deeply appreciated by the bishops. You are truly witnesses to Christ's love, and your pastors are thankful for your own loving presence and activity among those whom the Saviour loves with a special love . In the name of Jesus and in the name of his Church I thank you all. At the same time I would assure you that the transformation of the world and the building up of Christ's Kingdom of justice and peace can be effected only by grace and the power of God's love in us. Only love can transform hearts, and without love there can be no adequate reform of structures in society. The only violence that leads to the building up of the Kingdom of Christ is the sacrifice and service that are born of love.

I also express my gratitude to those of you who live the cloistered and contemplative life, so open to the presence of the living God, in the midst of a world that is so often confused and is groping to find the light. You are so deeply needed. And through your daily life of prayer and sacrifice, united with the oblation of Christ, you powerfully aid your sisters in the active apostolate. You are, moreover, of great assistance to the whole Church and its visible head in the mission of proclaiming Christ, and I tell you that I count very much upon your collaboration and your supplications to the Lord.

The mission of religious is thus a very important one. And in order to help you to respond to it ever more perfectly, I would like to mention three points of fundamental importance.

First, there is your task of being witnesses. By reason of your baptism, you must be a sign and instrument of union with God and of the salvation of the world. It is life in the Spirit that must come first, through listening to the word, through interior prayer, through the faithful accomplishment of the task given to you, through the gift of yourselves in service, and through the humility of repentance. Through your religious consecration, you are a visible testimony to the world of the deep mystery of Christ, for you represent him "in contemplation on the mountain, or proclaiming the kingdom of God to the multitudes, or healing the sick and maimed and converting sinners to a good life, or blessing children and doing good to all people, always in obedience to the will of the Father who sent him" *(Lumen Gentium, 46)*. Through your particular vocation, lived out in an Order or Congregation approved by the Church, you are a special sign of sanctification and apostolic work that gives you a specific role in the Church, a role with its own distinctive character. Always remain faithful to that vocation, in spite of temptations. Find your joy in preserving your interior identity and in being outwardly recognised for what you are.

The second point that I wish to mention is prayer. It is vital that everyone should appreciate the need for prayer and should actually pray, but religious, as people called to be specialists in prayer, must seek God and love him above all things; in all circumstances, they must strive to live a life hidden with Christ in God, a life from which love of neighbour springs and becomes a pressing need. You must, therefore, through Christ and with Christ and in Christ, intensify your personal and communal familiarity with the principal source of apostolic and charitable activity, and in this way you will be sharing intimately in the mission which takes its origin from the Father. As I said in my message to the Plenary Meeting of the Sacred Congregation for Religious and Secular Institutes, "your first duty is to be with Christ. A constant danger for those engaged in apostolic work is to become so engrossed in work for the Lord as to forget the Lord of the work". And so, in the taxing routine of your apostolic tasks, always make sure that you devote periods of each day to personal and community prayer. These times of prayer must be carefully guarded and suitably prolonged, and you must not hesitate to supplement them by periods of more intense recollection and prayer, at times especailly set aside for this purpose. You must always ensure that the natural centre of your communities is the Eucharist: you will accomplish this by your fervent daily participation in the Mass, and by community prayer in an oratory where the Eucharistic presence of Christ expresses and realises what must be the principal mission of every religious family.

The third point that I wish to mention is loving docility to the Church's magisterium, which is an obvious consequence of the special ecclesial position which is yours. As you know, religious life has no meaning except in the Church and in faithfulness to her directives. "It would be a serious mistake to make the two realities — religious life and ecclesial structures — independent one of the other, or to oppose one to the other as if they could subsist as two distinct entities, one charismatic, the other institutional. Both elements, namely, the spiritual gifts and the ecclesial structures, form one, even though complex, reality" *(Mutuae Relationes, 34)*. So I exhort you to be always ready to embrace the teaching of the Church, and, in fidelity to your charism, to collaborate in the pastoral activity of your local dioceses, under the direction of your bishops united to Peter and in union with Christ. Your adherence to the word of God as it is proclaimed by the Church will be the measure of your effectiveness in communicating the truth and the freedom of Christ. The same Holy Spirit who makes us attentive to the signs of the times has endowed Christ's Church with the apostolic and pastoral charism of magisterium, so that she may effectively transmit Christ's vivifying and liberating word of truth. Let us always remember the words of Jesus: "You will learn the truth and the truth will make you free" *(Jn 8:31)*.

It is so appropriate that our meeting takes place today in this Sanctuary dedicated to Mary, Mother of Perpetual Help, the title which reminds us that we are in constant need of her protection. As the Council teaches, the Mother of God is the Christian's model in faith, love and perfect union with Christ (cf. *Lumen Gentium, 63*): and in a special way she is the Mother and model of those who live the consecrated life.

You show your devotion to Mary by celebrating her feasts, by daily prayer in her honour and especially the Rosary, and by imitating her life. May that devotion grow stronger every day. Your consecrated life should mirror Mary's life: the "yes" which she uttered at the Annunciation was nothing but a confirmation of her previous attitude, and the point of departure for a journey in the Lord's company that lasted all her life. In this way, Mary reminds religious of the need to respond ever more generously to the Lord's plans for them. Each one will give this response in the first place by her openness to the Holy Spirit, by her continual conversion to Christ, by her chastity, poverty and obedience, in short by the unending discovery of her vocation and mission in the Church. And this constitutes that continued formation that for a number of years has been put forward as being so necessary.

The consecrated love of your religious life is lived in the context of an ecclesially approved Institute and for this reason has a community element. It concerns all religious, whatever their place in their communities. Each Institute has responsibility for the formation of its members according to its proper charism and in fidelity to the magisterium of the Church. In this regard the union among sisters, devotion to others, interest in the world's problems, and the wholesome organisation of daily life will sustain and foster the efforts of all concerned.

I would like to extend an earnest invitation to you to intensify your apostolic collaboration at the service of Christian families. This is in harmony with the conclusions reached by the recent Synod of Bishops. The links between families and the religious life are both profound and vital; the Christian family is the normal source of vocations to the religious life. Religious life will help families to become ever more Christian and to witness ever more clearly to the love of Christ, by assisting them in the Christian education of their children, in caring for the sick and in meeting the problems of life.

By your contact with families and through the example of holiness that you give in all your apostolates, you are able to be instruments of God's grace in regard to religious vocations. Indeed, you have been given this role to play: through prayer and your joyful lives of consecration to the Lord you are called to make the religious vocation in the Church something attractive to young girls and young women today. They must be able to perceive clearly — being convinced by the witness you give — that your lives are permeated with a personal love for your spouse Jesus Christ, a love that also embraces him in the whole of humanity. In my first Encyclical I mentioned that we "cannot live without love". We remain incomprehensible to ourselves if we do not experience it and make it our own (cf. *Redemptor Hominis*, 10). And it is when we do bear witness to a joyful and sacrificial love that our way of life becomes credible and the call of Christ, humanly speaking, becomes attractive and worth following. To be able to show the young that consecrated love for Jesus can itself fulfil the deepest aspirations of the human person is a great mission of faith, and, dear sisters, it is yours.

Finally, I thank you once again for your help in making this pilgrimage possible through your prayers and your ready aid. I entrust all your intentions to Our Lady of Perpetual Help, and I ask her to assist you to live your vocation ever more generously, for the coming of the Kingdom of her beloved Son, our Lord Jesus Christ. For in the words of Saint Peter: "Without having seen him, you

love him; though you do not now see him, you believe in him and rejoice with unutterable and exalted joy" *(1 P 1:8).*
Beloved Sisters: Praised be Jesus Christ!

O.R. 672. 23 February 1981

Homily at Mass for Men Religious, Manila
17 February 1981

.....At this time I wish to address a special message to the men religious — both priests and brothers — who are present here, and through them to all the men religious of the Philippines. May I begin, my brothers, by expressing my gratitude to the Lord for your presence in the Church and for your collaboration in the Church's mission of proclaiming the Gospel of our Lord Jesus Christ.

In the passage from Saint John which we have just heard, we are reminded of the essence of religious life. "You did not choose me, but I chose you and appointed you that you should go and bear fruit" *(Jn 15:16).* Through the initiative of the Saviour and your own free response, Christ has become the purpose of your life and the centre of all your thoughts. It is because of Christ that you made your profession of the evangelical counsels: and it is Christ who will sustain you in faithfulness to himself and in loving service to his Church.

Religious consecration is essentially an act of love: Christ's love for you and in return your love for him and for all his brethern. This mystery is proclaimed today in the Gospel when Jesus says to his disciples: "As the Father has loved me, so I have loved you; abide in my love" *(Jn 15:9).* Christ wants you to abide in him, to be nourished by him daily in the celebration of the Eucharist and to surrender your lives to him through prayer and self-denial. Trusting in his word and confident of his mercy, you respond to Christ's love. You choose to follow him more closely in chastity, poverty and obedience; and you want to share more completely in the life and holiness of the Church. You want to love all those whom Christ loves as brothers and sisters.

The world today needs to see your love for Christ. It needs the public witness of religious life. As Paul VI once said: "Modern man listens more willingly to witnesses than to teachers, and if he does listen to teachers, it is because they are witnesses" (*AAS 66 (1974), 5680*). If the non-believers of this world are to come to believe in Christ, they need your faithful witness — a witness which springs from your complete trust in the bountiful mercy of the Father and your persevering hope in the power of the Cross and Resurrection.

And so the ideals, values and convictions which underlie your commitment to Christ must be translated into the language of daily life. In the midst of the people of God, in the local ecclesial community, your public witness is part of your contribution to the mission of the Church. As St Paul says, "You are a letter from Christ... written not with ink but with the Spirit of the living God, not on tablets of stone but on tablets of human hearts" *(2 Co 3:3)*.

As religious brothers and priests you are engaged in a great variety of apostolic activities: proclaiming the word of God, administering the sacraments, teaching, catechising, caring for the sick, assisting the poor and orphans, exercising charity, serving by prayer and sacrifice, building up the local communities to reflect the Gospel and embody the kingdom of God. As you carry out these works of service with steadfast perseverance, remember the advice of St Paul: "Whatever you do, work at it with your whole being, do it for the Lord rather than for men" *(Col 3:23)*.

All these apostolic activities retain their importance today. They continue to be vital dimensions of evangelisation, bearing prophetic witness to God's love and contributing to full human advancement. I am sure that the community in general, as well as the ecclesial community, will be grateful to the religious for helping the Church to maintain her commitment to these diverse expressions of her pastoral activity.

At the same time, you rightly seek additional ways of bearing witness to Christ and serving his people. The Church must indeed be attentive to the needs of the men and women of our time. She cannot be indifferent to the problems which they face or to the injustices which they suffer. As you seek new ways of furthering the Gospel and of promoting human values, I offer you my encouragement and the assurance of my prayers. At the same time I ask you to observe this guideline: that each apostolic endeavour should be in harmony with the teaching of the Church, with the apostolic purposes of your individual Institutes and with the original charism of your founders. May I also remind you of my words at Guadalupe: "You are priests and religious; you are not social or political leaders or officials of a temporal power... Let us not be under the illusion that we are serving the Gospel if we dilute our charism through an exaggerated interest in the wide field of temporal problems". It is important for people to see you as "servants of Christ and stewards of the mysteries of God" *(1 Co 4:1)*.

Faithfulness to Christ in religious life requires a threefold fidelity: fidelity to the Gospel, fidelity to the Church, fidelity to the particular charism of your Institutes.

First of all, you must be faithful to the Gospel. We are reminded of this by the Second Vatican Council, which taught: "the fundamental norm of religious life is the following of Christ as it is presented to us in the Gospel" *(Perfectae Caritatis, 2)*. For this reason you make it your first priority to listen to the word of God, ponder it in your heart and seek to put it into practice. May you find time every day to meditate on its power to enlighten your minds and to bring to life within you the spirit of the Beatitudes.

Secondly, your religious consecration, in addition to strengthening your commitment to Christ, also binds you inseparably to the life and holiness of his spouse, the Church. And it is in the local ecclesial community that this is given concrete expression. This is the reason why it is so important for you to work in close collaboration with the clergy and laity of the local Church, and to accept willingly the authority and ministry of the local bishop as the focus of its unity.

In this connection I would like to underline two relevant expressions of this commitment to the local Church. The first is the relationship of religious priests with diocesan clergy. Religious priests should be happy to take part in the apostolate of the local Church, in a loyal and disinterested way, with the diocesan priests, whose tasks they are called to share, not by way of exception, but on a regular basis. The second is the relationship with the National Conference of Bishops. In the spirit of the document *Mutuae Relationes*, religious superiors should seek, accept and cultivate a frank and filial dialogue with the pastors whom the Holy Spirit has placed to govern the Church of God. In this sense it cannot be stressed too much how important are the relations between the National Conference of Bishops, whose task it is to work out and establish pastoral plans for the country, and the Associations of Major Religious Superiors, which assume the task of promoting the religious life, taking care that it should remain faithful to its deepest roots and to the charism that characterises it.

As religious you are in a position to make a special contribution to the promotion of the unity of the Church. Your experience of community life, common prayer, and corporate apostolic service prepares you for this task. May you dedicate yourselves to the great cause of unity with renewed vigour, seeking, in a spirit of openness and respect, to break down barriers of division and to encourage the progress of harmony and mutual collaboration.

Finally, may you always be faithful to the particular charisms of your individual Institutes. To illustrate this point I wish to acknowledge two events of great significance to the Church in the Philippines occurring this year: first, the 300th anniversary of the Christian Brothers of De La Salle. The instruction of young people in the Christian faith and in the other subjects remains as indispensable for the mission of Christ as at the time when this congregation was founded. And the Church in the Philippines has been greatly blessed through their consecrated lives and dedicated service.

The second event is the celebration of the 400th anniversary of the presence of the Society of Jesus in the Philippines. Through their missionary efforts, through their work in schools and parishes and through the spirituality of St Ignatius, the priests and brothers of the Society of Jesus have made a great contribution to the Philippines and throughout the world.

Similarly, all the religious families represented here today, each in a distinctive way, contribute to the holiness and life of the Church. An indication of the effectiveness of your contributions has been, and continues to be, your faithfulness to the spirit of your founders, to their evangelical intentions and to the example of their sanctity. May this faithfulness to your respective charisms always be seen as part of your fidelity to Christ.

In closing, may I say once again that your life of consecration and your partnership in the Gospel fill me with joy in my role as Pastor of the universal Church. I have come here to this Cathedral to celebrate with you and the entire ecclesial community the holiness of Christ's Church and the marvels of grace that have been accomplished in this archdiocese during the past four centuries of evangelisation. It is my prayer that the commemoration of this anniversary will be an added incentive for you to make your specific contribution as religious to the life of this local Church and to the life of the Church throughout the whole country. I pray that zealous religious will continue, as in the past four centuries, to serve the people of God faithfully by word and deed. And by your own generous and joyful example may young men be encouraged to carry on the traditions in this new era of grace.

May the Virgin Mary, Mother and model of all religious, assist you by her prayers. May she be your constant guide on the journey of faith to the heavenly Father, and may she help you to attain your highest goal: oneness in love with our Lord Jesus Christ.

O.R. 672. 23 February 1981

Address to Sisters at Nagasaki

26 February 1981

Beloved Sisters in Christ Jesus, to speak of Nagasaki to Japanese Christians is to evoke the heroic glorious beginnings of the establishment of the Church in this country. It is especially to evoke the memory of many martyrs who by the grace of Jesus Christ gave to him in this place the supreme witness of their love.

Nagasaki is thus a very special place, a place that is perfectly appropriate for our meeting today: for, since the early centuries of Christianity, the religious life has often been compared with martyrdom. Like martyrdom, the religious life is inspired by a deep love of the Lord above all else, shown by freely and generously giving up real values — property, a family, one's own free will — so as to make a complete gift to Christ. I am therefore particularly happy to meet you here and to greet you as one of the most precious treasures of the noble and worthy Church in Japan, a Church that is both venerable in its age and youthful in its missionary vitality.

It is very true to say that in this great country with its teeming millions of hard-working and cultivated people, the Church is like the mustard seed, or the little yeast that a woman places in several measures of flour until the whole dough is leavened. Your role is less conspicuous and more hidden than in many countries where Catholicism is more widespread; but it is no less important, even though the methods of evangelisation have to be very different.

In this situation, the testimony of your lives takes on a particular importance and value: even though it is not always possible to proclaim the Good News in words, it is always possible to present it through one's life. Moreover, many ancestral values of the Japanese people constitute stepping-stones for the Gospel: love of work, openness to others, the high level of human culture and above all the innate sense of recollection and contemplation, which is the distinctive mark of the peoples of the East.

The contemplative dimension is the true secret of the renewal of all religious life, and it is an element to which your fellow-citizens are particularly alert. Foster that dimension always. Make your houses centres of prayer, of recollection, of personal and community conversation with the One who is and must always be the One to whom you talk most throughout your busy days. Do not be led astray by the temptations to activism and distraction that the modern consumer society brings in its train, with all its materialistic overtones.

Without prayer, your religious life lacks meaning. It loses contact with its source, becomes emptied of its substance and cannot reach its goal. It is prayer that keeps you in contact with Christ your Spouse. The incisive words of *Evangelica Testificatio* deserve to be pondered: "Do not forget, moreover, the witness of history: faithfulness to prayer or its abandonment are the test of the vitality or decadence of religious life" *(no. 42)*.

With these words in mind, I address a special greeting and a word of encouragement to all the sisters who live the cloistered life in this country. You are living deeply at the heart of the Church. Your intense and unceasing prayer, based upon a rich spiritual and doctrinal heritage, is both a gift to the world and a challenge to that same world. It is also an answer to all those people today who are anxiously seeking for methods and experiences of contemplation.

The evangelical witness that you give by your consecration, lived in the practice of the counsels of chastity, poverty and obedience, and by the witness of the spirit of prayer that animates your communities, finds a fresh and particularly fruitful expression in your apostolic activities. I am thinking especially of your work among the poor, the sick, children and their families, in the vast field of teaching and catechesis. Your devotion to the training of the young is always very relevant. These activities of yours are a special means of evangelisation, of true human advancement. The exercise of this apostolate, with the mandate of your Congregations and in full cooperation with the local ecclesial communities, gives you a clear position in the Church, one that has its own specific role. Always be faithful to your role in spite of temptations, and be happy to preserve your interior identity and to be recognised outwardly for what you are.

At the same time, carefully maintain the constant respect and loving docility that you have always shown for the magisterium of the hierarchy. As you know, the religious life has no meaning except within the Church and in fidelity to her directives. So always be ready to welcome the teachings of the magisterium, and, in accordance with your particular charism, be ready to collaborate in the apostolic work of the local diocese, under the direction of your bishops united to the successor of Peter and in union with Christ. The word of Christ faithfully proclaimed by the Church with the assistance of the Holy Spirit will be for you the true source of holiness and freedom. Jesus assures us: "You will know the truth, and the truth will make you free" (*Jn 8:32*).

I would also like to urge you to increase your apostolic collaboration in the service of families, which are the special setting for the evangelisation and formation of the young. In doing so you will be acting in accordance with the conclusions of the recent Synod of Bishops.

Finally, I entrust you to the intercession of all the holy Martyrs of Nagasaki, and especially to the protection of Mary, Queen of Martyrs and Mother of the Church. She is indeed the Mother of all Christians, especially those who live the religious life, she who is so venerated in Japan as *Edo no Santa Maria* and as Our Lady of Otometoge. She it was whom Paul VI presented as the Virgin who listens, the Virgin who prays, the Virgin who begets Christ and offers him for the salvation of the world. May she be your guide along the sometimes difficult but always exhilarating path towards the ideal of complete union with Christ. This is my prayer to Mary on behalf of each of you and your communities, and I give you my Apostolic Blessing, praying that your joy may be full.

O.R. 674.   9 March 1981

Address to Episcopal Vicars for Religious from U.S.A.
20 March 1981

Dear friends in Christ, I wish to extend a very cordial welcome to each of you today. It is a joy for me to meet the vicars for religious from the United States, and all who work with them in a very important area of the Church's life and ministry.

In speaking of the role of episcopal vicars for Religious Institutes, the Holy See's document *Mutuae Relationes* shows that this task is a service of collaboration with the pastoral ministry of the bishop. Indeed, the mandate given to the episcopal vicar consists of helping to accomplish a task which of its nature pertains exclusively to the bishop, that is, a particular solicitude for religious life and the organic coordination of religious life within the pastoral activities of the diocese. All of you, in one way or another, are endeavouring to assist your bishops while offering support and encouragement to thousands of men and women who have generously given their lives to Jesus Christ, and who are striving to live out their ecclesial consecration with a persevering love that is worthy of their permanent commitment, and consistent with their sacred vows of chastity, poverty and obedience. Yours indeed is a splendid apostolate that can help sustain individuals and entire religious congregations in hope and fervour and in the very truth of their charisms.

All of you, whether you yourselves are religious or not, are called to offer your collaboration humbly as brothers and sisters who share with religious a common discipleship of Christ the Lord. You have with those whom you serve a common calling to holiness in the following of Jesus. At the same time the professional requirements of your apostolate entail a thorough understanding of religious life, especially in its essential ecclesial dimensions.

For this reason, you yourselves must repeatedly reflect on all the teaching of the Second Vatican Council that affects religious life, as well as on the papal postconciliar directives and those of the Sacred Congregation for Religious and for Secular Institutes. The document *Mutuae Relationes,* prepared jointly by the Sacred Congregation for Bishops and the Sacred Congregation for Religious and for Secular Institutes, is particularly relevant to the service that you are endeavouring to render in the Church.

It is important for you in the discussions and dialogue that you participate in, in the counsels you give, and in the decisions you may be called upon to take, to make constant reference to the essence of religious life. This will mean emphasising the value of consecration to the person of Jesus Christ — a consecration that is effected in his Church and by his Church, and in response to a personal vocation received from Christ through the working of his Spirit. Yours is the role of effectively drawing attention to the finality of the religious vows, showing how, in the words of the Second Vatican Council, they are directed to "a more vigorous flowering of the Church's holiness and the greater glory of the one and undivided Trinity, which in Christ and through Christ is the fountain and wellspring of all holiness *(Lumen Gentium, 47).*

Your own esteem for religious life and your deep appreciation of the individual values that it embodies for the good of the Church can be a powerful support for your brothers and sisters both in the ordinary circumstances of their daily lives and in moments of crisis. Being aware of the vital importance of religious in the Church, you will be in a position to help others to come to a serene realisation that this ecclesial institution, like the rest of Christ's Church, must undergo tribulation in the world. Indeed, it is no wonder that the sanctity of religious life would be opposed and even attacked by the devil. St Peter's call for calm vigilance is extremely relevant today: ''Your opponent the devil is prowling like a roaring lion looking for someone to devour. Resist him, solid in your faith...'' *(1 P 5:8f.).*

Because you yourselves have a special role of supporting and fostering religious life, you will be in a position to propose and re-propose to individual religious and to whole communities the perennial values inherent in consecrated religious life. It is an expression of your charity and part of your mission. Each of you will have opportunities to do this in one way or another: as the representative of a bishop in his pastoral concern for religious life in its relationship to the local and universal Church or simply as a friend, as a counsellor or confidant, an understanding fellow Christian, a spiritual director or a confessor.

By your contacts with them, you can be of great service to religious and to the Church as a whole by emphasising the importance of prayer in any genuine programme of renewal. Personal intimacy with Jesus Christ, sustained by prayer and the Eucharist, is an essential condition for the effective contribution of religious to the life of the Church. Society needs the incessant proclamation of the Beatitudes; and it needs to see them practised in the lives of religious.

Besides your personal contacts, many of you will undoubtedly be involved in one way or another in planning or coordinating meetings, classes or seminars at which religious will be in attendance. In all of these the Church's sublime teaching on religious life should be presupposed and appropriately manifested. The ontological condition of union with God, of being a new creature in Jesus Christ, consecrated to him by ecclesial vows, gives the religious a source of profound fecundity in the works of the apostolate. The lived renunciation that is linked to the Cross of Christ furnishes religious with a singular effectiveness in speaking to their brothers and sisters about the fullness of paschal life in the Risen Jesus. In embracing the poverty of Christ, religious have a real possibility of rendering genuine service to the poor and of being effective instruments of evangelisation in their regard. By a humble recognition of the limits of their personal insights, religious will be able to go forth with a fresh reassurance of the validity of the message they are trying to communicate. Through the generous renunciation of conjugal love, religious will be able to convince many people of the absolute primacy of Christ's love and of its profound power to fill the human heart with a joy that is contagious. Having surrendered their lives to Christ, religious can be truly open to his Holy Spirit, embracing in its entirety the word of God as it is proclaimed by the Church, thus being equipped for a real dialogue of salvation, which leads to the uplifting of humanity and the glory of Christ's name.

But, like every category in the Church, religious need support, understanding and love. They will find this in an eminent way in Mary, mother of Jesus and Mother of the Church, who as a model of holiness has a special relationship with all religious. At the same time, in the temporal sphere, this task belongs to all of you who are called by your bishops to foster religious life in the Church today. Yours is indeed an important apostolate in the Body of Christ. And may you yourselves find fresh strength and encouragement in the words of the Apostle Paul: "Help carry one another's burdens; in that way you will fulfil the law of Christ" *(Ga 6:2)*. May Mary help you all to do this for the glory of her Son, Jesus, who is the Saviour of us all.

O.R. 678.   6 April 1981

Address to Participants in a Congress on 'Mutuae Relationes'
30 April 1981

.....You are at the conclusion of a National Congress which had as its theme: "Communion and ecclesial co-responsibility in *Mutuae Relationes* in Italy', and in your reflections you have been helped by reports of excellent teachers. Certainly it is not for me, here and now, to propose to you a new lesson in addition to what you have already heard and then studied deeply in the discussions of the Congress. But the importance of the theme chosen for study and meditation prompts me to set forth to you a few brief considerations.

In the first place I am happy to recall that the charism of religious vocation has its own completely natural place in the life of the Church, natural because it is based on, and derived from, Jesus Christ's own will. In fact, if that first evangelical invitation addressed by Jesus to the rich young man, "If you would be perfect, go, sell what you possess..." *(Mt 19:21)*, did not meet, unfortunately, with any positive result, since he "went away sorrowful" *(ibid, 19:22)*, how many countless times, on the other hand, was it accepted in the history of the Church, with promptness, enthusiasm and great joy, by so many men and women, who made it their own shining reference point and their own *raison d'etre!* How many men and women religious have repeated and, even more, experienced the deep truth of the words of Paul the Apostle: "Sorrowful, yet always rejoicing; poor, yet making many rich; having nothing, and yet possessing everything" *(2 Co 6:10)*, since they knew and know that the words of the Author of the Book of Wisdom: "All good things came to me along with her" *(Wis 7:11)* are true, referring them to Christ.

It is a question, therefore, of a charism which deserves the greatest esteem on the part of the whole ecclesial community, not only because of the special consecration to the Lord, which distinguishes it, but also because it involves such a dimension of service and complete dedication to brothers, as to set it at the level of a new and incomparable motherhood and fatherhood, to which everyone owes respect, love and gratitude.

It is necessary, therefore, that religious life should fulfil its own fruitfulness by means of deep integration in the pastoral context of the Church, in a harmonious intermingling with the other charisms and ministries, first among which is the sacramental-hierarchical charism and ministry.

We read, in fact, in n. 20 of *Mutuae Relationes:* "The Church was not instituted to be an organisation of activities, but rather as the living Body of Christ in order to bear witness. However, it necessarily carries out a concrete work of planning and coordinating multiple offices and services, so that together they may converge in a unified pastoral action, in which it is established what are the choices to adopt and what are the apostolic commitments that have precedence over the others". Well, in this area of ideas and directives, religious life must closely collaborate with the life and mission of the whole Church, as it is interpreted and promoted by her legitimate pastors. Furthermore, only in this framework can the charism of religious consecration shine forth completely in its meaning and in its purpose as a sign and witness, albeit through the extremely different ways in which the members of the various institutes fulfil their own vocation. If, in fact, the seal of membership in the Church is necessary for every baptised person, who must therefore always seek and nourish communion with his own pastors, this is all the more necessary as the distinctive feature of those who, in the Church, make explicit profession of a belonging to Christ which goes beyond and completes what is already given in the Sacrament of Baptism.

A close understanding and collaboration of men and women religious with their bishops is, therefore, necessary. And this in a very concrete sense. In the first place, for a distribution or redistribution of the institutes, of consecrated persons and works, according to the real needs of the particular Church at the present time, giving precedence over other motives, however well-founded, to the ideal of the most effective service of the ecclesial community.

In the second place, agreement and an exchange of information with the diocesan pastors is highly opportune, when the respective organisms of men and women religious plan, even at the regional or national level, their meetings and their formation or renewal courses, especially when pastoral problems of common interest are dealt with on these occasions; and that for the purpose of not disuniting, or worse, opposing, initiatives which must aim at the building up of the Christian people.

In the third place, collaboration is necessary with regard to the social communications media. This need is particularly felt in Italy where the providential flourishing of these media is considerable. This applies particularly to the field of publishing that is carried on by religious. In this field, a very great deal of what is done certainly deserves the praise and gratitude of the bishops and of the whole Church because of the varied services rendered not only to devotional needs, but also to pedagogical, cultural or merely informational needs of the people of God. It is important, however, that the wide activity in this matter should take place according to criteria of effective building, that is, of positive construction of the people of God, on the basis of the norms already established or to be established with the Episcopal Conference. All the initiatives of the religious institutes must always be subordinated, in fact, to apostolic purposes, seeking the real good of souls and avoiding with vigilant care all that might disturb the faithful through condescension to attitudes of corrosive criticism, or to excessive pursuit of the new for the sake of the new. Certainly, Moses' wish: "Would that all the Lord's people were prophets!" *(Nb 11:29),* still holds good in the Church, but tempered by the words of the Apostle Paul, according to whom ''the manifestation of the Spirit'' must take place in the Church ''for the common good'' *(1 Co 12:7).*

Beloved brothers and sisters, while I thank you again for this visit today, I wish further to assure you and all your confreres and fellow sisters, whom you represent here, not only of my esteem, but above all of my affection and my firm confidence in the value of your respective ministries. My word, therefore, becomes one of deep encouragement to continue with generosity, intelligence and joy in the precious commitments which already absorb you or await you, for the benefit of the holy Church of God.

Rest assured that the Pope constantly thinks of you, prays for you and always commends you to the presence and the grace of the Lord, from whom he invokes the most abundant favours upon you.

A pledge of these is the Apostolic Blessing, which I willingly impart to you present, and which I am happy to extend to your dioceses and to your well-deserving religious families.

O.R. 683.   11 May 1981

Letter to the Superior General of the Vincentians 12 May 1981

Four hundred years ago — it was on 24 April 1581 in the village of Puoy in the Landes region — St Vincent de Paul was born. The Church is so indebted to this child of Jean de Paul and Bertrande Demoras that she must record this anniversary. Indeed throughout the centuries, even during their lifetime and much more after their death, the saints testify to the loving presence and salvific action of God in the world. The fourth centenary of the birth of Vincent de Paul is truly an occasion — for the religious families born of his charism as for the Christian people — to meditate on the marvels effected by the God of tenderness and mercy through a man who gave himself to him without reserve in the irrevocable bonds of the priesthood. Desiring ardently to manifest to the Congregation of the Mission, to the Company of the Daughters of Charity, to the Conference of St Vincent de Paul and to all the works of Vincentian inspiration, how much the Church appreciates the apostolic work which they accomplish in following their founder, I desire to express to them through you thoughts which this event suggests to me, and my most fervent encouragement always and everywhere to enkindle the fire of evangelic charity which burned in the heart of St Vincent.

First of all, the vocation of this genial initiator of charitable and social action still illumines today the path of his sons and daughters, of the laity who live of his spirit, of youth who seek the key to an existence which is useful and radically consumed in the gift of self. The spiritual itinerary of Vincent de Paul is fascinating. After his priestly ordination and a strange adventure of slavery in Tunis, he seemed to turn his back on the world of the poor, going to Paris in the hope of getting an ecclesiastical benefice. He succeeded in obtaining the post as one of the distributors of the alms of Queen Marguerite. This office brought him into contact with human misery, especially in the new Hospital of Charity. It was then that Father de Berulle, founder of the Oratory in France and chosen as spiritual guide by the young priest, began to give him, through a series of initiatives, apparently with little coherence, occasions for discoveries which would be the source of great accomplishment in his life. De Berulle first sent Vincent to exercise the function of curate in the Parisian suburb of Clichy-la-Garenne. Four months later he sent him to the de Gondi family as tutor for the children of the General of the Galleys. Providence had designs in this. Always accompanying the de Gondis to their chateaux and lands in the provinces, Vincent de Paul made there the disturbing discovery of the material and spiritual misery ''of the poor people of the fields''. From that time onwards, he asked himself if he still had the right to reserve his priestly ministry to the education of children of a good family, while the peasants were living and dying in religious abandonment. Knowing the misgivings of Vincent, de Berulle directed him to the parish of Chatillon-des-Dombes. In this parish, badly neglected, the new pastor had a decisive experience. Called one Sunday in August 1617 to a family, all of whose members were ill, he undertook to organise the devotion of the neighbours and persons of good will. The first ''Charity'', which would serve as the model for so many others, was born; and the conviction that the service of the poor must be his life remained with him until his last breath. This brief summary of the interior progress of Vincent de Paul during the first twenty years of his priesthood, shows us a priest extremely attentive to the life of his era, a priest who let himself be led by events, or rather, by Divine Providence, without ''striding on ahead'', as he liked to put it. Is not such availability, today as yesterday, the secret of peace and evangelical joy, the privileged path of sanctity?

In order to serve the poor better, Vincent wished "to join with other priests who were free of all benefices in order to apply themselves entirely, under the good pleasure of the bishops, to the salvation of the poor people of the fields, by preaching, catechesis and general confessions, without taking any remuneration of any kind whatsoever or in any manner". This group of priests, quickly named "Lazarists" from the name of the celebrated priory of St Lazare, acquired around 1632, developed rapidly and was established in some fifteen dioceses to give parish missions and to establish therein the "Charities". The Congregation of the Mission extended even into Italy, Ireland, Poland, Algeria and Madagascar. Vincent never ceased to inculcate in his companions "the spirit of Our Lord", which he summarised in five fundamental virtues — simplicity, meekness in regard to the neighbour, humility in regard to self, and then, as essential to these virtues, mortification and zeal which are, in a manner, the dynamic aspects of them. His exhortations to those whom he sent to preach the Gospel are full of spiritual wisdom and pastoral realism: it is not a question of being loved for oneself, but of making Jesus Christ loved. At a time when too many priests mixed Greek and Latin in complicated sermons, he required simplicity, convincing language full of imagery, in the name of the Gospel. May the Lazarists today — always faithful to their Father, St Vincent — sow abundantly the word of God by their preaching, and ceaselessly contribute to "fortify the priestly identity and its authentic evangelical dynamism" in the people of God, as I myself desired, Holy Thursday 1979, in my Letter to all the priests of the Church! May the example of Monsieur Vincent still stimulate all those who have the very grave responsibility of preparing, for the urban and rural Christian communities, the ordained ministers of whom they have absolute need!

In the course of the missions, Vincent de Paul also obtained proof that this method of evangelisation would bear fruit only if there was an instructed and zealous clergy on the spot. Thus very soon the Lazarists devoted themselves to the formation of priests, as well as to the popular missions, and founded seminaries conformable to the pressing appeals of the Council of Trent. The first retreat for ordinands, given by St Vincent himself in 1628 at the request of the Bishop of Beauvais, was the beginning of preparatory exercises for ordination, and also of some permanent formation for the clergy, thanks to the Tuesday ecclesiastical conferences at St Lazare. These initiatives, enthusiastically praised by Monsieur Olier, gave to the Church exemplary priests, among whom several, such as the celebrated Bossuet, were called to the episcopate. To the clergy of Paris and the provinces, Vincent de Paul communicated his evangelical spirit and his missionary inspiration, and he directed them to the practice of priestly fraternity and mutual aid in the service of the poorest, in a filial dependence on the bishops. How can we reveal the love of God to the world — he loved to repeat it — if the messengers of this love are not very united among themselves? Does not St Vincent today call all priests to live their priesthood in fraternal teams, indissolubly united in prayer and the apostolate, at the same time very open to collaboration with the laity and penetrated with the meaning of their ministerial priesthood which comes from Christ for the service of the Christian community?

In fact, another aspect of the dynamism and realism of Vincent de Paul was to give to the "Charities", which multiplied, a structure of unity and efficacy. Louise de Marillac, widow of Antoine Le Gras, first initiated into the spiritual life by Monsieur de Sales and then guided by Monsieur Vincent himself, was engaged by him for the inspection and support of the "Charities". She was marvellously suited for this, and her radiation contributed greatly in deciding several "good country girls" who were helping the "Charities" to follow her example of total oblation to God and to the poor. On 29 November 1633 the Company of the Daughters of Charity was born. Vincent de Paul gave it an original and very exacting rule: "You will have for monastery, the abode of the sick; for cell, a hired room; for chapel, the parish church; for cloister, the public streets; for enclosure, obedience; for grate, the fear of God; for veil, holy modesty." The spirit of the Company is summarised thus: "You should do what the Son of God did on earth. You should give life to these poor sick, life of the body and life of the soul." Following Louise de Marillac, thousands and thousands of women have consumed their entire life in the very humble service of the suffering, mendicants, prisoners, those on the fringe of society, the handicapped, the illiterate, abandoned children. Daughters of Monsieur Vincent, they are, after his example and like him, the heart of Christ in the world of the poor, and also of the rich whom they endeavour to render good to the poor. Without knowing the feminist movements of our time, Monsieur Vincent knew how to find in the women of his era intelligent and generous collaborators, faithful and constant. The history of the Company illumines in an exceptional manner the aspect of a woman that is undoubtedly the most profoundly feminine: that of her vocation to tenderness and mercy, of which humanity always has need. There are always the poor in our midst and modern societies are even giving rise to new forms of poverty.

This contemplative look at the Vincentian epic easily enables us to say that St Vincent is a modern saint. Certainly, if he were to return today, his field of activity would not be the same. There has been success in healing many illnesses which he had learned to care for. However, he would find at once the path of the poor, the new poor, in the urban concentrations of our time, as in the past in the country districts. Can one even imagine what this herald of the mercy and tenderness of God, would be capable of undertaking, utilising wisely all the modern means at our disposal? In a word, his life would be as it always was: a gospel opened widely, with the same procession of poor, sick, sinners, unhappy children, men and women devoting themselves also to love and to serve the poor — all hungry for truth and for love, as well as for earthly nourishment and bodily care — all listening to Christ still saying: "Learn from me for I am gentle and lowly in heart!" *(Mt 11:29)*.

May the fourth centenary of the birth of Vincent de Paul shine brightly on the people of God, reanimate the ardour of all his disciples, and make resound in the hearts of numerous young people the call to the exclusive service of evangelical charity! These are the sentiments and the desires which I wish to express to the great and dear family of Lazarists, Daughters of Charity, and all the Vincentian movements, and I join thereto my affectionate Apostolic Blessing.

O.R. 695.   3 August 1981

Letter to the Superior General of the Discalced Carmelites   14 October 1981

.....The time through which we are passing and which is distinguished by a renewed feeling for the Church and for prayer, seems to be a time of grace suited in a special way to the teaching and experience of Teresa of Jesus. Endowed with the strength which is drawn from her experience and her way of life, she invites all to love Christ and his Mystical Body, so that moved by the Holy Spirit, who loves it, in it they may "taste and see that the Lord is good" (cf. *Ps 34:9*).....

This invitation applies especially to those who with an added reason have vowed to follow Christ the virgin, who was poor and obedient and whom we have often reminded of their special connection with the Church, since it is never permissible, especially in the religious life, for "fidelity to Christ to be separated from fidelity to the Church" (cf. *AAS, 71, 1979, p. 1255*). While exhorting them to unite themselves to Christ through prayer, we stated that "the religious life without prayer has no meaning, it is cut off from its source, it loses its substance, and does not attain the end which is proper to it" *(ibid.)*.

As we commemorate St Teresa of Jesus we wish to address these words to all religious, but especially to those who have her as their mother and founder of the special form of life for which they are known in the people of God. For in her family, the model of a renewed life — which at no time is not characteristic of the saints — the mother who gave them their laws repeats to her spiritual sons and daughters these words which carry the weight of her office: "I am a daughter of the Church", and she reminds them of their chief obligation in the Church (cf. *"The Way of Perfection", 17,1*) — an obligation which we say is of the greatest importance — which is imposed on them by the rule (cf. *ibid., 4, 2*), according to which they are bound to pray without ceasing (cf. *ibid., 21, 10*), and that of living an interior and exterior life which is poor and austere (cf. *ibid., 4, 2*) which distinguishes them as true friends of Christ. St Teresa again addresses these words to them: "All of us who wear this holy habit of the Carmelites are called to practice prayer and contemplation" (cf. *Interior Castle, V:1, 2*). Indeed the Discalced Carmelites, both men and women, must be faithful to prayer and the habit of praying, and be consistent in it so that they may experience the living God, which gives them the title to their dignity, their special vocation and their salutary mission. They should strive more and more each day to become the adorers in spirit and in truth whom the Father seeks, being convinced, as the holy mother wrote, that the journey they have undertaken in this "way of perfection" is of benefit not only to themselves but to many souls (cf. *Autobiography, 11, 4*).

Observing even in this age the spirit of their rule, the Carmelite nuns should be faithful to those things which that "desert", as it were, demands of them in their daily life, in which according to their vocation and mission it is necessary for them to be completely contemplative in a special way. Their enclosure lacks meaning without this contemplative life which St Teresa shortly before her death described so very clearly in Chapter III of her book on *"Foundation of Monasteries"*. Our punctilious advice, which we also explained in the message to the Plenary Session of the Sacred Congregation for Religious and Secular Institutes in 1980, that "the enclosure should be observed with rightful rigour", seems to call to mind the instructions of St Teresa. Agreeing with her who was convinced that good does not remain hidden (cf. *"The Way of Perfection"*, 15, 6), we stated at that time that "the enclosure does not isolate...from the communion of the Mystical Body. On the contrary, it puts those who adhere to it at the heart of the Church" (cf. *AAS, 72, 1980, p. 211*). And so they should lovingly fulfil their mission and their vocation and strive after the example of St Teresa of Jesus "to be at the heart of the Church". They should remember her exhortation that "only by prayer and by the desire to sacrifice ourselves can we be useful to the Church".

But the male Discalced Carmelites, whom Teresa wanted to be "contemplative hermits" and "heavenly men", were also urged by her to engage in apostolic activity with a view to helping the Sisters to attain perfection according to the same rule, also that they might announce the Gospel to the lowly and humble, so that at the same time they might exert great influence in the theological and missionary field. For this reason she desired that there should be among them "teachers and prospective teachers" because she knew that a truly learned man never leads astray the souls he is counselling (cf. *Autobiography, 5, 3*). She was convinced that true learning when coupled with humility is very effective for following the way of prayer. St Teresa saw this brought to fruition in her first-born son, St John of the Cross — the teacher and guide in the ways of God. He first restored the renewed life of the Carmelites at the monastery in Duruelo. After his example the Discalced Carmelites should be leaders and teachers of men and women in the world today who are thirsting for communion with God and the experience of God. This is their mission which springs from their vocation.

The devout mother turns lovingly also to those Institutes and Congregations which follow her spirit and her form of perfection in the apostolic life to which they dedicate themselves and which is so fruitful in the Church and in the various fields of charity and social work. She urges their members to be men and women of prayer. They should be such that they turn any association with their brother into an invitation to communion with God. This exhortation of St Teresa seems, as it were, an incentive, urging them to prayer and action, while preserving the unity of life which fidelity to contemplation gives: "In this way anyone who is more advanced in prayer is to that extent the more eager to console and save his neighbour, especially their souls, and it seems that he will give many lives to lead even one soul from the state of sin" (cf. *Meditation on the Canticle, 7, 8*). Even now St Teresa lives and speaks in the Church. May our minds, stimulated by a renewed zeal, be effectively directed to her example and her teaching, especially to her memory, which has already begun.

In conclusion, we graciously impart the Apostolic Blessing, as a pledge of heavenly favours, to you, beloved son, to the friars and nuns of the Discalced Carmelites and to the other followers of the Teresian way of life.

O.R. 709. 9 November 1981

Address to the Congregation for Religious and for Secular Institutes

20 November 1981

It is always a great joy for me to know the work initiated and carried out by your Congregation to enable religious life to shine forth more brightly within the Church and to make its specific contribution to evangelisation. Precisely, for this Plenary Assembly, you had chosen the subject: to examine again the nature, the role and the operation of the Conferences or Unions of Major Superiors of Religious Institutes, on the national and supranational plane, in the light of conciliar documents and also especially of the document *Mutuae Relationes* on the relations between bishops and religious in the Church.

The ample consultation in preparation for this meeting provided valuable indications on the concern of religious to live their vocation better and better, and on the desire of pastors to promote their renewal by an attitude of benevolent encouragement, understanding interest, and reliable moral and doctrinal support. It showed at the same time the mutual efforts undertaken in the last three years, in the light of the document *Mutuae Relationes*, the publication of which was received by everyone with gratitude and readiness, manifested by serious study for its better implementation. I encourage you very willingly to continue along this way, by studying this important subject more deeply.

You have realised that the foundation of your work and your exchanges is the deep bond between Christ, the Church and evangelisation. It was the Church as such that received from Christ the task of evangelising; the diversity of ministries must contribute to the fulfilment of this mission which cannot be accomplished outside her; the meeting with Jesus Christ is bound up with the quality of ecclesial life.

In this Church, the bishops, successors of the Apostles, ensure, in union with Peter's successor and under his authority, the perennial quality of the work of Christ, the eternal Pastor. This ministry of bishops is the foundation of all ecclesial services: "No one has the power to exercise any function of teaching, sanctifying or governing, except by participation and in communion with them" *(Mutuae Relationes 9, a)*. Pastors of the whole flock, they are for everyone authentic teachers and guides of perfection and likewise the guardians of fidelity to religious vocation in the spirit of each institute, promoters of vocations and stout defenders of religious communities according to their specific character both in the spiritual and in the apostolic field.

On its part, the state of life constituted by the practice of the evangelical counsels, if it does not pertain to the hierarchical structure, belongs inseparably, however, to the life and holiness of the Church (cf. *Lumen Gentium, 44*). It is a precious treasure for the Church, the evident testimony of the complete gift of oneself to the love and service of God. As Paul VI recalls in the Apostolic Exhortation *Evangelica Testificatio (no. 3)*, "Without this concrete sign, the charity of the Church as a whole would run the risk of growing cold, the salvific paradox of the Gospel would be blunted, the 'salt' of faith would lose its savour in a world undergoing secularisation".

In the light of these principles and guidelines given by *Mutuae Relationes (nos. 60-65)*, you have examined the present situation of Unions and Conferences of Major Superiors (of men religious, women religious or mixed), their relations with the various ecclesial authorities, the fruits already gathered, the means of multiplying them, as well as the difficulties or the tensions that occur here or there, with the means of putting them right.

Bishops show themselves to be more and more aware of the value of religious life and of their responsibility in this connection. Their concern for better knowledge of the religious state as such and not only in its apostolic action, is manifested, among others, in their efforts to give seminarians and priests more and more deep and complete information. As I said in the message to the preceding

Plenary Assembly, it is essential that they should take care to procure for sisters spiritual aid of high quality, by means of outstanding priests. It is also necessary that the diocesan clergy should always respect their specific apostolic purpose and their community life. Only true religious can collaborate fruitfully in real evangelisation.

Guardians of the doctrine and liturgy, the pastors will take great care, therefore, to give all their flock, but especially this select portion comprising men and women religious, sound and rich spiritual and doctrinal nourishment, taking care to preserve them from doctrinal deviations and practical abuses which can harm apostolic fruitfulness and the very existence of consecrated life.

Although the subject of your Assembly does not directly concern contemplative life, I wish to repeat here the Church's entire gratitude for the inestimable help given to evangelisation by the prayers and sacrifices of monks and enclosed nuns. I know that the pastors all share this point of view and that each of them ardently desires to benefit from the presence of one or several monasteries in his diocese.

I also wish to bring particular encouragement to lay religious and to sisters associated with the pastoral work of bishops; their collaboration is of great value, especially for Christian education and catechesis of the young.

Religious must never be afraid of highlighting the essential elements of their life: union with God in prayer and contemplation, practice of the evangelical counsels, fraternal life. Pastoral concern must never unduly prevail over these fundamental values, but must be nourished by them.

They must also develop their ecclesial sense for better integration in the particular Church and in the universal Church. Above all, they must avoid a partitioning which would lead to dividing the Church into almost non-communicating compartments through an erroneous conception of exemption. The latter cannot cause difficulty in relations within the particular Churches, since religious, like all the faithful, are placed under the jurisdiction of the bishops for works of the apostolate.

This reference to the bishops is particularly necessary at the present time when quite a number of institutes are suffering from an insufficiency of vocations, and when it is a question for them of regrouping houses or restructuring work. Such measures must always be envisaged in collaboration with the Ordinary who bears pastoral responsibility for apostolic orientations. On all these points, the Unions of Major Superiors can prove to be very useful if they correspond adequately to the purpose established when they were set up. So it is desirable that they should periodically revise their action and their operation according to the conditions set out in the statutes.

The role of the Conference is of primary importance for reception of the guidelines of the Holy See; it often falls upon them to make them known, circulate them, and study them in a view of their better implementation by religious.

The subjects chosen on the occasion of General Assemblies will preferably be determined to highlight and promote the specific values of religious life.

The role of the Unions is particularly appreciable in the relations of the institutes with one another and with the hierarchy, as regards pastoral action. It is highly desirable that questions regarding the grouping of houses and the restructuring of work should be examined at the level of the Union in order that concerted action may permit a better distribution of evangelical workers.

The dialogue with the episcopate is greatly facilitated where there exist mixed commissions or similar organisms of bishops and religious and where the latter take part in pastoral councils. The forms of dialogue may be multiple and varied; they are fruitful when they rest on charity and mutual trust.

In conclusion, I hope with all my heart that pastors, religious superiors and their Unions will collaborate closely to help men and women religious to bear a faithful, generous and serene witness before the world today. They constitute in a special way the image of Christ, imitating more closely and representing continually through their state the form of life of the Lord and of his disciples (cf. *Lumen Gentium*, 44).

May the Virgin Mary, the Mother of the Church, the model of consecrated souls, help you all in carrying out this magnificent task. Such is my prayer for your intentions while I bless you willingly, and through you bless all those men and women who live as religious throughout the world.

O.R. 712.   30 November 1981

Address to the De La Salle Brothers

21 November 1981

The letter I addressed to you on 13 May 1980, for the opening of the year in commemoration of third centenary of the foundation of your Institute, expressed the essential part of my thought. For over a year you have celebrated this jubilee here and there, meditating on fidelity to the charism of your founder. This charism — is it necessary to recall? — is that of having conceived the school, put at the disposal of everyone, and particularly of the poor, as an educational community according to the Christian view, that is, based on love, capable of forming the souls as well as the minds of children and adolescents, thanks to duly qualified and competent teachers, themselves consecrated to God, familiar with prayer and living as brothers, in the school of the one Master, Christ Jesus. The Catholic school finds its inspiration and its model here.

As at your Institute's beginning, this apostolate is still of primary importance and even of burning relevance, all the more so that the shortage of devoted, competent and generous educators is felt everywhere, the status of the Catholic school needs to be reaffirmed — with different methods according to countries — and its educational project given new value.

I know how much you endeavour, in your educational action, to listen to the real needs of the young, through a pedagogy centred on persons. I congratulate you and thank you for this. I am sure that you make it a point to work with the parents and their associations.

The work you are carrying out, in union with other congregations of men and women consecrated to the formation of the young and with so many lay teachers, is part of a whole apostolate for which each bishop and the episcopal conferences are primarily responsible. As we said yesterday to members of the Plenary Assembly of the Congregation for Religious and Secular Institutes, trustful relations of understanding and collaboration must be more deeply established between bishops and religious and among the religious institutes themselves, to meet the present needs, particularly when problems of restructuring arise, while respecting, of course, your charism and your religious life.

As regards the spiritual way that you call upon the young to travel along with you, you will remember your holy founder: "The young whom God entrusts to you are sons of God; they have been consecrated to the Trinity, as well as you, since their baptism". Your role, therefore, is to develop the consequences of their spiritual membership, in a climate of trust, patience and rightly understood freedom, which means: awakening their faith, strengthening it or making them rediscover it through a living and renewed catechesis according to the directions of the hierarchy; training them in prayer, if need be by suitable retreats, helping them to accept the demands of the Gospel as ways of liberation, life and gift; teaching them to love the Church and to take an active place in it, to assume their responsibilities as men and Christians in their environment, in a spirit of service; encouraging their desire to help less privileged countries; appropriately cultivating their missionary concern. And for your pupils who do not share the Catholic faith, the witness of your competent dedication, your respect for consciences, the spiritual and moral values you teach, are also of vital importance: that is part of the evangelising mission of the Church.

For you, the educational service you render society and the Church is the work of religious. This means that you must derive from prayer and daily fidelity to your vows the soul of your apostolate. In my letter, I had laid stress on the life of prayer, which is essential. I would like to emphasise another fundamental element of your religious life, for which St John Baptist De La Salle is not only a teacher, but a model: I am thinking of community life.

The celebration of the third centenary has put before your eyes again the laborious beginnings of your Institute, full of external difficulties, but also internal ones: the first disciples, challenged on all sides, without any guarantee for the future, were assailed by violent temptations of discouragement and surrender. It was then that De La Salle, giving up his privileges as a canon, began to share their life style among them: he surrendered his comfort to adopt their material insecurity. Everything being shared from that time, the "School Masters", who had become "Brothers of the Christian Schools", had only one heart and one mind, in the image of the first Christian community.

What a precious source of meditation for you, dear brothers, inserted in a world which is rediscovering the community sense! I very cordially invite you to live this brotherly life intensely. The young people of our time are particularly sensitive to the witness of a community united in charity and the gift of oneself to others; they discover Christ there and his presence attracts them.

What a marvellous field of apostolate has been entrusted to you! It supposes that each of the brothers himself be strengthened inwardly, in contact with Jesus Christ, who asks him again incessantly, as he asked Peter: "Do you love me?", do you do that out of love?

Yes, may Christ — whom we will celebrate tomorrow as King of the Universe — reign in your hearts, and may his kingdom of love and holiness spread, thanks to all the Brothers of the Christian Schools! May he be your joy and strength! May he call new Gospel workers to work with you! May the Virgin Mary keep you in the school of Christ! May St John Baptist De La Salle sweep you along safely on ways at once old and new! I willingly bless the superiors of your congregation and, with them, all their brothers who are humbly carrying out their task all over the world.

O.R. 713. 7 December 1981

Apostolic Exhortation 'Familiaris Consortio'
22 November 1981

.....The contribution that can be made to the apostolate of the family by men and women religious and consecrated persons in general finds its primary, fundamental and original expression precisely in their consecration to God. By reason of the consecration, "for all Christ's faithful religious recall that wonderful marriage made by God, which will be fully manifested in the future age, and in which the Church has Christ for her only spouse" *(Perfectae Caritatis, 12)*.

Hence the possibility for men and women religious, and members of secular institutes and other institutes of perfection, either individually or in groups, to develop their service to families, with particular solicitude for children, especially if they are abandoned, unwanted, orphaned, poor and handicapped. They can also visit families and look after the sick; they can foster relationships of respect and charity towards one-parent families or families that are in difficulties or are separated; they can offer their own work of teaching and counselling in the preparation of young people for marriage, and in helping couples towards truly responsible parenthood; they can open their own houses for simple and cordial hospitality, so that families can find there the sense of God's presence and gain a taste for prayer and recollection, and see the practical examples of lives lived in charity and fraternal joy as members of the larger family of God.

I would like to add a most pressing exhortation to the heads of institutes of consecrated life to consider — always with substantial respect for the proper and original charism of each one — the apostolate of the family as one of the priority tasks, rendered even more urgent by the present state of the world.....

O.R. 715. 21-28 December 1981

Address to Superiors General of Men Religious
28 November 1981

Beloved brothers... I congratulate you in the first place on the choice of the subject of the meeting: "Understanding and application of the document *Mutuae Relationes*", in the light of which you have tried to study more deeply the doctrine and the relations of religious life with the universal Church and with the particular one, going into concrete matters through an examination of conscience of religious life today, and the presentation of some experiences between bishops and religious.

Along the lines of what was studied at your meeting last May: "The charism of religious life for the Church and for the world", you have dwelt on the identity of religious, because it is as such, that is, as consecrated persons, that they are called to take their place in the Church of which they are bearers of a specific charism, bestowed by the Holy Spirit to enable the Church herself "not merely to be equipped for every good work... but also to be adorned with the manifold gifts of her children, like the bride adorned for her husband" (*Perfectae Caritatis*, 1).

Religious, who ask bishops to be accepted as such, that is, for what they are (cf. *Part 1, chap. III of Mutuae Relationes*), will have to be the first to deepen their identity as consecrated persons and to make their identity manifest and credible through their lives and works, even when they wish to be closer to the needs of the modern world. The witness of consecrated life and fidelity to their own charism are the first form of evangelisation and also the most effective one, both for contemplative religious, and for those dedicated to works of the apostolate, since they are a call and a stimulus to overcome the three major temptations, those of pleasure, possessions and power, after the example of the saints, their founders. Conscientious and objective self-criticism has certainly helped you to realise if your way of living is such that the Church may "truly show forth Christ... to believers and unbelievers alike" *(Lumen Gentium, 46)*.

Also in the various works of the apostolate to which the religious dedicate themselves, according to the purposes of the Institute, their commitment to the radical following of Christ will have to be apparent: it would be a serious impoverishment for the Church if they did not want to distinguish themselves by their way of living and acting.

Fidelity to the charism of consecrated life must bring forth in religious a deep and sincere ecclesial awareness and therefore a constant effort to live with the Church, for the Church and in the Church. If the doctrine of religious life is part of ecclesiology, religious life lived is even more an expression of ecclesial life. On this is based the attitude of faith, love and docility of religious towards the pastors set to govern the Church, as well as the duty of taking their part in the life of the particular Church, enriching it with their own specific gifts, working within it and as part of it, and not merely as complementary forces.

From this is derived also the commitment of bishops, priests and other members of the diocesan family to consider religious as a living part of the particular Church, for which the pastor has a specific responsibility. From ecclesial awareness there spring also the communion that must unite priests with their religious confreres, who share in the one priesthood, and the duty of helping and assisting consecrated souls especially through the Sacrament of Reconciliation and spiritual direction, and, for everyone, the duty of encouraging and cultivating vocations to consecrated life, which are a sign manifesting the vitality of the particular Church.

In the recent address to members of the Plenary Session of the Sacred Congregation for Religious and Secular Institutes I urged bishops to supply seminarians and priests with "increasingly deep and complete information" for better knowledge of religious life as such.

The document *Mutuae Relationes* exhorts, in *no. 30,* that everything should be done that "men and women religious should be formed from the novitiate to have full awareness and solicitude for the particular Church" always in fidelity to their specific vocation. Deeper study also on the doctrinal plane of the bonds that tie religious to the universal Church and the particular one will help to harmonise their integration in the particular Church, making dependence on the Supreme Pastor felt and lived more, also by virtue of the vow of obedience, and will help them to understand his mission as sanctifier, perfecter and teacher with regard to consecrated persons.

A convinced ecclesial awareness, moreover, will facilitate the choices that religious are not infrequently called to make, in the framework of the pastoral plan, among the various forms of presence, even new ones, in the apostolic field and in the areas in which to commit themselves; a presence that will always have to be the result and sign of their consecrated life, renewed and deepened, though in necessary and opportune adaptation, thus avoiding the danger of secularism.

The Union of Superiors General, as also the Conferences of Major Superiors, can make a valuable contribution for this purpose. It will then fall to the superiors of the individual institutes, docile to the directives of the Church, and in liaison with the particular Church, to ensure the continuation of the works willed by the founder, renewing and adapting them according to the needs of the times, and to study and prepare new apostolic presences, taking into account the requirements of the pastoral mission and those of religious life.

Dear heads of congregations, I trust your wisdom and your zeal that this harmonisation between various forms of the apostolate may have concrete developments. That is a problem which has become extremely acute due to the increases of apostolic needs in the Church today and to the decrease in personnel. By force of circumstances, therefore, a vast field of collaboration between the bishops and religious institutes is opened, And in this evangelical work, really based on concerted action, it is important that each religious family should clearly preserve the sign of its consecrated life and its fidelity to the particular charism of the institute.

Finally, dear brothers, in all your endeavours to remain faithful to your charisms, faithful to your vocation to holiness, faithful to your ministry of salvation, you have Mary the Mother of Jesus to inspire you. She encourages you by her own example of fidelity; she supports you by her faithful prayers. Your love, like her must be expressed through fidelity — a fidelity to everything God asks of you through his Church: *Fiat voluntas tua!* For you, fidelity is the condition for being able to contribute effectively to the kingdom of God; it is the prerequisite for really sharing in evangelisation. The

Incarnation of the Word was linked to the fidelity of Mary, and the life of Jesus in the world today is linked to your fidelity. Your greatest contribution will undoubtedly be your love — a love manifested in sustained fidelity to Jesus Christ and to his Church.
With my Apostolic Blessing.

O.R. 714. 14 December 1981

Address to the Salesian Sisters

12 December 1981

.....I greet each of you who has come to pay a visit to the Vicar of Christ on the occasion of the XVII General Chapter, an important stage for the life of your Institute. From it, in fact, there must spring the new Constitutions which after the approval of the ecclesiastical authority, will provide you with reliable guidance for the fulfilment of your religious ideals in this society within sight of the third Christian millennium.

From the times of the Mornese community, from the heroic and promising beginnings of the Institute of the Daughters of Mary Help of Christians, a long way has been covered, marked by trials and sacrifices, but also crowned with consoling and precious fruits for your family and for the whole Church, for which we are grateful to the Lord from the depth of our hearts. The 200 or so Daughters of Mary Help of Christians left by St Maria Domenica Mazzarello at the moment of her death, the centenary of which is being celebrated this year, have become over 17,000, scattered in 62 nations, in every continent; and the houses, in the span of a century, have increased from about twenty-six to almost 1,500.

In the light of experience, the words of the then Bishop of Acqui, Mons. G. Sciandra, present at the ceremony of the first profession on 5 August 1872, sound prophetic today: "There is an accumulation of circumstances which show a special Providence of the Lord for this new Institute". Today you are carrying out your apostolate for youth in all sectors of formation, with regard to grades and schools, also at the university level, as well as in the missionary field, always in harmony with the aims of the charism of foundation. Before such a complex set of works, born from the impulse of Don Bosco and from the obedient fidelity of a girl humble in origin and poor in culture, but rich in the Holy Spirit, while on the one hand it is natural to note that God's finger is present in such growth, on the other hand your responsibility is challenged with regard to the young women of today, their problems and their hopes. In other words, you are called to ensure the continuity of your mission, aimed at involving also the daughters of this generation in the marvellous adventure of a life according to the Gospel, a mission that requires from you a joyful heart.

This joy is one of the well-known characteristics of the Salesian pedagogical charism completely assimilated by Mother Maria Domenica, with absolute fidelity and personal intuition. She was continually concerned, in fact, with the joy of her daughters, as if it were the principal proof of their holiness, and she used to ask each of them frequently: "Are you joyful?". It is a question of that joy which Jesus promised his followers and which was always recommended by St Paul, who considered it one of the first fruits of the Spirit: "the fruit of the Spirit is love, joy…" *(Ga 5:22).*

This attitude of joy is rooted above all in a profound sense of faith, in which the presence of the Lord dominates and is always prevalent as he who loves and saves, as the Father who, in his providence, looks after every affair of ours. If we do not deepen such an inner contact with the Heavenly Father, who shelters us from all our fears, doubts and torments, and who enables us to overcome them, it is vain to think of joy of the heart, much less try to express it. A forced and unconvincing attitude would result.

From intense contact with God, from a convinced spirit of faith, which finds concrete expression in constant adherence to the Church and to her magisterium, you will draw the deep motivations for your Salesian joy, and also the capacity of discernment of situations and particularly of the hearts of the young, an intelligent and supernatural discernment which unmistakably qualified the educational ministry of Don Bosco and Mother Maria Domenica.

In connection with this ministry I would now like to dwell for a moment on the well-known Salesian "preventive" system, contained in the triple concept: "reason-religion-love". Respect for the requirements of reason and religion — that is, a trustful attitude before the natural and supernatural values of the person — is certainly fundamental in an educational project. However, for lack of time, I will add only a word about the third characteristic of the "preventive" system, that is, that of love, or, to use Don Bosco's expression, "lovableness".

For him this is not only a cornerstone of his educational method, but we can say that it is its inspiring principle. A reflection of, and participation in, God's fatherhood, Salesian "lovableness" has its source in Christ's own heart and its model and inspirer in the Blessed Virgin. It is ardent zeal for the complete salvation of the girls; it is pastoral solicitude, extremely respectful of the person; it is affective power able to win the heart, which has a determinant value, according to the Salesian spirit, in the process of education.

Putting into practice the requirements of "lovableness", respect for the talents of the girls, that is, for the gifts and orientations of the Lord towards them, is at once seen to be fundamental. And this is an attitude of deep obedience to God's action, and of deep-rooted faith in him.

This trustful respect will inevitably lead to a second very important stage, that is, to be loved. In order that your solicitude for the girls may reach their hearts, it is necessary to make yourselves accepted, to show yourselves for what you are and be accepted as such. If this condition is not safeguarded, all zeal with regard to the girls runs the risk of being unsuccessful, without the desired fruits, because it will be impossible to arrive at the following stage, that is, the stage of being listened to and obeyed.

It is necessary, therefore, to make ourselves respected with the serene consistency of our witness with regard to all those values in which we believe and which we wish to share. This is a duty which cannot be shirked; nothing valid will pass from us to the young, we will not be able to transfer anything stable to them, if we are not concerned about being consistent with our consecration. In this connection I would like to draw your attention to the importance of even external witness, which embraces words, attitudes and even dress, as a sign of a mission and a belonging.

The girl needs models that attract also her sensitivity and thus make her disposed — as I mentioned above — to listen and to obey. This is a profound need of our young people, even if it is sometimes unconfessed and remote: to be guided towards a demanding formation by confidence in those who propose ideals of life to them.

Other reflections which might spring from further study of this subject I entrust to your discerning intuition, while I pray to Mary Help of Christians, whom you love so much, to suggest them to you and give them deep roots in your hearts. To her I entrust your whole family, willed by Don Bosco as "a living monument of Marian love", and I pray to her to protect you at every moment of your growth along your ways in the world.

As a token of these fervent wishes I willingly impart to you my Apostolic Blessing.

O.R. 719.   25 January 1982

Address to Religious in Ibadan, Nigeria
15 February 1982

Dear brothers and sisters in Christ, I am overjoyed to have this meeting with you, men and women of the different dioceses in Nigeria, who are living the religious life of consecration to Jesus Christ. Through your commitment of perfect charity you express the hope of the Church and become her crown and glory. You are a comfort for her. You are ambassadors for her. This encounter could not be omitted.

Having been already consecrated to God by baptism, you give special witness to Christ in the Church and in the world by your renunciation — for the sake of the kingdom of heaven — of marriage, earthly possessions and the doing of your own will. Through your vows you make this sacrifice freely, out of love for God and your fellow-man, in a spirit of dedication and service.

Consecrated chastity has great witness value in a world rampant with selfishness and the misuse of sex. In addition, in Nigeria and throughout Africa the sacrifice of fatherhood or motherhood is no small matter. Poverty calls people to give up attachment to money and what money can buy. And obedience swims against the world current of revolt, pride, vanity and oppression. As the Second Vatican Council says, the religious state is a proof that the kingdom of Christ and its overmastering necessities are superior to all earthly considerations (cf. *Lumen Gentium,* 44).

Even more important than the various works which you carry out is the life which you live: in other words, what you are. You are consecrated persons striving to follow Christ with great intensity of love.

Your love of God and union with him in prayer expresses itself in the activities of the apostolate. In many ways you are called to collaborate in the cause of evangelisation. Through multiplicity of works you strive to communicate Christ and to offer service in his name. Through a whole network of ecclesial initiatives you pursue the definitive aim of catechesis: "to put people not only in touch but in communion, in intimacy, with Jesus Christ" (*Catechesi Tradendae, 5)*. Wherever a child is in need, wherever a brother or sister feels alone or rejected, the religious has the opportunity to work for the kingdom of God. But prayer and union with God always remain the soul of your apostolate. Without Jesus you can do nothing.

I appreciate your efforts for continuing theological and spiritual formation of your members, your initiative of post-novitiate training centres, the regular meetings of your major superiors, and the area meetings which involve every religious. Through such activities you are able to reflect more deeply on religious life, grow in an understanding of charity and the meaning of your mission, consolidate unity among yourselves and coordinate your apostolate. Having been refreshed and renewed in faith and love, you will be in a position to give yourselves with ever greater availability to the service of the local and the universal Church.

I wish to make a particular mention of religious brothers and to praise them and to encourage them. Your vocation, my dear brothers, is not an easy one, especially because the spirit of the world does not appreciate evangelical poverty and humble service. You are called to follow Christ in a life of total self-giving which does not generally bring public acclaim.

Many people cannot understand your vocation because they cannot grasp how Christ's invitation, when accepted, can truly bring joy and deep fulfilment: "If any man would come after me, let him deny himself and take up his cross and follow me" *(Mt 16:24)*. The Christ who emptied himself is your model and your strength. You yourselves, then, must never begin to doubt your own identity. Your understanding of your vocation, your transparent happiness and infectious peace, and your zealous commitment to your apostolate and to the good of the people whom you serve are an eloquent witness to the power of Christ's grace and to the primacy of his love.

All religious, both brothers and sisters, must be aware that temptations will not spare them. Your three vows will sooner or later be tested in the crucible of problems, crises and dangers. Your intense love of Christ and his Church will teach you how to remain faithful. In particular, you will have to seek ever more authentic ways to live lives of evangelical poverty in a country in which the gap between the rich and the poor is widening all the time. In the Nigeria of today you are also expected to be a leaven in society through a spirit of humble service, exercised particularly among the poor. This type of consecrated service is the opposite of complacency, arrogance and privileged position.

In planning your apostolate and the professional training of your members, each congregation should take full account of the local Church or diocese. The diocese is a spiritual family of which the bishop is the father and head, and religious must avoid the temptation of running programmes parallel to those of the diocese. Rather the entire diocese — priests, religious and laity — should coordinate its apostolic plans and strategy and give corporate witness to Christ.

I wish to add a specific word to the monks and cloistered nuns of Nigeria, because of the specific contribution which their way of life makes to the Church and the nation. You rightly place particular emphasis on divine worship, on prayer and contemplation. The Church herself ratifies your vocation because of her conviction that apostolic fruitfulness is a gift of God. By assiduous prayer you are associated with Jesus, who is "living for ever to intercede for all who come to God through him" *(Heb 7:25)*. United with Jesus in his intercession, you are thus able to obtain graces for the active apostolate and for the whole world. I personally rely on your help.

You live lives of real self-sacrifice. You thereby give to all Christians, and indeed to all people, a silent but eloquent testimony of God's sovereignty and of Christ's primacy in your lives. By the work of your hands, and by your intellectual endeavours, you show the close relationship between work and prayer. At the same time you express your solidarity in work with all your brothers and sisters throughout the world.

Through monastic silence you help create an atmosphere for enabling people to listen to God and to receive his inspiration. It is no wonder that priests, religious and laity flock to your monasteries and convents for the sacred liturgy, prayer, spiritual retreats, recollection days, advice and even simply rest. In such ways you can help promote the maturity of your people in the Paschal Mystery of Christ's Death and Resurrection.

And to all of you, beloved religious of Nigeria, I wish to express my deep affection in Christ Jesus. I am very grateful to you for your lives of consecration and for all your generous service to the Church. I ask your continuing prayers for the intentions of the Apostolic See and for the needs of the universal Church. May our Blessed Mother Mary, our model of love for Jesus and of dedication to him, help you to live out faithfully your vocation of love and faith, of joy and hope. For in the words of St Peter, without having seen Jesus "you love him; though you do not now see him, you believe in him and rejoice with unutterable and exalted joy". Dear brothers and sisters, "set your hope fully upon the grace that is coming to you at the revelation of Jesus Christ" (*1 Pt 1: 8, 13*).

O.R. 723. 22 February 1982

Address to the Jesuit Major Superiors
27 February 1982

I am particularly pleased, dearest brothers in Christ, to welcome you today in this special meeting!... To these sentiments of sincere joy for your presence there should be added a due sentiment of recognition and gratitude, which — following in the steps of my predecessors — I wish to express to the whole Society of Jesus and to its individual members, for the historic contribution of apostolate, of service, of fidelity to Christ, to the Church and to the Pope, given over the centuries with an unwearying generosity and an exemplary dedication in all fields of the apostolate, in the ministries, in the missions. It is a recognition which I express today in the name of the whole Church to you, worthy heirs of these religious, who for four centuries and a half have taken as their motto and ideal "the greater glory of God".....

During this meeting of ours, as I look on your qualified group of the Sons of St Ignatius, there is offered to my consideration the vision of your Order and of its glorious history.

It is known to all those who are familiar with the history of the Church, how and to what extent the Society of Jesus, founded at the time of the Council of Trent, effectively contributed to the implementation of the directives of that Council, and to the vitality engendered by the Council.

However, it is opportune to reflect on your Order's past in order to grasp the fundamental marks of this process and the richest and most positive aspects of the way in which the Society contributed to it. They will be like guiding lights or beacons to indicate what the Society of today, impelled by the dynamism typical of its founder's charism, but genuinely faithful to it, can and must do to foster what the Spirit of God has brought about in the Church through the Second Vatican Council.

As one looks back over the four centuries and a half of its history, certain elements of genuine value emerge. They are those which characterise the life and mission of that body, which by the will of Ignatius is the Society of Jesus.

The first concern of Ignatius and of his companions was to promote an authentic renewal of the Christian life. The state of society and of the Church were such that only the work of men of God could have an influence and supply sanctifying vitality.

Following the example of Jesus who went about "all the cities and villages, teaching in their synagogues and preaching the Gospel of the kingdom" *(Mt 9:35)*, the first companions, sent out under obedience, went their pilgrim way to various cities, spreading the Good News and bringing a breath of saintly life. That was the beginning of those missions to the people which were destined to be of service to the Christian faithful, to instruct them in the faith and to lead them to a consistency of life. These missions to the people were subsequently to have a flourishing development and a vast influence for good. The spiritual exercises of St Ignatius which imprinted an indelible mark on the history of spirituality, proved to be a particularly efficacious means for a deeper renewal of the Christian life. The first companions and their successors were formed by the exercises, and with the exercises they became the spiritual guides of innumerable faithful; they helped them to discover their vocation according to God's plan and to become genuine, committed Christians, whatever their state in life might be.

Besides spiritual direction the Society had a solicitous concern for spreading the true Catholic doctrine among the learned and the unlearned, from the young to the oldest. The two Jesuit Doctors of the Church, St Peter Canisius and St Robert Bellarmine, were the authors of two celebrated catechisms for the young and they were, both of them, masters held in admiration, the former engaged in the theological discussions of the Council of Trent, and the latter a defender of the faith in the universities of Louvain and Rome.

For a similar reason St Ignatius, and after him the Society, took pains with the education of youth. They founded and multiplied colleges in which, following a new system of teaching — the famous *"Ratio studiorum"* — they aimed at providing an integral formation of the human person, in order to mould men who, while being eminent in study and in every profession, would also be outstanding Christians.

All this happened at a time when the world, and particularly Europe, was in a state of change, indeed at a decisive turning point in the literary and scientific field. In this process Jesuit scholars and men of science played a forceful part by performing a pioneering work *"ad maiorem Dei gloriam"*, that is to say, by fostering that Christian development of man which, when achieved, is to the glory of God.

Looking then at a sector of vital importance for the Church, St Ignatius and the Society after him were concerned about seminaries and higher centres of learning for the formation of the clergy. To St Ignatius is due the founding of the Roman College, later to become the Gregorian University, and likewise the founding of the Germanic College, which was followed, often with the collaboration of so many Jesuits, by the other national colleges in Rome, to prepare for the Church a flow of priests endowed with sound doctrine and solid virtue. These became zealous apostles in their own homelands, and not infrequently martyrs for the faith.

In connection with these centres of learning the Society has made a most valuable contribution in the field of the sacred sciences and has given a numerous band of Jesuit theologians, biblical exegetes, patrologists, Church historians, moralists and canonists, and scholars of so many other sciences connected with sacred studies.

But St Ignatius' vision opened on still wider horizons, as broad as the world, which, following upon the then recent geographical discoveries, had assumed larger dimensions. It is the yearning for Christ which throbbed in the heart of the Saint and in the hearts of those who, sharing his spirit, offered themselves entirely to "Our Lord, eternal king", whose "will is to conquer the whole world" *(Spiritual Exercises, n. 95)*.

The group of Ignatius' first companions was small; yet the Saint sent St Francis Xavier to the East, the first of that uninterrupted band of Jesuit missionaries who were "sent" to the East and the West to announce the Gospel. On fire with apostolic zeal they were ready to give their life as a witness to their faith, as is attested by the numerous martyrs of the Society. While the primary scope of their mission was to communicate the faith and the grace of Christ, they made every effort at the same time to raise the human and cultural level of the peoples among whom they worked, to promote a more just social life and one more in keeping with God's plans — because of which the famous *Reducciones* of Paraquay are still remembered in history.

The generosity and the spirit of the missionaries attracted new recruits; the letters of St Francis Xavier touched the hearts of the university students of Paris. The life and writings of so many other well-known apostles of Christ's kingdom had a similar effect. To them must be added a nameless host of holy religious who sacrificed their life in humility and in secret, in isolated mission lands......

Thus in the course of history the Society of Jesus, in every part of the world where it fought for Christ and for the Church, has been present with its finest sons, on fire with zeal, fortified with virtue, endowed with doctrine, and faithful to the directives of their head, of the Vicar of Christ, the Roman Pontiff.

This is the Society of Jesus which history places before our eyes; the Society of Jesus which the enemies of Christ persecuted until they obtained its suppression, but which the Church has made to rise again, realising the need of such valiant and devoted sons. Popes have trusted them in the past, and the Pope wishes to place his trust in them in the future.

If I have spoken about the Society of Jesus of the past, so as to bring together the distinctive features of its life and mission, that is because I am thinking of the Society as it is today and what the Church expects from it at present and in the future.

Whoever considers the contribution that your Order has made to the Church and to the world and appreciates its main objectives, cannot but see what was for St Ignatius one of the most characteristic features of the Order founded by him under the impulse of the Holy Spirit.

In fact, the Society of Jesus has always throughout its history, in all its many and varied forms of apostolic ministry, distinguished itself by the mobility and vigour which its founder infused into it, and which have made it capable of understanding the signs of the times and of being in the forefront of the renewal desired by the Church.

In view of the apostolic and missionary vocation which is yours, the members of this chosen body that you constitute by the will of St Ignatius and the Church, are, as Paul VI said to you, ''in the first line of the profound renewal which the Church, especially since the Second Vatican Council, desires to bring about in this secularised world. Your Society is, so to speak, a test of the Church's vitality throughout the centuries; it is in some sense a crossroads where, in a very significant manner, difficulties, temptations, efforts, undertakings, the durability and the successes of the entire Church all meet together'' (*Paul VI, Allocution to the Fathers of the 32nd General Congregation, 3 Dec. 1974*).

As my venerated predecessor already told you, the Church today wants the Society to implement effectively the Second Vatican

Council, as, in the time of St Ignatius and afterwards, it spared no effort to make known and apply the Council of Trent, assisting in a notable way the Roman Pontiffs in the exercise of their supreme magisterium.

Allow me to insist once more and solemnly on the exact interpretation of the recent Council. It was and still is an ecclesial renewal under the guidance of the Holy Spirit. On this most important point the conciliar documents are absolutely clear (cf. *Lumen Gentium, 4, 7, 9; Gaudium et Spes, 21, par. 5, and 43, par 6*).

This renewal of fidelity and fervour in all sections of the Church's mission — matured and expressed in the collective heeding of the Pentecostal Spirit — must be welcomed and lived today according to the same Spirit and not according to personal criteria or psycho-sociological theories. That is why, the better to accomplish this work in the bosom of the Church, contemplatives and religious who live the apostolic life have been called by the same Council to renew their evangelical life.

The decree *Perfectae Caritatis (2 and 3)* expressed clearly and fervently these criteria of renewal. Where there is fidelity, there is no room for deviations which are certainly harmful to the vitality of communities and of the entire Church. It seems to me that the Society of Jesus, ever more imbued with the spirit of true renewal, will be ready to play its part fully today as in the past and always: to be able to help the Pope and the Apostolic College to advance the whole Church along the great road marked out by the Council, and to convince those who are tempted, alas, by the ways of either progressivism or integralism, to return with humility and joy to unsullied communion with their pastors and brothers who suffer from their attitudes and their absence.

This patient and delicate task is surely the work of the whole Church, but faithful to St Ignatius and all his sons, you must rise like one man for this mission of unity in truth and charity.

The fourth vow of the Society was understood by St Ignatius precisely as the living and vital expression of the awareness that Christ's mission continues in time and space in those who, called by him to follow and share his works (cf. *Spiritual Exercises, nn. 91-98*), make his sentiments their own and thus live in intimate union with him and therefore with his Vicar on earth.

That is the reason why St Ignatius and his companions, wishing to share in Christ's mission which continues in the Church, decided to place themselves without reserve at the disposition of the Vicar of Christ, and to bind themselves to him by "a special vow, so much so that this union with the successor of Peter, which is the specific characteristic of the members of the Society, has always assured your communion with Christ, of which it is the sign; for Christ is the first and supreme head of the Society, which by definition is his — the Society of Jesus" (*Paul VI, Allocution to the Fathers of the 32nd General Congregation, 3 Dec. 1974*).

Because of this distinctive and characteristic feature of your Order, the Church first of all requires you to adapt the different forms of traditional apostolate which even today retain all their effectiveness, and to work for the renewing of the spiritual life of the faithful, the education of youth, the formation of the clergy, of men and women religious, and missionary activity.

This requires catechesis, proclamation of the word of God, the spreading of Christ's doctrine, Christian penetration into the culture of a world trying to establish division and opposition between science and faith, pastoral activity for those on the fringe of society, exercise of priestly ministry in all its authentic forms, not forgetting the new means of apostolic works provided by modern society, such as the press and the media, while bringing to perfection the use which the Society has already made of them during recent times.

Besides this, the Church wishes the Society to interest itself still more in the initiatives which the Second Vatican Council has particularly encouraged:

— ecumenism, in order to reduce the scandal of division among Christians. It is now more than twenty years since the Church instituted the Secretariat for Christian Unity. In a world becoming less Christian the collaboration between those who believe in God and in Christ is needed.

— the deepening of relations with non-Christian religions, carried out by the Secretariat for non-Christians, and the presentation of Christian life and doctrine in a manner adapted to the different cultures which tactfully keeps in mind their different characteristic traits and the richness of each one.

— studies and initiatives concerning the disturbing phenomenon of atheism, encouraged by the Secretariat for non-Believers, remembering the behest of Paul VI to "resist atheism vigorously and as strongly as possible" (*Allocution to the Fathers of the 31st. Congregation 7 May 1965*).

There is still one point to which I wish to call your attention. Today we feel with ever growing urgency the need to promote justice in the Church's evangelising action. When we think of the demands of the Gospel and at the same time of the influence of social conditions on practical Christian living, we easily understand why the Church considers the promotion of justice to be an integral part of evangelisation. It must be understood as an important sphere of apostolic action. In this domain not all have the same function, and as far as the members of the Society are concerned, it must not be forgotten that this necessary concern for justice must be exercised in conformity with your religious and priestly vocation. As I said on 2 July 1980 in Rio de Janeiro, priestly service, "if it is really to be faithful to itself, is essentially and *par excellence* spiritual. This must be even more emphasised in our times against the many tendencies to secularise the priest's work by reducing it to a purely philanthropic function. He is not a medical doctor, a social worker, a politician, or a trade unionist. In certain cases, no doubt, the priest can help, but in a supplementary fashion — as in the past priests have done with remarkable success. Today, however, these services are admirably rendered by other members of society, whilst our service is always more precisely and specifically spiritual. It is in the realm of souls, of their relation to God and their attitude towards their fellow-man that the priest has an essential function to fulfil. That is where he should use his talents with the people of today. Certainly, whenever there is need, he must also give material assistance through works of charity and by upholding justice, but, as I have said, in the last analysis, this must be a secondary service which must never obscure the principal service which is to help souls to discover the Father, to be open to him and to love him in all things".

The Second Vatican Council has already clarified the apostolate of the laity and has exhorted them to play their part in the Church's mission; but the role of priests and religious is different. They are not meant to take the place of the laity, and still less should they neglect the duty that is specifically theirs.

Your constitutions lay down clearly those prerequisites which are necessary if the Society of Jesus is to contribute efficaciously to the implementation of the conciliar decrees as the Church expects it to do.

First there is the prolonged, solid formation of the future apostles of the Society. In the very Formula of the Institute, after describing the way typical of the Society, Ignatius writes: "By experience we have learned that the path has many and great difficulties connected with it. Consequently we have judged it opportune to decree that no one should be permitted to pronounce his profession in this Society unless his life and doctrine have been proved by long and exacting tests." *(Formula of the Institute of the Society of Jesus, n. 9).*

You must not yield to the easy temptation of watering down this formation which has such importance in each and every one of its aspects, spiritual, doctrinal, disciplinary and pastoral; the ensuing damage would outweigh by far any results which could perhaps be achieved right away.

Remember that even in the days of your founder, the Society was faced with the anguishing problem which faces you today. Even then there were too few apostles, apt and ready, to cope adequately with the pastoral needs.

However, you must bear in mind that this long and exacting preparation has as its primary aim the formation of men who are outstanding because of their intimate union with God. In fact, Ignatius was convinced that all apostolic activity has value and is efficacious only if it flows from that "union between the instrument and God" of which he so often speaks. The primacy of the interior life is the very foundation of Ignatius' vision and spirituality; it constitutes the inner core of an authentic apostolic life, because the true apostle lives out his mission in total dependence of God in union with him.

Your founder and with him his first companions were indeed men of God; in answer to the freely-given call of the Eternal King *(Spiritual Exercises, 91-98),* and having understood interiorly the Spirit which animated Jesus himself, the One sent by the Father, they lived as the Lord asked his Apostles to live, when he said to them: "Abide in me, and I in you. As the branch cannot bear fruit by itself, unless it abides in the vine, neither can you, unless you abide in me. I am the vine, you are the branches. He who abides in me, and I in him, he it is that bears much fruit, for apart from me you can do nothing" *(Jn 15:4-5).*

Yet again, in virtue of what is the richest element in the spirit of your founder, I beg you to reflect on the deepest meaning of the "Contemplation for obtaining Love", by which the apostolic man lives in the awareness of the reality that "all gifts and benefits come from above. My moderate ability comes from the Supreme Omnipotence on high, as do my sense of justice, kindliness, charity, mercy and so on, like sunbeams from the sun or streams from their source..." *(Spiritual Exercises, 237).* Such is the spirit of the true apostle who lives his mission in total dependence on God and in union with him.

For this reason in apostolic religious life of which St Ignatius, under God's impulse, was one of the great founders, there should be no separation between the interior life and the apostolate. These are the two essential and constitutive elements of this life: they are inseparable, and they mutually influence and complement each other.

Together with solidity of virtue, your constitutions insist on a solidity and soundness of doctrine, such as is essential for an efficacious apostolate. Consequently "the Jesuits were universally considered to be a support for the doctrine and discipline of the whole Church. Bishops, priests and lay people used to look upon the Society as an authentic nourishment for the interior life" *(Letter of Cardinal Villot to Father Arrupe, 2 July 1973).* The same should remain true in the future by means of that loyal fidelity to the magisterium of the Church, and in particular of the Roman Pontiff, to which you are in duty bound.

In fact, a special bond binds your Society to the Roman Pontiff, the Vicar of Christ on earth. As I have already mentioned above, St Ignatius and his companions, having spiritually grasped the true meaning and value of the mission of Christ, and how it is prolonged in history, attached capital importance to this bond of love and service to the Roman Pontiff, so much so that they wished this "special vow" to be a characteristic element of the Society. Whilst describing their own interior disposition, and what they expected of those who would later be admitted to the professed body of the Society, they wrote those words which are, and must remain, engraved in the heart of every Jesuit worthy of the name: "For the sake of our greater devotion in obedience to the Apostolic See, of greater abnegation of our own wills, and of surer direction from the Holy Spirit, in addition to that ordinary bond of the three vows, we are obliged by a special vow to carry out whatever the present and future Roman Pontiffs may order which pertains to the progress of souls and the propagation of the faith; and to go without hesitation or excuse, as far as in us lies." *(Formula of the Institute of the Society of Jesus, n. 3).* It is evident that here we are touching upon the essence of the Ignatian charism, and upon what lies at the very heart of your Order. And it is to this that you must always remain faithful.

The Roman Pontiff to whom you are linked by this special vow is, in the words of the Second Vatican Council, "the Supreme Pastor of the Church" *(Christus Dominus, 5).* As such he has a particular ministry of service to exercise for the good of the universal Church, and in which he willingly accepts your loving, devoted and time-tested collaboration. But the same Roman Pontiff also accepts the collaboration that you offer him in his role as head of the Episcopal College, united with his brother bishops in a collegial ministry of discernment and harmony, which, in virtue of a distinctive charism, coordinates in docility to the Holy Spirit the other roles of ecclesial service (cf. *Mutuae Relationes,* 6) For this reason you are likewise linked to the members of the College of Bishops by a bond that calls you to be united with them in pastoral charity and in close practical collaboration. Precisely because of your special availability to the call of the Roman Pontiff, you are able to work ever more effectively with the College of Bishops and with its individual members, who in the Successor of Peter find their perennial and visible source and foundation of unity (cf. *Lumen Gentium* 5).

As the Second Vatican Council explained, the Roman Pontiff also employs the departments of the Roman Curia in the exercise of his service to the universal Church (cf. *Christus Dominus,* 9). This fact itself requires a loyal collaboration between the Society of Jesus and these departments. Because of the exigencies of your vows and the reality of my ministry, it could not be otherwise. Some of the special tasks assigned to the Society of Jesus and other important works that it has assumed in the postconciliar period correspond to the programmes of the Apostolic See that are coordinated by some of its new departments. Through collaboration with these various bodies, the Society of Jesus can find its rightful orientation in a number of issues and at the same time make an enormous contribution to the universal Church.

On his part the Roman Pontiff offers you, in the name of Christ, whose Vicar he is, the full measure of his grateful love for your collaboration with him personally, with the College of Bishops, and with the whole Roman Curia, which the Society of Jesus has been generously assisting in so many ways for years.

I shall not delay any longer these reflections, because I know that during these days you are considering...the wishes that I have expressed regarding the Society, and that in a spirit of faith and of fraternal collaboration, you are seeking the most suitable means of putting them into practice.

My only task is to encourage you to continue in this work which, while being of special importance for the good of your Society, will also be of great benefit for the whole Church which looks to the Society with a special interest and appreciation.

The exemplary nature of your religious life, the spiritual atmosphere of your communities, the austerity of your mode of life, and your fervour in apostolic works will be a cause of edification for the whole people of God, and will attract ever more numerous vocations to your Society — generous young people who aspire, not to mediocrity in the following of Christ, but to a radical consecration to him......

I shall accompany you in this work with my good wishes and my prayers that the Lord, through the intercession of her whom you are in the habit of invoking as Queen and Mother of the Society of Jesus and of your many saints and blessed, may bless your work and make it fruitful.

To these saints and blessed, already elevated to the honours of the altar, it is consoling to add also so many of your brothers who are awaiting the Church's official recognition of their sanctity. In this regard it is a pleasure for me to recall that precisely on 11 February of this year, I had the joy of declaring heroic the virtues of the humble and well-beloved coadjutor Brother, Francis Garate, who died some fifty years ago, a native of that land which saw the birth of your holy founder, Ignatius of Loyola.

The life of these religious of the Society as also of so many excellent Jesuits who live and work throughout the whole world in a spirit of faith filled with love and with a dedication to the service of man that is truly exemplary, is a clear proof that even in our times holiness continues to flourish in the Society.

It is a proof also of the continuing validity of the vocation of the coadjutor Brothers in the Society. Through their complete dedication to the service of the Lord in the carrying out of the various offices, these Brothers really cooperate with the Fathers in that priestly ministry which is proper to the Society. With these sentiments I impart to you with all my heart my Apostolic Blessing and through you I extend it to all the members of the Society as a pledge of divine gifts.

O.R. 726.   15 March 1982

Address to Priests and Religious at Montenero
12 March 1982

......The Virgin of Montenero is venerated as Our Lady of Grace and the Gospel on her feast is the canticle of the Magnificat. "My soul magnifies the Lord, and my spirit rejoices in God my Saviour, because he has regarded the humility of his handmaid...the Almighty has done great things in me and Holy is his name".

Dear priests and religious of the Diocese of Livorno, in this meeting of ours, we too, like Mary, in giving thanks to the Almighty, whose name is Holy, want to raise together the hymn of our exultation, because he has regarded the humility of his servants.

The Holy Virgin intones the Magnificat, aware that in order to fulfil his plan of salvation for all men, the Lord wished to associate her, a humble girl of his people. Following Mary's example, we are here to intone our Magnificat, knowing that we are called by God to a service of redemption and salvation, notwithstanding our inadequacy.

The grander the work to be accomplished, the poorer are the instruments chosen to collaborate in the divine plan. As it is true that the power of God's arm is emphasised by the weakness of the means employed, so too, the smaller the human persons who are invited to serve, the greater the things that the Almighty, through us, is disposed to accomplish.

It is for this reason that the rich are sent away empty-handed, the proud are confounded in the thoughts of their heart, while on the other hand, the lowly are exalted and the hungry are filled with good things. To accomplish the mission and render our service, what is asked of us is not so much a patrimony of material or human gifts, such as money, intelligence, culture, talent for organisation or efficiency, but rather the sense of our own uselessness and generous commitment in confident and complete abandon to the love of the Almighty. The salvation of mankind, in which even man is called to collaborate, is an eminently divine work, of such greatness that it surpasses the limits and possibilities of human powers. Therefore it can be achieved only if the human collaborators accept and develop the covenant with the omnipotence of God.

This is the meaning of the canticle and the Marian message that we want to accept and meditate on today. Our poverty is filled with the richness of God, our weakness with his strength, our "nothing" by him who is "everything".

"The Almighty has done great things in me", Mary states. She is fully aware of the greatness of her mission. But at the same time, seeing herself and remaining a "lowly handmaid", she attributes all credit for it to God the Saviour. The grandeur of the redemptive mission is achieved in Mary with the perfect accord between divine omnipotence and humble docility.

Dear priests and religious, these considerations arising from meditation on the essential contents of the Magnificat take on a significance of urgent moment if we pause to establish a relationship betwen the spiritual needs of modern society, of the universal and local Church, and the availability of collaborators' hands.

Certainly the work of salvation continues ceaselessly in the world, today as yesterday, and as it will tomorrow. And today too we must repeat with Jesus: "The harvest is great, but the labourers are few".

In our modern society there is so much to be done. To evangelise or re-evangelise. Even within the confines of your ecclesial community. The task is difficult, complex, and not of short duration. And it cannot be the result of mere human efforts. It is the work of God, even if God asks men's cooperation.

But God wants to save modern society, whatever be the nature of the social or ideological difficulties. God can do all things. He is not forgetful of his mercy, and the power of his arm is not weakened. And when he calls human collaborators to comply with his plan of evangelisation and salvation, he wants them in an attitude of humility and docility, like Mary.

Brothers and sisters, God has called you too, or rather he continually calls you. Since the time when the Lord's glance was cast with love on each one of you personally and you said "yes", you became apostles of the Gospel in permanent service.

Associating you in the work of salvation, God intends to accomplish "great things" through you. Things that certainly are impossible to man, but not impossible to Almighty God. Entrusting to you a portion of his vineyard, the Lord intends, together with you, to evangelise the modern world, your cities, your countries, of sea or mountain, all buffeted by ideological atheism or by the practical materialism of well-being.

If the difficulties are many, have no fear. God is with you.

You will fulfil your mission worthily, you will carry out your service, if, like the Holy Virgin, your dedication is total; if, placing yourselves in the attitude of humble and docile servants, you do not put your confidence in your own personal abilities, in the sciences or technologies of men, in the use of economic means, in the search for public acclaim, even if the wise use of human means can offer its own contribution. May your human insufficiency not frighten you. Keep your glance constantly fixed on the mercy and the power of God, who can raise up his children even from hearts apparently as hard as stones. Seek the kingdom of God. The rest will be given besides.....

You men religious in particular, without losing the characteristics of the original charism of your foundation, are called to lend a strong hand to the diocesan clergy, to become involved in the local Church, to give your substantial contribution to the development of the one Church.

In a special way, you sisters, so numerous at this meeting and so solicitous and ready in so many areas of diocesan life, have before you irreplaceable and appointed tasks to be fulfilled. I congratulate you very much for the precious help you offer the overall apostolate.

Dear brothers and sisters, may the Lord shower upon all of you, upon each one of you, the abundance of his graces. May the Virgin Mother be an example and an incentive for you; and may my special Blessing be a sign of divine favour.

O.R. 729. 5-12 April 1982

Address to Clergy and Religious at Fatima
13 May 1982

Dear Fathers, Brothers and Sisters, to you who are in God the Father and the Lord Jesus Christ, grace, mercy and peace, in the truth and love of the Holy Spirit who has been given to us! (cf. *1 Th 1:1; Rom 5:4*).

These words of the Apostle St Paul express my sentiments and anticipate my wishes this afternoon at this meeting, which has a particular importance for me and, I think I can say, also for you. It is a great joy and it is beautiful to be together with you — priests, men and women religious of Portugal — and to be able to greet and speak with you personally.

I feel full of joy, gratitude and hope when I can meet religious or those who are preparing for the religious life. It is for me a state of soul that has the intensity and vibration of a rare meeting, as though it could not be repeated again, with people very dear to me. I too, by divine grace, am a priest of Jesus Christ; and every day my respect for the priesthood and for the religious life grows, because they represent and contribute to the mission, life and treasury of the Church, the Mystical Body of Christ.

The communion of feelings that links me to you in brotherhood for life, at this moment makes me feel in a certain way the mysterious reality of the "Body" of our Holy Church illuminated by the maternally affectionate look of Our Lady. And here in Fatima, where she is so much loved and venerated, in greeting her with affection, I invite you to look to her stimulating example and, as your "older brother", in the name of all, I ask her maternal blessing, while praying: "Mother of mercy, show us Jesus, the blessed fruit of your womb!"

And with her blessing and patronage, we confidently raise our hearts to God our Father in thanksgiving: for he loves us "and it was he who first loved us" *(1 Jn 4:10)*. It was neither we nor our parents who took the initiative, who chose to be created, baptised and made members of his Church. The initiative came from the "original love", the first principle, from whom proceeds the Holy Spirit through the Son. Yes, it was by the most liberal initiative of the love of God the Father, who wanted to give of his goodness, that we were created through his extraordinary and merciful kindness and then gratuitously called to share in his life and glory in this ecclesial condition that is ours. Blessed be God.

And with our hearts in God, let us turn our attention anew to our Mother and let us imagine the tender blessing of her reply, when she says to us: "Jesus Christ? Look, and you can discover him in his signs. And there are so many of these signs!" And at this moment perhaps she might add — to my confusion — "the sign is the Pope. He goes beyond his own person because he only lends his image to him, to Jesus Christ". With this image, I want to say in all sincerity how limited I feel and at the same time how responsible before Christ and before you.

I see in my mind those moments of the Lord with his own, with those whom from that moment he no longer called servants but friends (cf. *Jn 15:14*), with whom he spoke in confidence, heart to heart; of his sorrow for the multitudes, "like a sheep without a shepherd", like "fields ready for the harvest", without hands to do the work *(ibid. v. 37)*; of the meaning of saying "yes" to this work — without material security *(Mt 10:9)*, personal capacities *(ibid. v. 27)*. Finally he spoke to his friends frankly of the things closest to their hearts.

And today the Pope wishes to do the same, without overlooking the "sign" of the great Friend of all of us.

You priests and religious consecrated your life to the service of the Gospel in a moment of generosity! You were "chosen" *(Jn 15:16)*; and today you are those "called" by God to whom he entrusted the marvellous gift of this special vocation, on behalf of the whole Church, to go forth and bear fruit, a fruit that will last. You are God's gift to the Church in Portugal. I congratulate you and thank the Lord for your generous presence in this always luxuriant "pasture" and for your collaboration in serving and proclaiming the Good News of salvation.

Look, God well knows the difficulties, the "weariness of the day and of its heat" *(Mt 20:21)*; and he, on his part, is faithful; the graces necessary for perseverance and a happy response to your vocation will never be lacking. And on your part I am sure that docility and generosity will never be lacking. And it could not be otherwise. After so many blessings received and so many others that we still await from God, would we not be ashamed — a holy bishop once asked — to deny the only thing which he asks in return: love for him and for our neighbour? Could we dare to close our hearts... to the Father and refuse to be truly his sons and serve others, our brothers? (cf. *St. Gregory of Nazianzus, Sermones, De Pauperum Amore, 23; PG 35, 887).*

I would like to linger with each one of you and speak about your loving dialogue with God; about that personal history, without doubt a beautiful history, which began with Baptism, up to the day when you left all things to follow Christ; and then continuing along your road with him, as ones chosen by God. But since that is not possible, I want to say to all of you, as if I were speaking to each of you individually, Christ is the only way, the measure and scope of your life; he is the Christ of the good news and of the completeness of the gift of oneself for the sake of the kingdom of heaven.

And we could run through different adventures without being able to choose, but let us bring forward as an example the spirit of poverty. "Blessed are the poor in spirit for the kingdom of heaven will be theirs" *(Mt 5:3)*.

In a society which gives value only to having, in which a constant desire for personal well-being and comfort seems to rule, and which is so often fascinated with luxury, in direct contrast with evident misery: in this society poverty, and especially the spirit of poverty, is a challenge. A challenge for all, for the rich and the poor in material goods, and a challenge especially for those who have made a profession of evangelical poverty.

Evangelical poverty is something more than the simple renunciation of material possessions; it is to abandon oneself, to lose oneself in God. Christ spoke one day about a merchant who chose a precious pearl and exchanged all that he had to buy it. He valued the choice of higher goods, those of great value given to those who can proceed with wisdom. Peter, after making this choice, dared to ask Christ about these higher values, for which he had left everything to follow his Master; and he received the famous reply: a hundredfold in this life and life everlasting (cf. *Mt 19:27-29*).

Thinking back to this exchange which we also make, in the light of the explanation obtained by St Peter, could we or others hesitate to verify the fulfilment of the Lord's promise? Our internal attitude and external behaviour which others see will always be that of serene possession of this "hundredfold" and of the hope of eternal life. Or will it more easily appear that we do not abandon everything — questions, "hypotheses" without hypotheses, human security, ties which do not allow us to throw aside all risks, etc. — and receive nothing more than any other "non-chosen" who totally commits himself to living this present life?

As you know, brothers and sisters, it is certainly not sufficient to abandon everything: it is necessary to follow Christ, with a continuous effort to identify oneself with him and with his cause. We are in the world without being of the world, representing among men the signs of the truth and of the presence of Christ in the world. We give him our whole being with its external features, that he may continue to exist, doing good.

This offering of ours, this giving up possessions has marked us with a particular sign, which has become our identity; with all our dignity as persons we are Christ's. All those who see us must be able to recognise without any difficulty this unique identity of ours. To facilitate mutual welcome at gatherings and meetings, it is current practice to display quite visibly one's photograph and personal data; and so without any embarrassment everyone is easily identified and called by name. It should always be the same for us also; our attitudes and external behaviour should allow others to begin a dialogue, private or open, with a priest, a male or female religious, or with a seminarian, who are all identified and called by name, as the chosen of God.

Just as it is difficult to live and to give witness of evangelical poverty in a society of consumerism and affluence, it is also difficult to be recognised as religious, in the Absolute of God, in an age of secularisation. The tendency towards levelling out, when it does not invert values, seems to favour anonymity of people: to be as most are, to go unnoticed. It is rather the characteristic of being "salt" and "light" (cf. *Mt 5:13 ff.*) in the world, that carries on Christ's call, especially for those who are consecrated to him. Likewise there remains in force the promise: "Whoever then will acknowledge me before men, I will acknowledge him before my Father in heaven" *(Mt 10:32).*

Beloved brothers and sisters: the "peculiarity" of the Master led him to be called things that were hardly flattering. And the disciples no less than the Master. The first disciples left us this testimony, showing themselves "full of joy that they had been found worthy of suffering dishonour for the sake of the Name" *(Acts 5:42)*; and the present generation of the Church must be the bearer of this testimony.

Fidelity to God and to men requires interior and spiritual freedom so that anyone can effectively share in the mission of Christ. Your vocation is a gift with regard this mission. You are called to work for the kingdom of God. And now I would like to speak to you on this reflection: the apostolic and pastoral commitment.

The tasks of the Church and in the Church are various: from the ministry to the simple and hidden services and to works that require culture, together with people of different conditions; but they are always close to man. For this reason many initiatives have come forth, inspired by the Holy Spirit, to respond to the various calls and needs of times and places. A simple glance at this assembly already shows what a variety of forms there are to this service of the Kingdom, while it shows the perennial vitality of the Church, with its constant solicitude, embodied in the founders of the religious families and by apostolic movements, each with its own role and merits.

But the common denominator, the first means and the most effective way to evangelisation by participating within the Church in the mission of Christ, remains the individual with the witness of his life. The other means and ways are carried out in works and initiatives, of greater or lesser favour among those being evangelised. But what you are, priests and religious, must never go unnoticed, much less forgotten. Even when for good reasons you might have to perform secular tasks, let this remain auxiliary and subordinate to your primary condition and function.

Never diminish this identity and do not forget the precise goal of the ministry and apostolic service to which you have been called: to lead your fellow man in our day to communion with the Most

Holy Trinity. In these days there is a growing temptation to seek security in property, knowledge, prestige and power. With your fidelity to all the obligations assumed with Holy Orders and with your consecration to Christ, generously alive in poverty, chastity and obedience, warn men against this false security; remember their eschatological dimension and point to the kingdom of heaven to which you consecrated your capacity to love.

The level of your pastoral and apostolic success will always be in proportion to the extent of your fidelity to Christ and your equal gift of love. It is this fidelity that frees the heart and inflames the spirit with total love for Christ and for his brothers and sisters in the world. And remember well that fidelity is achieved and maintained through union with the Lord, with the constant and profound renewal of prayer and the sacraments, so as to maintain the splendour of life in grace: "because without me you can do nothing" the same Lord says to us *(Jn 15:5)*.

Here, brothers and sisters, I would like to draw your attention to what is the fulcrum of my message to you today. If there is not a perfect balance between our life with God and our activity directed towards the service of men, we would compromise not only the work of evangelisation to which we are committed, but also our personal condition as people who have been evangelised. Prayer is the very soul of your work for the Kingdom: liturgical prayer centred in the Eucharist, received and lived with that purity of conscience that requires recourse to the Sacrament of Reconciliation, celebrated devoutly, for which there is no substitute; the Liturgy of the Hours, which signals the rhythm of continual adoration, in spirit and in truth, with the beloved presence of the Virgin in your prayer the Handmaid of God and model of whoever wishes to serve the Lord.

With the need for the witness of one's life, likewise the duty to proclaim salvation through Christ must be included, as St Peter said: "We cannot but speak of it" *(Acts 4:20)*. There will always be the chance to sow; but the seed can be only true and good; just as it will prove fruitful only if you have prayed and meditated on and studied the word of God, according to the reading of the authentic magisterium.

Today wonderful means of communication inform us of everything, and not always freely and objectively; so there are many things that we must clarify, direct and help people in choosing. The heart is always inclined to share knowledge and adhere to the truth, which you have already identified in Christ; and with love, faithful to the truth, you adopted the rule of St Francis of Assisi: to bring faith where there is doubt.

And it is above all in truth that unity is built: the communion of minds is easily transformed into the union of hearts, in the convergence of intentions towards the same cause. A kingdom divided against itself cannot survive. The divided apostolate comes to nothing by itself. And we know that it will be divided if you give in to the temptation of exclusivity, contrary to the just diversity of gifts and charisms, or to the temptation of isolation, disinterest or a standstill regarding the work of others, without following a programme or common pastoral plans.

If there is a diversity of gifts, services and operations, the source remains the same: "to each of us is given the manifestation of the Spirit for the common good" *(1 Co 12:7).*

When I began to study your beautiful language, I was impressed by the popular saying "It is through speaking that people understand each other". The union of the work forces of evangelisation requires a goal; and this in its turn will be found through an authentic dialogue, which also has its affective elements. How beautiful and important it is for us to meet as brothers, on a deeper level than mere communication of concepts! To meet in friendship, to share spiritual gifts, in affirmation of human fullness, in voluntary and genuine poverty of spirit. Every time these meetings occur — your experience will certainly tell you this — with our brothers in the ministry, the common life or the apostolate, our sense of living and participating in the mission of Christ is strengthened. After all, it was the Master who told us: "By this will all men know that you are my disciples, if you have love for one another" *(Jn 13:35).* And here would be the chance to broaden our considerations on the value of dialogue in charity and to a whole series of life's situations. I will limit myself to two points:

— the case of old people (priests, men and women religious) in this International Year of the Aged, and of the infirm: to them I address a word of deep understanding and a warm greeting, saying to them: You are important for the Church of Christ, today just as yesterday. With St Peter Chrysologus I ask you: make an altar of your hearts, and with every confidence offer your body as an offering to God, with faith and generosity! The Pope loves you and blesses you!

— relations with the coordinating authorities: here the dialogue, tranquil in docile and loyal cooperation and in obedience, achieves inestimable and mutual benefits which can be used for spiritual enrichment and for the treasury of the Church, and for the effectiveness of the work of evangelisation.

Enlarging on the concept of dialogue, I would say that to avoid the danger of the gradual impoverishment of the priestly and religious life, through difficulty if not through atrophy, we must maintain contacts with the sources of our initial basic formation, we must continue that training. Likewise, for the adequate proclamation of the Good News, there must be a dialogue with the culture of our environment, in a constant commitment to our chosen activity in order to gather together and transmit to others the reasons for the hope that inspires us (cf. *1 P 3:15*).

Something would be lacking in the joy of our meeting if we did not pay a brief visit in spirit to the brothers and sisters who have consecrated their life to contemplation and live in silent meditation, personally offering themselves in the cloister for love of the kingdom of heaven.

And what shall we say to them?

First of all, let us express our fraternal and joyful gratitude for what they are and what they represent for us, for the mission of the ecclesial community and for the world, placed as they are at the heart of the mystery of the Church. The comtemplative life is absolutely vital for the Church and for humanity, which is always in need of purifying and renewing oxygen of grace, breathed and distributed through these prayers and hidden immolations of our contemplative brothers and sisters.

But their silent immolation proclaims the Absolute of God and makes our fellow men ask themselves about the meaning of life. The love expressed in their adoration and supplication is lavished in the history of these same men: those who already know, and those who do not yet know, the Lord of history and the salvation that he offers. They all must more and more build a world of justice and brotherhood according to divine plans.

And I would like to repeat something that I feel very strongly on this pilgrimage to Fatima, and which is always in my heart when I address contemplatives: pray and sacrifice for us and for all those who pray, for those who cannot pray, for those who do not know how to pray and for those who do not want to pray! And may the God of peace be with you always!

And to the new brothers — seminarians or those who are about to embrace the religious life — I also want to address to you a word of deep affection, from my soul and with great confidence. You occupy a special place in the heart of the Pope, in the hope of the

Church and, in a special way, in the Church of this country, with so many worthy traditions with regard to priestly and religious vocations. In you I see and greet all those who aspire to the priesthood or the religious life in all of Portugal. And I can tell you what nostalgia I feel for my days as a seminarian and what a joy it is to be with you today!

But on the horizon of this joy, even here in Portugal, there are clouds, which bring to mind spontaneously the exclamation of the Lord, "the harvest is ripe but the labourers are few" *(Lk 10:2)*. And with this memory there comes from my heart an appeal to all those who are interested in this problem — to dedicate all their good will to the field of vocations: with constant prayers, with example, above all on the part of those already "chosen", and with adequate pastoral action, starting with the family, then through the various communities and through the school, and finally at the level of the complete pastoral programme. I know that you are already committed in this way and I want my words to comfort and encourage you.

And those in seminaries and houses of formation are giving the best of themselves to cultivate with the affection of Mother Church those plants destined to blossom into priests and men and women religious. I want to express all my esteem for you and repeat, even if they already know it: you are not alone in your generous and precious work; the whole Church is with you. Know that the Pope supports and appreciates you, as do your bishops and your religious superiors. May your work always be blessed by God!

And you, my young friends, cultivate the ideals, love this life and give it noble scope. You are at a point in life when you must speak much to God about men, so that later you can speak to men about God. There is a phrase that you are sure to know but which I would like to remind you of: "there are three 'much's' which three others can make up for: much study, much knowledge, much reflection, much wisdom, much virtue, much peace". Have courage!

Brothers and sisters, the poor in spirit is the one who believes in the Gospel of the love and mercy of God and lives it every day. The consecrated one is he who affirms and lives in himself the absolute dominion of God, who wishes to be everything to all men. The evangeliser is one who proclaims the Good News that he has in his heart and that transforms him interiorly and frees him spiritually. Be faithful to your sublime vocation!

And may the Virgin Mary, Mother of the Church — Our Lady of Fatima — be always present in your life, with her example and her protection, and may she give you the constant serenity, consolation and joy of her Son, Jesus Christ, in whose name I bless you with all my heart.

O.R. 739.   21 June 1982

Address to Men and Women Religious, London
29 May 1982

My dear brothers and sisters in Christ, ...the Second Vatican Council has addressed to you a call for appropriate renewal of religious life through a return to the original charism of each institute and through a healthy adaptation to meet the changed conditions of the times (cf. *Perfectae Caritatis, 2*).

My brothers and sisters, we can see what the Church, and indeed society at large, expects from you today. The people of our time look to you and repeat what the Greek-speaking visitors to Jerusalem said to the Apostle Philip: "We wish to see Jesus" *(Jn 12:21)*. Yes, in you the world wishes to see Jesus. Your public profession of the evangelical counsels is a radical response to the Lord's call to follow him. As a result, your lives are meant to offer a clear witness to the reality of the kingdom of God already present in the affairs of men and nations.

As you renew your religious consecration here this morning before God and the Church, in the sight of millions of your fellow-countrymen, I wish to meditate with you on the greatness and dignity of your calling.

To most people you are known for what you do. Visitors to your abbeys and religious houses see you celebrate the liturgy, or follow you in prayer and contemplation. People of all ages and conditions benefit directly from your many different services to ecclesial and civil society. You teach; you care for the sick; you look after the poor, the old, the handicapped; you bring the word of God to those near and far; you lead the young to human and Christian maturity.

Most people know what you do, and admire and appreciate you for it. Your true greatness, though, comes from what you are. Perhaps what you are is less known and understood. In fact, what you are can only be grasped in the light of the "newness of life" revealed by the Risen Lord. In Christ you are a "new creation" (cf. 2 Co 5:17).

At some time in your lives, the call of the Lord to a special intimacy and union with him in his redemptive mission became so clear that you overcame your hesitations. You put aside your doubts and difficulties and committed yourselves to a life of total fidelity to the highest ideals of the Gospel. Your free decision was sustained by grace, and your perseverance through the years is a magnificent testimony of the victory of grace over the forces that struggle to tarnish the newness of your life in Christ. This "newness of life" is a gift of Christ to his Church. It is proof of the Church's holiness, an expression of her vitality.

Through the profession of the evangelical counsels you are bound to the Church in a special way. Let me suggest to you, then, some of the aspects of your consecrated life that are especially significant in the present circumstances of the pilgrim people of God. Today there exists a widespread temptation to unbelief and despair. You, on the other hand, are committed to being men and women of deep faith and unceasing prayer. To you in a particular way may be addressed St Paul's exhortation to Timothy: "Fight the good fight of the faith: take hold of the eternal life to which you were called when you made the good confession in the presence of many witnesses" (1 Tm 6:12). Believe that Christ called you because he loves you. In moments of darkness and pain, believe that he loves you all the more. Believe in the specific inspiration and charism of your institute. Believe in your mission within the Church. Let your faith shine before the world, as a lamp in the darkness; let it shine as a beacon that will guide a confused society to the proper appreciation of essential values. May the spiritual joy of your personal lives, and your communal witness of authentic Christian love, be a source of inspiration and hope. Be recognisable as men and women religious. The secular city needs living witnesses such as you.

Today many people are tempted to live by a false set of values. You, on the other hand, are men and women who have discovered the pearl of great price, a treasure that does not fail. Through poverty voluntarily embraced in imitation of Christ — being poor in spirit and in fact, singly and corporately (cf. *Perfectae Caritatis, 13*) — you seek freedom from the tyranny of the consumer society. Chastity practised "for the sake of the kingdom of heaven" *(Mt 19:12)* is a special gift to you from Christ, and from you to the whole Church. Virginity or celibacy is not only a preferential love of the Lord, but also a freedom for a total self-giving in universal service, without conditions and without discrimination. Your chastity, when it is marked by genuine generosity and joy, teaches others to distinguish between true love and its many counterfeits. Through your obedience, which is a complete dedication of yourselves to the will of God, you seek to achieve the "mature measure of the stature of the fullness of Christ" *(Ep 4:13)*. Paradoxically, through self-renunciation, you grow to human and Christian maturity and responsibility. You show that many current ideas of freedom are in fact distorted. You help ransom society, as it were, from the effects of unbridled selfishness.

The witness of religious consecration has a special dimension for those of you who live the contemplative form of religious life. Your lives are hidden with Christ in God. In silence and through prayer and penance you praise him. You call down his graces and blessing upon God's people (cf. *Perfectae Caritatis, 7*). Many people have a vague idea of what you do, but very many more, including Catholics, fail to recognise the greatness of your special vocation and its irreplaceable role in the Church's life. Contemplative prayer sustains the Church in her struggle to bring mankind to a proper understanding of human dignity and spiritual values. In the name of the Church I thank you. I ask you to pray all the more for the pilgrim people of God and for the world. And to those who feel called to contemplative life, I repeat Jesus' invitation to two hesitant disciples: "Come and see". They came and saw and stayed with him (cf. *Jn 1:39*).

The hidden witness of contemplatives is flanked by the vigorous apostolic thrust of the active religious communities. In the footsteps of the Master, with zeal for his Father's will, and confident in your own particular charism, you "show wonderfully at work within the Church the surpassing greatness of the force of Christ the King and boundless power of the Holy Spirit" *(Lumen Gentium, 44)*.

Religious communities have a special responsibility to be sensitive to the signs of the times, and to try to meet such needs as are the proper concern of the Church's ministry. Imitate the faith and courage of your founders. Be ready to sacrifice yourselves as they did. Help the bishops in their pastoral ministry, with confidence in Christ's promise to protect and guide his Church.

Men and women religious, lift up your hearts! Give thanks to the Lord for your wonderful vocation. Through you Jesus wants to continue his prayer of contemplation on the mountain. He wants to be seen announcing God's kingdom, healing the sick, bringing sinners to conversion, blessing children, doing good to all, and always obeying the will of the Father who sent him. In you the Church and the world must be able to see the living Lord.

Do not be afraid to proclaim openly before the rest of the Church, especially the young, the worthwhileness of your way of life and its beauty. The Catholic community must be shown the high privilege of following Christ's call to the religious life. The young must come to know you more closely. They will come to you when they see you as generous and cheerful followers of Jesus Christ, whose way of life does not offer material rewards and accommodate itself to the standards of the world. They will be attracted by Christ's uncompromising, exciting challenge to leave all in order to follow him.

In concluding, I wish to greet the religious of the Anglican Communion who are present here. You too are inspired by the evangelical call to an ever closer following of Christ. You have expressed a desire to welcome the Pope and to hear him speak. I thank you. I commend to your prayers the ardent desire of millions of Christians throughout the world: that we may be fully one in faith and love.

To all of you I express my gratitude and respect. I entrust all the religious of England and Wales to the loving protection of Mary, Mother of the Church, the loftiest example of discipleship. May the Holy Spirit fill your hearts with his gifts. Rejoice in the Lord always! Again, I say, rejoice! May the public renewal of your religious vows help bring about a new Pentecost in your lives and in the Church in this land.

Praised be Jesus Christ!

O.R. 736   31 May 1982

Address to Priests and Religious at Edinburgh
31 May 1982

.....Brothers and sisters, members of the religious communities! How I wish I could greet each of you personally! To hear from each one of you the *magnalia Dei*, how the Holy Spirit works in your lives! In the depths of your hearts, in the struggle between grace and sin, in the various moments and circumstances of your pilgrimage of faith — in how many ways has Christ spoken to you and said: "Come, follow me"! Could the Pope come to Scotland and not say thank you for having answered that call? Of course not! So, thank you on behalf of the Church. Thank you for the specific witness you give and for all the gifts you contribute.

Because you have carried your baptismal grace to a degree of "total dedication to God by an act of supreme love" in religious consecration (cf. *Lumen Gentium, 44*), you have become a sign of a higher life, a "life that is more than food, a body that is more than clothing" (cf. *Lk 12:23*). Through the practice of the evangelical counsels you have become a prophetic sign of the eternal kingdom of the Father. In the midst of the world you point to the "one thing that is needed" *(Lk 10:42)*, to the "treasure that does not fail" *(Lk 12:33)*. You possess the source of inspiration and of strength for the various forms of apostolic work which your institutes are called to carry out.

Those of you who belong to contemplative communities serve the people of God "in the heart of Christ". You prophetically remind those engaged in building up the earthly city that, unless they lay its foundation in the Lord, they will have laboured in vain. Yours is a striking witness to the Gospel message, all the more necessary since the people of our time often succumb to a false sense of independence with respect to the Creator. Your lives testify to the absolute primacy of God and to the kingship of Christ.

And you, brothers and sisters, whose vocation is active work in ecclesial service, you must combine contemplation with your apostolic zeal. By contemplative prayer you cling to God in mind and heart; by apostolic love and zeal you associate yourselves with the work of redemption and you spread the kingdom of God. In your service to the human family you must take care not to confuse the *regnum Dei* with the *regnum hominis*, as if political, social and economic liberation were the same as salvation in Jesus Christ. Your prophetic role in the Church should lead you to discover and proclaim the deepest meaning of all human activity. Only when human activity preserves its relationship with the Creator does it preserve its dignity and reach fulfilment.

Your communities have been engaged in the process of renewal desired by the Second Vatican Council. You are trying to be ever more faithful to your role within the ecclesial community, in accordance with your specific charisms. Proceeding from the original inspiration of your founders and following the magisterium of the

Church, you are in an excellent position to discern the promptings of the Holy Spirit regarding the needs of the Church and the world today. Through appropriate exterior adaptation accompanied by constant spiritual conversion, your life and activity, within the context of the local and universal Church, becomes a magnificent expression of the Church's own vitality and youth.

In the words of St Paul: "I thank my God through Jesus Christ for all of you, because your faith is proclaimed in all the world" *(Rm 1:8).*

Brothers and sisters, there is one who walks beside us along the path of discipleship: Mary, the Mother of Jesus, who pondered everything in her heart and always did the will of the Father. In this Metropolitan Cathedral dedicated to her, I wish to return to the thoughts and sentiments that filled my heart at Fatima on 13 May. There I once again consecrated to her myself and my ministry: *Totus Tuus Ego Sum.* I reconsecrated, and entrusted to her maternal protection, the Church and the whole world, so much in need of wisdom and peace.....

And to each priest and deacon, to each religious brother and sister, to each seminarian, I leave a word of encouragement and a message of hope. With St Paul I say to you: "This explains why we work and struggle as we do: our hopes are fixed on the living God..." *(1 Tm 4:10).* Yes, dear brothers and sisters, our hopes are fixed on the living God!

O.R. 737. 7 June 1982

Letter to the Discalced Carmelite Nuns
31 May 1982

With profound joy and particularly deep affection I address you, the Discalced Carmelite Nuns, on the occasion of the fourth centenary of the blessed death of St Teresa of Jesus, your foundress and Doctor of the Church, which took place at Alba de Tormes on 15 October 1582. You, her daughters, and the Discalced Carmelite Fathers have wished to prepare for this event by dedicating an entire year to the memory and honour of your venerated Mother.....

On this occasion, therefore, so full of significance for you, I want to express to you my heartfelt gratitude, while at the same time offering you a word of warm encouragement.

Yes, in the first place I want to thank you, because I am aware of all you do for the glory of God and for the world by means of your life of prayer and sacrifice. With regard to this, I am pleased to recall to your minds the words of your holy Mother who, referring to the need of saving souls, thus addressed her daughters: "This is why he — the Lord — has gathered you here together. This is your vocation. These must be the business matters you are engaged in. These must be the things you desire, the things you weep about; these must be the objects of your petitions" *(Way of Perfection, 1,5)*.

And with expressions still so very timely, she added: "The world is all in flames; they want to sentence Christ again, so to speak, since they raise a thousand false witnesses against him; they want to ravage his Church" (ibid).

Hence, for her, the purpose of the reform and of the foundations was above all that of procuring the glory of God and the "good of his Church" *(Way of Perfection, III, 6)*.

Only the Lord knows all that the daughters of St Teresa, in the course of these 400 years, have done in achieving this good. Nevertheless, glancing over the chronicles of your monasteries and admiring the luminous examples of sanctity offered us in the past — for all let St Therese of the Child Jesus, heavenly patroness of the missions, serve as an indication — as also the present-day witness to evangelical perfection offered by your religious families, we do succeed in obtaining a glimpse of this mysterious fruitfulness in the Church and for the Church. And so it is that I cannot refrain from expressing, in the name of Christ and of the Church, my gratitude to you, daughters of so great a Mother, for all you have achieved and continue to achieve for the salvation of souls and the coming of the kingdom of God.

Hand in hand with these expressions of dutiful gratitude, I want to offer you my warm encouragement to continue always with ever greater conviction and success along the path traced out by St Teresa, so as to offer the Church and the world all they expect from you.

The Second Vatican Council confirmed the legitimacy in the Church of institutes which, like your own, "are entirely devoted to contemplation, in such wise that their members attend solely to God in solitude and in silence, in continual prayer, and intense penance..."; the Council reaffirmed their utility for the Church herself, to which "they give increase by a mysterious apostolic fruitfulness", so that they constitute for her "a glory and a fountain of heavenly graces". At the same time, the fundamental conditions for this fruitfulness were indicated and attention was called to the fact that the work of updating of the said institutes be done ''with respect for their separation from the world and for the exercises proper to the contemplative life'' (cf. *Perfectae Caritatis, 7*).

Now you will readily find in these Council norms the teaching and the directives of your holy Mother. Was it not in order to obtain a life ''entirely ordained to contemplation ''that she undertook the reform?

She had in truth fully accepted the pressing call of the Lord: ''I will have you converse, not with men, but with angels'' *(Life, XXIV, 5)* and she had dedicated long hours contemplating the example of Jesus who ''teaches us to pray in solitude'', *(ibid., 4)*, so that she warned her daughters: ''We have to separate ourselves from all so as to approach God interiorly'' *(ibid., 5)*.

Better than anybody else, your foundress knew that such solitude is only a means and, referring to this, she said: ''It would in truth be a great pity if we could only pray in the little corners of solitude'' *(Foundations, V, 16)*. But at the same time, she knew by experience the importance of this means, and she was well aware that the desert is the place par excellence for meeting the Lord, as Sacred Scripture says: ''That is why I am going to lure her and lead her out into the wilderness and speak to her heart'' *(Ho 2:16)*. This explains her continual insistence on the observance of the enclosure, which is the concrete means for actualising this contemplative solitude; an observance for which I also, in my address to the participants at the Plenary Session of the Congregation for Religious and for the Secular Institutes, strongly recommended ''appropriate austerity'' (24 March 1980).

And together with enclosure and the external signs of which it is composed, the holy Mother forcefully recommended all the other means, which guarantee separation from the world, among which excels that silence which ''highly facilitates prayer, the foundation of the monastery'' *(Way of Perfection, V, 9)*.

Then as regards the ''intense penance'' indicated by the Council as a characteristic — together with prayer — of a purely contemplative life, more than by her exhortations, it is the very life and constitutions of St Teresa which tell you of its importance or rather of its absolute necessity.

Hence, an updating that would lead to a lessening of penance, that is to say, to a less joyful, less complete sacrifice of yourselves, would certainly not be in keeping with the Council or with the charism of your holy Mother.

In fact, fidelity to the practice of penance also promotes the exercise of fraternal charity, total detachment and authentic humility which remain the three hinges of the way of perfection *(Way, IV, 4)*: at the same time, penance denotes that characteristic and essential element of Carmelite experience which St John of the Cross, intrepid cooperator with St Teresa in the reform of your Order, has with masterly skill expressed in the absolute of the *todo-nada*.

I have no doubt but that the Carmelite nuns of today, no less than those of yesterday, tend with joyful hearts towards the attainment of this absolute, so as to offer an adequate response to the generous inspirations that are born of an exclusive love for Christ and of a total consecration to the mission of the Church.

Along this path, let the most Blessed Virgin be your help and your guide, since she is an incomparable example for all contemplatives and especially for you, daughters of an Order which from the very beginning took an entirely Marian shape, in keeping with the motto of your Fathers of the Middle Ages: *Totus marianus est Carmelus.*

In her purpose of bringing back the Order to its original fervour, your holy Mother had as her one aim to work "for the Lord's service and the honour of the habit of his glorious Mother" *(Life XXXVI, 6)* and in founding the monastery of St Joseph in Avila, her most burning desire was that "the Rule of Our Lady and Empress he observed with the perfection with which it was observed when initiated" (Way). Our Lord himself comforted her in this sense, when having achieved this foundation, "he thanked her for what she had done for his Mother" (cf. *ibid., 24*).

Numerous other circumstances of her life witness to the extent to which the charism of Teresa of Jesus bore the sign of Mary, From her, in the year 1562, the great Saint received, so to speak, her investiture of reformer, and in her hands she once renewed her profession. Hence, it does not surprise us to hear St Teresa repeatedly calling her nuns "daughters of the Virgin" and exhorting them with these words: "Imitate Our Lady and consider how great she must be and what a good thing it is that we have her for our Patroness".

After the example of your reformer, meditating on the mystery of Mary whose Heart, in virtue of her intimate union with Christ, is a fountain of life for the Church, you penetrate ever more deeply into the radiant light of your vocation, and of its demands for solitude, silence and total sacrifice, convincing yourselves, at the same time, of its secret fruitfulness, which appears to you all the more urgent today, in that, more so than 400 years ago, "the world is on fire" and threatened by very grave dangers.

Dearly beloved daughters of St Teresa and of the Virgin of Mount Carmel, while thanking you once again for all you do for the Church, for its bishops, priests and missionaries, of whom you are the hidden, silent but necessary helpers, I exhort you to live ever more generously this dimension of your vocation. May the Teresian Year help to deepen your correct understanding of fidelity to the charism of your holy Mother and obtain for you the indispensable graces for an ever greater commitment.

As a pledge of this, and as a sign of my special favour, I impart to all of you my Apostolic Blessing.

Address to the General Chapter Members of the Capuchins   5 July 1982

Beloved brothers, I am happy to be here today with you, who as Chapter Fathers not only represent all the Capuchins scattered through the world, but are carefully reconsidering your Constitutions. This is taking place in the year of the eighth centenary of the birth of St Francis, whose disciples you are and to whom I cordially commend you.

Therefore, this circumstance adds a further note of relevance and interest to our meeting, while I deeply thank you for having desired it.

In the Decree *Perfectae Caritatis* from the Second Vatican Council, it is written that "the appropriate renewal of religious life involves the continuous return to the source of all Christian life and to the original inspiration of the institutes, and at the same time the adjustment of the institutes themselves to the changed conditions of the times" *(no. 2)*. Of these two fundamental requirements — the return to the sources and the adjustment to the conditions of the times — during the years immediately following the Council, there was especially emphasised, and for understandable reasons, the second aspect, and that is the adjustment to what the conciliar text itself calls "the needs of the apostolate,... the requirements of a given culture, the social and economic circumstances" *(no. 3)*. Along these lines, you Capuchins have also reviewed in various stages your Constitutions and your life in order to make them correspond more closely to the requirements of the times and to the directives drawn up by the Church in the Second Vatican Council.

However, now that this effort to update has been brought to an end in its essential aspects, you too have felt the need — as also many other institutions in the Church — to address with renewed commitment that other primary requirement which the conciliar text calls the "continuous return to the sources", not in order to repudiate or set aside the legitimate adjustments and the new values discovered and tested during these years, but rather to give new life to them also, grafting them on to the living trunk of tradition, from which your Order derives its character and strength.

Precisely to encourage such a balance between the two requirements, during the present General Chapter, after having elected the new superiors, you have wanted to review the Constitutions in order to give them, now that the trial period is over, the form which — following the approval of the Apostolic See — should become definitive and permit your Institute to undertake with renewed energy and without any kind of uncertainty a new stretch along its path in the service of the Church and of the world.

You have discovered your original inspiration by reflecting with new sensitivity upon the very name received in legacy from your Father, St Francis; that is, "Friars Minor". Indeed, within that name the Saint included what was closest to the heart of the Gospel: brotherhood and humility, brotherly love and choosing for himself the last place, following the example of Christ, who came not "to be served, but to serve" *(Mt 20:28)*. In this is seen how the return to the sources is often the best way, even with the purpose of adapting to the expectations and signs of the times. A truly fraternal life, lived under the banner of evangelical simplicity and charity, open to the meaning of the universal brotherhood of all men and, better yet, of all creatures, and in which each person — young or old, learned or unlearned — is accorded equal dignity and attention is, in fact, perhaps the most up-to-date and most urgent witness that can be given of Christian newness to a society so marked as ours is by inequalities and by the spirit of domination.

You have made a great effort to re-propose these two fundamental characteristics of your Franciscan identity — brotherhood and humility — to the younger generations in the light of the Capuchin tradition, which confers upon them that unmistakable mark of spontaneity and simplicity, of joyfulness along with gravity, of drastic detachment from the world along with great closeness to people, which have made the Capuchin presence so effective and incisive in the midst of Christian peoples and in the missions, and produced such an extensive array of saints, among whom St Crispin of Viterbo, whom I myself had the joy of adding to the roll of heroic saints of the Church.

Speaking of the first example of renewal, which is a return to the sources, the Decree *Perfectae Caritatis* emphasises that it is not only a question of a return to the original inspiration of the Institute itself, but it is necessarily also a "continuous return to the source of all Christian life", and that is to Jesus Christ, to his Gospel and to his Spirit. This is the meaning of the words with which all the religious of the Church, regardless of which Order they belong to, are exhorted to consider the supreme rule, the following of Christ, to choose him as the only thing necessary, in short, to live for God alone.

Aware of this, you have rightly reaffirmed in every way the primary place which prayer and, according to your most authentic tradition, especially contemplative prayer, must occupy in your lives, both personal and community. Of all the "roots", this is the "mother root", that which absorbs mankind in God himself, which keeps the branch joined to the vine and assures to religious that constant contact with Christ without which — as he himself states — we can do nothing, and with his Spirit of holiness and grace.

The eighth centenary of the birth in the world of your founder, Francis of Assisi, with the extraordinary echo it has aroused, has shown how much today's world is still sensitive to the call of the *Poverello,* how much it needs and, one could say, misses him. It is up to you, in a very special way, to keep this hope always alive in the world and, what is more, make it even more visible and recognisable. This will happen, as far as your Order is concerned, if after having renewed your Constitutions with so much dedication and seriousness, each of you and each of your fellow religious feel urged to translate them into practice, in remembrance of those words spoken by Christ to his disciples: "Knowing these things, blessed are you if you do them" (*Jn 13:17*).

Indeed, it now seems that the time has come for religious institutes to pass with resolution from the phase of discussion about their own legislation to that of putting into practice certain and fundamental values, from preoccupation with the letter to that of the spirit, from words to life, and this in order not to fall into that dangerous illusion that St Francis himself denounces in one of his Admonitions when he writes that "those religious are killed by the letter who do not want to follow the spirit of the Holy Scripture, but want to know only words and explain them to others".

The due truthfulness and sincerity before God demands of an Institute a renewed will for conversion and for fidelity to its own vocation in order that the image of itself which it has given to the Church and to the brethren by means of its own Constitutions be always as authentic as human weakness allows.

Beloved brothers and sons, receive these words as a sign of my esteem for you. At the same time, be assured that you enjoy a special place in my prayers. I entrust to the Lord you and the entire praiseworthy family of the Friars Minor Capuchins. The Holy Church and the world itself, which have already benefitted greatly from your zeal, still expect from you a generous and intelligent contribution of shining evangelical witness.

May the Lord fill you with his graces, and in the spirit of St Francis, continue, joyful and certain.

May you always be accompanied by my Apostolic Blessing, which I impart to you, Chapter Fathers, with special thought to your new Minister General, and which I extend to all the beloved members of your Order.

O.R. 746. 9 August 1982

Address to Cloistered Nuns at Avila

1 November 1982

My dear sisters, cloistered religious of Spain, while making this pilgrimage in the footsteps of St Teresa of Jesus, I come with great satisfaction and joy to Avila. There are many Teresian places in this city, such as the monastery of St Joseph, the first of the "dovecotes" which she founded; and this monastery of the Incarnation, where St Teresa took the habit of Carmel, made her religious profession, had her definitive "conversion", and lived her experience of total consecration to Christ. It can well be said that this is the sanctuary of the contemplative life, a place of great mystical experiences, and the centre from which radiate other monastic foundations.

I am pleased to meet you here, cloistered Spanish nuns, who represent the various contemplative families which enrich the Church: Benedictines, Cistercians, Dominicans, Poor Clares, Capuchins, Religious of the Immaculate Conception, besides the Carmelites.

This occasion demonstrates how diverse paths and charisms of the Spirit are complementary in the Church. This is a unique experience for the cloistered convents and monasteries which have opened their doors so that these religious might come in pilgrimage to Avila, to give due honour, in company with the Pope, to St Teresa, that exceptional woman, Doctor of the Church, yet nevertheless "totally enveloped in humility, penace and simplicity", as my predecessor, Paul VI, said *(Homily, 4 October 1970)*.

I thank God for such a sign of ecclesial union, and for my being able to fulfil this visit with you who are spread out before my eyes like one great Spanish cloister.

The contemplative life has occupied and will continue to occupy a place of honour in the Church. From the cloister "your life is hidden with Christ in God" *(Col 3:3)*; it is dedicated to prayer and to silence, to adoration and penance. Your consecrated life has its foundation in the gift received in baptism and continues to unfold. By the Sacrament of Baptism God, who has chosen us in Christ "before the foundation of the world so that we might be holy and immaculate before him in charity" *(Ep 1:4)*, has saved us from sin and has incorporated us in Christ and in his Church so that we might "live a new life" *(Rm 6:41)*.

That new life bears fruit in you through the radical following of Jesus Christ in virginity, obedience and poverty, and is the foundation of the contemplative life. He is the centre of your life, the reason for your existence: "Good of all goods and my Jesus", as St Teresa would sum up.

The experience of the cloister makes still more absolute this following of Christ until you are identified in your religious life with Christ: "your life is Christ", and St Teresa, making her own the exhortation of St Paul (cf. *Col 3:3*). For the religious this becoming one with Jesus constitutes the focal point of the consecrated life and the seal which identifies it as contemplative.

In silence, in the framework of a humble and obedient life, your vigilant waiting for the Bridegroom is changed into a friendship which is pure and true: "I can relate to him as a friend even though he is the Lord" (St Teresa). This relationship, cultivated day and night, is prayer, the fundamental duty of the religious and an indispensable path for her identification with the Lord: "they begin to be servants of love... those who go by this path of prayer to him who loved us so" *(ibid)*.

The Church knows well that your silent and separate life in the exterior solitude of the cloister is a leaven for renewal and for the presence of the Spirit of Christ in the world. That is why the Council said that contemplative religious "occupy an eminent place in the Mystical Body of Christ... In effect, they offer to God an outstanding sacrifice of praise, they illumine the people of God with the richest fruits of holiness; they animate it with their example, and they extend it by the mystery of their apostolic fecundity. Therefore, they are the honour of the Church and fountainhead of heavenly graces" *(Perfectae Caritatis, 7)*.

That apostolic fecundity of your life proceeds from the grace of Christ which absorbs and integrates the total oblation of your life in the cloister. The Lord has chosen you; and as he identifies you with his Paschal Mystery, he joins you with him in the work that sanctifies the world. As branches grafted on to Christ, you can give much fruit through the wonderful and mysterious reality of the communion of saints.

This should be your perspective of faith and ecclesial joy for every day and every action of yours: your prayer and meditation, your praise in the Divine Office; your life in your cell or at work; your mortifications, whether in your rules or voluntary; your sickness or suffering; all should be joined to the Sacrifice of Christ. For him, with him and in him, you will be an offering of praise and of sanctification for the world.

"So that you will not have any doubt in this respect", as I said to your sisters in the Carmel of Lisieux, "the Church, in the name of the same Christ, took possession one day of all of your capacity to live and to love. It was the day of your monastic profession. Renew it often! And, following the example of the saints, consecrate yourselves, immolate yourselves each time more, without pretending to know how God will use your cooperation".

Your life in the cloister, lived in full fidelity, does not separate you from the Church nor does it impede an effective apostolate. Recall the daughter of Teresa of Jesus, Therese of Lisieux, from her cloister so near to the missions and missionaries of the world. Like her, may you be the love in the heart of the Church.

Your virginal fecundity ought to be the life in the bosom of the universal Church and of your particular Churches. Your monasteries are communities of prayer in the midst of Christian communities, to which you offer support, encouragement and hope. They are sacred places and can be also centres of Christian encounter for those persons, especially the young, who are often searching for a simple and transparent life, in contrast to that offered to them by the consumer society.

The world needs, more than it even believes at times, your presence and your witness. It is necessary, therefore, effectively to demonstrate the authentic and absolute values of the Gospel to a world which often exalts the relative values of living, and which, choked off by an excessive estimation of what is material, of what is passing, of what does not know the joy of the Spirit, runs the risk of missing the meaning of what is divine.

You will do so by showing to the world the evangelising message which sums up your life and which finds an echo in those words of Teresa of Jesus; "Disappear then, worldly goods... even though I lose all things, God alone is enough".

Today, as I look on so many cloistered religious, I cannot do less than think of the great Spanish monastic tradition, its influence on Spanish culture, customs and life. Is it not here that we find the basis of continual references to the moral strength and spirit of Spain?

Today the Pope invites you to continue cultivating your consecrated lives through a liturgical, biblical and spiritual renewal, following the norms of the Council. All of this requires a continuing spiritual formation, having a solid doctrinal, theological and cultural foundation. In this way you will be able to give the evangelising response which so many young persons of our time seek, who today also approach your monasteries, attracted by a life of generous commitment ot the Lord.

In this regard I call on the Christian communities and their pastors, reminding them of the irreplaceable importance which the contemplative life has in the Church. We all ought to value profoundly and appreciate the commitment of the contemplative souls to prayer, to praise, and to sacrifice.

You are very necessary for the Church. You are the prophets and living teachers of all: you are the front line of the Church moving to the Kingdom. Your attitudes before realities of the world, which you contemplate in the light of the wisdom of the Spirit, enlighten us about the meaning of ultimate goods and make us feel the gratuity of the saving love of God. I exhort everyone, then, to strive to develop vocations among youth for the monastic life, with the certainty that these vocations enrich the whole life of the Church.

I must bring this visit to a close, even though it is so delightful for the Pope to be with you, faithful daughters of the Church. I conclude with a word of encouragement: Maintain your fidelity! Fidelity to Christ, to your contemplative vocation, to your founding charism.

Daughters of Carmel: may you be living images of your mother Teresa, of her spirituality and humanism. May you truly be, as she was and wanted to be called, and as I want her to be called, Teresa of Jesus.

All contemplative religious: may your founders and foundresses also be seen through you.

Live your ecclesial vocation with joy and pride; pray for one another and help one another; pray for religious vocations, for priests and for priestly vocations. And pray also for the fruitfulness of the ministry of the Successor of Peter who speaks to you. I know that you do and I thank you sincerely.

I present to the Lord yourselves and your intentions. I entrust you to the Most Holy Mother, model of contemplative souls, so that she will make you, from the Cross and glory of her Son, a joyous gift to the Church.

Carry my cordial greetings to your sisters who have not been able to come to Avila. And to all of you I give my blessing with love in the name of Christ.

O.R. 760.   22 November 1982

Address to Men Religious at Madrid
2 November 1882

Dear brothers, this prayerful meeting on this afternoon in Madrid, nearly at the beginning of my apostolic pilgrimage through Spain, is a great joy for me. I am meeting persons who are very dear, whose existence, consecrated by the three evangelical vows, "belongs in an unquestionable way to the life and holiness of the Church" *(Lumen Gentium, 44).*

You belong to that great living spring which has flowed with such generosity, in the land of Spain, and which has made the evangelical seed abundantly fruitful among a multitude of peoples in all parts of the world. As religious belonging to families of long traditions, or of more recent origin, you have served all men of all races and of all languages with a magnanimous heart; and, now as then, you give strength to the living tree of the Church already 2,000 years old.

I speak to you with the words of St Paul: "I give thanks to God always for you because of the grace of God which has been given you in Christ Jesus, that in every way you were enriched in him with all speech and all knowledge — even as the testimony to Christ was confirmed among you'' *(1 Co 1:4-6)*. The Pope also appreciates having the opportunity of this meeting which St Teresa of Jesus has made possible for me because she has provided the desired occasion to speak to your heart.

You are a great treasure of spirituality and of apostolic initiatives in the bosom of the Church. On you depends in great measure the fate of the Church.

This places a grave responsibility on your shoulders and requires that you have a profound awareness of the greatness of the vocation which you have received and of the necessity of continually making yourself equal to it. It means, in effect, to follow Christ and, with an affirmative response to the call which you have received, to serve the Church joyfully in holiness of life.

Your vocation is a divine initiative; it is a gift given to you and at the same time a gift given to the Church. With confidence in the fidelity of the one who called you and in the strength given by the Spirit, you have placed yourselves at God's disposition by the vows of poverty, consecrated chastity, and obedience; and this not for a limited time, but for your entire life through an irrevocable commitment. In faith you have pronounced a ''yes'' for everything and for always. Thus, in a society which frequently lacks the courage to make commitments, and in which many prefer in vain to live a life without bonds, you give testimony to a life of definitive commitments through a decision for God which embraces the whole of life.

You know how to love. The quality of a person can be measured by the class of his commitments. Therefore it can joyfully be said that your liberty has been freely bound to God in a voluntary service, in loving servitude. And in so doing, your humanity becomes mature. ''Mature humanity means full use of the gift of freedom received from the Creator when he called to existence the man made 'in his image, after his likeness'. This gift finds its full realisation in the unreserved giving of the whole of one's human person, in a spirit of the love of a spouse, to Christ and, with Christ, to all those to whom he sends men and women totally consecrated to him in accordance with the evangelical counsels. This is the ideal of the religious life, which has been undertaken by the orders and congregations both ancient and recent...'' *(Redemptor Hominis, 21)*.

Always give thanks to God for the mysterious call which one day sounded in the depths of your hearts: "Follow me". "Sell what you possess and give to the poor, and you will have treasure in heaven; and come, follow me; *(Mt 19:21)*. This call and your response — which God himself with his grace has placed in your will and on your lips — are found at the foundation of your personal journey; it is, never forget, the reason for your every action.

Revive now and again in prayer this personal encounter with the Lord who throughout your life continues to insist: "Follow me". I say to you with St Paul: "The gifts and the call of God are irrevocable" *(Rm 11:29)*. God is faithful and he will never regret having chosen you.

And when in the daily ascetical struggle contrition and conversion are necessary, remember the parable of the prodigal son and the happiness of the father. "This joy indicates a good that has remained intact: even if he is a prodigal, a son does not cease to be truly his father's son; it also indicates a good that has been found again, which in the case of the prodigal son was his return to the truth about himself" *(Dives in Misericordia, 6)*. Frequent the Sacrament of Penance, with the regularity counselled and indicated by your Rules and Constitutions.

Your vocation is an essential part of the deepest truth about yourselves and your destiny. "You did not choose me," says the Lord in words which are applicable to you, "but I chose you and appointed you that you should go and bear fruit and that your fruit should abide" *(Jn 15:16)*. God has chosen you!

Your commitment, perhaps made a long time ago, or even recently, ought to be strengthened always in the Lord. I ask you for a renewed fidelity, one which will make love for Christ blaze in your hearts, make your self-giving more sacrificial and joyful, your service more humble, knowing — I quote to you the words of St Teresa of Jesus — that "whoever truly begins to serve the Lord cannot give less than his own life" *(Way of Perfection, 11,2)*.

For this there is required attentive listening to the mystery of God, the daily entering into the love of Christ crucified, a committed cultivation of prayer under the sure guidance of the pure sources of Christian spirituality. Read assiduously the works of the great masters of the spirit. How many treasures of love and faith you have at hand in your beautiful language! And, especially, savour with faith and humility the Sacred Scriptures in order to reach the "supreme advantage of knowing Christ" *(Ph 3:8)*. Only in him, through his Spirit, will you find the necessary strength to overcome the weakness now and again experienced.

Keep alive the certainty that yours is a divine vocation through a profound vision of faith nourished by prayer and the sacraments, especially by the holy mystery of the Eucharist, the source and apex of authentic Christian living. Thus you will easily overcome all incertitude about your identity, and you will progress in fidelity, identifying yourselves with the Christ of the beatitudes and witnessing, at the same time, to the kingdom of God in the present world.

This fidelity implies before all else, and as a foundation of all else, a growing desire of friendship with God, of a loving union with him. The consecrated person — I say this with St John of the Cross — "God wants to be such a religious that he will have finished with everything and that all will be regarded as worthless by him, because he himself wants to be his riches, his consolation and his delightful glory" *(Letter 9)*. Those desires for union with God will make you experience the truth of the words of the Lord: "My yoke is easy and my burden is light" *(Mt 11:30)*. His yoke is love and his burden is a burden of love. And that same love will make sweet its weight.

This dimension of total self-giving and of permanent fidelity to love constitutes the basis of your witness before the world. In fact, the world seeks from you a sincere lifestyle and a kind of work in keeping with what you really are. The witness is not simply a teacher who teaches what he has learned, but he is one who lives and acts in conformity with a profound experience of what he believes in.

As consecrated persons you are, above all, consecrated precisely by the profession and practice of the evangelical counsels; therefore your life should offer an essentially evangelical witness. You must continually turn to Christ, the living Gospel, and reproduce him in your life, in your way of thinking and of working.

One must recover confidence in the value and current importance of the evangelical counsels which have their origin in the words and example of Jesus Christ (cf. *Perfectae Caritatis, 1*) You must be poor as Christ was poor, obedient, accepting this attitude of the heart of Christ, who came to redeem the world not by doing his own will but that of the Father who sent him; living a life of perfect continence for the kingdom of heaven with all its consequences as a sign and stimulus of charity and as a source of apostolic fruitfulness in the world. Today the world needs to see the living examples of those who, in leaving all, have embraced as an ideal the life of the evangelical counsels. It is the real sincerity in the radical following of Christ which will attract vocations to your institutes because youth is searching exactly for that evangelical radicalness.

The Gospel is definitive and does not pass away. Its criteria are for ever. You cannot re-read the Gospel according to the times, conforming yourselves to whatever the world asks. On the contrary, you must read the signs of the times and the problems of the world today in the indefectible light of the Gospel.

A decisive factor in every age in which the Church has had to undertake great changes and reforms has been the fidelity of the religious to her doctrine and norms. Today we live in one of those epochs in which it is necessary to offer the world the witness of your fidelity to the Church.

Christians have a right to expect the consecrated person to love the Church, to defend her, to strengthen her and to enrich her with his support and obedience. That fidelity should not be merely external, but principally internal, deep, joyful and self-sacrificing. You have to avoid anything that might lead the faithful to believe that there exists in the Church a double magisterium, the authentic one of the hierarchy and another of the theologians and thinkers; or that the norms of the Church have lost their force today.

Not a few of you are dedicated to the theological formation of the faithful, to the management of educational or relief centres, and some of you direct information and formation publications. Through all of these means seek to give an integral education, inculcating a profound respect and love for the Church and encouraging a true adherence to her magisterium. Do not be bearers of doubts or of ideologies, but rather of the certainties of faith. The true apostle and evangeliser, declared my predecessor Paul VI, "will be a person who even at the price of personal renunciation and suffering always seeks the truth that he must transmit to others. He never betrays or hides truth out of a desire to please men, in order to astonish or to shock, not for the sake of originality or a desire to make an impression. He does not refuse truth" (*Evangelii Nuntiandi*, 78).

All of this must be kept especially in mind when you address women religious who attend your courses and listen to your conferences. Above all, you must faithfully transmit the doctrine of the Church, that doctrine which has been expressed in such rich documents as those of the Second Vatican Council. In the renewal of the consecrated life, which these new times call for, fidelity to the thought and to the norms of the Church must be safeguarded; more specifically, in the sphere of doctrine and in liturgical matters avoid certain critical postures which are full of bitterness, which obscure the truth, and which disconcert the faithful and even consecrated persons themselves. Fidelity to the magisterium is not a brake put on proper investigation, but a necessary condition for the authentic progress of true doctrine.

The community life is an essential element, not of the consecrated life as such, but certainly of the religious form of that consecration. God has called religious to sanctify themselves and to work in community. Community life has its foundation not in human friendship, but in the vocation from God who has freely chosen you to form a new family, one whose finality is the fullness of charity and whose expression is the observance of the evangelical counsels.

Some of the elements of a true community life are: the superior who possesses authority (cf. *Optatam Totius, 14*) which he ought to exercise in an attitude of service; the rules and traditions which shape the religious family; and, finally, the Eucharist, which is the principle of unity in every Christian community; in effect when we partake of the Eucharist we all eat the same Bread, we drink the same Blood, and we receive the same Spirit. For this reason the centre of our community life cannot be other than Jesus in the Eucharist.

The community dimension ought to be present in your apostolic activity. The religious is not called to work as an isolated person or on his own account. Today, more than ever, it is necessary to live and work in unity; first, within each religious family, and then by collaborating with other consecrated persons and members of the Church. Union makes for strength. Furthermore, community life offers an extraordinary sphere for the sacrifice of oneself, for forgetting self and thinking of one's brother, embracing all in the love of Christ.

The consecrated person is one who, by renouncing the world and himself, completely devoted to God, and filled with God, returns to the world to work for the kingdom of God and for the Church.

The consecrated person is profoundly marked by this exclusive belonging to God, while having as the object of his service both mankind and the world. The life and activity of the consecrated person cannot be reduced to an earthly horizontalism, forgetful of his consecration to God and of his obligation to impregnate the world with God. In all of your activities this theological purpose must be present.

There exist within the Church diverse charisms, and consequently, diverse services, which are mutually complementary. It would not be just that religious should enter the sphere proper to seculars: the consecration of the world from within it (cf. *Lumen Gentium, 31; Guadium et Spes, 43*).

This does not mean that your religious consecration and your eminently religious ministries should not have a profound repercussion in the world and in the changing of its structures. If the hearts of men do not change, the structures of the world will not be able to change in any effective way. The ministry of religious is ordered principally to achieve the conversion of hearts to God, the creation of new men and to point out those areas in which seculars, consecrated or simple Christians, can and ought to act to change the structures of the world.....

Reflecting on the theme of the coming Synod, I would like to invite you who are religious priests to value as one of your primary ministries the Sacrament of Confession. In the hearing of confessions and the forgiving of sins you are effectively building the Church, spreading over it the balm which heals the wounds of sin. If there is to be achieved in the Church a renewal of the Sacrament of Penance, it will be necessary that the religious priest dedicate himself with joy to this ministry.

Before concluding, I want to remind you of a characteristic of Spanish religious which is perhaps undergoing a temporary eclipse and which it is necessary to restore in all its ancient splendour: I refer to the missionary generosity with which thousands of consecrated Spaniards gave their lives for the apostolic work of establishing the Church in lands not yet evangelised. Do not allow the ties of flesh and blood nor the affection which you justly nourish for your homeland where you were born and learned to love Christ, to become bonds which curtail your liberty and jeopardise the fullness of your surrender to the Lord and his Church. Always remember that the missionary spirit of a determinate portion of the Church is the exact measure of its vitality and authenticity.

Finally, always maintain a tender devotion to the Holy Mother of God. Your piety for her should retain the simplicity of its first moments. May the Mother of Jesus, who is also our Mother, model of surrender to the Lord and to his mission, accompany you, make sweet the cross for you, and bestow on you, in whatever circumstances of your life, that joy and unalterable peace which only the Lord can give. In pledge of which, I affectionately impart to you my cordial Blessing.

O.R. 774. 7 March 1983

Address to Sisters in Palermo Cathedral
21 November 1982

Beloved sisters,... I cordially greet all of you. I would like to do this individually and have a word with each one, but this is clearly not possible. At least accept this sincere desire of mine. I am thinking of, and send my greeting to, particularly those of you who are tried by suffering or by difficulties. I greet with deferential respect those sisters who have been spending themselves for a long time in the Lord's vineyard. I greet with admiration and satisfaction those who, in the vigour of their strength, generously give themselves in the service of God and their brethren. My greeting is meant to be hope and encouragement for the young who are probing and inspecting their path and their choice. I thank all of you, in the name of the universal Church whose shepherd I am, for your response to God's call, and for your will to continue to work and to suffer for the sake of the kingdom of Christ, to whom you want to be exclusively consecrated, for the purpose of offering to men, even here below, through your fraternal communion and the practice of works of charity, the firstfruits of that kingdom of ''justice, peace and joy in the Holy Spirit'' *(Rm 12:17)*.....

I am here among you to congratulate you for what you are already doing, to assure you of my total support in the initiatives of charity that you undertake or carry on, and to express to you my sincere participation in your sufferings and your difficulties. I am here above all to give you a word of encouragement and hope, to give new strength to your enthusiasm, to open new ways to you, to help you remove obstacles.

Most of all, the recommendation I would want to give you is this: preserve and foster a correct and lofty concept of religious life and consecration, according to what the Master always taught and still teaches. The Church today certainly encourages secular and lay forms of consecrated life which if properly understood are a great blessing for the people of God and for the world. The Council made clear the dignity of the earthly values and the spirituality of the laity. Nevertheless, the same Council, stressing the unique value of the religious vocation, takes care not to depreciate it with the distortion of a misunderstood secularism, forgetting that the religious life achieves a perfection beyond baptismal consecration.

It certainly is not a matter of feeling, with vain presumption, that one is on a level higher than the simple laity, since, as St Thomas already taught *(Summa Theologica, II-II, 184, 4)*, not everyone who is in the "state of perfection" is necessarily perfect. On the contrary, more is required of the religious, precisely because she has received more: greater humility, greater gratitude to God, greater awareness of her Christian duties, a greater commitment to charity, since "when much has been given a man, much will be required of him. Much more will be asked of a man to whom more has been entrusted" *(Lk 12:48)*.

The superiority of the religious state certainly does not depend on the Christian's relationship with the final end, which is the same for everyone: blessedness in God, attained in the sanctity and the perfection, which as such are superior to those deriving from baptismal consecration, sufficient to characterise the secular or married state. The religious, however, if she wants to attain that greater intimacy with Christ that characterises her vocation, must make wise and persevering use of those special means that are at her disposal.

This eminence of the religious life is attested to in words and above all in works: it is proven in deeds, that the world may see and believe.

For this reason, the concept and practice of religious life that one has are immediately and consequentially reflected in the activity that is carried out for the promotion of vocations, which I know you have discussed in your fifth regional convention.

The human heart instinctively seeks the best, that which is most elevated and is the loftiest: and if you do not give that "witness of the Transcendent", about which your Cardinal Archbishop spoke in a recent letter, that is, if you are not a "sign" of that which goes beyond this world and its perishability, and of that which is most greatly elevated — the divine and eschatological realities — you will not be able to exercise a true attraction to the religious life on young girls who today are searching for the Absolute.

Therefore do not be afraid to propose to the world the ideal of a life that transcends the present. Remember that the profound meaning of your consecration is that of being, together with your confereres, the prefiguring signs of future mankind, of the "new man" and the "new woman" of the resurrection. Through your very behaviour be living and concrete proof of the existence of God, of his goodness, of the kingdom of peace that he has promised us with his cross!

In the second place, do not forget your specific role as women, within the Church and in the service of mankind. Help yourselves and help the Church, with the assistance of the Holy Spirit and with your considered reflection, to put this role always in better light. As Mary Most Holy is an integral part of the divine plan of salvation, so the woman, especially if she is a religious, is the image of Mary, the Ideal of woman, and therefore she too has her own essential part in the salvation of mankind. Reproducing in herself, then, the Marian mystery, the woman religious is also an image of the Church, of which Mary, as the Council says *(Lumen Gentium, 63)*, is figure and type.

If you are always convinced that this role you fulfil cannot be substituted, you will feel a wholesome and humble pride in it, without being tempted to desire other roles or functions that would pervert your features in the bosom of the Church.

But the choice of consecration according to the model of femininity cannot be an end in itself: it must be rooted on what is the truly fundamental value, that of active and generous charity, which made St Paul say, "The love of Christ impels us" *(2 Co 5:14)*.

I have had other opportunities to say that the profound essence of religious consecration is an act of love for Christ. Religious, male and female, are called to reproduce more closely to Christ this same love. They are a sign, as I have said, of resurrection. But they can be this only in so far as their love shines through their oblation and their spirit of sacrifice, like Christ's, "who gave himself for us as an offering to God, a gift of pleasing fragrance" *(Ep 5:2)*. They must be dead to the world in order to be "raised up in company with Christ" *(Col 3:1)*.

You too, dear sisters, like the Apostles, are "the light of the world and the salt of the earth" *(Mt 9:50)*. You are the hope of the world. Your very existence disproves the bitter and sometimes hypocritical fatalism of one who, believing injustices to be insuperable, is tempted to follow the examples of the violent and evildoers. It is not asked of you to overcome these injustices with severity and the force of interventions, which do not form part of your mission. Nevertheless, you have weapons which, while they may be less conspicuous, are no less effective: the weapons of prayer, of persevering dedication, of responsible obedience, of an educative and charitable mission, of purity of life, of the honest and sincere word, of Christian patience, full of a hope of immortality. These are the very weapons of Christ, King of ages; Christ, the Lamb who is King of kings. They are the weapons of his Most Holy Mother. They are the weapons that have conquered the world.

May my blessing accompany and sustain you.

O.R. 763. 13 December 1982

Address to the General Chapter Members of St John of God Brothers

17 December 1982

Beloved brothers in Christ, as the crowning point of your General Chapter you desired a special meeting with the Pope to express concretely your fidelity and your devotion to the Church, and to have a word of encouragement for your religious life. I am very happy to welcome you, and while I extend my respectful greeting to those of you present and to all your confreres scattered throughout the world, I also express to you my gratitude for the work that your Order carries out in the Church.

In the history of every order and every congregation the General Chapter is always an event of great importance, since it not only permits casting a glance at the comprehensive progress of religious life according to its own constitutional charism, but above all it is an incentive to new spiritual fervour and to a more decisive consecration to its proper ideal: the past is meditated upon, the present is considered, and proposals are made for the future.

Every General Chapter must be considered a true grace of God, and consequently also a responsibility not only of the superiors, who must decide for the best, but also of the individual members. This is my heartfelt wish for you, religious of the Hospitaller Order of the Fatebenefratelli, which for more than four centuries has cared for the sick with supernatural love and total dedication. When on 8 March 1550 St John of God's earthly life came to an end in the city of Granada, the small following of disciples who had joined him did not let die the work he had begun, so necessary during that age that unfortunately was insensitive to the lowly and the poor; they made the humble seed sown by the founder bear much fruit. After many historical events and many troubles of the times and of men, through difficulties and consolations, your Order now numbers 191 houses, 1,721 religious, among whom are 116 priests. Thanks to the Lord for all the good that you have been able to do, and may you also be thanked and blessed, that you may continue caring for the sick with courage and with love.

Together with the deep satisfaction for the work carried out, I next address to you the exhortation to persevere in your ideal and always to improve in making hospital work and the medical profession more human and sensitive. You doubtlessly have a great mission to carry out which presupposes a vocation and is known to be ever more valid and necessary.

It is a relevant mission, as it was relevant during the time of Renaissance humanism and, subsequently, during the era of Illuminism. In fact, despite scientific progress and social development, pain remains, and disease, physical and moral suffering, misfortune remain; the race for well-being does not eliminate illness. The thirst for pleasure crashes into the unrelenting wall of pain! From this tragic and permanent contradiction is born the danger of putting aside those who suffer because illness becomes a burden, an irritation, an annoyance. Sometimes the sick are not considered as persons. And their care can become a "job". Therefore, you are called to humanise sickness, to treat the sick as a creature of God, as a brother in Christ. You recall the dramatic and moving scene of the Passion, when Pilate, pointing to Jesus, wounded, scourged, crowned with thorns, says to the crowd: "Look at the man" (*Jn 19:5*). You, when you are in hospitals, in the infirmaries, in the pharmacies, see the person who is suffering, bewildered and in pain, in the light of faith, and say: "Look at Christ!". It is without doubt a difficult and demanding mission which takes up your whole life and each one of your days, spent beside those who are suffering in the mystery of sickness and misfortune. But it is also a consoling mission, because always, but especially during our age, men ask the "why" of pain and of life itself, and many sometimes reach the abyss of despair, finding neither comfort nor meaning. You, by your presence and by your patient and loving charity, make faith in Christ and in the fatherhood of God credible. You open new horizons and new perspectives. You are of spiritual help not only to the ill but also to the doctors and hospital personnel. May you always be where there is suffering man, following the example of St John of God! And therefore, given the present needs of society, I wish from my heart for numerous vocations in your Hospitaller Order! May the Lord inspire many young university students to give their lives and their abilities among the ranks of your members consecrated to the service of suffering mankind.

In order to be in this way a true help and example to the sick and to the doctors, you essentially need to maintain an intense conversation with Christ, through personal and liturgical prayer, meditation, community life in understanding mutual affection. May the General Chapter make itself the apostle and guarantor everywhere of a profound interior life, sole function and sole basis of every authentic apostolate.

I would like to conclude by offering for your consideration the significant person of Blessed Richard Pampuri, whom I personally had the honour and consolation to elevate to the glory of the altars in October of last year. An affable, sensitive, refined, sympathetic person, heroic in carrying out his duty as a doctor, he stated in a letter to his sister: "The greater I feel my inadequacy the more deeply and completely I place my confidence in God"; and a short time before his death in Milan on 1 May 1930, at only 33, he confided to his relatives: "I am content and happy to have always done the will of the Lord".

I want to wish such joy to you and to all the religious of St John of God: may the joy of Christmas accompany you always, with the special protection of Mary Most Holy and with my Apostolic Blessing.

O.R. 768.   24 January 1983

Address to Cloistered Nuns at Greccio

2 January 1983

On the joyous occasion of my visit to Greccio and in the mystic and gentle atmosphere of this locality, so intimately Franciscan and therefore Christian, I am very pleased to be able to address a particularly cordial greeting to you, cloistered religious, assembled here to meet me, remembering and imitating well the love and the veneration towards the Roman Pontiff that St Francis always felt and taught.

I thank you, moved by your presence, so affectionate and expressive, and I also wish to renew for you the sentiments I feel for your total consecration to the contemplative life. This gift of yours to the Absolute, which requires a vocation and which uniquely has love as its ideal, is a typical way of being the Church, of living in the Church, of accomplishing the illuminating and saving mission of the Church. I intend to emphasise strongly the essential value of your presence in the providential plan of Redemption and to confirm you in the validity of your proposals of prayer and penance for the salvation of mankind.

Your ideal is first of all a sign for modern man who is troubled by thousands of problems and tormented by so many social and political events. Cloistered nuns, with their life of prayer and austerity, propose to the world the words of Jesus: "Seek out instead his kingship over you, and the rest will follow in turn" *(Lk 12:31)*; and the words of the Letter to the Hebrews: "For here we have no lasting city; we are seeking the one which is to come" *(Heb 13:14)*. Your real and concrete example therefore becomes an exhortation and an invitation to man to re-enter himself, to leave superficiality, dissipation, the hunger for efficiency, to feel that in effect our heart — as St Augustine said — is made for the Infinite, and it finds peace and rest only in him. For you the words that St Teresa of Jesus wrote in her autobiography are also of value: "After having seen the great vision of the Lord, there was no longer anyone who in comparison would seem so pleasing to me as to occupy my mind any longer..." *(Life, 37,4)*. It is the continual challenge which, with your choice, you throw down to the world.

Your total consecration to Love is also a warning for all Christians, for priests, religious, theologians, and leaders of the Church. Certainly, for the proclamation of the Gospel and for the salvation of souls, the various means of the apostolate are necessary: the search for new methods, creativity, novelty, active dynamism, updating ideas and proposals... But personal prayer, the entreaty for light and strength for oneself and for the entire world, remains essential, just as the fundamental concern must always be the maintenance and the defence of the deposit of truth which Jesus, by being born in Bethlehem, revealed and then entrusted to the Church.

Being a few months away from the beginning of the commemorative Jubilee of Christ's Redemption, I entrust to you, dearest cloistered sisters, the successful outcome of this initiative, which I feel so necessary for reflection and conversion. I entrust to your prayers and to your spiritual fervour the entire Jubilee Year, and in a particular way, two events which are near to my heart: the Italian National Eucharistic Congress and the Synod of Bishops on the theme "Reconciliation and Penance".

May the Divine Saviour always fill you with the holy joy which St Francis of Assisi felt here at Greccio! May the Holy Virgin and St Joseph accompany you with their heavenly protection! And may my Apostolic Blessing, which I heartily impart to you, help you.

O.R. 770.   7 February 1983

Address to Women Religious of Costa Rica

3 March 1983

Dear Sisters,... during this meeting of faith, prayer, and spiritual communion with Peter's Successor, to whom your consecration binds you in affection, obedience and apostolic collaboration, my words are intended to bring you a message of joy and hope to confirm your identity and open up new ways to your ecclesial commitment, now strengthened by my presence among you.

As the Church has always done with regard to Christian virgins since the earliest days of Christianity, I would like to remind you of your bond with Jesus Christ, your Lord and Spouse, whose love and whose cause you have embraced at the same time.

You are disciples, because you have followed him with the evangelical counsels of chastity, poverty and obedience. Along with St Paul, you can say: "Life to me, means Christ" *(Ph 1:21)*, because you have personally consecrated yourselves to him and you have been called to feel this communion of love fully, so as to be able to say that this is he who lives in you and who communicates true life to you. You have identified yourselves with his cause and for this reason, leaving everything behind, as the Apostles did, you have chosen to be witnesses to the values and obligations of the Kingdom.

Your contribution is very precious to the Church. I know that you enthusiastically bear a good part of the burden of many parochial activities, of evangelisation, of teaching, of works of mercy, of community inspiration, of ecclesial presence and witness among the poorest, the alienated, the needy; with the ability to make the Church present with an authentically maternal appearance, with sensibility and affection, with wisdom and balance. In this dimension you feel the joy of the consecration through which you can say, paraphrasing the words of St Paul: For me, life is being the Church.

At a moment in history when woman is acquiring in society a place which belongs to her, with an advance which gives her dignity, I see with satisfaction your qualified presence as messengers and witnesses of the Gospel. This movement which is now acquiring greater form of expression in the pastoral community has its foundation and roots in the very attitude of the Teacher towards the women who followed him (cf. *Lk 23:55)*, who enjoyed his friendship, like Martha and Mary of Bethany (cf. *Jn 12:1-8)* and who were messengers of his resurrection, like Mary Magdalen (cf. *Jn 20:18*) or were invited to recognise him as the Messiah, like the Samaritan woman (cf. *Jn 4:39*).

The Church also entrusts to you the service of the word and catechesis, education in the faith, cultural and human advancement; therefore she requires of you an adequate preparation, more intense every time, in biblical and dogmatic theology, liturgy, spirituality and science; and at the same time she recognises with what enthusiasm and generosity you bring the Gospel among the poor, the most simple, the restless youth of this geographical area.

However, the Gospel is life, and in your heart, consecrated to Christ, you carry the instinct for life, for charity — which is the very life of God — which takes on flesh in the works of welfare and advancement. The Christians of these lands rightly claim your irreplaceable presence near the sick-bed, in school, in the various manifestations of the evangelical mercy proper to religious creativity. In these places, in these environments, you are the very presence of the love of Christ, you are the face of the Church, which shines before men through his love, translated into goodness, help, consolation, liberation and hope.

Looking concretely at the situation of your peoples, the restlessness which agitates society, the fragile balance of peace, the commitments to promote justice which is yet to be realised, I can do no less than reaffirm my confidence in your mission.

At this time, I would like to re-echo the words of the Second Vatican Council in its message to women: "You, consecrated virgins, in a world where egoism and the search for pleasure would become law, be the guardians of purity, unselfishness, and piety... you to whom life is entrusted at this grave moment in history, it is for you to save the peace of the world" (*Message to Women, 8,11*).

Your mission could seem to be too exacting for you, too great for your abilities. In many cases, since you are near the people, you hold in your hands the education of children, young people and adults; by nature and evangelical mission, you must be sowers of peace and concord, of unity and fraternity; you can disengage the mechanisms of violence through an integral education and a promotion of man's authentic values; your consecrated life must be a challenge to egoism and oppression, a call to conversion, a factor of reconciliation among men.

To be able duly to fulfil this mission, remain firm in the radical nature of your faith, in the love of Christ and in ecclesial awareness. Thus in the necessary preferential, but not exclusive, option in favour of the poor, you will avoid possible deviations and using the Gospel as a tool.

Do not let yourselves be deceived by party ideologies; do not succumb to the temptations of choices which one day could cost you the price of your freedom. Have confidence in your pastors and always be in communion with them. In this communion with the Church, in the identification with its guiding principles, you will find the norm for sure action. You too collaborate in being able to discern the reality upon which the light of the Gospel must fall. Almost through supernatural instinct, always direct the authenticity of your apostolic choices with the compass of the direction of the Church, composed of sincere communion with its magisterium, in unity with its pastors.

With this guarantee, embrace the cause of the poor; be present where Christ suffers in his needy brothers; arrive with your generosity in places where only the love of Christ knows how to perceive the lack of a friendly presence. Be patient and generous in the hope of a better society, sowing the seed of a new humanity which builds rather than destroys, which transforms the negative into the positive, as an announcement of resurrection.

The Holy Spirit, who has stirred up the charism of religious life in the Church and has also stirred up the charism of each one of your institutes, will give you light and creativity to know how to incarnate it into new values and new situations, with the charge of evangelical newness which possesses every charism inspired by the Spirit, when it remains in ecclesial communion.

As points of this meeting for you to reflect on, I want to leave you some reasons for fidelity which will broaden your heart and give you the full joy of an authentic disciple of Jesus, even in the midst of persecution, lack of understanding, the apparent ineffectiveness of your apostolic efforts.

First of all, fidelity to Christ, through loving communion with him through prayer, for which you must reserve long and frequent periods in your life, however much apostolic necessities may press upon you. Your prayer must seek the experience of Christ, followed, loved and served.

Fidelity also to the Church. Your consecration unites you to the Church in a special way; and in the perfect communion with her, with her mission, with her pastors and her faithful, you will find the full meaning of your religious life. As consecrated women, continue to be the honour of Mother Church.

Carry her sorrows and pains in your heart and in your life; be capable of reflecting at every moment the evangelical countenance of the Spouse of Christ.

Remain united to the fidelity of your charism. In this way the

Church shows the beauty of the various evangelical expressions assumed by your founders and foundresses. In communion with your institutes, contribute a universal dimension in the particular Church, a dimension which your religious families have. By living in communion with your sisters, you realise this first communion which assures the presence of Jesus in your midst and guarantees a community's apostolic fruitfulness.

Also live in communion between the various institutes, in order to offer the people of God the example of an evangelical unity which reflects the union of the Mystical Body, where all the charisms are united by the same Spirit.

Finally, be faithful to your people, to your particular Churches, to their efforts and to their hopes for justice and advancement, so that the Church may appear with you completely incarnate in the various nations, in their characteristics, in their values and traditions, in the ambience of the One, Holy and Catholic Church.

All that I have wanted to entrust to you has its suitable application, respecting the kind of life proper to them, to the religious of a contemplative life. They live silently and give witness to the value of union with God, in penance and in total sacrifice. With their prayer they embrace the needs of the poor, they assume the concerns of the universal Church and of the particular communities. They are the tangible manifestation of the fact that your peoples have an authentic contemplative capacity.....

Dear sisters: I cannot leave you without showing you the perfect model of this fidelity which I have just asked of you: the Virgin Mary. In her you will find the first disciple and the first word of presence in the midst of her people. She is the expression of all the charisms and the Mother of all the consecrated.

Your peoples are devoted to Our Lady and perceive in the preaching of the Gospel the mark of catholicity when she is spoken of, or its absence if she is not spoken of. By loving the Virgin, by speaking of her, you will enter into the heart of your people. Above all, however, if you know how to reflect her in your life, you will be these qualified messengers of the Gospel which the Church in Central America needs.

May she keep you faithful to the Gospel. I entrust you to her, so that with your word and your life you may be able to say to everyone, only and always, Jesus Christ is the Lord. Amen.

O.R. 777. 28 March 1983

Address to Men Religious at Guatemala

7 March 1983

Dear brothers, I have saved a special meeting to be able to be with you. First of all I wish to express my gratitude to you for your ecclesial presence in this land, where you are in the service of particular Churches.

Many of you are sons of this land. Others have come from near and far. But all of you are urged on by the same love for these peoples from whom you have also received much, through their simple faith, their sincere life of piety, their generous affection.

The special situations which these people are living and their very closeness favour an intense communion between you. For my part, I would like to encourage the efforts for ecclesial communion, for collaboration with your bishops, for the search for your better insertion into the ecclesial life in these sister nations, in order to be, as religious, a sign of communion and reconciliation.

You are committed to making the supreme rule of your life the following of Christ according to the Gospel. Allow me to remind you of this: you must be the specialists of Jesus' Gospel vitally identified with his words and with his example.

The distinctive mark of religious life in the Church must consist in maintaining the purity of the Gospel not only in the vows which are characteristic of your consecration, but above all in perfect charity towards God and your neighbour, which is the essence of the Gospel; in the beatitudes which affirm their originality with respect to the mentality of the world, and in these specific manifestations of the Gospel which are the charisms of your founders.

Fidelity to the Gospel assures the vitality of religious life, of which my predecessor Paul VI opportunely spoke: "Thanks to their consecration they are eminently willing and free to leave everything and to go and proclaim the Gospel even to the ends of the earth. They are enterprising and their apostolate is often marked by an originality, by a genius that demands admiration. They are generous: often they are found at the outposts of the mission, and they take the greatest risks for their health and their very lives" *(Evangelii Nuntiandi, 69)*.

Thus, be faithful to the perennial youthfulness of the Gospel which Christ has entrusted to the life-giving action of the Holy Spirit and his charisms.

The awareness of your consecration to Christ in the Church is a guarantee of fidelity. Yes, one does not embrace the Gospel merely as a just cause or as a utopia. The Gospel is a person: it is Jesus Christ, the Lord. He who "was handed over to the death for our sins and raised up for our justification" *(Rm 4:25)*. He has called you to follow him to the cross; and one cannot follow him with fidelity, if one does not first of all love him deeply. For this religious consecration vitally unites you to Jesus and becomes a bond of love which requires friendship, communion with him, nourished by the sacraments, especially the Eucharist and Penance, by the meditation of his word, by prayer, identification with his very sentiments.

Embracing the counsels for the kingdom of heaven means serving the kingdom of Christ, which is the Church. Thus, religious life directly signifies a bond "with the Church and her mystery" and is developed for its benefit (cf. *Lumen Gentium, 44*).

However, always remember that in Christ's plan one cannot conceive of religious life as being independent of the bishops, or as indifferent to the hierarchy; because there cannot be charisms except in the service of communion and the unity of the Body of Christ. Consequently, not only must any type of apostolate or magisterium parallel to that of the bishops be excluded, but it must also be emphasised that it is the very nature of religious life by all means to increase communion, to promote it in the faithful, to solidify it where it loses vigour. This has been the characteristic which all the founders have evidenced.

Yes, dear religious. I know that by mentioning the founders of your institutes you feel within you this type of family spirit which identifies you with them and with your brothers. It is the feeling that the charism is something alive, vital, animated by the Spirit, made flesh and blood in your experience of formation and of religious life.

You are the trustees and the ones responsible for this experience of the Spirit which is the charism of the founders. You are the sons of these "men of the Spirit", their living presence in the Church of today, in this land.

The faithful recognise you by your union with these saints. And these same faithful expect you to be and act as true sons of these saints; united with God, and through him committed to promoting justice, to elevating man culturally and humanly, in the cause of the poor. Remember, however, that in working first of all on their behalf, you must not exclude anyone.

One cannot think of the founders' work without seeing in them the incarnation of the Gospel, as extending through the geography and the history of the Church.

From this clear evangelical perspective, they offer you the example of a presence alongside the people and their suffering. Without allowing themselves to be carried away by temptations or currents of a political nature, they are a valid example for you even today; because, as I said to the priests and religious of Mexico, "you are not social directors, political leaders or officials of a temporal power". Your founders were able to embody Christ's charity effectively, not only with words, but with generous gestures, with services and institutions. In this way they have left a trace in history, they have made culture, they have sown truth and life, from which we continue to gather the fruits.

This remembrance, my dear brothers, allows me to ask you for complete fidelity to the Gospel and to the spirit of your founders, so that, today as yesterday, religious may live in perfect charity with a profound sense of faith, with generous dedication to the task of evangelisation, which is the first task entrusted to you, without ever permitting manipulating ideological motivations to replace your evangelical identity or inspire your action, which must always be that of the Church. Starting from this clear conviction, also work with enthusiasm for man's dignity.

With this evangelical charity which, as your founders demonstrated, is the most concrete and complete of any human ideology, and which concerns itself with man in his spiritual, material and social dimension, I exhort you to renew the fervour of your life and your works. The children of the Church who live in this land ask this of you. They want to feel that you are near, first of all as spiritual guides, as specialists in Christ's charity, which urges one to love others and to commit himself with all strength for man's justice and dignity.

Before your eyes, there are the tasks of evangelisation and of the formation of the Christian communities. With your generosity, make up for the lack of vocations or for distances between ecclesial groups, so much more in need of your presence the further away they are from the great urban or rural centres. Also educate popular piety so that it may bear the fruits of this simple and generous faith which animates it.

Continue to train a mature laity that will responsibly assume its place in the Church and give itself with clear-sightedness to the mission which belongs to it: to transform civil society from within. And give to the poor first of all — as I indicated to you before — the bread of the word, the defence of his rights when he is oppressed, promotion, integral education and every possible assistance which will help him live with dignity. In this, follow the indications of the Church's social teaching just as she proposes it, and have confidence in this social teaching of the Church. The times in which we live give us historic proof of its validity.

I ask you to give particular attention to youth. Your young people are generous; they expect the sympathy and the help of those who have received from their founders a special mission of Christian, cultural, working, human education. Therefore, may your presence not be missing from education centres of all levels, where the values which inform those who one day will rule the destinies of your peoples are determined.

In this important field, as in all apostolic activity — as an individual, as a religious community or institute or as associates in the widest sense — faithfully follow the directions of your bishops and demonstrate your love for the Church with the respect, communion and collaboration which they deserve as the pastors of the particular Churches. Through them you will be united with the visible head of the Church, to whom Christ entrusted the charism of confirming his brothers in the faith. Also be generous in helping and collaborating with the diocesan clergy.

With these requests the Pope renews his confidence in you, he encourages you towards a fruitful growth in your charisms and towards an enthusiastic dedication which must be the distinctive sign of your radical option for Christ, for the Church, and for man, our brother.

Do you want a key to apostolic fruitfulness? Live unity, the source of a great apostolic strength (cf. *Perfectae Caritatis, 15)*. In fraternal communion there is, in fact, the guarantee of the presence of Christ and of his Spirit, to put your responsibilities into practice, following the rules of your institutes.

The young people who knock on your doors want to find an ecclesial life that is characterised by the fervour of prayer, by the family spirit, by apostolic commitment. These young people are sensitive to community values and expect to find them in religious life. Be capable of welcoming them and guiding them, carefully cultivating new vocations, whose search must be one of your principal concerns.

My dear brothers: all of your institutes profess a special love for the Virgin Mary; under various titles and with various emphases, the Virgin appears as the reflection of a living Gospel, and therefore as the Mother of all religious. In her name I ask that you be able to maintain mutual appreciation for your charisms and collaboration in your work of the apostolate.

I entrust you to her, to preserve and increase your fidelity to Christ and to the Church. I ask her for the flowering and perseverance of abundant vocations for your religious families. The Church of this geographical area needs your presence, to live this fullness of the Gospel which belongs to religious life. May Mary, the Virgin who is faithful and solicitous about man's needs, grant you this grace. Amen.

O.R. 779.   11 April 1983

Letter to the Bishops of the U.S.A.
3 April 1983

In this Extraordinary Holy Year which has just begun, the whole Church is seeking to live more intensely the mystery of the Redemption. She is seeking to respond ever more faithfully to the immense love of Jesus Christ, the Redeemer of the world.

In the Bull of Indiction of the Jubilee, I pointed out that "the profound meaning and hidden beauty of this Year... is to be seen in the rediscovery and lived practice of the sacramental economy of the Church, through which the grace of God in Christ reaches individuals and communities" (*Aperite Portas Redemptori, 3*). While these words have a personal meaning for everyone, they are particularly relevant to individual men and women religious and to each religious community. It is my profound hope and ardent prayer that the grace of the Redemption will reach religious in great abundance, that it will take possession of their hearts, and become a source of Easter joy and hope for them — that the Holy Year will be a fresh beginning for them to "walk in newness of life' *(Rm 6:4)*.

By their very vocation, religious are intimately linked to the Redemption. In their consecration to Jesus Christ they are a sign of the Redemption that he accomplished. In the sacramental economy of the Church they are instruments for bringing this Redemption to the people of God.

They do so by the vitality that radiates from the lives they live in union with Jesus, who continues to repeat to all his disciples: "I am the vine, you are the branches" *(Jn 15:5)*. Religious bring the people of God into contact with the Redemption by the evangelical and ecclesial witness they bear by word and example to the message of Jesus. Their communion with their local Churches and with the universal Church has a supernatural effectiveness by reason of the Redemption. The important collaboration they give to the ecclesial community helps it to live and perpetuate the mystery of the Redemption, especially through the Eucharistic Sacrifice in which the work of the Redemption is repeatedly actuated.

The Church presents the Year of the Redemption to all the people of God as a call to penance and conversion, because ''there is no spiritual renewal that does not pass through penance and conversion'' *(Aperite Portas Redemptori, 4)*. But this call is linked in a particular way with the life and mission of religious. Thus the Jubilee Year has a special value for religious; it affects them in a special way; it makes special demands on their love, reminding them how much they are loved by the Redeemer and by his Church. Especially relevant to religious are these words of the Apostolic Bull: ''The specific grace of the Year of the redemption is therefore a renewed discovery of the love of God'' *(no. 8)*. In this regard, as pastors of the Church, we must proclaim over and over again that the vocation to religious life that God gives is linked to his personal love for each and every religious. It is my earnest hope that the Holy Year of the Redemption will truly be for religious life a year of fruitful renewal in Christ's love.

If all the faithful have a right — as they do — to the treasures of grace that a call to renewal in love offers, then the religious have a special title to that right.

During this Jubilee of the Redemption you will be coming to Rome for your *ad limina visits*, and I shall have an opportunity to consider with you some of the aspects of religious life as you see them. This makes my thoughts turn at this time in a special way to the religious of the United States. In reflecting on their history, their splendid contribution to the Church in your country, the great missionary activity that they have performed over the years, the influence they have exerted on religious life throughout the world, as well as the particular needs which they experience at the present time, I am convinced that, as bishops, we must offer them encouragement and the support of our pastoral love.

The religious life in the United States has indeed been a great gift of God to the Church and to your country. From the early colonial days, by the grace of God, the evangelising zeal of outstanding men and women religious, encouraged and sustained by the persevering efforts of the bishops, have helped the Church to bring the fruits of the Redemption to your land. Religious were among your pioneers. They blazed a trail in Catholic education at all levels, helping to create a magnificent educational system from elementary school to university. They brought into being health care facilities remarkable both for their numbers and quality. Working towards the establishment of justice, love and peace, they helped to build a social order rooted in the Gospel, striving to bring generation after generation to the maturity of Christ. Their witness to the primacy of Christ's love has been expressed through lives of prayer and dedicated service to others. Contemplative religious have contributed immensely to the vitality of the ecclesial community. At every stage in its growth, the Church in your nation, marked by a conspicuous fidelity to the See of Peter, has been deeply indebted to its religious: priests, sisters, brothers. The religious of America have also been a gift to the universal Church, for they have given generously to the Church in other countries; they have helped throughout the world to evangelise the poor and to spread Christ's Gospel of peace. This generosity has given evidence of a strong and vital religious life, ensured by a steady flow of vocations.

And because I have stressed the pastoral character and the full participation of the local Churches in the celebration of the Holy Year, I now turn to you, the bishops of the United States, asking you during this Holy Year to render special pastoral service to the religious of your dioceses and your country. I ask you to assist them in every way possible to open wide the doors of their hearts to the Redeemer. I ask that, through the exercise of your pastoral office, as individual bishops and united as an episcopal conference, you encourage the religious, their institutes and associations to live fully the mystery of the Redemption, in union with the whole Church and according to the specific charism of their religious life. This pastoral service can be given in different ways, but it certainly includes the personal proclamation of the Gospel message to them and the celebration of the Eucharistic Sacrifice with them.

It will likewise mean proclaiming anew to all the people of God the Church's teaching on consecrated life. This teaching has been set forth in the great documents of the Second Vatican Council, particularly in *Lumen Gentium* and *Perfectae Caritatis*. It has been further developed in *Evangelica Testificatio*, in the addresses of Paul VI and in those which I myself have given on many occasions. More recently still, much of this doctrinal richness has been distilled and reflected in the revised Code of Canon Law promulgated earlier this year. The essential elements are lived in different ways from one institute to another. You yourselves deal with this rich variety in the context of the American reality. Nevertheless, there are elements which are common to all forms of religious life and which the Church regards as essential. These include: a vocation given by God, an ecclesial consecration to Jesus Christ through the profession of the evangelical counsels by public vows, a stable form of community life approved by the Church, fidelity to a specific founding gift and sound traditions, a sharing in Christ's mission by a corporate apostolate, personal and liturgical prayer, especially Eucharistic worship, public witness, a lifelong formation, a form of government calling for religious authority based on faith, a specific relation to the Church. Fidelity to these basic elements, laid down in the constitutions approved by the Church, guarantees the strength of religious life and grounds our hope for its future growth.

I ask you, moreover, my brother bishops, to show the Church's profound love and esteem for the religious life, directed as it is to the faithful and generous imitation of Christ and to union with God. I ask you to invite all the religious throughout your land, in my name, and in your own name as bishops, in the name of the Church and in the name of Jesus, to seize this opportunity of the Holy Year to walk in newness of life, in solidarity with all the pastors and faithful, along the path necessary for us all — the way of penance and conversion.

In their lives of poverty, religious will discover that they are truly relevant to the poor. Through chastity they are able to love with the love of Christ and to experience his love for themselves. And through obedience they find their deepest configuration to Christ in the most fundamental expression of his union with the Father — in fulfilling his Father's will: "I always do what pleases him" *(Jn 8:29)*. It is especially through obedience that Christ himself offers to religious the experience of full Christian freedom. Possessing peace in their hearts and the justice of God from which that peace flows, they can be authentic ministers of Christ's peace and justice to a world in need.

In those cases, too, where individuals or groups, for whatever reason, have departed from the indispensable norms of religious life, or have even, to the scandal of the faithful, adopted positions at variance with the Church's teaching, I ask you, my brother bishops, sustained by hope in the power of Christ's grace and performing an act of authentic pastoral service, to proclaim once again the Church's universal call to conversion, spiritual renewal and holiness. And be sure that the same Holy Spirit who has placed you as bishops to shepherd the Church is ready to utilise your ministry to help those who were called by him to a life of perfect charity, who were repeatedly sustained by his grace and who have given evidence of a desire — which must be rekindled — to live totally for Christ and his Church in accordance with their proper ecclesial charism. In the local Churches the discernment of the exercise of the charisms is authenticated by the bishops in union with the Successor of Peter. This work is a truly important aspect of your episcopal ministry, an aspect to which the universal Church, through me, asks you to attach special priority in this Jubilee Year.

As an expression of my solidarity with you in this area of your pastoral service, acknowledging the special links between religious life and the Holy See, I am hereby appointing Archbishop John R. Quinn of San Francisco as Pontifical Delegate to head a special Commission of three bishops whose task it will be to facilitate the pastoral work of their brother bishops in the United States in helping the religious of your country whose institutes are engaged in apostolic works to live their ecclesial vocation to the full. Associated with him in the Commission are Archbishop Thomas C. Kelly of Louisville and Bishop Raymond W. Lessard of Savannah. Working in union with the Sacred Congregation for Religious and Secular Institutes and following a document of guidelines which the Congregation is making available to them and to you, the Commission has authority to set up a suitable programme of work which, it is hoped, will be of valuable help to the individual bishops and to the Episcopal Conference. I would further ask the Commission to consult with a number of religious, to profit from the insights that come from the experience of religious life lived in union with the Church. I am confident that the religious of contemplative life will accompany this work with their prayers.

In asking the Commission to be of assistance to you in your pastoral ministry and responsibility, I know that it will be very sensitive to the marked decline in recent years in the numbers of young people seeking to enter religious life, particularly in the case of institutes of apostolic life. This decline in numbers is a matter of grave concern to me — a concern which I know that you and the religious also share. As a result of this decline, the median age of religious is rising and their ability to serve the needs of the Church is becoming increasingly more limited. I am concerned that, in a generous effort to continue manifold services without adequate numbers, many religious are overburdened, with a consequent risk to their health and spiritual vitality. In the face of this shared concern, I would ask the Commission, in collaboration with religious, utilising the prayerful insights of individual religious and major superiors, to analyse the reasons for this decline in vocations. I ask them to do this with a view to encouraging new growth and a fresh move forward in this most important sector of the Church's life.

And in addressing the many issues affecting the consecrated life and ecclesial mission of religious, these bishops will work closely with you, their brother bishops. Besides having as an aid the document on the salient points of the Church's teaching on religious life prepared by the Sacred Congregation for Religious and Secular Institutes, you and they will have my full fraternal and prayerful support. The *ad limina* visits of the American bishops will truly offer an excellent opportunity for you and me to speak personally about the pastoral service that we wish to render together in the name of Jesus, Chief Shepherd of the Church and Redeemer of the world.

By requesting that this call to holiness, to spiritual renewal and to conversion and penance be initiated during the Jubilee Year of the Redemption, I am trusting that the Lord Jesus, who always sends labourers into his vineyard, will bless the project with his redeeming love. The power of the Holy Spirit can make this call a vital experience for all who respond to it, and a sign of hope for the future of religious life in your country. May Mary the patroness of the United States, the first of the redeemed and the model of all religious, support your episcopal ministry with her motherly prayer, so that it may come to fruition, bringing renewed joy and peace to all the religious of America, and offering ever greater glory to the Most Holy Trinity.

O.R. 793.   18 July 1983

Address to the Union of Mothers General
13 May 1983

Beloved sisters in Christ, accept my most heartfelt greeting! It is always a reason for joy for me to meet female religious and to express openly the Church's deep esteem for their lives of total consecration to the Lord, the keen interest and the faith which the Holy See has in them and in their mission.

But today's meeting assumes an altogether special importance because of its universal nature: in fact, in the persons of the superiors general of the various religious institutes spread throughout the world, in a certain way there is expressed the presence in Rome of all female religious and their desire to witness to their devotion to the Church and to the Pope, and to accept personally his teachings and directives.

Therefore, through you, I send a heartfelt special blessing to all the female religious in the world: to the contemplatives; to those who in humble generosity are dedicated to the service of the brethren; to those tried by age, by sickness of body or mind. The sacrifices of all of them have an incomparable value in the eyes of the Lord.

To you, gathered in Rome to examine the "Apostolic Spirituality of Religious". I want above all to offer a word of encouragement and comfort, which is required by such an important, such a delicate, but at the same time such a pastoral mission, conferred on you by your very election: that of building up in Christ a fraternal community where, above all, God may be sought and loved (cf. *Canon 619*).

The theme of your work in preparation for some years, is rich in teachings and offers you the opportunity not only to treat of your apostolic activities but even more to draw from the sources which must nourish them.

Moreover, I strongly advise you to meditate on the teachings of the new Code of Canon Law bearing on this subject. It will offer you valuable insights into a fundamental part of your lives.

In fact, the Code recalls in the first place (cf. *canon 673*) that the apostolate of religious consists above all in giving witness by their consecrated lives, nourished by prayer and penance. This basic affirmation is of particular importance since it places the apostolic role of religious in its true place. Precisely through their innermost being they join the dynamism of the Church, thirsty for the absolute of God, called to sanctity. Above all, they are called to witness to this sanctity (cf. *Evangelii Nuntiandi, 69*).

Before being translated into proclamation or action, the apostolate is the revelation of God present in the apostle. And this revelation postulates that the religious be in intimate and constant contact with the Lord. In this way, it matters little whether she be in the fullness of her strength or infirm, young or advanced aged, active or without any direct activity: evangelisation is real and deep to the degree that Christ's life is reflected through her personal life. The great evangelisers were primarily prayerful souls, interior souls: they always knew how to find the time for prolonged contemplation.

At this historical moment when you all have reason to suffer from the lack of apostolic workers, it is especially well to pause and meditate on this truth, in the belief that "being" has more value than "doing", which is always limited and imperfect. Moreover, be certain that your courageous and joyful fidelity to the fundamental demands of consecrated life will offer a pressing invitation to young women, always ready to be generous, to follow the Lord along the path marked out by you.

In this perspective, although they are not present among you, I want to reaffirm strongly the eminently apostolic role of cloistered nuns. To leave the world to devote oneself in solitude to deeper and constant prayer is none other than a special way of living and expressing Christ's Paschal Mystery, of revealing it to the world and, therefore, of being an apostle. It would be an error to consider cloistered nuns creatures separated from their contemporaries, isolated and as if cut off from the world and the Church. Rather, they are present to them, and in deeper way, with the same tenderness of Christ, as *Lumen Gentium (no. 46)* affirms. It is therefore not surprising that the bishops of the new Churches solicit, as an eminent grace, the possibility of receiving a monastery of contemplative religious, even if workers for the active apostolate are still in such insufficient number.

Sisters of the contemplative life! May your vocation be dear to you; it is more precious than ever in today's world, which seems unable to find peace. The Pope and the Church need you; Christians count on your fidelity.

May you who are consecrated to the works of the active apostolate always be more greatly convinced of the Council's teachings, so appropriately recalled in the Code. Live them! That is, may your lives be steeped in the apostolic spirit and may your every apostolic action be inspired by an evangelical spirit.

In this way your activities will constitute an authentic service, humbly respectful of persons, concerned with avoiding undue pressures and every intolerable overbearing characteristic.

I exhort you again never to forget that the religious apostolate is, by its nature, communitarian: the witness given by a religious cannot be purely individual; it is communitarian in nature, and all religious are called to exercise the apostolate along the line of the charism recognised by the Church and through the mandate of their lawful superiors.

It is not a matter of a simple disciplinary dependence, but of a reality of faith. We must ceaselessly remind ourselves that we are in the Church, intimately incorporated in it, ordained to its mission, inseparable from its life and from its sanctity, as *Lumen Gentium* teaches.

This conception must stimulate in religious the will to work in strict and profound union with the Church's magisterium and its hierarchy. Certainly, in carrying out the multiple, traditional forms of your apostolate you must not fail to listen to your contemporaries in order to understand well their problems and their difficulties and be better able to help them.

Never forget, however, that the schools, the hospitals, the relief centres, the initiatives directed towards service of the poor, cultural and spiritual development of peoples not only preserve their relevance but, appropriately brought up to date, often are revealed as special places for evangelisation, witness and authentic human promotion.

Sometimes it may be necessary to abandon works or activities in order to be able to dedicate oneself to others, to create more limited communities in order to answer the most pressing needs of the poor in certain regions. I know your ardent desire to be present to the poor, and I appreciate your efforts in this regard. However, as I said recently to the religious of Sao Paulo (3 July 1980), it seems opportune to recall here certain norms for new forms of presence.

First of all, these efforts must always be conducted in a climate of prayer. The soul which lives constantly in the presence of God and lets itself become permeated with the warmth of his charity will easily escape the temptation of individualism and the contradictions which risk division; it will be able to interpret in the light of the Gospel the option for the poor and for the victims of the selfishness of men, without yielding to socio-political radicalism which, sooner or later, produces effects contrary to those hoped for and engenders new forms of oppression. Finally, the person in touch with God will find the way to come close to people and to become part of their milieux, without losing her own religious identity, and neither hide nor disguise the uniqueness of her vocation which is to follow Christ, poor, chaste and obedient.

Moreover, these experiences must also be prepared for by serious study in a constant dialogue in the heart of the institute, with responsible superiors and in collaboration with concerned bishops. In this way, the programmes will be worked out after examining the possibilities of success, without running risks, but always acting in conformity with the most urgent needs and according to the nature of the institute.

In conclusion, it will be important always to pursue such experiments in accord with the hierarchy, attempting humbly and courageously, if necessary, to correct them, to set them aside or to adapt them in a more suitable manner.

Above all, always and in everything, behave as loving daughters of the Church, generously and faithfully adhering to its authentic magisterium, the guarantee of fruitfulness. The fidelity promised to Christ can never be separated from fidelity to the Church: "He who hears you, hears me" *(Lk 10:16)*.

The Holy Year which we have been celebrating since 25 March, and the preparation for the Synod of Bishops next September, are of invaluable assistance to you in carrying out your mission of evangelisation.

The Holy Year invites us to rediscover the riches of salvation, and so it calls us to a personal commitment to renewal, through penance and conversion.

The celebration of this event is, for all Christians and therefore for religious, an earnest appeal to repentance and conversion. It makes us rediscover a sense of sin and to become aware of the fact that we are sinners. It makes us rediscover a sense of God. This attitude of conversion will especially show itself in a more sincere approach to the sacraments, and it will impel us to practise a charity that is based on truth and that promotes justice. I would like to emphasise at this point the real and profound link that exists between the fraternal life of religious and the very theme of the Holy Year. This is perfectly highlighted by the new Code of Canon Law: "By their fraternal communion, founded and rooted in charity, religious will give an example of universal reconciliation in Christ" *(canon 602)*.

In this same spirit of communion and joy, I wish to repeat my cordial welcome to all of you who have come to Rome for this meeting. My contact with the members of the two international Unions of Superiors General is a valued way of reaching the religious of the world and of maintaining a continuing contact with the development of religious life. On Tuesday of this week I had the pleasure of meeting the executive committee of the Union of Superiors General. Today I meet you and I hope to have further contact with both unions in the future. When you go home, carry with you my special blessing to the sisters of your congregations. The Blessed Virgin Mary, the first of the redeemed, the first to have been closely associated with the work of the Redemption, will always be your guide and model. Like Mary the Mother of Jesus, who was totally consecrated to the person of her Son and to the service of the Redemption, so you and your sisters will learn to know nothing except the Crucified Jesus, who became for us wisdom, justice, sanctification and redemption.

O.R. 787. 6 June 1983

Address to Women Religious at Milan.
20 May 1983

Beloved Religious from Milan and Lombardy: my visit to this archdiocese on the occasion of the National Eucharistic Congress has a well qualified and significant characteristic: it is a journey of witness, of catechesis and of adoration of the Most Blessed Sacrament of the Altar. Therefore I could not omit a special meeting with you religious who are consecrated precisely to Christ, present in the Eucharist, and who have prepared for this great event with intense prayer.

I greet you cordially and express to you my gratitude and esteem for the enormous and careful work carried out by you and by your individual congregations in the service of this local Church and of the Lombardy region. How many spiritual and also social fruits your love for Christ and for the brethern has produced! An immense array of consecrated souls from century to century has spread everywhere goodness, love, charity, relief, joy, well-being, consolation. Children have been received and educated, parents helped and advised, young people loved and guided, the sick cured and comforted, the poor helped and consoled, those discriminated against and those gone astray have been lovingly taken in and cared for. Certainly it has not been possible to relieve every suffering and eliminate all distress; perhaps there have been deficiencies and defects. But it is impossible not to recognise sincerely the immense work carried out in this land with love and with dedication, at times heroic, by the sisters of the various congregations, by you, who find strength and happiness, serenity and courage in the intimate union with the Eucharistic Jesus. Wherever your love and your smiles pass, through the grace of God, good flourishes! For all of this, let us together thank the Lord, who has called you and chosen you for such dignity and given you such a noble and ever authentic mission. And at the same time let us pray that, also through your fervent witness, he may give to today's Church numerous and holy vocations, so necessary for modern society, which above all needs love, understanding, mercy and hope.

My greeting becomes a wish and an exhortation to be ever more fervent in the commitment to your sanctification and fraternal charity, and it is extended to all your fellow sisters who could not be present at our meeting because of unbreakable commitments and reasons of health. My greeting goes with special affection to the numerous cloistered nuns who, in continual prayer and self-giving, are an irreplaceable and fruitful part of the Church and of the social organism itself.

The important event of the National Eucharist Congress which urged me to come as a pilgrim to Lombardy also suggests to me the recommendation I leave you this evening: that your Eucharistic spirituality may always be deeply dogmatic.

The Eucharistic dogma affirms the true, real, substantial presence of Christ who offers himself to the Father as a sacrifice in our name and who is intimately united with us in Communion. The Council of Trent, recalling and interpreting with definitive authority the words spoken by Jesus both in the discourse on the bread of life *(Jn 6)* and at the Last Supper, expressed itself in this way: "The Church of God always had this faith: immediately after the consecration, under the appearance of bread and wine there is the true Body of our Lord and the true Blood, together with his soul and his divinity. His Body exists under the appearance of Bread and his Blood under the appearance of wine by virtue of the words of consecration. His Body is under the appearance of bread, his Blood under the appearance of wine and his soul under both appearances by virtue of that connection and natural concomitance which holds united all the parts of Christ the Lord, who rose from the dead never to die again. Finally, his divinity is found present through his admirable hypostatic union with his body and soul. It is therefore very true that as much is contained under one of the two species as under both. In fact, just as Christ is whole and entire under the appearance of bread and under every part of the same appearance, he is also whole and entire under the appearance of wine and under its parts" *(Sess. XIII, 3).*

Then, interpreting the affirmations of the Apostles, of the Letter to the Hebrews, and of the whole early Church, the Council of Trent affirms and explains that the Eucharist is the sacrificial presence of Christ in time, that is, the Eucharist is the renewal of the Sacrifice of the Cross. The Second Vatican Council reaffirms the same truth: "As often as the Sacrifice of the Cross in which 'Christ our passover has been sacrificed' *(1 Co 5:7)* is celebrated on an altar, the work of our redemption is carried on" *(Lumen Gentium, 3; cf. Sacrosanctum Concilium, 47).*

Therefore nourish your spirituality and your catechesis with dogmatic truths! Read and meditate on the great and fundamental doctrinal documents of the Church regarding the Eucharist, the encyclicals, and statements of qualified and authentic teachers, the experiences of the saints and mystics! There can be no confusion or mystification about the Eucharist!

St Thomas Aquinas well said that the truth of the Eucharist "cannot be grasped with the senses, but only with faith, which is based on the authority of God" *(Summa, III, 75, 1).* And St Ambrose, the great Bishop of Milan (334-397), wrote: "Not without significance do you say 'Amen', since now in your spirit you confess that you receive the Body of Christ. Therefore, when you come up to request it, the priest says to you: 'The Body of Christ', and you answer: 'Amen', that is, 'It is true'. One's inner conviction safeguards what the tongue confesses" *(De Sacramentis, IV, 5, 25).*

The Christian is convinced that as a creature he must pray to and adore God, the Creator and Lord of the universe and of his life; but enlightened by faith he knows that true adoration, perfectly valid, worthy of the infinite sanctity of God and of his own personal intelligence, is possible only through the Sacrifice of the Mass, to which every other prayer is linked. One cannot live without adoring and therefore one cannot live without the Mass! The Christian knows that Jesus is present in the form of food and drink, because he gave himself totally to man and wants to unite himself intimately with us to strengthen us in faith and will, to console us during tribulations, to transform us into himself, to inflame us with love towards all creatures. Only from the Eucharistic dogma, precisely understood and totally lived, comes the true meaning of Christian existence, the strength of the religious vocation, the authentic commitment to the transformation of society, the enlightened sense of unity in Christ, in truth and in charity.

In the same work on the sacraments, St Ambrose wrote: "Receive every day what must do you good every day!... Whoever has been wounded goes to be healed. Our wound is this, that we are under sin, and the medicine is the heavenly and adorable sacrament" *(ibid., V, 4 25)*.

May the Eucharist, that is the Holy Mass and Holy Communion, truly be the effective and dynamic centre of your consecrated life and of each of your communities so that the very virtues of Christ may always shine in you: strength, patience, goodness, generosity, total gift of self and supernatural joy. Sometimes this all means heroic and enduring sacrifice! But it also means always feeling more need for the Eucharist and a longing for heaven. In *The Way of Perfection*, St Teresa wrote this of Jesus: "The soul which intensely desires to feed on this food will find in the Most Blessed Sacrament spiritual delight and consolation, and as soon as one has begun to taste it there will no longer be trials, persecutions or toils which he cannot bear easily" *(XXXIV, 2)*.

Beloved! May the Most Holy Virgin be close to you and sustain you. As St Ambrose exhorts, may she be "the model for your lives" (cf. *De virginibus, 1, II, 2, 6*).

In one of her apparitions to St Catherine Labouré, Our Lady said to the young sister, frightened by the greatness and the difficulty of the mission which had been entrusted to her: "It is here at the foot of the Tabernacle that you must seek strength and consolation!" The heavenly Mother addresses the same words to each of you. With the Eucharist, near the Tabernacle, may you be holy and fearless sisters, today and for the rest of your lives!

With this wish, I impart to you my heartfelt Apostolic Blessing.

O.R. 787.   6 June 1983

Address to the Chapter Members of the Conventual Franciscans
9 July 1983

I greet you all with sincere affection, members of the General Chapter of the Friars Minor Conventual... The deep affection which I have for your Franciscan family — evidenced by my two pilgrimages to the tomb of St Francis, respectively the day after my election to the chair of Peter, and on the occasion of the eighth centenary of the birth of the saint — moves me to express to you some thoughts inspired in my soul by your presence.

You are Friars Minor Conventual and you want to preserve and to live authentically the charism left to you as a heritage by your inspired founder. To this end, immersed as you are in a society in continual transformation, it is important to question yourselves on what is essential and irreplaceable in the type of life you have embraced in responding to the Franciscan vocation. It seems to me that one thing which cannot be changed or substituted is above all the spirit of renunciation, like that of the *Poverello* of Assisi. You cannot live your charism fully without accepting discipline with perfect joy, without loving the rule which makes you strong and free, without embracing self-denial, the vigilance over your own thoughts and behaviour, and above all without keeping deeply impressed in your heart the words of Christ: "None of you can be my disciple if he does not renounce all his possessions" *(Lk 14:33)*

The Friar Minor Conventual is a man detached from the greed to possess and therefore does not share the common form of life founded on the search for temporal prosperity: following the example of the Seraphic Father, he flees what the world seeks, searching rather for what the world despises, that is, joyful poverty, interior recollection, the candid and chaste life, voluntary penance and serene submission to superiors, who are the manifest signs of God's will.

In order to be reliable witnesses to the eternal truths in the midst of this world, the Friar Conventual must make his own the experience of St Paul, and for that matter, of all the saints, and repeat with them: "We do not fix our gaze on what is seen but on what is unseen. What is seen is transitory; what is unseen lasts forever" *(2 Co 4:18)*. The pivots, therefore, on which his whole life must turn are the search for God and prayer, which free man from all earthly conditioning, restoring his true identity to him. To this end, St Francis "spent all his time in holy recollection, in order to imprint wisdom in his heart; he was afraid of regressing if he was not always making progress. And if at times visits from the laity or other matters were pressing, he cut short more than ended them, in order to take refuge again in contemplation. Because to him, who was feeding on heavenly sweetness, the world proved to be tasteless, and the divine delights had given him no appetite for the coarse foods of man" *(2 Celano LXI, 94, FF 1, p. 629)*.

May this wonderful example be for you a constant incentive to react against certain modern tendencies which, in religious life, would want to put in second place conversation with God, whether it be individual or communitarian, as well as the sacramental and liturgical rites, in order to give a certain preference to other horizontal purposes which, although good in themselves and worthy of being followed, are nevertheless always dependent on the primary end, namely, the spiritual end, which must inspire the whole life and work of the Christian and particularly of the religious.

Another aspect which seems to me to constitute an essential part of the Franciscan charism is total and generous fidelity to the Church. It is a question of adhering lovingly and firmly, not to an imaginary Church, which each one could conceive and structure in his own way, but to the Catholic Church, as it is, that is, as Christ willed it and instituted it with its purposes, its laws, its means of salvation and its indispensable structures. What is expected today from the spiritual sons of St Francis is that they be able to enliven from within this one true Church of Christ, that they fortify it and enrich it with their complete fidelity, with their absolute obedience: in a word, with all those ascetic virtues which are proper to the Franciscan tradition.

Always have before your eyes the great problems which today occupy and concern the Church: priestly and religious vocations, the missions, the advancement of the lowly, the poor and the weak, the defence of justice and peace; in other words, the proclamation of the Good News to everyone of good will. Bring your specific contribution to attaining these great goals. Like your Seraphic Father, you too be ever more resplendent with the most ardent love for "Holy Mother Church" *(XXI, FF I, 134)*. In so doing you will reproduce in yourselves his dear paternal image, you will conform your life to his and you will be true servants of the people of God, capable of lighting everywhere the lamp of hope, of confidence and of optimism, which finds its source in the same Lord.

The Jubilee Year of the Redemption now in progress recalls to mind the specific message of pardon and reconciliation which was entrusted to the sons of St Francis with the Portiuncula Indulgence. This is a message of grace and mercy of which you yourselves are the first beneficiaries. Therefore, above all, cherish in this Jubilee the great pardon which Francis implored from Christ, through the intercession of the Queen of Angels. In the spirit of the Holy Year, renew in yourselves the humble and joyous invocation of the grace of the reconciling God, and always be more clearly aware of your debt to him, who offered to you "once for all" *(Heb 9:12)* and continually makes present to you, with unchanged goodness, a pardon, to which no one has a right, and he pours into you the joy of living your consecrated life in depth. May this fruit of the

Indulgence be among the spiritual fruits of your General Chapter.

May the examples of the great Assisian and of all the saints of the Franciscan tradition who have honoured the Church assist you. May the shining and courageous figure of St Maximilian Maria Kolbe, martyr of charity and exemplary model of Franciscan life for our time, whom I myself had the joy of numbering among the heavenly company of saints, and whose "City of the Immaculate" I had the joy of revisiting during my recent apostolic pilgrimage to Poland, be of particular comfort to you. In his footsteps, may the Immaculate Virgin Mary, the Queen of the Franciscan Order, always shine before your eyes and dispose you to an ever more generous dedication to the new and multiple apostolic activities which await you.

May you be sustained also by my prayers for the success of your religious works, above all, those most demanding ones you carry out in Lebanon, Turkey, China and in the mission territories.

May the Apostolic Blessing, invoking abundant heavenly graces, descend upon all of you here present and upon all the members of your Order.

O.R. 798. 22-29 August 1983

Address to Women Religious at Lourdes

My dear sisters, I have just reminded priests of their sublime and demanding ministry of reconciling sinners to God, which completes their Eucharistic ministry. Your vocation is not to administer these sacraments, although you often play an important role in preparing souls to receive them.

I often remind lay people, the baptised, of their prophetic and royal mission to show their faith around them, be it in family, social, professional, political, artistic or scientific circles, and to insert evangelical values into these complex human realities. Baptised, you also share in this role, especially if you are dedicated to active life. In this last instance, you are being told more and more often that you represent enormous vital strength for the Church which counts on you to complete and support the parish ministry of the priests: to fulfil educational, medical and social functions which correspond so closely to ecclesial charity; to accompany the faithful in catechesis or various organisations; for all kinds of missionary work, etc. The choice of apostolate is so vast, and you offer such availability and such competence!

And yet, my dear sisters, this is not what defines you. Your religious life is first of all a life consecrated to God, and I would say that a sign of this consecration is unselfish love. You are primarily for the world privileged witnesses of this gift of love, and this is no doubt what God wants most for this world, before any consideration of your "usefulness" to society. And this is what the Church expects from you, for its own witness, before considering your many useful and effective services.

Yes, first of all, the vocation which you received and which was tested by your congregation is a free gift of God's love. Why you, rather than your sister or your friend? Mary was freely chosen by God. And so was Bernadette, to carry his message. Like them, are you sufficiently thankful to the Lord for this tremendous gift?

And your loving response to the Lord must be equally free. By the gift of your life to Christ, as to the Spouse, you show that the Lord deserves to be loved for himself, that the kingdom of God according to Jesus, with its apparent "folly", warrants the dedication of our life to it, and that the realities of the hereafter are so strong as to make you want to share in them even now.

For you who are contemplatives, this aspect is evident: the free choice of your life of prayer and penance stuns, seduces or irritates the world, but never leaves it indifferent, especially today. But, even if you lead an active life, people must also be able easily to recognise the One to whom you consecrated your life.

Unselfish love must also inspire the many services and apostolates which you perform in the Church. You want to serve the men and women around you. And many of your congregations have not hesitated to reach out to the poorest, to those on the fringes of society, to those whose health is most affected, to those neglected by many sectors of society as "unproductive", but whom you love for themselves, thereby witnessing to the fact that human life is always deserving of love and respect because Christ loves it. And it is the same for all those who devote themselves without measure so that the souls of children, young people and adults will freely accept the faith.

In your community life also, you try to live with deep charity among sisters who did not choose each other.

Your religious vows help you precisely to live this donation:

obedience makes you available to others, poverty makes you unselfish, chastity frees you from possessive relationships.

At the heart of your consecrated life is the Eucharist, received every day and adored in an oratory of your house or close by. It is in this sacrament that your contemplative prayer and your apostolic or charitable action find their nourishment. For, just as the Holy Spirit transforms the offerings at Mass into the Body and Blood of Christ, so must he transform you, to make of you an offering to his glory, a free offering. This gift will be your joy and your primary witness.

Certainly your activity will be fruitful in the Church. And even perhaps the most fruitful! But you do not have to seek after this success, even apostolic, at any cost: it will come in addition. As in the life of the Virgin Mary. As in the life of Bernadette, for whom to live was enough. Her religious life seemed miserable as far as health was concerned, and useless, when she was at Nevers. And yet! In fact, the witness she left to the world is especially strong, pure and clear.

This is what I wish for you, as I bless you with all my heart, you and the congregations which you represent. I bless also the sisters who are ill and those who could not come here. Go in the peace and joy of Christ!

O.R. 798. 22-29 August 1983

Address to Chapter Members of the Augustinians
25 August 1983

Dear brothers, I am very happy to receive you in this special audience that is reserved for you, the participants in the General Chapter of the Augustinian Order... The first thought that comes out from my heart in this important moment is that of gratitude to the Lord, the giver of every grace, who throughout the many centuries and in the midst of the many adverse winds of history willed to keep your Order alive and dynamic; your Order which includes a long list of saints and mystics, which has inspired thinkers and pastors of great talent and universal renown, and which now counts in its membership 3,400 confreres of whom 2,570 are priests. You well know the fundamental importance of prayer in general and of thanksgiving in the life and teaching of St Augustine! He who rose so high in the contemplation of divine truth and descended so deeply into the abysses of the mysteries of God and man understood the absolute necessity of prayer that is humble and totally trusting. As sharp as the intelligence of man may be, mystery always infinitely surpasses it and prayer then becomes a need of the soul: *"Fit in oratione conversio cordis"*, says the holy bishop, *"et in ipsa conversione purgatio interioris oculi..."* (*De Sermone Domini in Monte*, II, 3, 14).

My second thought is an entreaty: you need supernatural light for the deliberations you must carry on for the good of your Order in the future years and also for the good of the whole Church. In fact, in this chapter there is the election of the Prior General and his immediate collaborators, but above all there are decided those activities and initiatives that have the purpose of promoting the spiritual and apostolic vitality of all the members of the Order. They are events of fundamental importance that demand a great sense of responsibility and also a particular gift of far-sightedness.

There are three special events that give an even greater weight to your assembly: the Holy Year of the Redemption that is now involving the universal Church; the 450 years since the arrival in America — and specifically in Mexico — of the first group of Augustinian missionaries; and finally, the preparation for the celebration of the 16th centenary of the conversion of St Augustine (386-387). In order effectively to promote the spiritual and apostolic vitality of the Order, the chapter has set before itself an attentive examination of continuing formation, which should include in a serious and methodical manner the individual and communal levels, with special theological, pastoral and spiritual courses as well as live-in gatherings of Augustinians, as stated expressly in your Constitutions *(n. 110)*. This is a question of the highest importance especially today in the modern world that so rightly demands religious persons who are doctrinally firm and spiritually well formed. This need regards not only you Augustinians but also the clergy, religious of other congregations and laity engaged in the apostolate. It is a question of a continuing formation that is not simply intellectual, necessary as that is, but of an integral formation that includes the whole man, intellect, will, and feelings; a formation that can truly be called "Augustinian", that is always bringing about renewal whether in the style of communal life of the Order or in the updating of the religious sciences.

For all these projects you have a great need of prayer: "Pray in hope, pray with faith and love" — wrote our saint — "pray with constancy and patience" *(Ep 130, 19)*. Prayer is as necessary as the grace it obtains. Your Order has as a principal obligation the task of keeping alive and attractive the fascinating quality of Augustine also in modern society: a stupendous and stimulating ideal, because the exact and heartfelt knowledge of his thought and life excites the thirst for God, the attraction of Jesus Christ, the love of wisdom and truth, the need for grace, prayer, virtue, and fraternal charity, and the yearning for the happiness of eternity.

I too accompany you with my prayer, because I am convinced that you have a great mission to unfold in the modern world, that of making felt the love and the mercy of Christ with the same passionate and burning accents of your father and master. "Late have I loved you, O Beauty ever ancient, ever new, late have I loved you" cried St Augustine with quiet grief; but once the truth had been reached, he consecrated himself radically to it and lived for it alone. He bore witness to it, preached it, defended it, sacrificing himself totally for it: *"O aeterna veritas, et vera caritatis et cara aeternitas! Tu es Deus meus tibi suspiro die et nocte!" (Confessions VII, 10, 16)*; thus he expressed himself in the Confessions, and in the Soliloquies: "At last I love you alone, I follow only you, I search only for you, I am ready to follow only you because you alone rule justly and therefore I want to be yours... Tell me what I must do to be able to see you, with the hope of being able to accomplish all the commands you have given" *(Sol. 1, 5)*. These should be your sentiments also, to be able to realise the task which you have chosen and which has been entrusted to you.

At the threshold of the chapter I tell you and all the members of the Order with the same intensity of St Augustine: "Love truth totally and with all your heart";

— love truth before everything, and feel a deep understanding of the modern society in which we live. Today's humanity is full of people who, like Augustine, are searching for the truth, that is, the sense of their own lives, the meaning of history that is always turbulent and unforeseeable, and now the reason for the universe itself that slips away from the definitive knowledge of science. Remember what the Saint wrote in the Confessions: "I have become a great enigma to myself; I asked my soul why it was sad and why it tormented me so, but it could answer me nothing" *(IV, 3)*. How these words sound so real today! Twenty years ago, in the opening talk of the Second Vatican Council, Paul

VI said: "A look at the world fills one with sadness because of its many evils: atheism is invading a part of humanity and creating an imbalance of the intellectual, moral and social order, of which the world has lost the notion. At the same time that the light of the science of things grows, there is spread darkness about the science of God and consequently about the true science of man. As progress wonderfully perfects the instruments that man can use, his heart declines towards emptiness, sadness and desperation" (*Teachings of Paul VI, 1963, p. 182*). Dramatic statements, sadly true! However, there remains still true and ever more stirring the cry of St Augustine: "You have made us for yourself, O Lord, and our heart is restless until it rests in you" (*Conf. I, 1*). Out of the striking phenomenon of secularisation there must rise the phenomenon of the maturation of the faith, that is, of personalisation by means of inquiry and individual persuasion. Problematic man who is searching and the Christian body who demands clarity and certainty must be understood, and loved and helped.

— love truth then above all with the scruple of orthodoxy, eagerly listening to the Master who speaks within, and staying closely united to the Church, the Mother of salvation. "Let Christ be in your heart, so that your heart be never alone or thirsty or have other springs to drink from. So, the master who teaches is within; it is Christ! If his inspiration and his anointing are not there, words outside sound in vain" (In *Ep. 10. 3, 13*). But it is the Church that must guide along the road of truth. In this regard St Augustine is clear and categorical: "*Quantum quisque amat Ecclesiam Christi, tantum habet Spiritum Sanctum*" (In *Joann. 32, 8*). "*Non habent Dei caritatem, qui Ecclesiae non diligunt unitatem*" (*De Baptismo III, 16, 21*).

Act in such a way as to be and sow always "good grain", so that whoever hears your word and your counsels can feel himself confirmed in truth, comforted in the love of Christ and the Church, happy to walk towards the heavenly city.

— finally, love truth by dedicating yourselves precisely to the work of your perfection. The contemplative dimension is the principal one of your Order, in function then of the active life, in teaching and in charity. St Augustine teaches that the apostle must first of all be "one who prays", then a preacher (*De Doctrina Christiana, IV, 15, 32*). In this regard it is necessary to underline the need for austerity of life, a certain seriousness, sense of discipline, and a holy courage whether in making demands in the name of Christ and the Church, or in obeying. An Augustinian must particularly remember that he is an instrument and collaborator of the grace of God. It seems that St Augustine in all his works, inexhaustible mines for meditation, wants to tell us continually that though there is always need for a greater understanding, there is even more a need for greater love. "The more you love, the more will you ascend" (En. in *Ps 21, 5*). Therefore, to love the truth signifies in the concrete to love sanctity. "When you begin to feel disturbed in yourself," he admonishes us, "waken Christ who sleeps: rouse up your faith and know that he does not abandon you" (En. in *Ps. 90, 11*).

Friends! To bring to a close this pleasant encounter, I want to follow up again the teaching of the holy Doctor and instil in you a tender and profound love for Mary, the most holy. In his work that treated of virginity he wrote: *"Maria cooperata est caritate ut fideles in Ecclesia nascerentur, quae illius capitis membra sunt; corpore vero ipsius capitis mater" (De sancta virginitate, 6)*. Mary cooperated with her love to give us supernatural love. May she enlighten you and inspire you in these days of intense work; may she above all protect and comfort the Augustinian Order in its journey towards him who is the "end of our desires", whom, on the "sabbath with no evening", we shall see without end, we shall love without boredom, we shall praise without growing tired. "See what will be at the end without end. And what other end is ours if not that of the coming of the kingdom of God which has no end" (cf. *City of God, XXII, 30*).

May you be accompanied by the Apostolic Blessing which I now impart from my heart to you and to all the Brethern of the Order.

O.R. 799. 5 September 1983

Address to the General Congregation of the Jesuits
2 September 1983

My dear brothers, I am happy to find myself in your midst, as you have wished, to concelebrate the Eucharistic Sacrifice and in this way to beg for an outpouring of the Holy Spirit's gifts on the General Congregation that you are opening.

On this occasion, the words of Paul to the Ephesians, that you heard in the first reading, take on a prophetic meaning. And it is with these same words that I address myself to you with heartfelt emotion. Just as the Apostle did, so I too exhort you to conduct yourselves in a manner worthy of the vocation you have received, to preserve attentively the unity of spirit by the peace that binds you together.

In greeting you I greet all Jesuits of the world, engaged on every frontier in the life of the Church: indeed this is a great family, called by a special vocation to serve the Name of Christ, with a total availability for all the concerns of his Kingdom. At this moment, I feel it is present right here, united by the same ideals, by the same calling of the Spirit, that Christ spills out from his breast upon you, as on all the Church: From his breast shall flow fountains of living water.

In this spirit of an outpouring of hearts, in an attentiveness to the divine activity, today the General Congregation begins. It is an official action in the life of your religious family, an important moment to live in unity of spirit. This is a unity of ecclesial spirit because you are rooted vitally in the Church, One, Holy, Catholic and Apostolic, that you have pledged yourselves to serve with total fidelity, with an awareness that it is a universal sacrament of salvation through the riches of the truth and divine life that it imparts to mankind. A unity of the Ignatian spirit, because that special charism, one that makes the Society a privileged instrument of the Church at all levels, is the all-embracing and distinctive element that the founder himself wanted for your activity and your mission.

And this unity is born out of one faith, one baptism, one Christian and religious vocation, that is its logical and austere flowering. It is nourished by the trinitarian, theological reality, that is, by the life of the one Father, the one Lord, the one Spirit. And today, we are experiencing that in a special way: One body, one Spirit, just as you were all called into one and the same hope when you were called.

Here you have the theological and spiritual roots of today's events. For having offered me the consolation of experiencing them together with you I give you my heartfelt thanks, my very dear brethren.

This General Congregation takes on, then, a special importance by reason of its twofold objective. In the first place, it must provide a successor to the revered Father Arrupe, whom I am delighted to greet here in person and to express to him the gratitude of all for having continued to sustain the Society by his example, by his prayer and by his sufferings.

Your Congregation has, in addition, the task of setting the orientations, of spelling out the guidelines in the years immediately ahead so that there may be an ever better realisation, in the special circumstances of the present moment, of the ideal of the Society as it is set forth in the Formula of your Institute: "To serve as a soldier of God beneath the banner of the Cross... and to serve the Lord alone and the Church, his spouse, under the Roman Pontiff, the Vicar of Christ on earth" *(Apostolic Letter, Exposcit Debitum, 21 July 1550).*

Such a twofold task is certainly weighty; and it is important that you should keep in mind the orientations and recommendations that my revered predecessors, Paul VI and John Paul I, communicated to you on the occasion of your most recent Congregations, and that I myself expressed to you on the occasion of the meeting of your Provincials in February of last year. They are orientations and recommendations that retain their full weight and that you should have in mind in the work of the Congregation in order to guarantee the happy outcome on which the vitality and development of your Institute depends. Hence the need to call on the Holy Spirit: "Come, Holy Spirit, and fill the hearts of your faithful".

Your General Congregation is an event that is destined also to have some important repercussions in the life of the Church. This is why I take an active interest in it. The Society of Jesus is still the most numerous religious Order; it is spread out to every part of the world; it is engaged, for the glory of God and the sanctification of men and women, even in the most difficult spheres and in key ministries that are of great benefit to the service of the Church. On that account, very many keep their eyes on you, whether they be priests or lay persons, men religious or women religious; and what you do often has some reverberations that you do not suspect.

Thus my predecessors have many times underlined the vast influence that the Society's actions exercise in the Church. In particular, Paul VI, of revered memory, did not hesitate to state that "a very special bond links your Society to the Catholic Church; your fortune, in a certain measure, has an impact on the fortune of the entire Catholic family" *(21 April 1969; cf. AAS, 61 (1969), p. 317).* If this responsibility weighs on all members of the Society of Jesus, it weighs today in a special fashion on you who have been chosen as members of this General Congregation. This is why the Pope in this moment is especially close to you in prayer with his best wishes and his fatherly encouragement. And he repeats this with the words of the Letter to the Ephesians: "I implore you therefore to lead a life worthy of your vocation. Bear with one another charitably, in complete selflessness, gentleness and patience. Do all you can to preserve the unity of the Spirit by the peace that binds you together" (Ep 4:1-3).

To this end, I am certain that you will keep well in mind the providential nature and the specific purpose of the Society. As I have said, it is engaged in a wide range of difficult ministries. In the course of the meeting with the Provincials in February of last year, I had rapidly sketched out a picture of the activities that you have been called to exercise: involvement in the renewal of Christian life, in the spread of authentic Catholic doctrine, in the education of young people, in the formation of the clergy, in deepening of research in the sacred sciences and in general even of secular culture, especially in the literary and scientific fields, in missionary evangelisation.

For this array of such differing apostolic tasks, in forms that are both traditional as well as new, in response to the needs of the times that have been underlined by the Second Vatican Council, I address once again to you my words of encouragement, with full confidence, just as you were all called into one and the same hope when you were called.

The Pope counts on you, he expects so much of you.

On that account, the very special link that the Society maintains with the Pope, who is responsible for the unity of the Church in its entirety, assures to the Society itself an effectiveness and certainty when it expends itself, with full availability and complete fidelity, in the struggle on all these fronts of ecclesial action, today as in the days of its origin.

At that moment, your founder, desirous of dedicating himself totally to the service of Christ the Lord, at the same time as his first companions, under the mysterious guidance of Providence made his way to Rome, in the days of Pope Paul III, in order to place himself completely at his disposition and to accomplish the mission that the Pope would point out to him, and to do that in the place that he would determine; you know how Paul III accorded a very willing reception to this proposal, while seeing in it a special sign of divine action.

In this perspective, the fourth vow takes on a special meaning. It certainly does not tend to put a check on generosity, but only to assure a sphere of activity that is deeper and broader, in the certainty that the most inward and most secret motivation for this religious obedience, of this bond with the Pope, is that of being able to respond in the most incisive way and with a much greater dedication, "immediately, without delay, without any manner of excuse", to the needs of the Church, in apostolic fields both old and new.

While expressing to you my thankfulness for all that the Society has accomplished during more than four centuries of fruitful activity, I am sure that I can continue still in the future to rely on the Society for support in the exercise of my apostolic ministry and to count always on your faithful collaboration for the good of the entire people of God.

You know that the Pope is with you and prays for you so that, in constant fidelity to the voice of the Spirit, the Society of Jesus may continue to draw from God's grace the strength and the drive to carry on its vast and varied apostolate.

The Church has always considered your Society as a group of religious, prepared spiritually and doctrinally, who are ready to do what is asked of them in the context of the Church's universal mission of evangelisation.

The Supreme Pontiffs throughout the centuries have not failed to entrust these missions to you, looking at the most urgent needs of the Church and trusting in your generous availability. To limit myself to the most recent times, I wish to recall the mission that my venerable predecessor Paul VI committed to you on 7 May 1965, "to resist atheism vigorously with united forces", a mission which I urgently re-propose to you, for as long as this "tremendous danger that hangs over humanity" continues *(AAS, 57, 1965 p. 514)*.

In November 1966, after the Second Vatican Council which had just ended, the same Pope asked you to cooperate in that deep renewal which the Church is facing in this secularised world. And I myself, in the above-mentioned discourse to your Provincials, confirmed that "the Church today expects the Society to contribute effectively to the implementation of the Second Vatican Council, just as, at the time of Saint Ignatius and also afterwards, it strove with every means to make known and to apply the Council of Trent and to help in a special way the Roman Pontiffs in the exercise of their supreme magisterium". To this end I invited you, and today I renew this invitation, to adapt to the different spiritual necessities of the present day "the various forms of the traditional apostolate that even today retain all of their value" and to pay ever greater attention to "the initiatives which the Second Vatican Council especially encouraged", like ecumenism, the deeper study of the relations with non-Christian religions, and the dialogue of the Church with cultures. In this regard, I am acquainted with and approve your commitment to inculturation, so important for evangelisation, provided that it is joined to an equal commitment to preserving Catholic doctrine pure and intact.

Speaking of your apostolate I did not fail at that time to call to your attention the necessity that is found within the evangelising action of the Church to promote the justice connected with world peace, which is an aspiration of all peoples. But this action must be exercised in conformity with your vocation as religious and priests, without confusing the tasks proper to priests with those that are proper to lay people, and without giving in to the "temptation to reduce the mission of the Church to the dimensions of a simply temporal project... (to reduce) the salvation of which she is the messenger... to material well-being" *(Evangelii Nuntiandi, 32)*. This is the magnificent field of an apostolate open before you, to work with renewed zeal, faithful to the mandate received from the Pope, under the leadership of the new Superior General, and in close collaboration among yourselves.

The generous realisation of this ideal will increase ever more your apostolic thrust; it will help you to overcome the difficulties that in the mysterious plan of Providence are usually connected with the works of the Lord; and it will raise up numerous vocations of generous young men who, listening to the voice of the Holy Spirit, desire also today to consecrate their own lives for an ideal which deserves to be lived and thus to cooperate actively in the divine work of the redemption of the world.

The redemption of the world! Indeed, it is here that your General Congregation is being held by coincidence with the extraordinary Holy Year during which the Church tries to live more intensively the mystery of Redemption. Your vocation consists precisely in seeking to follow Christ, Redeemer of the world, by being his collaborators in the redemption of the entire world. Consequently you should excel in the service of the divine King, as stated in the offering that concludes the Contemplation of the Kingdom of Christ in the Spiritual Exercises of St Ignatius.

My very dear brothers! May this be, for you, the special fruit of the Jubilee Year: a renewed drive in your vocation, that invites you above all to a personal conversion: "Open wide the doors to the Redeemer", to allow penetration by the love of Christ and by his Spirit, bringing to pass what is said in the petition that St Ignatius recommends in the second week of the Exercises: "to know the Lord intimately in order to love him and to follow him ever more closely". Intimate knowledge, strong love and the closer following of the Lord are the soul of your vocation. In other words, you ought to be a Society of contemplatives in action who strive in every way to see, to know and to experience Christ, to love him and to make him loved, to serve him in every way and in all things and to follow him even up to the Cross.

On the other hand, one does not know the Lord — and you who are masters of the spiritual life teach that to others — without at the same time placing oneself with total docility and abandonment under the influence of the Holy Spirit whom Christ has poured out over humanity, as a majestic and ever flowing river. As we have heard in the Gospel of St John, Christ calls us to come to him and drink: "If anyone thirst, let him come to me and drink". This thirst should impel us to enter into intimate contact with Christ to contemplate with him the Heavenly Father and thereby to draw strength, light, perseverance, fidelity in exterior action.

In order to reach this state of contemplation, St Ignatius demands of you that you be men of prayer, in order to be teachers of prayer; at the same time he expects you to be men of mortification, in order to be visible signs of Gospel values. The austerity of a simple and poor life should be a sign that Christ is your sole treasure. The renunciation, with joyful fidelity, of ties of family affection should be a further sign of your universal love which opens your hearts in purity of spirit to Christ and to the brethren. Obedience on the grounds of faith should be a sign of your close imitation of Christ who was obedient even to death on the Cross. Unity of spirits in a fraternal community life that overcomes any possible differences or conflicts should be an example in the Church, in this year when we celebrate not only the Jubilee of Redemption, but also the Synod of Reconciliation.

I also ask you that the young men who are recruited to your Society be formed from the novitiate on in this renewed spirit of commitment to exemplary religious life.

That, my dear brothers, is what the events of today suggest to us for common reflection. I hope that in this General Congregation, which is taking place in the Jubilee Year of Redemption, you may truly follow the voice of the Holy Spirit that calls you to "do all you can to preserve the unity of the Spirit by the peace that binds you together" (Ep 4:3).

Together with this fidelity may generosity in the service of Christ the Lord and of the Church his spouse, in union with his Vicar on earth, be the characteristic of every true Jesuit. May it be the impetus to the works of the General Congregation which starts today. May it be the commitment of the government of the new General you are about to elect. All this the Church expects from you. The same expectation is shared by the Pope who participates in this solemn ritual, who unites himself with you in fervent prayer and who blesses you by imploring with you:

"Come, Holy Spirit, fill the hearts of your faithful, and enkindle in them the fire of your love".

O.R. 800. 12 September 1983

Address to the General Chapter Members of the Dominicans 5 September 1983

Dear Friars Preachers, members of the General Chapter, on two occasions, according to the primitive chronicle of the Order, Brother Dominic set out from Toulouse, where, with a handful of brothers, he made the Sacred Preaching a reality, having begun amid sacrifice and solitude in Prouille, and undertook the difficult and perilous crossing of the Alps in order to reach the Eternal City. He came first in 1215, to request of Pope Innocent III that his little family "could be called, and in reality be, an Order of Preachers" *(Legenda Petri Ferrandi, c. 27).* He was back in December 1216, in order to receive from Pope Honorius III, newly elected to the Chair of Peter, the Bull of approval of the Order for which he had yearned so much. We know with what veneration and paternal affection he was received by the Popes on each of these two occasions.

I recall these two visits by Dominic de Guzman to the Pope for I, too, wish to associate myself with my two distant and illustrious predecessors in the joy and affection with which I receive you today....

To you all, I want once more to make clear the attachment which, for many reasons, I have to your Order. Let me even say that, among you, I feel as part of the family. I am sure that the Church, and he who is its universal Pastor, can count on your collaboration (as always before) in the arduous task of the evangelisation of the world.

Indeed, it was with this task in mind that your Order was founded by St Dominic. For this, too, your Order was approved and sent out by the Church. Your mission still remains the same. My predecessor, Pope Honorius III, writing to St Dominic on 18 January 1221, recognised that his mission was inspired by "him who allows his Church to beget ever new offspring". This mission is "to dedicate oneself to the preaching of the word of God, proclaiming worldwide the name of our Lord, Jesus Christ" (cf. *MOPH XXV, p. 144*).

"In fact, the Order of Friars Preachers founded by St Dominic 'has from the very beginning, as is known, been specially instituted for preaching and for the salvation of souls'. Which is why our friars, following the mandate of the founder, 'like men desirous of seeking their own salvation and that of others, should behave honestly and religiously, as Gospel men, in the footsteps of their Saviour, speaking either with God or about God among each other and to their neighbour" (*Constitutio fundamentalis par. II*).

"Now, in order to be perfect in the love of God and neighbour by means of this *sequela Christi*, we, bound to our Order by religious profession, consecrate ourselves totally to God and we dedicate ourselves to the Church in a new way, wholly devoted to the preaching of the word of God in its entirety" (*Constitutio fundamentalis par. II*). To the extent that the Order will be faithful to such needs in the future as it has been in the past, it will be an intimate partner in the universal Church's activity and will be specially close to the Bishop of Rome.

In order to carry out its mission, your Order must hold firm to a number of guiding ideas which arise from the fundamental text I have read to you. These are principles of faith, developed in theology by the great Doctors, among whom St Thomas Aquinas shines with particular brilliance. The Church continues to suggest that these principles are foundation-stones of Christian wisdom and hinges of the apostolate. It is your role as Capitular Fathers to appreciate the dynamism of these principles in order then to translate this dynamism into regulations or orientations for the spiritual life and work of the Order.

The first of these principles is that which affirms the absolute primacy of God in the intelligence, in the heart, in the life of man. You know well how St Dominic responded to this requirement of faith in his religious life: "He spoke only with God or of God".

You also know how, on the level of doctrine, St Thomas Aquinas, beginning with the Sacred Scriptures and the Fathers of the Church, envisaged this primacy of God and how he supported it with the force and consistency of his metaphysical and theological thought, using the analogy of being which permits the recognition of the worth of the creature, but as dependent on the creative love of God.

And then, on the level of spirituality, St Thomas is completely of the school of his Father, Dominic, when he defines the religious as "those who place themselves totally at the service of God, as if offering a holocaust to God" *(Summa, II, II, 186, art. 1 and art. 7)*. If one does not accept this subordination, if one exalts the greatness of man to the detriment of the primacy of God, one arrives at the failure of the ideologies that postulate the self-sufficiency of man and give rise to the proliferation of errors of which the modern world bears the burden and of which it does not succeed in breaking the cultural and psychological yoke. The foundations of moral and social life are shaken whereas, at the religious level, a kind of insensitivity or indifference is frequently manifested in regard to God. One could even speak of the incapacity to face this "struggle with God", which, as the story of Jacob teaches us, expresses in the highest degree the tension of man called to go forward towards a goal that transcends history, where he must live, work, confront trials, and overcome the challenges of time which passes and of death which follows. One could speak of an alienation of man from himself: he loses his dignity and capacity for hope, even when the ideologies would promise him liberation.

You Dominicans have the mission of proclaiming that our God is alive, that he is the God of life and that in him exists the root of the dignity and the hope of man who is called to life.

You do it as religious by the witness of your lives "totally consecrated as a holocaust to God". You do it as masters and preachers if your theology and your catechesis, like the *kerygma* of the apostles, produces a shock, a break in the closed system where man is on the way to losing himself at the frontier of annihilation. Your proclamation must be addressed to man just as he is constituted by culture, social life, his personality and his conscience, and it must bring him the liberating power of God.

Every other study and every other task, in the different domains of the human sciences, economics, social action, etc., are justified if, for you, as religious called to witness and to preach the kingdom of God, it finds its finality and its measure in the higher apostolic goal — taken in its totality — of the Church and of your Order.

Your Constitutions give priority to the ministry of the word in all its oral and written forms, and the link between the ministry of the word and that of the sacraments is its crowning.

And from this priority also comes the missionary character of your Order.

In this sense, your Constitutions contain strong exhortations: "In imitation of St Dominic, who was full of solicitude for the salvation of each individual and all peoples, may the brothers know that they are sent to all people, believers and non-believers, and especially to the poor..., to evangelise and establish the Church among non-believing peoples and to instruct and strengthen the faith of the Christian people *(L.I. c.IV, art. 1, no. 98)*.

The Church today cannot but confirm these laws of yours, bless such projects and encourage your universal missionary commitment, because she knows well that, everywhere, in every place as in each human heart, there is need of God!

To this need, this yearning for God, he has responded throughout history. Through faith we have come to know the work of salvation, which finds its central point, its axis and its fullness in Jesus Christ. And we never slacken in our proclamation of the fact that salvation comes to us through Christ, a proclamation in accordance with the festive declaration by Peter and the other Apostles: "There is no other name under heaven given to men by which we must be saved" *(Acts 4:12)*.

This was precisely St Dominic's proclamation, in the footsteps of the Apostles. As St Catherine of Siena said, Dominic received the "ministry of the word" *(Dialogue, 158)*. In responding to this task, he returned passionate love to the Crucified One. This is marvellously portrayed in Fra Angelico's famous painting: it shows the saint, pressing his hands on the Cross, as he embraces, in a look, the form of Christ, so that drops of the Saviour's blood run down over him, too. Basing himself on the foundation of the Gospel, St Dominic in his preaching insistently proclaimed Jesus Christ.

My thoughts turn today to the innumerable brothers, known or not, who during the past 760 years, and even now, dedicate themselves to biblical studies, patristics, systematic theology, either as teachers and preachers, as editors and people otherwise involved in the media, as promoters of the Rosary and as missionaries, in pastoral work and in particular offices of the Holy See.

All of these have but one aim: with all their strength and with generous heart to do their duty in the service of salvation in today's world.

The Successor of Peter expresses to the Order of St Dominic the joyful gratitude of the Church for all it has done until now. And he encourages you today (your General Chapter is, after all, taking place halfway through the 1983 Holy Year) to open up new possibilities of study and of preaching Christ Crucified for your brothers, in the tradition of your forefathers.

That which has been taught by the Second Vatican Council on ecclesiastical studies, combined with the indications and guiding principles of my predecessor, Paul VI, on evangelisation in the Apostolic Letter *Evangelii Nuntiandi,* and also my own indications in the Encyclical Letter *Redemptor Hominis* and in the Apostolic Letter *Catechesi Tradendae* illustrate a steady plan of work which I earnestly pray your Order to make its own, so that you may be fellow workers in the vanguard of the Church's teaching office and also be prepared to unfold before the world the Kingship of Christ, who died for us and was raised.

We come to the third principle that justifies the existence of a religious Order and orients its activity: its vital relationship with the Church. As is indicated in the Code of Canon Law and your own Constitutions, there is a demand for catholicity, unity and apostolicity if one wishes to be the Church and work on a universal level; one has to make ever more real and visible the fourth mark of the Church, holiness. The link with the Pope is the best guarantee of this ecclesial character; it legitimates the action of an Order extended throughout the world, guarantees its freedom, and keeps intact its conformity with the norms that regulate the activity of the religious within the local Churches.

Thus I am sure that your Order will never be without its traditional and full obedience to the Successor of Peter, its sincere respect for the magisterium and that complete fidelity to the Holy See that has always been a characteristic note of your religious family.

My desire for your Order (whose motto is Truth) is that you may form numerous sons ready to serve the Church, to work in truth and in obedience, always remembering this beautiful text from your own Constitutions:

"From the moment in which by obedience we unite ourselves to Christ and the Church, every effort and all mortification that we undertake to put this into practice is like a continuation of the self-offering of Christ and acquires a value of sacrifice, as much for us personally as for the Church: in the consummation of this sacrifice is realised all the work of creation" (*L.I., art II, no. 11*).

The vital relationship between the Order and the Church has another essentially theological dimension that flows from its finality and its nature, which are recognised by the Holy See.

As one reads in your Fundamental Constitution, you are a "clerical Order" in the Church, an Order that has a "priestly and prophetic function" *(Nos V, VI).*

Your history is proof that there is no opposition between the priestly and the prophetic vocations: rather, both are found together to give to the Order its identity and integrity, just as St Dominic desired. It is also true that, owing to the different cultural and religious conditions of peoples and even more, perhaps, to personal attitudes and charisms, one or the other of these functions in particular stands out. Your history, in any case, your rule also, your doctrine conclude that in teaching, in preaching, in the exercise of the pastoral ministry, the prophetic charism within your Order has received the particular seal of theology, understood in the full sense by St Thomas as a wisdom that bases thought and action on contemplation: this stimulates action, inspires it and rules it *(Summa theologiae I, q.6, art. 6; II, q. 45, art. 3)*. Following St Dominic, St Thomas himself was not only the teacher but also the exemplar of this life of wisdom, towards which it has always been possible for your Order to look as into a mirror of its own "prophetic function", which consists in "proclaiming everywhere the Gospel of Jesus Christ by word and example", according to the text of your own Fundamental Constitution.

On this day I should like to say to you, Capitular Fathers, and to all your brethren in religion: be faithful to this mission of theology and of wisdom in your Order, no matter in what form you are called to exercise it — whether specialised or popular, academic or pastoral, scientific or catechetical. But certainly a place of privilege in the first line of your work (be this work scientific or apostolic) must be accorded to a deepening of the theological and philosophical work of St Thomas Aquinas. More so for you than for other Orders, it is necessary to cultivate familiarity with the thought and the writings of this incomparable master and to renew and enrich his teaching.

Your theological function assures to the Order that vital relationship with the ecclesial community, from which emerges a variety and richness of chrisms which are ordained towards unity by the Spirit, with a view to the building up of the Body of Christ.

Lastly, dear Father Capitulars, and still following a path indicated by your Constitutions, I wish to remind you that the secret of a profitable carrying out of your mission in the Church and in the world, the secret, even, of your numerical and qualitative recovery after the crisis which did not spare even your Order in recent years, consists in fidelity to "the apostolic life in the full sense of the word, in which preaching and teaching should gush forth from the abundance of contemplation" *(Fundamental Constitution, IV)*.

It is the fourth principle (but in order of importance the first) on which you will be able to build a present and a future for the Order worthy of its past. It is a principle which becomes concrete in matters you are familiar with and which need only be mentioned here briefly for your reflection and, if deemed necessary, for the resolutions of your Chapter. These are the spirit of prayer, the interior life, zeal, correctness and fidelity in the celebration of the liturgy and, in general the regular observance of common life, the practice and spirit of the vows and penitence.

Pope Honorius III summed all this up in his letter to St Dominic and his first companions when he said that God had "inspired in them the loving desire to embrace poverty and to put regular life into practice" for the sake of the reform of the world and the preaching of the faith *(Letter of 18 January 1221, in MOPH XXV, p. 144; cf. Fundamental Constitution, I).*

This divine inspiration pointed out the path that must remain yours today. That inspiration has not been modified in any essential way and must not be endangered by structural or functional adaptations or innovations which you have introduced and still do introduce into the organisation of the Order in loyalty and in harmony with the Church's directives. Many trial experiments are possible, as long as one does not abandon the correct road. It may even be that, realistically weighing up what has already been tried by way of experiment, it appears to Chapter that, in relation to some points, a process of re-thinking is necessary.

In particular, allow me to suggest that you pay renewed attention to the qualities of conventual life: silence (traditionally seen among you as the "father of the preachers"), the habit ("as a distinctive sign of your consecration" L.I., c.1. art. V. no. 51), the correct importance of cloister, laid down by your Constitutions "so that... the friars may better attend to contemplation and study, so that the intimacy of the family may grow and so that the temper of your religious life and your fidelity to it may be expressed" *(ibid., no. 41).* Strengthened by community life, the friars will be enabled to carry out their tasks on the roadways of the world, without hiding their identity, but giving witness to the values of a religious life freely chosen for the sake of the kingdom of God.

Dear Capitular Fathers, how many more things there are which I should wish to share with you with all my heart and as an expression of my affection and appreciation of your Order! May what I say be an encouragement to walk in the steps of your confreres who have marked the history of the Order, indeed one might say, of the Church, with their lives.

Since I must finish, I wish to do so by repeating with you a few sentences from the "Prayer to Blessed Dominic" which was written by his successor Master Jordan and with which you must be quite familiar. I repeat this prayer here as if I were with you before the tomb of your founder in San Domenico at Bologna, where I have in fact often been.

"You, once you had begun the path of perfection, left all, in order to follow, naked, the naked Christ, preferring to store up treasures in heaven. But you renounced your own self with even greater strength, manfully carrying your cross, and you dedicated yourself to following in the footsteps of our only true guide, the Redeemer.

"You, inflamed by divine zeal and supernatural ardour, in the overflowing of your charity and with an immense outpouring of generosity, gave yourself totally to perpetual poverty, to the apostolic life and to the preaching of the Gospel. And to further this great work, and not without divine inspiration, you founded the Order of Friars Preachers...

"You, who so zealously sought the salvation of the human race, come to the aid of the clergy and of the Christian people ..."

"Be for us truly a *'dominicanus'*, an attentive custodian of the Lord's flock..." (cf. ed. *Scheben, ASOP XVIII (1929) pp. 564-568*).

Dear Friars Preachers, I commit you and your entire Order to the care of your Holy Father Dominic, and I refer to the entire Dominican family, including, as well as the friars, the cloistered nuns, the sisters of active life, the secular institutes associated with the Order and the numerous lay people and priests who form part of the fraternities.

And with all my heart I impart to you my Blessing, calling down upon you the divine assistance in the work of the Chapter and even more abundant graces for the life of the Order which is so dear to you and to me.

O.R. 800.   12 September 1983

Homily to Priests and Religious at Mariazell
13 September 1983

.....Today's Gospel culminates with the verse: "Blessed is she who has faith that the Lord's promise would be fulfilled" *(Lk 1:45)*. With these words the Evangelist takes us back from the house of Elizabeth to the room at Nazareth, from the dialogue of the two women to the words of God. It is God who opens the dialogue with the Holy Virgin, with mankind. God is always the first to speak. "In the beginning was the Word" *(Jn 1:1)*. Therefore, dear priests and religious, the first thing we must do in our spiritual life is listen. First we must listen to the word of God, only then can we respond; first we must listen, only then can we obey. Silence and recollection, reading and contemplation are indispensable elements of our vocation and service as those who listen to and proclaim the Word made Flesh. Herein Mary is our example and our help. The Gospels paint Mary as the one who remains silent, who listens in silence. Her silence is the womb of the Word. She keeps everything in her heart and allows it to ripen. As in the Annunciation, listening to God quite naturally turns into a dialogue with God, in which we may talk to him and he listens to us. Therefore, talk to God, tell him what troubles you! Thank him joyously for the mercy he has shown you and for what he gives to others, through you, every day. Lay before him your concern for the people entrusted to you, children and youths, husbands and wives, the aged and the sick! Lay before him the difficulties and failures you experience in your ministry, lay before him your anxiety and suffering! Dear priests and members of religious orders, prayer is an indispensable part of our calling. It is so essential that many other — seemingly more urgent — things may or even must come second to it. Even if your daily lives in the service of man require more work from you than you seem to be able to do, there still must be enough time for silent contemplation and prayer. Prayer and work must never be put asunder. If we go before God every day to reflect on our work and commend it to him, work itself will finally turn into prayer.

Learn how to pray! Draw above all on the wealth of the breviary and the Eucharist, which should accompany your daily work more than anything else. In the school of our Lord, learn to pray in such a way that you yourselves become masters of prayer and can teach those entrusted to your care how to pray. By teaching people how to pray you will make their — often inarticulate — faith speak again. Through prayer you will lead them back to God and will again give purpose and meaning to their lives.

As I look at you, dear candidates for Holy Orders, dear novices, I am filled with hope. Your seminaries and novitiates should be places of recollection, of prayer, of preparation for an intimate relationship with God. I know how much you want to pray in the right way, and I know that you are looking for new ways to have your lives even more deeply imbued with prayer. Together with you, we all wish to re-learn how to pray. Let us be carried away by the Psalmist of the Old Testament and his prayer: "One thing have I desired of the Lord, that will I seek after: that I may dwell in the house of the Lord all the days of my life, to behold the beauty of the Lord and to contemplate his temple" *(Ps 27:4).*

Dear brothers and sisters! The word of God leads us to silence, to our inner selves, to the meeting with him, but it does not separate us from one another. The word of God does not isolate, but unites. In the silence of the dialogue with the Angel, Mary learns of Elizabeth's maternity. From the silence of this dialogue she sets out and goes straight to her in the hill country of Judea. Mary knows what God has done for Elizabeth and she tells her what God has done for herself. To that hour we owe precious prayers. "Blessed art thou among women and blessed is the fruit of thy womb". This is Elizabeth's reply to Mary's greeting, and our daily Magnificat is Mary's reply to Elizabeth. Let us remember from the Gospel of today's Mass: God not only calls us, but he helps those who receive his call to understand and accept each other in their different callings.

Jesus wants those he has called to be with him, not as isolated individuals, but as a community. All the people of God and all the individuals that receive his call are in communion with the Lord and with one another. As in the case of Mary and Elizabeth, this communion embraces both the life of faith and everyday life. This is particularly evident in the case of you religious. You, more than others, live by the example of the ancient Church, when "those who believed were of one heart and one soul" *(Acts 4:32).* The more you succeed in living together in your communities in true charity, the more convincingly will you bear witness to the credibility of the Christian message. In the words of the Council, "the unity of the brethren is a symbol of the coming of Christ and is a source of great apostolic power" *(Perfectae Caritatis, 15)...*

The celibacy which you priests and religious have chosen for the sake of the kingdom of heaven makes you freer for communion with Christ and for the service of mankind. Yet it also makes you freer for closer and deeper communion with each other. Do not let yourselves be tempted by anyone or anything to diminish or renounce this generous readiness to serve. Rather, bring it to full fruition for your lives and your service for the salvation of man.....

The stronger the community spirit in the lives of religious and priests, the more effective their service will be. The way in which they live in community will also determine whether or not more young people will dare to follow the calling to become a religious or a priest. Wherever convents are full of life, wherever pastoral ministers live together in brotherhood, wherever priests and laity are bound together in the unity of the Body of Christ — it is there that we also find the most vocations!

Dear brothers and sisters, it affords me deep joy and satisfaction to address these words to you in the presence of the holy image of the Blessed Mother of Mariazell. As the Mother of God and Mother of the Church, Mary is also above all the Mother of all those who continue the mission of her Son in history. In her calling, in her unconditional acceptance of the message of the Angel, and in her praise of God's forgiving mercy in the Magnificat, we recognise the mystery and the significance of our own calling. In faithful acceptance of her election and mission, the Word of God became a historical reality in her. In this way God's eternal plan was carried out, about which St Paul speaks in today's second reading: "For those whom he foreknew he also predestined to be conformed to the image of his Son, in order that he might be the first-born among many brethren" *(Rm 8:29)*. By her trusting obedience to the word of the Angel, the Virgin Mary was placed at the centre of God's plan of salvation. By her maternity, the Son of God became a brother to all of us, so that we can conform to his image in justice and glory. For St Paul also tells us today: "Those whom God called, he also justified; and those whom he justified he also glorified" *(ibid.)*. The raising of man all the way to his participation in the glory of the Most Holy Trinity takes place through Christ, the Son of God, who became the Son of Man through the faithful *fiat* of the Virgin Mary. Indeed, "blessed is she who believed", for behold, henceforth all generations will call her blessed.

Yes, dear brothers and sisters, we too will be blessed that we have believed, if like Mary, we set out from our own personal encounter with God to proclaim today to the inhabitants of the mountains and valleys of all countries and continents the marvels God has performed — in Mary's womb, in Christ, her Son, and in us, his brothers. For, as the Prophet Isaiah tells us in the first reading, "Darkness shall cover the earth and thick darkness the peoples, but the Lord will arise upon you, and his glory will be seen upon you" *(Is 60:2)*. Through the faith of the Blessed Virgin, God's light began to shine and illuminate the new Jerusalem. It is the shining of the glory of the Most High, of that light which in the beginning illuminates every man, but which seeks to shine its full radiant splendour to everyone in Jesus Christ. This is why we are commissioned to proclaim: "Arise, shine; for your light has come, and the glory of the Lord has risen upon you" *(Is 60:1)*.

Whoever has a spiritual vocation is called to this mission of the Church in a special way. Christ called his followers to himself, and he sent them out among the people, far from his reassuring presence (cf. *Mk 3:14)*. "Go into all the world and proclaim the Gospel to the whole creation" *(Mk 16:15)*. In this connection I should particularly like to mention all of your priests, brothers and sisters in the missions, who, together with the Church's development aid volunteers proclaim the Good News throughout the world in word and in social action. Whoever you are and wherever you work, your spiritual task is always the same, i.e., to shine with the "radiant light from above" on all who "sit in darkness and shadow of death" (cf. *Benedictus*). This is your mission, whether you are priests in a city parish or have charge of a small rural community, whether you are religious working in a school or caring for the sick and the poor, or whether you are condemned by sickness or old age to a life of seeming inactivity.

Indeed, it is you sick and and elderly priests and religious to whom I feel particularly attached in this hour — I shall even have the opportunity afterwards to greet some of you personally. The entire Church throughout the world commends itself to your concern and your prayer. For your mission there are no longer any boundaries of space. Your language is prayer and suffering, accepted always with renewed courage. To you also the Lord entrusts ever new missions. Your special service — of prayer and suffering — is an irreplaceable part of the mission of the Church. At the end of his life the Lord, too, no longer preached. Rather, he took up his cross and carried it and endured it, until finally everything was finished.

Dear brothers and sisters who are already priests and religious, and all of you who are preparing yourselves for this spiritual vocation! The Lord has chosen you so that you may be with him in prayer and recollection; so that you may live out your calling in community, and so that you carry his salvation to the poeple. At the end of the celebration of the Eucharist, I shall ask the Blessed Mother of Mariazell for her motherly protection and support for this, your mission.

To summarise what I would like you to take with you from our common pilgrimage, what Mary herself would like to give you — and me — from this shrine of hers, to accompany us on our way, I have chosen a phrase that she herself often prayed in her life, a verse from today's responsorial psalm...: "Hope in the Lord, be strong! Have steadfast courage and hope in the Lord!" Amen.

O.R. 803. 3 October 1983

Address to a Group of U.S. Bishops
19 September 1983

Dear brothers in our Lord Jesus Christ, I have recently spoken to other groups of American bishops about two important aspects of the great mystery of the Church: the episcopate and the priesthood. I would now like to reflect with you on yet another special gift of God to his Church, and this gift is the religious life.

So much is religious life a part of the Church, so intimately does it touch her constitution and her holiness, that it must form an integral part of the pastoral solicitude of the Pope and the bishops, who have a unique responsibility for the entire life of the Church and are meant to be signs of her holiness. In speaking about religious life we are speaking about an ecclesial reality which concerns the bishops by reason of their office.

At every moment, but especially during the Holy Year of the Redemption, the Church offers the call to conversion to all her members, particularly to religious. This call to conversion goes out to religious so that they may acquire the full benefits of the Redemption and be ever more faithful witnesses of that Redemption; so that they may be ever more authentic channels of the Redemption for the people of God through their own spiritual vitality which, in the Communion of Saints, is a supernaturally effective contact with the Redemption; and so that through conversion they may live more faithfully the unity of the Church, which is itself the effect of the Redemption and a participation in it.

For this reason I wrote to all the bishops asking for their special pastoral service to the religious of the United States in the context of the Holy Year of the Redemption. In my letter I stated: "It is my earnest hope that the Holy Year of the Redemption will truly be for religious life a year of fruitful renewal in Christ's love. If all the faithful have a right — as they do — to the treasures of grace that a call to renewal in love offers, then the religious have a special title to that right".

The whole thrust of my initiative was formulated as an invitation, a call to be extended to the religious, to open wide the doors of their hearts to the Redeemer. In this regard I wrote: "I ask you to invite all the religious throughout your land, in my name, and in your own name as bishops, in the name of the Church and in the name of Jesus, to seize this opportunity of the Holy Year to walk in newness of life, in solidarity with all the pastors and faithful, along the path necessary for us all — the way of penance and conversion".

This pastoral endeavour is of such importance that it could be fulfilled only by a full collegial commitment on the part of all the bishops of the United States. At that time I promised you my fraternal and prayerful support. I also named a Commission headed by Archbishop John Quinn whose task it would be to assist you in the exercise of collegiality and to facilitate your pastoral work of "helping the religious of your country whose institutes are engaged in apostolic works to live their ecclesial vocation to the full". I am deeply grateful to the Commission for the generosity and zeal with which they are striving to formulate a suitable programme that will effectively assist the body of bishops who have the main responsibility in this matter. As guidelines for both the Commission and yourselves in this important work, I approved a summary of the salient points of the Church's teaching on religious life prepared by the Sacred Congregation for Religious and for Secular Institutes.

Since then I have also had the opportunity, as I had hoped, to speak personally with so many bishops about religious life, hearing their viewpoints and learning about their own devoted pastoral service to religious. I am deeply grateful to our Lord Jesus Christ that this initiative has been so zealously undertaken by the Commission and by individual bishops, and that it is seen for what it is, an application — an extremely important application — of the principle of collegiality, a principle so forcefully enunciated by the Second Vatican Council. In proposing this initiative to your pastoral zeal, my first intention has been to affirm collegial responsibility for the state of religious life, which is intimately linked to the mystery of the Church and to the mystery of the episcopate. Religious need the support and assistance of the bishops in their lives of consecrated witness to the holiness of Christ and to the primacy of God. Your collegial collaboration is not only a means of giving general support to religious and of assisting them in solving particular problems that inevitably touch their lives; it also signifies an authentic and vital relationship between the episcopate and the religious.

The collegial service that you, as bishops, are asked to render to religious in the precise area of episcopal competence is, above all, to proclaim a call to holiness, a call to renewal and a call to penance and conversion. In other words, in the name of the Redeemer to extend the call of the Holy Year, asking for the greatest possible response of love. In my letter to you I mentioned that "this call is linked in a particular way with the life and mission of religious... it affects them in a special way; it makes special demands on their love, reminding them how much they are loved by Christ and his Church".

This initiative of pastoral care for religious is one aspect of the great dialogue of salvation, which begins with an awareness of God's love, made visible in the Incarnation, and leads to the fullness of salvation effected by this love. The whole dialogue of salvation is directed to the full acceptance, through *metanoia*, of the person of Jesus Christ. In the case of the religious, as in the case of the faithful, the process is the same: in the very moment in which we bishops recognise our own need for conversion, the Lord asks us to go out to others — humble and repentant, yet courageous and without fear — to communicate with our brothers and sisters. Christ wants to appeal through us, to invite and call his people, especially his religious, to conversion. The aim of all dialogue is conversion of heart.

It is not my intention on this occasion to speak about all the essential elements of the Church's teaching on religious life, as described in my letter and in the document of the Sacred Congregation. I am convinced that you will continue to reflect on all of these points, which are taken from authentic sources, so as to be able to explain and promote them all. At this time I would like to emphasise only a few points intimately linked to the theme of conversion and holiness of life in the context of religious life and of the pastoral responsibility of the bishops, who are "entrusted with the duty of caring for religious charisms, all the more so because the very indivisibility of their pastoral ministry makes them responsible for perfecting the entire flock" (*Mutuae Relationes, 9,c*). Bishops must proclaim the nature of religious life as teachers of the faith and representatives of the Church that guarantees the charism of religious. This proclamation is both an instruction for the people of God and an encouragement for the religious.

In selecting certain aspects of religious life for special reflection, the notion of prayer stands out immediately. The new Code of Canon Law states that the first and principal duty of all religious is the contemplation of things divine and constant union with God in prayer (cf. *can. 663, par. 1*). The question of religious being united with God in prayer precedes the question of what activity they will perform. The idea of prayer is again underlined as it touches the apostolate. The Code insists that the apostolate of all religious consists primarily in the witness of their consecrated life, which they are bound to foster through prayer and penance (cf. *can. 673*).

All of this tells us something very profound about religious life. It speaks to us about the value of living for God alone, of witnessing to his Kingdom, and of being consecrated to Jesus Christ. Through the vows of chastity, poverty and obedience, religious consecrate themselves to God, personally ratifying and confirming all the commitments of their Baptism. But even more important is the divine action, the fact that God consecrates them to the glory of his Son; and he does this through the mediation of his Church, acting in the power of the Spirit.

All of this emphasises the esteem that we bishops must have for the religious and for the immense contribution that they have made to the Church in the United States. And yet this contribution is more a contribution of what they are than of what they have done and are doing. In speaking of religious, we must say that their greatest dignity consists in this: that they are persons individually called by God and consecrated by God through the mediation of his Church. The value of their activity is great, but the value of their being religious is greater still.

Hence one of the bishop's contributions is to remind the religious of their dignity and to proclaim their identity before the people of God. This enables the laity to understand more clearly the mystery of the Church, to which the religious offer so much.

The ecclesial dimension is absolutely essential for a proper understanding of religious life. The religious are who they are because the Church mediates their consecration and guarantees their charism to be religious. Although their primary apostolate is to witness, their other apostolates involve a multiplicity of works and activities performed for the Church and coordinated by the bishops (cf. *can. 860*).

Since the value of the consecration of religious and the supernatural efficacy of their apostolates depend on their being in union with the Church — the entirety of which has been entrusted to the bishops' pastoral care for governing (cf. *Acts 20:28*) — it follows that bishops perform a great service to the religious by helping them to maintain and deepen their union with the Church, and by assisting them to harmonise all their activities with the life of the Church. The fruitful living of the religious charism presupposes the faithful acceptance of the Church's magisterium, which in fact is an acceptance of the very reality and identity of the Episcopal College united with the Pope. The College of Bishops as the successor of the Apostolic College, continues to enjoy the guidance of the Holy Spirit; the words of Jesus apply still today: "He who hears you hears me, and he who rejects you rejects me, and he who rejects me rejects him who sent me" *(Lk 10:16)*.

Venerable and dear brothers, in the dialogue of salvation I would ask you to speak to the religious about their ecclesial identity and to explain to the whole people of God how the religious are who they are only because the Church is what she is in her sacramental reality. And I would ask you to emphasise the special feminine role of women religious: in the Church and personifying the Church as the Spouse of Christ, they are called to live for Christ, faithfully, exclusively and permanently, in the consciousness of being able to make visible the spousal aspect of the Church's love for Christ.

And may everyone realise that the greatest misunderstanding of the charism of religious, indeed the greatest offence to their dignity and their persons, would come from those who might try to situate their life or mission outside its ecclesial context. Religious are betrayed by anyone who would attempt to have them embrace teaching against the magisterium of the Church, who conceived them by her love and gave them birth in her liberating truth. The acceptance of the reality of the Church by religious and their vital union — through her and in her — with Christ is an essential condition for the vitality of their prayer, the effectiveness of their service to the poor, the validity of their social witness, the well-being of their community relationships, the measure of the success of their renewal and the guarantee of the authenticity of their poverty and simplicity of life. And only in total union with the Church does their chastity become the full and acceptable gift which will satisfy the craving of their hearts to give themselves to Christ and to receive from him, and to be fruitful in his love.

Dear brothers, through our collegial action, especially in the Holy Year of the Redemption, let us manifest our pastoral love in a special way to the religious of the United States. And let us lead the way in the sacrifice and love demanded by conversion. As bishops we must help ensure for this generation and for those to come that the magnificent contribution made by the religious of the United States to the mission of the Church will continue.

But, above all, what is at stake in the collegial service of our pastoral love is to confirm the religious of America in their charism to be religious, and to be ever more the expression of Christ's holiness in the mystery of the Church. May they live for Christ, as Mary lived for Christ, in renunciation, sacrifice and co-redemptive love, filling up "what is lacking in the sufferings of Christ for his body, the Church" *(Col 1:24)*. The first and principal duty that springs from their being religious will always be "the contemplation of things divine and constant union with Christ in prayer" *(can 663, par. 1)*.

Finally, for the benefit of all, let us recall those memorable words of Paul VI that apply to every age of the Church's life: "Do not forget, moreover, the witness of history: faithfulness to prayer or its abandonment is the test of the vitality or decadence of the religious life" *(Evangelica Testificatio, 42)*.

All of this is part of the ministry whereby we, as bishops, live the mystery of the Church, encouraging the religious, whom we love and for whom we live and are willing to die, to strive to become ever more "the very holiness of God" *(2 Cor 5:21)*.

O.R. 803.   3 October 1983

Address to the Major Religious Superiors of Europe   17 November 1983

Dear brothers and sisters, I am very happy to receive you. This is the first official meeting of the Pope with the representatives — men and women — of the conference of Major Religious Superiors of Europe, which is still in its initial stages.

Here we are gathered together at the moment when the Church is preparing to celebrate the feast of Christ, King of the Universe, light that shines to the end of men's path, he who alone is able to bring all peoples the benefits of unity and of peace. Your coming together has as its precise goal to help the religious of Europe to bear witness to the Gospel, more intensely and in a manner ever more adapted to peoples' needs, in order to establish the Kingdom of Christ.

And how could you fail to be stimulated by the experience of the past? Your predecessors, the European religious, truly accomplished a work of evangelisation in every sense of the term. Not only did they win over their brothers of immediate geographical proximity, but they carried the Gospel and the message of Christ into numerous regions which became, thanks to them, authentic lands of Christianity, spiritually rich and fruitful.

You are located in the privileged situation of the European continent, with perceptible differences according to its various regions. Despite the present decline of vocations in many countries, the traditional role of the religious creates for them today serious and grave obligations in the area of evangelisation.

Your vocation itself is for your religious, men and women, a privileged means of evangelisation; you witness to the holiness of the Church by incarnating her profound longing to give herself over to the radicalism of the Beatitudes. By your life, you are signs of a total self-surrender to God, for the Church, for the brethren. The first means of evangelisation for religious is to conform their lives more and more to the person and to the message of Jesus Christ. Before any proclamation of the word, it is their life itself that should reveal Jesus Christ and his Gospel. At certain moments of their life, and even constantly in the case of contemplative institutes, this witness will be the only form of evangelisation, a very fruitful one as well, as is revealed by the case of St Thérèse of the Child Jesus, who in her Carmelite monastery became Patroness of the Missions, and as is likewise attested by the numerous religious, unknown during their lifetime, whose prayer and sacrifices, often continuing right up till their death, have been in all truth an admirable witness to the fecundity of the Gospel and a Christian seed. Suffice it to mention here the case of St Maximilian Kolbe and that of Blessed Maria Gabriella, the Trappistine and apostle of unity! It was in this sense that I spoke to the religious at Lourdes of the gratuitousness of love.

The primordial role of your meeting should be to assist the religious of Europe to realise better their evangelical mission by living their own vocation more fully. Your national conferences and all the religious have a right to expect assistance, encouragement and collegial support from their brothers and sisters of other nations, in order to confront the problems that transcend national frontiers and affect the religious life of the continent. In this way you will be in a better position to implement an effective collaboration between the national conferences of religious. This action should be accomplished of course with due respect for the legitimate autonomy of these national conferences and institutes, as also for the legitimate diversities of cultures, of customs, of life-styles and without any reference to political considerations. Above all, it should contribute to the development and to the affirmation of the proper character of the religious life.

Indeed, that which differentiates the members of the Church from one another constitutes a reciprocal complementarity and is ordered to the unique communion and to the mission that belongs to the whole body. Care must then be taken that the religious life preserve its proper characteristics and its visibility. If the Church requires visibility in order to give witness, so does religious life. The attenuation to the point of virtual disappearance to the eyes of the world of that which characterises the religious life is not good for the religious, or for the Church or for evangelisation. This respect for the specific riches of the religious life should take account of the particular nature of the institutes such as it had been recognised by the Church at the time of their official approval.

The fact that several countries of Europe are experiencing an increased de-Christianisation, with baptised persons living practically outside the Church, poses more acutely for Christians and for religious the question of their witness and of their apostolate. Certainly the reasons are complex and stem in part from difficulties external to the Church. But one may ask oneself: have these Christians had sufficient evangelisers, and their witness, like that of European religious, has it been sufficiently authentic and visible? More than all others, the religious should take care not to allow the "salt" of the Gospel to become insipid through secularising practices and attitudes, sacrificing prayer to an all too human pattern of activity, adopting socio-political behaviour determined by criteria that are not always evangelical. I know well that you are convinced of this; is it not one of the aspects of spiritual renewal that you are seeking by a revision of your constitutions?

The authentic evangelical witness of religious concerns also an everyday more significant number of non-Christian immigrants from other continents seeking more favourable living conditions in Europe. It is of the highest importance that these poor people find in religious a reflection of the charity of Christ. This is a new way of continuing what the missionaries of preceding generations accomplished in distant lands.

This fraternal charity ought to be lived first of all among the religious themselves. Canon 602 sees in the "fraternal union of the members, rooted and based in charity, an example of universal reconciliation in Christ", a theme developed by the recent Synod of Bishops. If union within the religious family is a powerful evangelical witness, division among brothers, among sisters, is a stumbling block for evangelisation. Now disunity is not only to be found among the different Christian communities in Europe; it is also encountered among the faithful of the Catholic Church and sometimes even in religious houses where polarisations constitute a by no means negligible obstacle to the witness of fraternal charity.

Moreover, these divisions derive most often from a practical forgetfulness of the ecclesial nature of evangelisation; the latter must always be carried out in the name of the Church, in communion with its pastors and not according to individualistic criteria and perspectives. Fraternal unity lived in fidelity to the magisterium will contribute to implanting the Church which cannot exist without the respiratory function which is the sacramental life culminating in the Eucharist.

Yes, it is in the perspective of the Church's mission, confronted with its most urgent needs, such as the responsible pastors see them, that the multiple apostolic services of which your institutes are capable must be viewed. For the Church counts on you, she needs you and she knows that she finds in you, in your institutes, immense and marvellous resources for the various forms of her direct and indirect proclamation of the Gospel.

At the present time, the Gospel must be proclaimed to a world which is suffering from hunger and privation. Despite discernible differences between the regions, the European continent remains privileged on the economic level; it must not happen that religious, allowing themselves to be won over by the pursuit of comfort and the selfishness of many people around them, close their eyes to the underprivileged categories of society and to the regions of the world that are plunged in misery. They must by their availability and their disinterestedness turn to the help of the deprived of every sort. But I will not press the point, because I know to what extent many institutes, many religious — both men and women — are making an effort today to live poor and among the new poor that our society hides away. On the other hand, this form of witness does not prevent the undertaking of true responsibilities that are a service. Indeed, the educational and social action of the institutes, according to their proper charism recognised by the Church and in organic collaboration with the laity, always remains relevant, especially if the religious preserve in this area a concern for the poor, for those on the fringe of society, for the immigrants, refugees, etc. Their activity in this direction is more than ever a necessity for evangelisation, being a visible manifestation of the love of God for mankind.

The larger view your union affords of the world, the fruitful relationships it establishes with the Council of European Episcopal Conferences, should enable it to help the national conferences of religious and the various institutes to offer an ever more effective evangelical witness by impregnating the different cultures with the Good News brought by Jesus Christ, without being enslaved by any one of them.

On the morning of Pentecost, the Virgin Mary, Mother of the Church, was present in prayer at the beginnings of the evangelisation that took place under the inspiration of the Holy Spirit. May she ever remain the Star that guides religious in their mission and renders them generous and joyously faithful to the Gospel and to the Church!

Confident that your meeting here will be effective in helping the religious of the European continent to be ever more credible witnesses to the Gospel, I bless you with all my heart.

O.R. 816. 9 January 1984

Homily to Religious

2 February 1984

"A revealing light to the Gentiles, the glory of your people Israel" (Lk 2:32).

Today, dear brothers and sisters, I want to borrow these words of the old man Simeon in order together with you to adore the Light: Christ the Light of the world!

We are meeting in St Peter's Basilica in the Year of the Redemption, in the year of the extraordinary Jubilee. We are meeting in that great and multiform community which you all make up, brothers and sisters from so many religious orders, congregations and institutes. Individuals and communities consecrated to God!

This meeting brings together the representatives of the religious families who live in Rome and, at the same time, extends to all those fellow brothers and sisters with whom the unity and the identity of your vocation unites you. And through this unity and identity you are bound also by a special union of mission in the Church, a mission in the midst of the people of God in every country and on every continent, to the ends of the earth.

Today, in this great universal community, you join the Bishop of

Rome and the Successor of Peter to cry out in the spirit of today's Liturgy: "A revealing light to the Gentiles!" The light: Christ the Light and glory of the people of God throughout the world!

With this cry you want to respond to the spirit of the liturgy of this special feast, and at the same time you want to express what constitutes the interior mystery of each and every one of you. In fact, because of your vocation you walk in a special way in this Light which is Christ, and, in addition, you bear witness to it in a special way.

Today it is manifested by the lighted candles which in a short time you will hold in your hands. Each of these recalls above all the Sacrament of Baptism, through which Christ began to illuminate your life with the light of the Gospel and with the light of the Redemption: Christ received through faith into the community of the Church. Christ passed down from day to day in the life of your Christian family, surroundings and school. The full flowering of Baptism is the Eucharist; and, at the same time the constant renewal of its purifying power is the Sacrament of Penance and Reconciliation.

Then, each of these candles reminds you — against the background of the liturgy of today's feast — of the moment of your consecration: religious profession, the choice of the way of life according to the evangelical counsels of poverty, chastity and obedience.

The light of Christ shone then with an especially brilliant flame. The flame of faith and hope joined the vivid flame of charity concentrated on the Heart of the Divine Spouse and, at the same time, opened it widely through this concentration.

Just as this Divine Heart is opened widely in the mystery of the Redemption, which we know is universal, embracing everyone and everything.

Depth and universality — these are the two characteristics of the religious vocation which attest to its being rooted in the mystery of the Redemption in the light of Christ.

Today, the liturgy of the Feast of the Presentation of the Lord leads you towards this light. So, you enter the temple, just as Mary and Joseph once did, who took Jesus to Jerusalem to offer him to the Lord. The law of the Old Testament provided that every first-born son be consecrated to the Lord, and this consecration was accompanied by a sacrifice of a pair of turtledoves or two young pigeons.

Today, beloved brothers and sisters, you enter this temple to renew — in the light of the Presentation of Christ — your offering to God in Jesus Christ: your consecration to be his exclusive property.

From the depths of the mystery of consecration springs this particular belonging to God himself: a belonging of which only the person, the knowing and free subject, is capable. This belonging has the nature of a gift. It responds to a gift and at the same time expresses the gift.

In the light of Christ each one of you perceives, with penetrating clearness, that all of creation is a gift and you perceive in creation the special gift of your own humanity, and with the gift of this entire and indivisible humanity you desire to respond to the gift of the Creator, of the Redeemer, of the Spouse.

In this way, there is inscribed in the human "I" of each one of you a special bond of communion with Christ and, in him, with the Most Holy Trinity; with the Father, with the Son and with the Holy Spirit.

Entering the temple, then, along with Mary and Joseph — where the rite of the Presentation of Jesus provided for by the law will take place — we encounter two persons wholly consecrated to God, dedicated to the expectation of Israel, or rather, to mankind's greatest hope of all times: they are Simeon and Anna.

Simeon, inspired by the Holy Spirit, has gone to the temple.

Does this not perhaps bring to mind a similar "inspiration" with which you were once moved: the inspiration of the Spirit? Yes! Since the Holy Spirit, in the power of Christ's Redemption, is the author of all sanctity, he is also author of that special call on the way to sanctity which is contained in the religious vocation.

Today, when you renew your profession in your hearts, remember that interior "inspiration" of the Spirit which was at the beginning of your path. Remember how this "inspiration" came, how it became stronger, how, perhaps, it returned again after a certain amount of time, until you recognised in it the clear voice of God and the power of the nuptial love of the Lord who was calling you.

Remember this today, in order to give thanks with a renewed heart, to profess "the marvels of God" (*Acts 2:11*). This inspiration from the Spirit cannot be extinguished. It must endure and mature, along with the religious vocation, during your entire lives.

You can never separate yourselves from this salvific inspiration from the Spirit, caring for it in that interior temple which each of you is!

How eloquent are the words concerning the prophetess Anna in today's Gospel: "She was constantly in the temple, worshipping day and night in fasting and prayer. Coming on the scene at this moment, she gave thanks to God and talked about the child to all who looked forward to the deliverance of Jerusalem" *(Lk 2:37-38)*. Simeon leans over the child and utters the prophetic words: "This child is destined to be the downfall and the rise of many in Israel, a sign that will be opposed so that the thoughts of many hearts may be laid bare" *(Lk 2:34)*. He addresses these words to Mary, his Mother.

And he adds: "And you yourself shall be pierced with a sword" *(Lk 2:35)*.

A strange prophecy! It is perhaps the most concise and at the same time the most complete synthesis of all Christology and of all soteriology.

Dear brothers and sisters, may this prophecy reach your souls today with new strength!

Welcome Christ, who is the Light of the world: Christ in whom God "has prepared salvation in the presence of all peoples" (cf. *Lk 2:31)*.

Welcome Christ, who is also a "sign of opposition". This "opposition" is inscribed in your vocation. Do not try to remove it or to erase it. This "opposition" has salvific significance. The salvation of the world is achieved precisely along the path of this opposition offered by Christ. You too, by welcoming Christ, are a manifestation of this salvific opposition. It cannot be otherwise. Precisely in the name of the salvific opposition there is inscribed in your Christian and religious "I" the profession of poverty, chastity and obedience.

The world needs the authentic "opposition" of religious consecration as a constant leaven of salvific renewal.

You will carry in your hands the lighted candles of today's liturgy.

They say that Christ is the light which enlightens every man who comes into this world.

They are the testimony of your indivisible dedication to Christ and to God, they are the testimony of your consecration.

These candles also illuminate human life, the life of each one of us. As the candle gradually burns, the wax melts and the candle is consumed.

May your lives burn in the light of Christ!

May yours be lives of total nuptial dedication to his service!

May the life-giving current of the mystery of the Redemption pass through this life, reaching the world and man and directing all our human existence towards the eternal light: the light of vision and glory.

Simeon said to Mary, Mother of Jesus: "And you yourself shall be pierced with a sword!"
Dear brothers and sisters, receive Christ from the hands of Mary! May the mystery of the Redemption reach you through her soul! May all the salvific plans of consecrated hearts always be manifest before the heart of the Mother! United with her. With your glance focused on her. In her there is a special resemblance to Christ, the Spouse of your souls.

O.R. 822.   20 February 1984

Apostolic Exhortation "Redemptionis Donum"
25 March 1984

Dear brothers and sisters in Christ Jesus!

The gift of the Redemption, which this extraordinary Jubilee Year emphasises, brings with it a particular call to conversion and reconciliation with God in Jesus Christ. While the outward reason for this extraordinary Jubilee is of an historical nature — for what is being celebrated is the 1950th anniversary of the Crucifixion and Resurrection — at the same time it is the interior motive that is dominant, the motive that is connected with the very depth of the mystery of the Redemption. The Church was born from that mystery, and it is by that mystery that she lives throughout her history. The period of the extraordinary Jubilee has an exceptional character. The call to conversion and reconciliation with God means that we must meditate more deeply on our life and our Christian vocation in the light of the mystery of the Redemption, in order to fix that life and vocation ever more firmly in that mystery.

While this call concerns everyone in the Church, in a special way it concerns you, men and women religious, who, in your consecration to God through the vows of the evangelical counsels, strive towards a particular fullness of Christian life. Your special vocation and the whole of your life in the Church and the world take their character and their spiritual power from the same depth of the mystery of the Redemption. By following Christ along the narrow and hard way, you experience in an extraordinary manner how true it is that "with him is plenteous redemption" *(Ps 130(129):7)*.

Therefore, as this Holy Year moves towards its close, I wish to address myself in a particular way to all of you, men and women religious, who are entirely consecrated to contemplation or vowed to the various works of the apostolate. I have already done so in numerous places and on various occasions, confirming and extending the evangelical teaching contained in the whole of the Church's Tradition, especially in the magisterium of the recent Ecumenical Council from the dogmatic Constitution *Lumen Gentium* to the Decree *Perfectae Caritatis,* in the spirit of the indications of the Apostolic Exhortation *Evangelica Testificatio* of my predecessor Paul VI. The Code of Canon Law, which recently came into force and which in a way can be considered the final conciliar document, will be for all of you a valuable aid and a sure guide in concretely stating the means for faithfully and generously living your magnificent vocation in the Church.

I greet you with the affection of the Bishop of Rome and Successor of St Peter, with whom your communities are united in a characteristic way. From the same See of Rome there also reach you, with an unceasing echo, the words of St Paul: "I betrothed you to Christ to present you as a pure bride to her one husband" *(2 Cor 11:2)*. The Church, which receives after the Apostles the treasure of marriage to the divine Spouse, looks with the greatest love towards all her sons and daughters who, by the profession of the evangelical counsels and through her own mediation, have made a special covenant with the Redeemer of the world.

Accept this word of the Jubilee Year of the Redemption precisely as a word of love, spoken by the Church for you. Accept it, wherever you may be: in the cloister of the contemplative communities, or in the commitment to the many different forms of apostolic service: in the missions, in pastoral work, in hospitals or other places where the suffering are served, in educational institutions, schools or universities — in fact in every one of your houses where, gathered in the name of Christ, you live in the knowledge that the Lord is in your midst.

May the Church's loving word, addressed to you in the Jubilee of the Redemption, be the reflection of that loving word that Christ himself said to each one of you when he spoke one day that mysterious "Follow me" from which your vocation in the Church began.

"Jesus looking upon him loved him" *(Mk 10:21)* and said to him,

"If you would be perfect, go, sell what you have, and give to the poor, and you will have treasure in heaven; and come, follow me" *(Mt 19:21)*. Even though we know that those words, addressed to the rich young man, were not accepted by the one being called, their content deserves to be carefully reflected upon; for they present the interior structure of a vocation.

"And Jesus looking upon him loved him". This is the love of the Redeemer: a love that flows from all the human and divine depths of the Redemption. This love reflects the eternal love of the Father, who "so loved the world that he gave his only Son, that whoever believes in him should not perish but have eternal life" *(Jn 3:16)*. The Son, invested with that love, accepted the mission from the Father in the Holy Spirit, and became the Redeemer of the world. The Father's love was revealed in the Son as redeeming love. It is precisely this love that constitutes the true price of the Redemption of man and the world. Christ's Apostles speak of the price of the Redemption with profound emotion: "You were ransomed... not with perishable things such as silver or gold, but with the precious blood of Christ, like that of a lamb without blemish or spot", writes St Peter (1 Pet 1: 18-19). And St Paul states: "You were bought with a price" (1 Cor 6:20).

The call to the way of the evangelical counsels springs from the interior encounter with the love of Christ, which is a redeeming love. Christ calls precisely through this love of his. In the structure of a vocation, the encounter with this love becomes something specifically personal. When Christ looked upon you and loved you, calling each one of you, dear religious, that redeeming love of his was directed towards a particular person, and at the same time it took on a spousal character: it became a love of choice. This love embraces the whole person, soul and body, whether man or woman, in that person's unique and unrepeatable personal "I". The One who, given eternally to the Father, gives himself in the mystery of the Redemption, has now called man in order that he in his turn should give himself entirely to the work of the Redemption through membership in a community of brothers or sisters, recognised and approved by the Church. Surely it is precisely to this call that St Paul's words can be applied: "Do you not know that your body is a temple of the Holy Spirit...? You are not your own; you were bought with a price" *(1 Cor 6:19-20)*.

Yes, Christ's love has reached each one of you, dear brothers and sisters, with that same "price" of the Redemption. As a consequence of this, you have realised that you are not your own, but belong to Christ. This new awareness was the fruit of Christ's loving look in the secret of your heart. You replied to that look by choosing him who first chose each one of you, calling you with the measurelessness of his redeeming love. Since he calls by name, his call always appeals to human freedom. Christ says: "If you wish...". And the response to this call is, therefore, a free choice. You have chosen Jesus of Nazareth, the Redeemer of the world, by choosing the way that he has shown you.

This way is also called the way of perfection. Speaking to the young man, Christ says: "If you wish to be perfect...". Thus the idea of the "way of perfection" has its motivation in the very Gospel source. Moreover, do we not hear, in the Sermon on the Mount: "You, therefore, must be perfect, as your heavenly Father is perfect" *(Mt 5:48)*? The calling of man to perfection was in a certain way perceived by thinkers and moralists of the ancient world and also afterwards, at the different periods of history. But the biblical call has a completely original nature: it is particularly demanding when it indicates to man perfection in the likeness of God himself. He must therefore seek the perfection proper to him in the line of this image and likeness. As St Paul will write in the Letter to the Ephesians: "Therefore be imitators of God, as beloved children. And walk in love, as Christ loved us and gave himself up for us, a fragrant offering and sacrifice to God" *(Eph 5:1-2)*.

Thus the call to perfection belongs to the very essence of the Christian vocation. On the basis of this call we must also understand the words which Christ addressed to the young man in the Gospel. These words are in a particular way linked to the mystery of the Redemption of man in the world. For this Redemption gives back to God the work of creation which had been contaminated by sin, showing the perfection which the whole of creation, and in particular man, possesses in the thought and intention of God himself. Especially man must be given and restored to God, if he is to be fully restored to himself. From this comes the eternal call: "Return to me, for I have redeemed you" *(Is 44:22)*. Christ's words: "If you wish to be perfect, go, sell what you have, and give to the poor..." clearly bring us into the sphere of the evangelical counsel of poverty which belongs to the very essence of the religious vocation and profession.

At the same time these words can be understood in a wider and, in a sense, essential way. The Teacher from Nazareth invites the person he is addressing to renounce a programme of life in which the first place is seen to be occupied by the category of possessing, of "having", and to accept in its place a programme centred upon the value of the human person: upon personal "being" with all the transcendence that is proper to it.

Such an understanding of Christ's words constitutes as it were a wider setting for the ideal of evangelical poverty, especially that poverty which, as an evangelical counsel, belongs to the essential content of your mystical marriage with the divine Spouse in the Church. Reading Christ's words in the light of the superiority of "being" over "having", especially if the latter is understood in a materialistic and utilitarian sense, we as it were touch the very anthropological bases of a vocation in the Gospel. In the framework of the development of contemporary civilisation, this is a particularly relevant discovery. And for this reason the very vocation to "the way of perfection" as laid down by Christ becomes equally relevant. In today's civilisation, especially in the context of the world of wellbeing based on consumerism, man bitterly experiences the essential incompleteness of personal "being" which affects his humanity because of the abundant and various forms of "having"; he then becomes more inclined to accept this truth about vocation which was expressed once and for all in the Gospel. Yes, the call which you, dear brothers and sisters, accepted when you set out on the way of religious profession, touches upon the very roots of humanity, the roots of man's destiny in the temporal world. The evangelical "state of perfection" does not cut you off from these roots. On the contrary, it enables you to anchor yourselves even more firmly in the elements that make man man, permeating this humanity, which in various ways is burdened by sin, with the divine and human leaven of the mystery of the Redemption.

Vocation carries with it the answer to the question: Why be a human person — and how? This answer adds a new dimension to the whole of life and establishes its definitive meaning. This meaning emerges against the background of the Gospel paradox of losing one's life in order to save it, and on the other hand saving one's life by losing it "for Christ's sake and for the sake of the Gospel", as we read in Mark (8:35).

In the light of these words, Christ's call becomes perfectly clear: "Go, sell what you possess and give to the poor, and you will have treasure in heaven; and come, follow me". Between this "go" and the subsequent "come, follow me" there is a close connection. It can be said that these latter words determine the very essence of a vocation. For a vocation is a matter of following the footsteps of Christ (*"sequi"* — to follow, hence *"sequela Christi"*). The terms "go... sell... give" seem to lay down the precondition of a vocation. Nevertheless, this condition is not "external" to a vocation but is already inside it. For a person discovers the new sense of his or her humanity not only in order to follow Christ but to the extent that he or she actually does follow him. When a person sells what he possesses and gives it to the poor, he discovers that those possessions and the comforts he enjoyed were not the treasure to hold on to. The treasure is in his heart, which Christ makes capable of giving to others by the giving of self. The rich person is not the one who possesses but the one who gives, the one who is capable of giving.

At this point the Gospel paradox becomes particularly expressive. It becomes a programme of being. To be poor in the sense given to this "being" by the Teacher from Nazareth is to become a dispenser of good through one's own human condition. This also means to discover the treasure. This treasure is indestructible. It passes together with man into the dimension of the eternal. It belongs to the divine eschatology of man. Through this treasure man has his definitive future in God. Christ says: "You will have treasure in heaven". This treasure is not so much a reward after death for the good works done following the example of the divine Teacher, but rather the eschatological fulfilment of what was hidden behind these good works here on earth, in the inner treasure of the heart. Christ himself, in fact, when he invited his hearers, in the Sermon on the Mount, to store up treasure in heaven, added: "For where your treasure is, there will your heart be also" *(Mt 6:21)*. These words indicate the eschatological character of the Christian vocation. They indicate even more the eschatological nature of the vocation that is realised through spiritual marriage to Christ by the practice of the evangelical counsels.

The structure of this vocation, as seen from the words addressed to the young man in the Synoptic Gospels, is traced little by little as one discovers the fundamental treasure of one's own humanity in the perspective of that treasure which man has in heaven. In this perspective the fundamental treasure of one's own humanity is connected to the fact of being, by giving oneself. The direct point of reference in such a vocation is the living person of Jesus Christ. The call to the way of perfection takes shape from him and through him in the Holy Spirit, who continually recalls to new people, men and women, at different times of their lives but especially in their youth, all that Christ has said, and especially what he said to the young man who asked him: "Teacher, what good deed must I do to have eternal life?" *(Mt 19:16)*. Through the reply of Christ, who looks upon his questioner with love, the strong leaven of the mystery of the Redemption penetrates the consciousness, heart and will of a person who is searching with truth and sincerity.

Thus the call to the way of the evangelical counsels always has its beginning in God: "You did not choose me, but I chose you and appointed you that you should go and bear fruit and that your fruit should abide" *(Jn 15:16)*. The vocation in which a person discovers in depth the evangelical law of giving, a law inscribed in human nature, is itself a gift! It is a gift overflowing with the deepest content of the Gospel, a gift which reflects the divine and human image of the mystery of the Redemption of the world. "In this is love, not that we loved God but that he loved us and sent his Son to be the expiation for our sins" *(1 Jn 4:10)*.

Your vocation, dear brothers and sisters, has led you to religious profession, whereby you have been consecrated to God through the ministry of the Church, and have been at the same time incorporated into your religious family. Hence the Church thinks of you, above all, as persons who are consecrated: consecrated to God in Jesus Christ as his exclusive possession. This consecration determines your place in the vast community of the Church, the people of God. And at the same time this consecration introduces into the universal mission of this people a special source of spiritual and supernatural energy: a particular style of life, witness and apostolate, in fidelity to the mission of your institute and to its identity and spiritual heritage. The universal mission of the people of God is rooted in the messianic mission of Christ himself — Prophet, Priest and King — a mission in which all share in different ways. The form of sharing proper to consecrated persons corresponds to your manner of being rooted in Christ. The depth and power of this being rooted in Christ is decided precisely by religious profession.

Religious profession creates a new bond between the person and the One and True God, in Jesus Christ. This bond develops on the foundation of the original bond that is contained in the Sacrament of Baptism. Religious profession "is deeply rooted in baptismal consecration and is a fuller expression of it" *(Perfectae Caritatis, 5)*. In this way religious profession, in its constitutive content, becomes a new consecration: the consecration and giving of the human person to God, loved above all else. The commitment undertaken by means of the vows to practise the evangelical counsels of chastity, poverty and obedience, according to the determinations proper to each religious family as laid down in the Constitutions, is the expression of a total consecration to God and, at the same time, the means that leads to its achievement. This is also the source of the manner proper to consecrated persons of bearing witness and of exercising the apostolate. And yet it is necessary to seek the roots of that conscious and free consecration and of the subsequent giving of self to God as his possession in Baptism, the sacrament that leads us to the Paschal Mystery as the apex and centre of Redemption accomplished by Christ.

Therefore, in order to highlight fully the reality of religious profession, we must turn to the vibrant words of St Paul in the Letter to the Romans: "Do you not know that all of us who have been baptised into Christ Jesus were baptised into his death? We were buried therefore with him by baptism into death, so that as Christ... we too might walk in newness of life" *(Rm 6:3-4)*; "Our old self was crucified with him so that... we might no longer be enslaved to sin" *(Rm 6:6)*; "So you also must consider yourselves dead to sin and alive to God in Christ Jesus" *(Rm 6:11)*.

Upon the sacramental basis of Baptism in which it is rooted, religious profession is a new burial in the death of Christ: new, because it is made with awareness and by choice; new, because of love and vocation; new, by reason of unceasing conversion. This burial in death causes the person buried together with Christ to walk like Christ in newness of life. In Christ crucified is to be found the ultimate foundation both of baptismal consecration and of the profession of the evangelical counsels, which — in the words of the Second Vatican Council — "constitutes a special consecration". It is at one and the same time both death and liberation. St Paul writes: "Consider yourselves dead to sin". At the same time he calls his death "freedom from the slavery of sin". Above all, though, religious consecration, through its sacramental foundation in holy Baptism, constitutes a new life "for God in Jesus Christ".

In this way, simultaneously with the profession of the evangelical counsels, in a much more mature and conscious manner "the old nature is put off" and likewise "the new nature is put on, created after the likeness of God in true righteousness and holiness", to use once more the words of the Letter to the Ephesians *(4:22-24)*.

Thus, then, dear brothers and sisters, all of you who throughout the Church live the covenant of the profession of the evangelical counsels: renew in this Holy Year of the Redemption your awareness of your special sharing in the Redeemer's death on the Cross — that sharing through which you have risen with him, and continually rise with him to a new life. The Lord speaks to each of you, just as he once spoke through the prophet Isaiah: "Fear not, for I have redeemed you; I have called you by name, you are mine" *(43:1)*.

The evangelical call: "If you would be perfect... follow me" guides us with the light of the words of the divine Teacher. From the depths of the Redemption there comes Christ's call, and from that depth it reaches the human soul. By virtue of the grace of the Redemption, this saving call assumes, in the soul of the person called, the actual form of the profession of the evangelical counsels. In this form is contained your answer to the call of redeeming love, and it is also an answer of love: a love of self-giving, which is the heart of consecration, of the consecration of the person. The words of Isaiah — "I have redeemed you... you are mine" — seem to seal precisely this love, which is the love of a total and exclusive consecration to God.

This is how the special covenant of spousal love is made, in which we seem to hear an unceasing echo of the words concerning Israel, whom the Lord "has chosen as his own possession" *(Ps 135(134):4)*. For in every consecrated person the Israel of the new and eternal covenant is chosen. The whole messianic people, the entire Church, is chosen in every person whom the Lord selects from the midst of this people; in every person who is consecrated for everyone to God as his exclusive possession. While it is true that not even the greatest saint can repeat the words of Christ: "For their sake I consecrate myself" *(Jn 17:19)* in the full redemptive force of these words, nevertheless, through self-giving love, through the offering of oneself to God as his exclusive possession, each one can through faith stand within the radius of these words.

Are we not reminded of this by the other words of the Apostle in the Letter to the Romans that we so often repeat and meditate upon: "I appeal to you therefore, brethren, by the mercies of God, to present your bodies as a living sacrifice, holy and acceptable to God, which is your spiritual worship" *(Rm 12:1)*? These words are as it were a distant echo of the One who, when he comes into the world and becomes man, says to the Father: "You have prepared a body for me... Lo, I have come to do your will, O God" *(Heb 10:5,7)*.

In this particular context of the Jubilee Year of the Redemption, let us then go back again to the mystery of the body and soul of Christ, as the complete subject of spousal and redemptive love: spousal because redemptive. For love he offered himself, for love he gave his body "for the sin of the world". By immersing yourselves in the Paschal Mystery of the Redeemer through the consecration of the religious vows, you desire, through the love of total giving, to fill your souls and your bodies with the spirit of sacrifice, even as St Paul invites you to do in the words of the Letter to the Romans, just quoted: ''to offer your bodies as a sacrifice''. In this way the likeness of that love which in the Heart of Christ is both redemptive and spousal is imprinted on the religious profession. And such love should fill each of you, dear brothers and sisters, from the very source of that particular consecration which — on the sacramental basis of holy Baptism — is the beginning of your new life in Christ and in the Church: it is the beginning of the new creation.

Together with this love, may there grow deeper in each one of you the joy of belonging exclusively to God, of being a particular inheritance of the Most Holy Trinity, Father, Son and Holy Spirit. Now and then repeat with the Psalmist the inspired words:

''Whom else have I in heaven?
And when I am with you,
the earth delights me not.
Though my flesh and my heart waste away,
God is the rock of my heart
and my portion for ever'' *(Ps 73(72):25-26).*
or:
''I say to the Lord: my Lord are you
Apart from you I have no good.
O Lord, my allotted portion and my cup,
You it is who hold fast my lot'' *(Ps 16(15):2,5).*

May the knowledge of belonging to God himself in Jesus Christ, the Redeemer of the world and Spouse of the Church, seal your hearts, all your thoughts, words and deeds, with the sign of the biblical spouse. As you know, this intimate and profound knowledge of Christ is actuated and grows deeper day by day through the life of personal, community and liturgical prayer proper to each of your religious families. In this too, and especially so, the men and women religious who are dedicated essentially to contemplation are a powerful aid and a stimulating support for their brothers and sisters devoted to the works of the apostolate. May this knowledge of belonging to Christ open your hearts, thoughts and deeds, with the key of the mystery of the Redemption, to all the sufferings, needs and hopes of individuals and of the world, in the midst of which your evangelical consecration has been planted as a particular sign of the presence of God for whom all live, embraced by the invisible dimension of his Kingdom.

The words "Follow me" spoken by Christ when he looked upon and loved each one of you, dear brothers and sisters, also have this meaning: you take part, in the most complete and radical way possible, in the shaping of that new creation which must emerge from the redemption of the world by means of the power of the Spirit of Truth operating from the abundance of the Paschal Mystery of Christ.

Through your profession, the way of the evangelical counsels opens up before each one of you. In the Gospel there are many exhortations that go beyond the measure of the commandment, indicating not only what is necessary but what is better. Thus for example the exhortation not to judge, to lend expecting nothing in return, to comply with all the requests and desires of our neighbour, to invite the poor to a meal, to pardon always and many other invitations. If, in accordance with tradition, the profession of the evangelical counsels has concentrated on the three points of chastity, poverty and obedience, this usage seems sufficiently clearly to emphasise their importance as key elements and in a certain sense as a summing-up of the entire economy of salvation. Everything in the Gospel that is a counsel enters indirectly into the programme of that way to which Christ calls when he says: "Follow me". But chastity, poverty and obedience give to this way a particular Christocentric characteristic and imprint upon it a specific sign of the economy of the Redemption.

Essential to this economy is the transformation of the entire cosmos through the heart of man, from within: "For the creation waits with eager longing for the revealing of the sons of God... and will be set free from its bondage to decay and obtain the glorious liberty of the children of God" *(Rm 8:19-21)*. This transformation takes place in step with that love which Christ's call infuses in the depth of the individual — that love which constitutes the very substance of consecration: a man or woman's vowing of self to God in religious profession, on the foundation of the sacramental consecration of Baptism. We can discover the bases of the economy of Redemption by reading the words of the First Letter of St John: "Do not love the world or the things in the world. If any one loves the world, love for the Father is not in him. For all that is in the world, the lust of the flesh and the lust of the eyes and the pride of life, is not of the Father but is of the world. And the world passes away, and the lust of it; but he who does the will of God abides for ever" *(1 Jn 2:15-17)*.

Religious profession places in the heart of each one of you, dear brothers and sisters, the love of the Father: that love which is in the Heart of Jesus Christ, the Redeemer of the world. It is love which embraces the world and everything in it that comes from the Father, and which at the same time tends to overcome in the world everything that does not come from the Father. It tends therefore to conquer the threefold lust. The lust of the flesh, the lust of the eyes and the pride of life are hidden within man as the inheritance of original sin, as a result of which the relationship with the world, created by God and given to man to be ruled by him, was disfigured in the human heart in various ways. In the economy of the Redemption the evangelical counsels of chastity, poverty and obedience constitute the most radical means for transforming in the human heart this relationship with the world: with the external world and with one's personal "I", which in some way is the central part of the world in the biblical sense, if what does not come from the Father begins within it.

Against the background of the phrases taken from the First Letter of St John, it is not difficult to see the fundamental importance of the three evangelical counsels in the whole economy of Redemption. Evangelical chastity helps us to transform in our interior life everything that has its source in the lust of the flesh; evangelical poverty, everything that finds its source in the lust of the eyes; and evangelical obedience enables us to transform in a radical way that which in the human heart arises from the pride of life. We are deliberately speaking here of an overcoming as a transformation, for the entire economy of the Redemption is set in the framework of the words spoken in the priestly prayer to the Father: "I do not ask you to take them out of the world, but to guard them from the evil one" *(Jn 17:15).* The evangelical counsels in their essential purpose aim at the renewal of creation: the world, thanks to them, is to be subjected to man and given to him in such a way that man himself may be perfectly given to God.

The internal purpose of the evangelical counsels leads to the discovery of yet other aspects that emphasise the close connection of the counsels with the economy of the Redemption. We know that the economy of the Redemption finds its culminating point in the Paschal Mystery of Jesus Christ, in whom are joined self-emptying through death and birth to a new life through the Resurrection. The practice of the evangelical counsels contains a deep reflection of this paschal duality: the inevitable destruction of what in each of us is sin and its inheritance, and the possibility of being reborn each day to a more profound good hidden under the action of grace, towards which the practice of chastity, poverty and obedience renders the human soul particularly sensitive. The entire economy of Redemption is realised precisely through his sensitivity to the mysterious action of the Holy Spirit, the direct author of all holiness. Along this path the profession of evangelical counsels opens out in each one of you, dear brothers and sisters, a wide space for the "new creation" that emerges in your human "I" precisely from the economy of the Redemption and, through this human "I" also into the interpersonal and social dimensions. At the same time it emerges in humanity as part of the world created by God: that world that the Father loved anew in the eternal Son, the Redeemer of the world.

Of this Son St Paul says that "though he was in the form of God... he emptied himself, taking the form of a servant, being born in the likeness of men" *(Phil 2:6-7)*. The characteristic of self-emptying contained in the practice of the evangelical counsels is therefore a completely Christocentric characteristic. And for this reason also the Teacher from Nazareth explicitly indicates the Cross as the condition for following in his footsteps. He who once said to each one of you "Follow me" has also said: "If any one would come after me, let him deny himself and take up his cross and follow me" (that is to say, walk in my footsteps) *(Mk 8:34)*. And he said this to all his listeners, not just to the disciples. The law of renunciation belongs therefore to the very essence of the Christian vocation. But it belongs in a particular way to the essence of the vocation linked to the profession of the evangelical counsels. To those who walk the way of this vocation even those difficult expressions that we read in the Letter to the Philippians speak in a comprehensible language: for him "I have suffered the loss of all things, and count them as refuse, in order that I may gain Christ and be found in him" *(Phil 3:8-9)*.

Renunciation therefore — the reflection of the mystery of Calvary — in order to be more fully in the crucified and risen Christ; renunciation in order to recognise fully in him the mystery of one's human nature, and to confirm this on the path of that wonderful process of which the same Apostle writes in another place: "Though our outer nature is wasting away, our inner nature is being renewed every day" *(2 Co 4:16)*. In this way the economy of the Redemption transfers the power of the Paschal Mystery to the level of humanity, docile to Christ's call to life in chastity, poverty and obedience, that is to a life according to the evangelical counsels.

The Paschal character of this call makes itself known from various points of view, in connection with each individual counsel.

It is indeed according to the measure of the economy of the Redemption that one must also judge and practise that chastity which each of you has promised by vow, together with poverty and obedience. There is contained in this the response to Christ's words, which are at the same time an invitation: "There are eunuchs who have made themselves eunuchs for the sake of the Kingdom of heaven. He who is able to receive this, let him receive it" *(Mt 19:12)*. Prior to this Christ had emphasised: "Not all men can receive this saying, but only those to whom it is given" *(Mt 19:11)*. These last words clearly show that this invitation is a counsel. To this also the Apostle Paul devoted a special reflection in the First Letter to the Corinthians (cf. 7:28-40). This counsel is addressed in a particular way to the love of the human heart. It places greater emphasis on the spousal character of this love, while poverty and still more obedience seem to emphasise primarily the aspect of redemptive love contained in religious consecration. As you know, it is a question here of chastity in the sense of "making themselves eunuchs for the sake of the Kingdom of heaven", a question, that is, of virginity or celibacy as an expression of spousal love for the Redeemer himself. In this sense the Apostle teaches that they "do well" who choose matrimony but they "do better who choose virginity". "The unmarried man is anxious about the affairs of the Lord, how to please the Lord, and "the unmarried woman or girl is anxious about the affairs of the Lord, how to be holy in body and spirit".

There is contained neither in the words of Christ nor in those of Paul any lack of esteem for matrimony. The evangelical counsel of chastity is only an indication of that particular possibility which for the human heart, whether of a man or of a woman, constitutes the spousal love of Christ himself, of Jesus the Lord. "To make themselves eunuchs for the sake of the Kingdom of heaven" is not in fact merely a free renunciation of marriage and family life but a charismatic choice of Christ as one's exclusive Spouse. This choice not only specifically enables one to be "anxious about the affairs of the Lord" but — when it is made "for the Kingdom of heaven — it brings this eschatological Kingdom of God close to the life of all people in the conditions of temporality, and makes it in a certain way present in the midst of the world."

In this way, consecrated persons accomplish the interior purpose of the entire economy of the Redemption. For this purpose expresses itself in bringing near the Kingdom of God in its definitive, eschatologial dimension. Through the vow of chastity, consecrated persons share in the economy of the Redemption through the free renunciation of the temporal joys of married and family life; on the other hand, precisely by their having made themselves "eunuchs for the sake of the kingdom of heaven", they bring into the midst of this passing world the announcement of the future resurrection and of eternal life: life in union with God himself through the beatific vision and the love which contains in itself and completely pervades all the other loves of the human heart.

How very expressive in the matter of poverty are the words of the Second Letter to the Corinthians which constitute a concise synthesis of all that we hear on this theme in the Gospel! "For you know the grace of our Lord Jesus Christ, that though he was rich, yet for your sake he became poor, so that by his poverty you might become rich" *(2 Co 8:9)*. According to these words poverty actually enters into the interior structure of the redemptive grace of Jesus Christ. Without poverty it is not possible to understand the mystery of the gift of divinity to man, a gift which is accomplished precisely in Jesus Christ. For this reason also it is found at the very centre of the Gospel, at the beginning of the message of the eight Beatitudes: "Blessed are the poor in spirit". Evangelical poverty reveals to the eyes of the human soul the perspective of the whole mystery, "hidden for ages in God" *(Ep 3:9)*. Only those who are poor in this way are also interiorly capable of understanding the poverty of the one who is infinitely rich. The poverty of Christ conceals in itself this infinite richness of God; it is indeed an infallible expression of it. A richness, in fact, such as the Divinity itself, could not have been adequately expressed in any created good. It can be expressed only in poverty. Therefore it can be properly understood only by the poor, the poor in spirit. Christ, the God-man, is the first of these: he who "though he was rich became poor" is not only the teacher but also the spokesman and guarantor of that salvific poverty which corresponds to the infinite richness of God and to the inexhaustible power of his grace.

And thus it is also true — as the Apostle writes — that "by his poverty we have become rich". It is the teacher and spokesman of poverty who makes us rich. For this very reason he says to the young man of the Synoptic Gospels: "Sell what you possess and give... and you will have treasure in heaven" *(Mt 19:21)*. In these words there is a call to enrich others through one's own poverty, but in the depths of this call there is hidden the testimony of the infinite richness of God which, transferred to the human soul in the mystery of grace, creates in man himself, precisely through poverty, a source for enriching others not comparable with any other resource of material goods, a source for bestowing gifts on others in the manner of God himself. This giving is accomplished in the context of the mystery of Christ, who has made us rich by his poverty. We see how this process of enrichment unfolds in the pages of the Gospel, finding its culmination in the paschal event: Christ, the poorest in his death on the Cross, is also the one who enriches us infinitely with the fullness of new life, through the Resurrection.

Dear brothers and sisters, poor in spirit through your evangelical profession, receive into the whole of your life this salvific profile of the poverty of Christ. Day by day seek its ever greater development! Seek above all the Kingdom of God and his righteousness, and the other things shall be yours as well. May there be accomplished in you and through you the evangelical blessedness reserved for the poor, the poor in spirit!

Christ, "though he was in the form of God, did not count equality with God a thing to be grasped, but emptied himself taking the form of a servant, being born in the likeness of men. And being found in human form he humbled himself and became obedient unto death, even death on a Cross" *(Ph 2:6-8)*.

Here, in these words of the Letter of St Paul to the Philippians, we touch the very essence of the Redemption. In this reality is inscribed in a primary and constitutive way the obedience of Jesus Christ. Other words of the Apostle, taken this time from the Letter to the Romans, confirm this: "For as by one man's disobedience many were made sinners, so by one man's obedience many will be made righteous" *(Rm 5:19)*.

The evangelical counsel of obedience is the call which derives from this obedience of Christ "unto death". Those who accept this call, expressed by the words "Follow me", decide — as the Council says — to follow Christ "who, by an obedience which carried him even to death on the Cross, redeemed humanity and made it holy" *(Perfectae Caritatis, 14)*. By living out the evangelical counsel of obedience they reach the deep essence of the entire economy of the Redemption. By fulfilling this counsel they desire to gain a special sharing in the obedience of that one alone by whose obedience all will be made righteous.

It can therefore be said that those who decide to live according to the counsel of obedience are placed in a unique way between the mystery of sin and the mystery of justification and salvific grace.

They are in this place with all the sinful background of their own human nature, with all the inheritance of the pride of life, with all the selfish tendencies to dominate rather than to serve, and precisely by means of the vow of obedience they decide to be transformed into the likeness of Christ, who redeemed humanity and made it holy by his obedience. In the counsel of obedience they desire to find their own role in the Redemption of Christ and their own way of sanctification.

This is the way which Christ marked out in the Gospel, speaking many times of fulfilling the will of God, of ceaselessly searching for it. "My food is to do the will of him who sent me, and to accomplish his work" *(Jn 4:34)*. "Because I seek not my own will but the will of him who sent me" *(Jn 5:30)*. "He who sent me is with me; he has not left me alone, for I always do what is pleasing to him" *(Jn 8:29)*. "For I have come down from heaven, not to do my own will, but the will of him who sent me" *(Jn 6:38)*. This constant fulfilling of the will of the Father also reminds us of the messianic confession of the psalmist in the Old Testament: "Behold I come; in the written scroll it is prescribed for me. To do your will, O my God, is my delight, and your law is within my heart" *(Ps 40(39): 8,9)*.

This obedience of the Son — full of joy — reaches its zenith in the face of the Passion and Cross: "Father, if it is your will, take this cup from me; yet not my will but yours be done" *(Lk 22:42)*. From the prayer in Gethsemane onwards, Christ's readiness to do the will of the Father is filled to the very brim of suffering, becoming that obedience "unto death, even death on a Cross" spoken of by St Paul.

Through the vow of obedience consecrated persons decide to imitate with humility the obedience of the Redeemer in a special way. For although submission to the will of God and obedience to his law are for every state a condition of Christian life, nevertheless in the religious state, in the "state of perfection", the vow of obedience establishes in the heart of each of you, dear brothers and sisters, the duty of a particular reference to Christ "obedient unto death". And since this obedience of Christ constitutes the essential nucleus of the work of the Redemption, as is seen from the words of the Apostle quoted above, therefore also in the fulfilling of the evangelical counsel of obedience we must discern a particular moment in the economy of the Redemption which pervades your whole vocation in the Church.

From this derives that "total availability to the Holy Spirit" who is at work above all in the Church, as my predecessor Paul VI puts it in the Apostolic Exhortation *Evangelica Testificatio (no. 6),* and who is likewise manifested in the Constitutions of your institutes. From this derives that religious submission which in a spirit of faith consecrated persons show to their legitimate superiors, who hold the place of God. In the Letter to the Hebrews we find on this theme a very significant indication: "Obey your leaders and submit to them; for they are keeping watch over your souls, as men who will have to give account". And the author of the Letter adds: "Let them do this joyfully, and not sadly, for that would be of no advantage to you" *(Heb 13:17).*

On the other hand, superiors will bear in mind that they must exercise in a spirit of service the power conferred on them through the ministry of the Church, and they will show willingness to listen to their brothers or sisters in order to discern more clearly what the Lord asks of each one. At the time they retain the authority proper to them to decide and order what they consider appropriate.

Hand in hand with submission-obedience thus conceived goes the attitude of service which informs your whole life after the example of the Son of Man, who "came not to be served but to serve, and to give his life as a ransom for many" *(Mt 10:45).* And his Mother, at the decisive moment of the Annunciation-Incarnation, entering from the very beginning into the whole salvific economy of the Redemption, said: "Behold, I am the handmaid of the Lord; let it be to me according to your word" *(Lk 1:38).*

Remember also, dear brothers and sisters, that the obedience to which you committed yourselves by consecrating yourselves without reserve to God through the profession of the evangelical counsels is a particular expression of interior freedom, just as the definitive expression of Christ's freedom was his obedience unto death: "I lay down my life, that I may take it again. No one takes it from me, but I lay it down of my own accord" *(Jn 10:17-18).*

In the Jubilee Year of the Redemption the entire Church wishes to renew her love for Christ, the Redeemer of man and of the world, her Lord and also her divine Spouse. And so in this Holy Year the Church looks with special attention to you, dear brothers and sisters, who, as consecrated persons, occupy a special place both in the universal community of the people of God and in every local community. While the Church wishes also your love for Christ to be renewed through the grace of the extraordinary Jubilee, at the same time she is fully aware that this love constitutes a special possession of the whole people of God. The Church is aware that in the love that Christ receives from consecrated persons, the love of the entire Body is directed in a special and exceptional way towards the Spouse, who at the same time is the Head of this Body. The Church expresses to you, dear brothers and sisters, her gratitude for your consecration and for your profession of the evangelical counsels, which are a special witness of love. She also expresses anew her great confidence in you who have chosen a state of life that is a special gift of God to the Church. She counts upon your complete and generous collaboration in order that, as faithful stewards of this precious gift, you may think with the Church and always act in union with her, in conformity with the teachings and directives of the magisterium of Peter and of the pastors in communion with him, fostering, at the personal and community level, a renewed ecclesial awareness. And at the same time the Church prays for you, that your witness of love may never fail, and she also asks you to accept in this spirit the present message of the Jubilee Year of the Redemption.

Precisely in this way the Apostle Paul prayed in his Letter to the Philippians, "that your love may abound more and more... with all discernment, so that you may approve what is excellent, and may be pure and blameless for the day of Christ, filled with the fruits of righteousness" *(Ph 1:9-11)*.

Through the work of Christ's Redemption "God's love has been poured out into our hearts through the Holy Spirit which has been given to us" *(Rm 5:5)*. I constantly ask the Holy Spirit to grant to each one of you, according to your own gift, to bear special witness to this love. May "the law of the Spirit that gives life in Christ Jesus..." be victorious within you, in a way worthy of your vocation, that law that has "set us free from the law of death" *(Rm 8:2)*. Live then this new life in the measure of the different gifts of God which correspond to the vocation of your individual religious families. The profession of the evangelical counsels shows each of you how with the help of the Spirit you can put to death everything that is contrary to life and serves sin and death; everything that is opposed to true love of God and others. The world needs the authentic contradiction provided by religious consecration, as an unceasing stimulus of salvific renewal. "Do not be conformed to this world but be transformed by the renewal of your mind, that you may prove what is the will of God, what is good and acceptable and perfect" *(Rm 12:2)*. After the special period of experimentation and renewal provided for by the Motu Proprio *Ecclesiae Sanctae*, your institutes have recently received or are preparing to receive the Church's approval of your renewed Constitutions. May this gift of the Church encourage you to know them, to love them and, above all, to live them in generosity and fidelity, remembering that obedience is an unambiguous manifestation of love.

It is precisely this witness of love that the world today and all humanity need. They need this witness to the Redemption as this is imprinted upon the profession of the evangelical counsels. These counsels, each in its own way, and all of them together in their intimate connection, bear witness to the Redemption which, by the power of Christ's Cross and Resurrection, leads the world and humanity in the Holy Spirit towards that definitive fulfilment which man and, through man, the whole of creation find in God, and only in God. Your witness is therefore of inestimable value, you must constantly strive to make it fully transparent and fully fruitful in the world. A further aid to this will be the faithful observance of the Church's norms regarding also the outward manifestation of your consecration and of your commitment to poverty *(Code: can. 669)*.

From this witness of spousal love for Christ, through which the entire salvific truth of the Gospel becomes particularly visible, there also comes, dear brothers and sisters, as something proper to your vocation, a sharing in the Church's apostolate, in her universal mission, which is accomplished contemporaneously in every nation in many different ways and through many different charisms. Your specific mission is in harmony with the mission of the Apostles, whom the Lord sent to the whole world to teach all nations, and it is also linked to the mission of the hierarchial order. In the apostolate which consecrated persons exercise, their spousal love for Christ becomes, in an organic way as it were, love for the Church as the Body of Christ, for the Church as the people of God, for the Church which is at one and the same time Spouse and Mother.

It is difficult to describe, or even to list, the many different ways in which consecrated persons fulfil through the apostolate their love for the Church. This apostolate is always born from the particular gift of your founders, which, received from God and approved by the Church, has become a charism for the whole community. That gift corresponds to the different needs of the Church and the world at particular moments of history, and in its turn it is extended and strengthened in the life of the religious communities as one of the enduring elements of the Church's life and apostolate. In each of these elements, in each field — both of contemplation, so fruitful for the apostolate, and of direct apostolic action — the Church's constant blessing accompanies you, as does at the same time her pastoral and maternal solicitude, with regard to the spiritual identity of your life and the correctness of your activity in the midst of the great universal community of the vocations and charisms of the whole people of God. Through each of the institutes separately and through their organic integration in the whole of the Church's mission, special emphasis is given to that economy of the Redemption, the profound sign of which each one of you, dear brothers and sisters, bears within himself or herself through the consecration and profession of the evangelical counsels.

And thus, even though the many different apostolic works that you perform are extremely important, nevertheless the truly fundamental work of the apostolate remains always what (and at the same time who) you are in the Church. Of each one of you can be repeated, with special appropriateness, these words of St Paul: "For you have died, and your life is hid with Christ in God" *(Co 3:3)*. And at the same time this "being hidden with Christ in God" makes it possible to apply to you the words of the Master himself: "Let your light so shine before men, that they may see your good works and give glory to your Father who is in heaven" *(Mt 5:16)*.

For the sake of this light with which you must shine before men, of great importance among you is the witness of mutual love, linked to the fraternal spirit of each community, for the Lord has said: "By this all men will know that you are my disciples, if you have love for one another" *(Jn 13:35)*.

The fundamentally community nature of your religious life, nourished by the teaching of the Gospel, by the sacred liturgy and above all by the Eucharist, is a special way of accomplishing this interpersonal and social dimension: by caring for one another, by bearing one another's burdens, you show by your unity that Christ is living in your midst. Important for your apostolate in the Church is every kind of sensitivity to the needs and sufferings of the individual, which are seen so clearly and so movingly in today's world. For the Apostle Paul teaches: "Bear one another's burdens, and so fulfil the law of Christ" *(Ga 6:2)*; and he adds that "love is the fulfilling of the law" *(Rm 13:10)*.

Your mission must be seen! Deep, very deep must be the bond which links it to the Church! Through everything that you do, and especially through everything that you are, may the truth be proclaimed and reconfirmed that "Christ loved the Church and gave himself up for her" *(Ep 5:25)*; the truth that is at the basis of the whole economy of the Redemption. From Christ, the Redeemer of the world, may the inexhaustible source of your love for the Church pour forth!

This Exhortation which I address to you on the Solemnity of the Annunciation in the Jubilee Year of the Redemption is meant to be an expression of that love which the Church has for men and women religious. You, dear brothers and sisters, are truly a special treasure of the Church. And this treasure becomes more understandable through meditation on the reality of the Redemption, for which the present Holy Year offers a continuous opportunity and a welcome encouragement. Recognise, therefore, in this light, your identity and your dignity. May the Holy Spirit — through Christ's Cross and Resurrection — "having the eyes of hearts enlightened", enable you "to know what is the hope to which he has called you, what are the riches of his glorious inheritance in the saints" *(Ep 1:18)*.

These "eyes enlightening the heart" the Church unceasingly asks for each one of you who has already taken the road of the profession of the evangelical counsels. The Church, together with you, asks for the same "enlightened eyes" for many Christians, especially for young men and women, that they may discover this way and not be afraid to enter upon it, that — even in the midst of the adverse circumstances of life today — they may hear Christ's "Follow me". You too must strive for this through your prayer and also through the witness of that love whereby "God abides in us and his love is perfected in us" *(1 Jn 4:12)*. May this witness become present everywhere and universally clear. May the people of our times, in their spiritual weariness, find in it both support and hope. Therefore serve your brethren with the joy that wells up from a heart in which Christ has his dwelling. "And may the world of our time...be enabled to receive the Good News not from evangelisers who are dejected and discouraged... but from ministers of the Gospel whose lives glow with fervour, who have first received the joy of Christ" *(Evangelii Nuntiandi, 80)*.

The Church, in her love for you, does not cease "kneeling before the Father" that he may effect in you"... the strengthening of the inner nature" (cf. *Ep 3:14, 16*), and as in you, so also in many others of your baptised brothers and sisters, especially young people, so that they may find the same way to holiness which in the course of history so many generations have travelled together with Christ, the Redeemer of the world and Spouse of souls, often leaving behind them the bright radiance of God's light against the dark and grey background of human existence.

To all of you who travel this road in the present phase of the history of the Church and the world there is addressed this fervent hope of the Jubilee Year of Redemption, that "you, being rooted and grounded in love, may have the power to comprehend with all the saints what is the breadth and length and height and depth, and to know the love of Christ which surpasses knowledge, that you may be filled with all the fullness of God" *(Ep 3:17-19).*

On the feast of the Annunciation in this Holy Year of the Redemption, I place the present Exhortation in the Heart of the Immaculate Virgin. Among all the persons consecrated unreservedly to God, she is the first. She — the Virgin of Nazareth — is also the one most fully consecrated to God, consecrated in the most perfect way. Her spousal love reached its height in the divine Motherhood through the power of the Holy Spirit. She, who as Mother carries Christ in her arms, at the same time fulfils in the most perfect way his call: "Follow me". And she follows him — she, the Mother — as her Teacher of chastity, poverty and obedience.

How poor she was on Bethlehem night and how poor on Calvary! How obedient she was at the moment of the Annunciation, and then — at the foot of the Cross — obedient even to the point of assenting to the death of her Son, who became obedient unto death! How dedicated she was in all her earthly life to the cause of the Kingdom of heaven through most chaste love!

If the entire Church finds in Mary her first model, all the more reason do you find her so — you as consecrated individuals and communities within the Church! On the day that calls to mind the inauguration of the Jubilee of the Redemption, which took place last year, I address myself to you with this present message, to invite you to renew your religious consecration according to the model of the consecration of the very Mother of God.

Beloved brothers and sisters! "God is faithful, by whom you were called into the fellowship of his Son, Jesus Christ our Lord" *(1 Co 1:9).* Persevering in fidelity to him who is faithful, strive to find a very special support in Mary! For she was called by God to the most perfect communion with his Son. May she, the faithful Virgin, also be the Mother of your evangelical way: may she help you to experience and to show to the world how infinitely faithful is God himself!

With these hopes I bless you with all my heart.

O.R. 828.   2 April 1984

Address to the Chapter Members of the Salesians
3 April 1984

Dearest Chapter Members,..... I would like to express the sincere congratulations of the whole Church for the work accomplished by the Salesians, beginning from that far-off day in 1858 when Don Bosco was here in the Apostolic Palace for the first time, in audience with Pius IX, to whom he presented a plan of rules for the Society he wanted to found. It was the beginning, small and hidden like the seed described by the Gospel, of the Society of St Francis de Sales, which was then officially realised with the definitive approval of the Constitutions in 1874, and which spread throughout the world, with admirable ranks of priests, missionaries, teachers, lay brothers, students and alumni, from Don Bosco's first successor, Blessed Don Rua, to the martyrs Monsignor Luigi Versiglia and Don Callisto Caravario, both of whom I had the joy of beatifying last year. A profound and sincere feeling of gratitude to the Lord must arise in your souls when you observe how during this long period of years, in the midst of so many adverse and stormy events, Don Bosco has always remained present among you, in your houses, among the young people entrusted to you, in the various initiatives and activities of your many institutions. The increase in vocations is also a reason for hope and consolation. Of course for your congregation too, there are difficult problems and complex issues; but it is very comforting for me to know that you are spurred on by the concern to be faithful to the spirit of Don Bosco, wherever you may be.

Thus, together with my thanks for your visit and for the sentiments of fidelity and devotion which inspire it, I also add the strong exhortation to fervent and courageous perseverance. The revision of the Constitutions must be for you and for the entire congregation a reason and an incentive for an ever more convinced and decisive apostolic commitment.

Let no one lose heart! Let no one let himself be dismayed in times of difficulty and possible defeats! Let no one allow himself to be conquered by the temptation to think his efforts are useless in the face of a secularised society which often forgets transcendent values! Remember what Don Bosco wrote to a disheartened parish priest: "Calm down then. Do not talk about freeing yourself from the parish. There is work to do! I will die working'like a good soldier of Christ'. Am I not good at much? 'I can do all things in him who strengthens me'. Are there thorns? Angels will weave a crown in heaven for you with thorns changed into flowers. Are times difficult? They were always so, but God's help was never lacking. 'Christ yesterday and today'. (Turin, 25 October 1878)

Never becomes discouraged! Look at Don Bosco, at his life, at his total dedication to souls! Read his writings; listen to his teaching, which is still valid; pray to him perseveringly and devoutly, so that his spirit may always be alive and present in you and in your educational, catechetical, parochial, athletic and recreational activities: "Everything for the Lord — he repeated. Let us do what we can 'for the greater glory of God'. We will rest in Paradise". Trained in the school of the great saints and the great mystics, with daring and far-sightedness he kept the rudder of his life and his plan in hand and he was not afraid to affirm categorically: "I intend that all Salesians work for the Church until the last breath!" (*Mem. B. XIV, 229*). On 7 December 1887, expressing his last wishes to Monsignor Cagliero, he said; "May everyone work zealously and ardently; work, work! Always strive tirelessly to save souls!" (*ibid., XVIII 477*). In this regard, I like to offer the example of Cardinal August Hlond, Primate of Poland, spiritual son of Don Bosco, who had to suffer so much because of the tragic events of the last World War: "In the Salesian congregation — he said — I learned that work is neither a burden nor a cross, but a joy..." "Every brick is a cross, every stone a suffering. Tears cement them together. This is how the saints built. This is how Don Bosco built. I have placed all my confidence in Don Bosco and in Dominic Savio" (cf. "*A Shepherd of the Church during Difficult Times*", *Salesianum, no. 4, 1982*).

With regard to the work of the education and formation of youth, which is the Salesian congregation's charism, I ardently exhort you to intend to build on the firm rock of God's will as Don Bosco did. It is important to emphasise and always keep in mind that Don Bosco's pedagogy had an extremely eschatological value and perspective: as Christ repeatedly said in the Gospel, it is essential to enter the kingdom of heaven. But, paraphrasing Christ's words, neither mere sentimental invocation, nor ideological planning, nor social and utopian activism can give entrance to the kingdom of heaven, but rather the fulfilment of God's will: the rains fall, the winds blow, the torrents come, they buffet that house, but it does not collapse because it is solidly set on rock. Thus, it is necessary to erect the building of education also on the rock of God's will: this was the primary and constant intention of Don Bosco, who certainly cannot be accused of abstract mysticism or spiritual selfishness! And this must be the Salesians' never-ending commitment: God's will is certainly the knowledge of the person and message of Christ, the Revealer of the Father and the Redeemer of mankind, as proclaimed by the Apostles and taught by the Church; God's will is certainly the life of grace, and that is, the Christocentric education which is pivoted on frequent confession and on the Eucharist. Today too, Don Bosco repeats to everyone: "Remember your last days and you will never sin" *(Sir 7:36)*. Young people today need and feel the necessity for spiritual, serious, enlightened, constructive guidance: this is the supreme responsibility of every priest and this is also the supreme joy!

Families anxiously await your help, your collaboration, in preventing evil, in forming Christian consciences, in realising the work of Redemption in individuals. Don Bosco, though a man so committed in earthly values that he could so marvellously utilise his talents for dynamism and organisation, could nevertheless be defined "the man of eternity"! The will of God is certainly charity which makes one totally fulfil his duty, obeying the authority of the Church and of one's superiors, and it expands one's heart to universal love. One day, Don Bosco gave this answer to young Prince Czartoryski, who turned to him as his spiritual director: "I pray. You pray too that God keep all of us steadfast on the road which can better assure Paradise for us" *(Epistolario, vol. IV, 378)*. The supernatural view of existence is Don Bosco's radical teaching and it is the only way to build truly on the rock!

Reading the biography and writings of St John Bosco, one is impressed by the continuous reference to the presence of Mary Most Holy. It can be truly stated that he conceived everything and did everything in dependence on Mary and surrounded by her maternal and often even visible protection! In 1862 he confided to Don Cagliero: "Our Lady wants us to honour her under the title of Mary Help of Christians: times are so sad that we truly need the Virgin to help us preserve Christian faith". These are grave and serious words which we can repeat even today, strengthening our love and our trust in Mary Help of Christians ever more. Put your trust in Mary! Every day entrust all your activities and your anxieties to her maternal care!

With the wish that your Chapter decisions bear abundant and effective fruits, I impart my Blessing to you, which I willingly extend to the entire Salesian congregation.

O.R. 830.   16 April 1984

Address to the Religious of Switzerland at Fribourg

13 June 1984

.....Together we have directed praise and intercession to the Father, through his Son our only Mediator and Redeemer, by the inspiration of the Holy Spirit. And now I would like to comment on the exhortation made by the Apostle Paul to the Christians of Ephesus, which we heard earlier: "I implore you therefore to lead a life worthy of your vocation. Bear with one another charitably, in complete selflessness, gentleness and patience. Do all you can to preserve the unity of the Spirit by the peace that binds you together" *(Ep 4:1-2)*.

Your congregations and communities are concerned, I know, by the decrease in candidates to the religious life. This objective statement, partially explained by reasons of a socio-cultural order but also by reasons of a religious nature, is not an inevitable fate, and above all must never lead you to discouragement. A renewal is possible, and, with the help of the Lord, you are able to do all that it requires. In fact, St Paul's encouragement to the Ephesians is for all of you an urgent call to let yourselves be convinced that a renewed vitality of your institutes implies among other things and necessarily, a renewal of community life.

The past has known numerous communities, with the advantages and perhaps certain burdens inherent in this style of life. Today, these same communities are reduced in number because of advanced age and the death of their members, a decrease of entrants, and at the same time by the rise of numerous more restrictive fraternities which desire to adopt new forms of presence to the world of man. At this time it seems that a happy medium should be found or rediscovered.

To have the power to attract, a religious community must be alive and visible, composed of sufficient numbers who are complementary in their gifts and their functions; it is also important that it be marked by a great spirit of humble and authentic togetherness in seeking the Lord, in apostolic joys and sufferings, and reasonably open to appropriate initiatives.

Today's young people are not, as is too easily said, closed to the evangelical call. They can certainly move more spontaneously towards new institutes; however, they are no less attracted to older congregations who demonstrate vitality and remain faithful to radical and adequately presented demands. We have long had proof of this: we need only to consult the history of the Church. Often adaptations are necessary, but those possibly inspired by a relaxation or which lead to it, absolutely cannot attract the young who carry deep within themselves the capabilities for radical giving, even if at times these capacities seem hesitant or blocked.

This renewal can be greatly helped by an active, trusting, intensified collaboration among your religious families, especially when they have the same spirit, customs and goals, The federations, associations and also the unions, already pointed out by Popes Pius XI and Pius XII, encouraged by the Council and by Pope Paul VI, following the directions given by the Decree *Perfectae Caritatis (no. 22)* and by the Motu Proprio *Ecclesiae Sanctae (nos. 39, 40 and 41)*, always with respect for the freedom of individuals, can be beneficial to the life of the Church and to the institutes themselves.

In any case, community life cannot survive and grow without renunciation of self, without humility. This is how it bears fruit, such as the purification of sensitivity, the increasing maturity of persons, the authentic development of human and spiritual qualities. In a divided world where particular interests, individual and collective selfishness, disrespect for the person and his rights often triumph, the Gospel can be made credible by the witness of true religious communities united by the Holy Spirit and living a real fraternity, thus constituting for the world a powerful sign of hope.

I would also like to emphasise how much the renewal of religious community life finds its source and dynamism in the Eucharist, "sacrament of love, sign of unity, bond of charity" (cf. *Const. Sacrosanctum Concilium, n. 47*). The Eucharist is the sure way to communion, that is, to union and unity with God in Christ, the sure way to the communion of all, one with another, in fraternal love. The Eucharist will make community "one Body and one Spirit" *(Ep 4:4)*. The Eucharist permits each member and the entire community to accomplish progressively its Passover, its passage from an existence more or less impregnated by selfishness or weakness to a life more fully given to God and to others. Dear religious, always give priority to the daily Eucharistic celebration, whether it be a question of the time reserved for the celebration or of the dignity, the recollection and the active participation which must characterise every Eucharistic celebration and edify those who occasionally attend. A religious community gives witness to its authenticity, its fervour, first of all by the manner in which it celebrates, venerates and receives the Body and Blood of the Lord.

This reality which is at the centre of your life cannot minimise or replace other times and other forms of contact with God, which are exercises of spiritual nourishment absolutely indispensable to the life of every man and woman religious. We all know that insufficient nourishment is detrimental to physical health, and sometimes disastrous. Help one another to safeguard or to restore to its proper place the Liturgy of the Hours, personal prayer, the reading of Scripture and the Fathers, Eucharistic adoration, Marian piety which is in conformity with the teaching of the magisterium, the monthly retreat, regular and devout reception of the Sacrament of Reconciliation, which generates a renewed movement of conversion. Each religious family should seek to find a balance between these ways of approaching the Lord.

For those of you who, under the guidance of the bishops, are engaged in various apostolic activities, the Eucharist and other spiritual exercises are the source of a joyful fidelity to the Lord and a dedication according to his Spirit; fidelity and dedication which inspire and enliven pastoral action in parishes, hospitals, schools or in society.

And you, dear religious who have dedicated yourselves to contemplative life, draw from the Eucharist and the other forms of community and individual prayer in your monasteries the secret of your silent influence on retreatants or passing visitors. May the secret of your own happiness lie in having left everything for the Lord and in accomplishing your spiritual mission, in the name of the Church, for a humanity which lets itself be totally absorbed in difficult tasks and intense worries, as well as in the mirage of worldly goods.

For you, brothers and sisters whom age or illness has forced to give up generous apostolic activities, either in your own country or in mission lands, and who feel, at least sometimes, a bit useless, be led by the Eucharist and at every moment of prayer to deepen and to live the mysterious fruitfulness of the oblation of Christ, who knew the immobility of the Cross.

Yes, may the Eucharist model your persons, fundamentally consecrated by baptism and later by religious vows, according to the mystery of Christ Jesus radically available to God his Father and totally given to all his brothers and sisters especially the poorest!

Dear religious from all parts of Switzerland, have courage and confidence, keeping in mind the greatness and the importance of your religious vocation, for yourselves, for the Church of today and also for contemporary society!

In the Apostolic Exhortation *Redemptionis Donum* which I greatly desired to publish at the end of the recent Holy Year, I wanted to re-read and ponder with religious of the whole world Jesus' words concerning a vocation, among which the following are at least overwhelming: "And looking at him, Jesus loved him" *(Mk 10: 21)* and said to him, "if you wish to be perfect, go, sell what you have and give the money to the poor and you will have treasure in heaven; then come, follow me" *(Mt 19:21)*. The glance and the call of Jesus are always directed to a particular person. It is a love of choice which takes on a spousal character. The love of Christ embraces the whole person, soul and body, whether man or woman, in that person's absolutely unique and personal "I" (cf. *Redemptionis Donum, no. 3*).

Through your personal and free response to Jesus of Nazareth the Redeemer of the world, you have consented to abandon a way of life centred on "having" in order to commit yourselves along the narrow and magnificent paths of "being". I deeply wish and ask the Lord that each of you discover the splendour and the timeliness of your religious profession.

In its humble daily realisation, it can and must be prophetic, in the sense that it can and must show men and women of this time what in truth builds up the human person. Thanks to the search, discernment, acquisition and development of convictions and ways of being which transcend changes of time and customs, your vocation, just as the Christian vocation, yet at a much more decided level, is eschatological.

It should help the world escape from the quicksand in which it is caught by consumer goods and a certain number of anti-values. Yes, the contemporary world, and especially the young, should discover through your communities and their style of life the value of a life which is poor in service of the poor, the value of a life freely committed to celibacy in order to give oneself to Christ and with him to love especially the unloved, the value of a life where obedience and fraternal community discreetly oppose the excesses of an often capricious and sterile independence.....

Having come among you as the servant of unity and truth, I pray to God who is Light, Love and Life, to breathe into your communities and fraternities a new evangelical spirit. And I confide the fervour and perseverance of each one of you to the Virgin Mary, model of the consecrated life. May my prayer accompany you always. You, too, be so good as to accompany my apostolic service with your spiritual support.

In the name of the Lord, I warmly bless you, your institutes, your monasteries and your service of the Gospel.

O.R. 840. 25 June 1984

Homily: Mass for Contemplative Nuns, Hull, Canada
19 September 1984

"The Spirit and the Bride say 'Come'... Come, Lord Jesus" *(Rv 22:17, 20)*. The Church, inspired by the Spirit present in her, continues to address this call to the Lord Jesus. She awaits his return. The Church awaits him, as a bride yearning after her beloved husband who is at the right hand of the Father. She has already washed her robes in his redeeming blood. She hopes to feed on the tree of life. She knows that she already shares in his life in a mysterious and partial way, through faith, the sacraments, prayer and charity. It is with him that she works to renew this world according to his Spirit. But she is impatient for a complete renewal, for the full vision of her spouse. For the moment, her life is hidden in God.

The whole Church must live in this expectancy and bear witness to it. But consecrated souls have made "a charismatic choice of Christ as the exclusive spouse". This choice already enables one "to be anxious about the affairs of the Lord" but also — when it is made "for the kingdom of heaven" — it brings this eschatalogical reign of God closer to the life of all people. Consecrated persons bring into the midst of this passing world news of the resurrection to come and of eternal life (cf. my letter *Redemptionis Donum, no. 11*).

All men and women religious have this charism at the heart of the Church. But it is even more obvious in the case of cloistered sisters who give up all activity in the world in order to be present to the Lord alone. And in this place it is first of all to you that I speak, dear contemplative sisters. The Church considers your place in the Mystical Body of Christ essential to the life of the Church, to its full development, and this, even in the young Churches whose energy is monopolised by the tasks of evangelisation (cf. *Perfectae Caritatis no. 47*, and *Ad Gentes, no. 40.*). In fact, the prayer of contemplatives has played a considerable role in the deepening of faith in Canada. That was certainly the insight of Father Mangin and Sister Marie-

Zita de Jesus when they founded here, almost 100 years ago, the Servants of Jesus and Mary. These women religious honour in a special way the Sacred Heart of Jesus in the Eucharist, the supreme gift of his love, before which they keep a continuous vigil. Your spiritual apostolate, dear sisters, is it not to support the ministry of priests and to collaborate in the eternal plan of the covenant for all believers: "that they might be one"? I think also of all the men and women who have established the contemplative life in Canada according to complementary spiritualities. So, in addition to all the religious here today, I greet with affection and I encourage all those who lead a monastic life in Canada. "The Kingdom of heaven will be like this: ten bridesmaids took their lamps and went to meet the bridegroom. Five of them were foolish and five were wise". My sisters, wait for the groom as these wise virgins did. Always be ready. Always be open. In your waiting for the Lord, be on watch.

Your convent life is organised in such a way as to encourage the experience of God. Your withdrawal from the world, with its solitude; your silence, which is a listening silence, a silence of love; asceticism, penance, the tasks which lead you to share in the redemptive work; fraternal communion which is always being renewed; the daily Eucharistic celebration that unites your offering to that of Christ.

May the weariness, routine and monotony involved in your convent life not make you lose your vigilance, may the occasional impression that God is absent or temptations or even the normal trials of growing in mystical union with Christ not discourage you! May the lamp of your prayer, of your love, never stop burning! Keep it well supplied with oil, day and night.

For, even within a community, your path is still a personal one. Just as the wise virgins were incapable of making up for the carelessness of the foolish virgins, no one else can take your place in welcoming the Trinitarian life into the depth of yourself there, where the love received responds in adoration, praise and gratitude to love. It is then that you make your own the prayer of the psalmist we were reading a moment ago: "God, you are my God, I am seeking you, my soul is thirsting for you, my flesh is longing for you, a land parched, weary and waterless; I long to gaze on you in the sanctuary and to see your power and glory. Your love is better than life itself... all my life I will bless you... I meditate on you all night long... I sing for joy in the shadow of your wings. My soul clings close to you, your right hand supports me" *(Ps 63(62): 2-5, 7-9)*.

This ineffable meeting with the personal and living God can take place only in the darkness of faith. The groom stands behind the door while you are still outside in the night. It is always in the light of faith that God gives himself. But the signs of God are so discreet in the ordinariness of your everyday life that you must be vigilant if you are to persevere and grow in faith in imitation of Mary. The treasure that awaits you in heaven will only be the eschatological fulfilment of what is hidden in the inner treasure of the heart (cf. *Redemptionis Donum, no. 5*).

Your lives have a hidden but assured fruitfulness. "Whoever remains in me... bears fruit in plenty" *(Jn 15:5)*. In the solidarity that unites all the members of Christ, you are like the heart, as St Therese of the Child Jesus put it. Without your love, charity would grow cold. In the Church that prays, suffers and evangelises, your part is the link with God. Your offering makes you like Christ so that he can use your whole being for the work of redemption according to the pleasure of his love. And God hears the prayer of praise and intercession that rises up from your hearts and pans out his grace, without which there would be neither conversion to the Gospel, growth in faith nor vocations of apostolic workers in the Church.

The Christian community in Hull seems to have clearly understood your vocation, as has the neighbouring community of the city of Ottawa. People are attached to your monastery and support it. They do not hesitate to entrust you with their sorrows and their joys, their plans and their prayer intentions.

More and more people — and among them, many young people — are seeking places of grace, of prayer, of contemplation. They are thirsting for the absolute. Some come to your monasteries in search of spiritual values. To all these seekers after God, show by the truth and the transparency of your persons that belonging to Christ makes you free and that experience of God fulfils you. Without shirking the requirements of contemplative life, find ways of expressing for the culture of our time your radical option for God. To those who say: "We do not know how to pray", say again and again by your existence that dialogue with God is possible for "the Spirit too comes to help us in our weakness" *(Rm 8:26)*. To those who want to do something great with their life, testify that the path to holiness is the most beautiful of adventures. It is not just the work of our efforts, but that of the infinite tenderness of God in the vastness of human misery. May your monasteries allow passers-by to approach the sources of living water: "Then let all who are thirsty come: all who want it may have the water of life and have it free" *(Rv 22:17)*!

My meditation seems to be focused on cloistered nuns. But, all along, I have had in mind all the women who have devoted themselves to God in religious life in Canada. There are almost 40,000 them! What I said about the spirit of consecrated life is also valid for all the sisters dedicated to an active or apostolic life. Circumstances have not permitted a special meeting with them as a group, and I regret that. I have seen many of them at every stage of my visit, with the people of God. But I was waiting for this opportunity and now, this evening, I am happy to greet them all from this place of contemplation and to address to them this message.

Dear sisters, in the Church, you carry out services that are precious to Christian communities and to the world: among others things, you are involved in teaching catechism, in education, in hospital care, in supporting the elderly and in parish activities... Happy are the villages and the cities where sisters are still present! You exercise a certain professional activity, with preference for activity which allows you to express charity and to give witness to faith, and that, in a community way.

But that is not the original mystery of your life. You freely consecrated yourself to the Lord who was the first to choose you. Your religious vows are intimately rooted in the consecration of Baptism but express it with greater fullness. You share in a special and permanent way in the Redeemer's death on the Cross and in his Resurrection. The Paschal nature of your life is evident in each of the evangelical counsels which you have committed yourselves to practise in a radical way. At the same time you become truly free in order better to serve. You stake your all, not on "having" but on the quality of being, the quality of the person renewed in Jesus Christ.

More than ever before, our world needs to discover in your communities and in your lifestyle the value of a simple and poor life in the service of the poor, the value of a life freely committed in celibacy in order to consecrate itself to Christ and, with him, to love especially those deprived of love, the value of a life where obedience and community life silently protest the excesses of an independence that is sometimes irresponsible and barren.

Above all, the world needs witnesses to the free gift of love of God. To those who doubt God or who have the impression that he is absent, you show that the Lord is worth seeking and loving for himself, that the kingdom of God, despite its apparent foolishness, is worth devoting one's life to. Thus, your lives are a sign of the indestructible faith of the Church. The free giving of your life to Christ and to others is perhaps the protest that most urgently needs to be made to a society where profit-making efficiency has become an idol. Your life amazes, questions, interests or irritates the world, but it never leaves it indifferent. In any case, the Gospel is always the sign of contradiction. You will not be understood by all. But never be afraid to manifest your consecration to the Lord. It is your honour! It is an honour to the Church! You have a special place in the Body of Christ where everyone has his or her role to assume, his or her own charism.

If, with the Holy Spirit, you seek the holiness which corresponds to your state of life, do not be afraid. He will not abandon you. Vocations will come to you, and you, you will keep the youthfulness of your soul, which has nothing to do with age. Yes, my dear sisters, live in hope. Keep your eyes on Christ and walk firmly in his steps in joy and in peace.

I cannot develop any further now this message to all the Canadian nuns. On 25 March of this year I wrote a special letter to you and to all men and women religious, entitled *Redemptionis Donum*.

This evening, at the end of my long apostolic journey across Canada, I am very happy to be... the guest of the sisters. As Jesus loved to withdraw to Bethany to the home of Mary and Martha — the one more contemplative, the other more active — I have come to your home in order to pray with you. As Peter and the other Apostles withdrew to the Cenacle, together with Mary the Mother of Jesus, I come to invoke the Holy Spirit. May he pour out his light and his power upon all the inhabitants of this dear country, so that the Church here may grow in holiness! Pray with me for all religious, for all those who are consecrated, for the men and women who are members of Secular Institutes. Let us pray for the priests, who are the ministers of the Eucharist and the guides of consciences. Let us pray for those who educate people in the faith. Let us pray for those who undergo persecution for their faith... Let us pray for all those who must contribute to establishing more justice, more peace and more fraternity, in Canada and in the less privileged countries.

Lord Jesus, may your kingdom come! Amen.

O.R. 8 October 1984

Address to the Chapter Members of the Redemptorists

18 November 1985

It is with true joy that I welcome you today, dear sons of St Alphonsus, who have come together for your General Chapter in order to renew and to fortify your mission in the Church and in the world.

I first of all wish to greet Father Juan Manuel Sasso de la Vega y Miranda, the new Superior General, and to give him my best wishes for the mandate which has been given to him by this Chapter, and which he has generously accepted in a spirit of faith. I likewise thank, in the name of the Church, Father Joseph Pfab, who, during the twelve years of his generalate, worked tirelessly in favour of the Redemptorist family and the Church, also actively and effectively collaborating as a member of the Congregation for Religious and Secular Institutes.

Beloved friends, you have recently celebrated the two hundred and fiftieth anniversary of the congregation's founding, and you have received the Church's approval of your renewed constitutions, as called for by the Council. In addition, one of your brothers was beatified in May of 1982, Fr Peter Donders, a tireless and intrepid missionary. All of this testifies to the fact that the foundation of St Alphonsus is a timely and efficacious instrument for the sanctification of its members and for the evangelization of the world. Faithful from the very beginnings to the charism of St Alphonsus, you Redemptorists have always sought to be particularly attentive to the poor, the abandoned, the oppressed, and the Lord has blessed your work such that today you serve the Church in vast numbers, covering sixty countries of the five continents.

According to the desires which emerged from the 1979 Chapter, you have deliberately chosen to live ever more intensely the project of your Holy Founder: "to follow the example of Jesus Christ, preaching the word of God to the poor".

You have consequently striven to intensify the explicit proclamation of the Word of God through the traditional "popular missions" so dear to St Aphonsus, through catechism, through missionary work in the midst of peoples who have not received the gospel message, adapting your efforts to the particular situations that present themselves. Continue this apostolate courageously and with perseverance, united in close and loyal collaboration with the local Churches and their pastors.

You are aware of the fundamental importance of personal and community prayer as the one source of apostolic life, of the witness of faith and of hope. You are also fully aware that a religious community that does not pray cannot last: you will thus need to be able to programme the means for activating and consolidating this prayer personally and in community, in order to give effective support and fraternal help to one another.

It is not individually, in fact, that you exercise your apostolate, but as a community, in a spirit of fraternal communion, bringing together prayer and reflection, work and suffering, neither allowing yourselves to be puffed up by successes nor depressed by failures, but directing everything towards the service of the Gospel. In this spiritual brotherhood — which certainly requires effort and sacrifice on the part of everyone, but which constitutes one of the essential elements of religious life — you will find the energy indispensable to apostolic work, thus manifesting Christ's charity to the world. St Alphonsus's whole life was a witness of pastoral and fraternal charity for the spreading of the Gospel.

The lay brothers are intimately joined, in number and quality, to the apostolic work of the priests and, like them, are full-fledged religious through the profession of the evangelical counsels and the witness of their generous commitment.

They participate in the pastoral mission entrusted to the Institute by the Church in the way proper to them; it is therefore only right that their theological and spiritual formation be provided for.

You who are members of a congregation that takes its name from the Divine Redeemer, strive ever more intensely to actuate in your lives the Christian and religious vocation, in the light of the Mystery of the Redemption. The faithful, generous and serene practice of the evangelical counsels constitutes an inexhaustible witness to the power of the Cross and Resurrection of Christ, the only power which can lead humanity towards its total fulfilment in God, and only in God (cf. *Redemptionis Donum*, n. 14).

May the Virgin Mary — who is intimately joined to her Divine Son in the mystery of the Redemption, and who is particularly invoked by the members of your religious family, as well as by the faithful who benefit from your apostolate, with the title of Our Lady of Perpetual Help — sustain you always, both in your consecrated and apostolic life, and may she obtain for your congregation numerous vocations, generous and fervent, for the realisation of the mission which it is called to carry out in the Church and in the world. I give you my heartfelt blessing.

O.R.   23-30 December 1985

Address to the Congregation for Religious and for Secular Institutes

24 January 1986

With great joy I greet you, dear members of the Plenary Assembly of the Congregation for Religious and for Secular Institutes, In these past days you have studied a topic that is particularly close to me and is so important for religious life as a whole: "The identity and mission of Brothers in lay and clerical Institutes".

With the following words the Second Vatican Council desired to confirm the lay religious in the value of their religious vocation: "The lay religious life, for both men and women, constitutes a state which of itself is one of total dedication to the profession of the evangelical counsels" (PC 10). Twenty years after that ecclesial event, you have desired to examine the situation of the male lay religious life to verify the progress, the difficulties, the new perspectives of this type of life in the Church today.

I am convinced that this style of religious life, which has rendered the Church so much service throughout history, remains even today very adapted to the new apostolic challenges that the proclamation of the Gospel message must face. You have therefore wanted to shed new light upon the great possibilities contained in the Code of Canon Law for the development of this vocation in the Church; you desire to ensure that the People of God can understand the dignity and usefulness of the lay religious vocation.

Religious life began with a typically lay configuration. It grew out of the desire of some Christian faithful to "derive more abundant fruits" from baptismal grace and, by the profession of the evangelical counsels, to free themselves from those obstacles which might have drawn them away from the fervour of charity and the perfection of divine worship (cf. LG 44).

Some clerics desired to participate in this life which imitated with particular accuracy and perpetually exemplified in the Church the form of life which the Son of God embraced (cf. LG 44), whether to dedicate themselves more intensely to their own sanctification or to exercise their apostolate more effectively. The clerical institutes accepted lay religious who, helping the priests, shared in the charism of the Institute. Some founders were inspired to create exclusively lay congregations in order to exercise better "the pastoral work of the Church by educating the young, caring for the sick, and discharging other services" (PC 10) that spring from the baptismal consecration. Other founders established institutes in which the lay and priest religious could work together, in union without confusion, for the Kingdom of God.

Thus the lay religious life in the Church, as an expression of total consecration to the Kingdom, is an expression of the holiness of the Spouse of Christ and contributes in an efficacious and original way to the fulfilment of the Church's mission of evangelisation and her many apostolic ministries. We cannot imagine religious life in the Church without the presence of this particular lay vocation, still open to so many Christians who can consecrate themselves in it to the following of Christ and the service of humanity.

The Second Vatican Council authorised the lay religious institutes who so desired to ordain some of their members as priests, without losing their proper character (PC 10). The same Council spoke of institues that are "not exclusively lay" (PC 15). All of this shows us how the Holy Spirit, who is always at work in the Church, causes new structures, institutes and lay ministries to grow from the ever young roots of baptism and the ancient trunk of the evangelical counsels. Affirming that the "state of consecrated life by its nature, is neither clerical nor lay" (CIC 588, 1), the Code of Canon Law recognizes this reality, leaving room for the possibilities which the Spirit of God may suggest to meet the new needs of the apostolate.

Nevertheless, it is always necessary that the institutes observe the norm of Canon 578 regarding fidelity to the intention of the founders and their plan, as officially recognised by the Church. The Congregation for Religious and for Secular Institutes has the task of watching over the fulfilment of these important requirements.

Dear members of this Plenary Assembly, tell the brothers — I use this term consecrated by use, notwithstanding the fact that, within an institute, all the members, lay and priest religious alike, are "brothers" in a common vocation; tell the brothers to deepen continually the baptismal roots of their religious consecration. In 1980, receiving in audience the lay religious men of Rome, I said to them: "Your religious profession is set, in the first place, in the line of baptismal consecration, and expresses the biopolarity of the universal priesthood, which is based on this consecration. In life as lay religious, in fact, there takes place the offering of the spiritual sacrifice, the exercise of worship in spirit and truth, to which every Christian is called; at the same time, there rings out in it before the world a very clear proclamation of the marvels of salvation. A double direction, therefore, towards God and towards men, characterises your life; and at the basis of both there is the same one baptismal priesthood, in both there is expressed the same love spread in the heart by the Spirit (cf. Rom 5:5), in both there is lived in fullness the identical charism of the 'laity', conferred by the grace of the sacraments of Christian initiation'' (*L'Osservatore Romano*, English Edition, 4 February 1980, p. 9).

It is necessary for the lay religious to be aware of the fact that they are responsible, along with their priest brothers, for all that can help strengthen the vitality of their own institute. The Code of Canon Law opens to them many possibilities for participation in the life and mission of their own religious family, except, of course, those aspects that derive strictly from the priestly character. It will be the task of the General Chapters to study more precisely and to apply these possibilities in the light of the norms of the universal law and in a renewed dedication of fidelity to the founding charism and to the specific mission of each institute in the present needs of the Church.

I would like to remind all the religious — laymen and priests — of the complementarity of their respective paths within the same religious life. The religious priest, involved in many pastoral activities, is reminded by his lay brother that religious life has a community dimension which he must not overlook. To the brother, involved in humble domestic chores or in tasks of secular service, the priest recalls the apostolic dimension of what he is doing. Furthermore, fulfilling one another in the respective service which they render to the human person, they are a living witness that "the salvific mission of the Church in relation to the world must be understood as an integral whole'', as the Extraordinary Synod has emphasized (Final Relatio, II, D 6) (*L'Osservatore Romano*, English Edition, 16 December 1985).

I also want to express my gratitude, as well as that of the entire People of God, for the work of the brothers in those areas of the apostolate so rooted in the tradition of the Church and for which the Spirit has always raised up charisms to meet the needs. I refer to the education of youth, the care of the sick, and their many missionary functions. These are charisms and services still irreplaceable for an effective presence of the Gospel and a striking witness to the spirit of the Beatitudes.

In the face of the beauty of the vocation of brothers in the Church, of the fullness of their religious identity and in the renewed possibilities for their presence, I make a twofold wish. The first is that all Pastors of the Church promote the specific vocation of religious consecration, without which something would be lacking in the vitality of the individual Churches, especially in the young ones. The second wish is for an adequate theological formation step by step with their professional and technical training, which the brothers need today to fulfil adequately their apostolic task.

To the religious brothers I especially say that the Church and the world expect from them the witness of a holy life and that perfection of charity to which the evangelical counsels lead. This charity has frequently been that "odour of Christ" which so many lay brothers have mysteriously spread in the life of the Church.

One of the greatest satisfactions of my pontificate has been the elevation of a great many lay religious to the honours of the altar; they are all eminent for the quality of service and the heroism of their virtues. Saint Miguel Febres Cordero, a professor and member of the Academy of Languages of Ecuador, his country; Blessed Riccardo Pampuri, a doctor; Blessed André Bessette, a miracle-worker; Blessed Albert Chmielowski, a painter, engineer, and founder; Blessed Jeremiah of Valachia, a nurse; Blessed Isidore de Loor, gardener and cook; Blessed Francisco Garate, the "perfect porter".

This simple list clearly shows that all human activities, from the simplest to the loftiest in the world's esteem, can take on the dimension of authentic "lay ministries", which, rooted in baptism and in religious consecration, sing the praises of God and contribute to the "realisation of this civilisation of love, which is God's design for humanity as it awaits the coming of the Lord" (Message of the Extraordinary Synod to the People of God, IV) (L'*Osservatore Romano*, English Edition, 16 December 1985, p. 5).

May Mary, the humble Virgin of Nazareth, model of service and consecration, to whose protection all religious families turn, be for all the brothers a mother and teacher of evangelical fidelity. To her I entrust the work of your Plenary Assmbly, that she may obtain the help and light to find more suitable means to confirm, renew and promote among the People of God the lay religious vocations, so necessary for the present and the future life of the Church.

O.R.   24 February 1986

Address to the Society of St Paul

22 March 1986

Dear Chapter Members of the Society of St Paul,

I am delighted to meet you, who have gathered for your General Chapter, and my thoughts go in a special way to Father Renato Perino, whom you have confirmed as Superior General.

I extend my heartfelt greeting to the entire Congregation, and I assure the whole Pauline family of my prayers. I am certain that your venerated founder, Father Giacomo Alberione, accompanies and protects you from heaven. I know that you are present in twenty-five nations, where you carry on with zeal the apostolate of the means of social communication. It is — as you know — a great mission of exceptional responsibility: it requires fine professional capabilities, but above all presumes a deep doctrinal and spiritual formation, since only on these conditions are the press, the microphone and film capable of being authentic pulpits of Truth, schools of the apostolate and efficacious means of salvation, as Father Alberione wished. He recognised the risks of these arts and feared their deviations. Already at the beginning of this century, he considered the ''mass media'' to be the new instruments which the Church would have to use in her preaching in the modern era, and he suffered much in defence of this ideal; but with anxious foresight he said to his followers: ''Be persuaded that in these apostolates a greater spirit of sacrifice and a deeper piety are required. . . We need saints going before us along these untrodden paths which in part are even uncharted'' (October 1950). And he added: ''Let us save souls, but let us first save ourselves!''

The stage that you have now reached with the confirmation of the Superior opens a new phase of life in the history of your Congregation, and, as such, lends itself to some reflections that we might make together and which can serve you as directives.

Without a doubt, the Society of St Paul deserves great praise for the apostolic effort made in this century in its vast and erudite editorial work. Taking a glance at the past, one can only note with admiration the magnificent series of books dealing with Sacred Scripture, theology, hagiography, philosophy, psychology, sociology, literature and pedagogy that have been published with careful and timely selection and in the form of worthy and accessible editions; nor can we forget the many works dealing with the Liturgy, catechesis for all categories of persons, homiletics, pastoral work, and general culture in line with various tastes and public interest.

And everything was always done in the light of Jesus the Master, who has revealed himself as the Way, the Truth and the Life.

With all possible earnestness, I exhort you to continue following the path pointed out to you by Father Alberione! Do not allow yourselves to be confused by the ideologies that weave their way through the modern world! Show spiritual wisdom, be acutely critical, apostolically balanced and astute! Remember what St Paul wrote: "Whatever is true, whatever is honourable, whatever is gracious, if there is any excellence, if there is anything worthy of praise, think about these things" (Phil 4:8). Recall also what Father Alberione said: "Everything for the Gospel, everyone for the Gospel, everyone to the Gospel!" Times have changed; this is a new era and it is necessary to use means which are up-to-date and suited to today's men and women; but the doctrine revealed by Christ does not change, it is valid always and for everyone, and, as your founder added, "we must lead souls to Paradise. Our apostolate is to preach Jesus Christ, and thus to accompany the Church, indeed, to be part of the Church that has entrusted us with this mission". Feel intensely the duty always to illuminate souls, never instilling doubt, never spreading confusion; avoid whatever might create disorientation, or whatever might be dictated by the desire to follow cultural fashions alien to the Gospel. Never let yourselves be influenced in your decisions by motives of human interest.

May docility to the Magisterium of the Church be your commitment and your spiritual joy, and may you sustain the Magisterium in the difficult but necessary task of defending orthodoxy and spreading the Truth. In your decisions may you be guided only by the desire to proclaim the Gospel and serve the Church.

You Paulines, who are priests and men of culture and modern refinement, well know that the faithful live in an age in which they hear taught and see practised doctrines that are often deformed versions of the Gospel message. Many are so upset as to vacillate in their faith. You understand how much more urgent, important and delicate your mission becomes! You — like the Good Samaritan of the Gospel parable — must bend down to these wounded and suffering souls, with love and extreme trepidation, in order to bring them the word of Truth, which grants light to the understanding, and gives the solace of supreme certainties.

You have great opportunities and great abilities: put them all at the service of Truth. We know that Christ's message is the "Revelation" of God, and therefore that Truth which is ever valid and timely. The cultural updating that you must continuously carry out in the theological, social, and literary fields must therefore always be measured against the Truth that does not pass away: today's Christians, and all men in general, feel the need for certainty and doctrinal clarity, and for this reason everything you produce must be clear, logical, convincing, illuminating and consoling. In addition, history itself teaches that man, even when he walks in darkness or obstinately remains in error, has need of light, and suffers by not possessing it; he yearns for Truth and envies those who have it. Sooner or later he feels Christ's call and therefore wishes to meet him in a priest, in the Church, in the minister of Truth and Grace.

You have been called to a stupendous mission, and with your books and magazines you can given interior light to so many souls, bringing Christ to them, giving them the joy and the consolation of meeting the Divine Master, Friend and Saviour.

In order to succeed in realising this magnificent goal, you need a firm and sound doctrinal and ascetic formation. This was Father Alberione's deep desire: he well knew that the secret of success for the Society founded by him lay in the intimacy of his followers with Christ. A man of action and initiative, he was nonetheless a contemplative accustomed to praying for hours on end, even at night, kneeling in the church before the tabernacle: "The world, the Church, souls" — he said — "have a supreme need of God: prayer calls him to you". He had but one passion: "to give God to men and men to God through Jesus Christ". A man of methodical study and of meditation, he became convinced that "everything begins and ends in Jesus Christ". He therefore desired that in the proclamation of the Gospel and in the witness of Christian life, every Pauline have as his model the Master Jesus Christ, "the Way, the Truth and the Life".

Follow the example and the directives of your founder, so that you may truly be "all things to all people" in faith, charity and works.

May the Most Holy Virgin, the Queen of the Apostles, who plays such an important and irreplaceable part in the formation of every member of the Society of St Paul, make you feel in a special way her maternal love and intercession; and you, repeat daily with great confidence and filial commitment the sweet prayer: "Virgin Mary, Mother of Jesus, make us saints!"

May my Blessing, which I extend with affection to all your confreres, go with you, along with my wish for a Holy Easter!

O.R.   14 April 1986

Address to Superiors General of Women Religious

14 May 1987

Dear Sisters,

It is a great joy for me today to receive such qualified representatives of the consecrated life. You come from many countries, from various cultures, bearing the concerns and the hopes of your sisters and of the peoples among whom your institutes carry out their apostolate.

The first sentiment that rises in my heart and in the heart of the Church is one of lively gratitude to God. Religious life is, indeed, an integral part of the Church which benefits as a whole from this charism of the consecrated life. Through you, the Church's gratitude reaches all your communities.

Your principal responsibility as superiors general is to assume in the course of daily existence the maternal function of spiritual animation of so many consecrated souls. This is the primordial role of your service. No one can replace you in the accomplishment of this mission which invites you to be attentive and full of affection for the individuals entrusted to you.

The more you yourselves are imbued with the filial spirit the better you will be able to fulfil this task. Are you not above all daughters of God, living each day in a spiritual joy and in trusting abandonment to the goodness of the heavenly Father? You are also daughters of your founders and foundresses, reflecting in the present situation the characteristic traits of their particular spirituality. You are daughters of your communities which bore you to the religious life and which sustain you daily in your personal sanctification.

You are also sisters as it were for our contemporaries whose sufferings and hopes you share. It is your desire to walk with them in the light of the Gospel message. The precise purpose of your meeting in Rome is to do some in-depth study of what forms should be assumed by the prophetic mission of religious life in the Church and in the world.

I think it would be opportune to share with you some reflections in relation to the theme of your study on the directives recalled by the Council and repeated on various occasions by my prdecessors.

The Gospel should be incarnated in every epoch in concrete

situations, in the vicissitudes of peoples and of cultures, while avoiding the snares of possible unilateral or arbitrary theories to which a growth process is always exposed.

Attentive as you are to the needs of our contemporaries, you are very conscious of the evils from which society is suffering in your various countries. In one place, there is extreme poverty, hunger, endemic threats to health; in another, unemployment, drug addiction, the suffering of all categories of the marginalised, and of the newly impoverished. Sometimes a political or economic enslavement, a lack of freedom, various assaults on the dignity of persons exist. You are rightly sensitive to the dramas that affect the lives of families. It is those in charge of civil society who generally concern themselves with all these things, and many efforts are being made to supply remedies. However, there are other miseries of which you are very aware: moral disorders, the relativism that affects concsciences, religious indifference, even unbelief, which are becoming widespread in certain circles.

The ascertaining of these evils, while stimulating the reaction of all believers, finds in your institutes forces that are more lively, more courageous, more ready to denounce them, to make people aware of them, and above all to help supply effective remedies. The study which you have undertaken, with the help of experts, is aimed at discerning the forms and methods of action most suited to your consecrated state.

It is in fact your role to enhance and to reinforce the meaning, the dignity and the creative power — which nothing can replace — of the interior life. The contemplative dimension of the consecrated life should find its vital space in your families of active life, so as to transcend the horizontalism of an apostolate wrongly understood. If the necessary solidarity with neighbour does not spring from a contemplative life animated by the love of God, nourished by meditation on and participation in the redemptive suffering of Christ, it risks remaining barren, or failing to bring to others the salvation they have a right to expect. When a person realises fully a true vertical relationship with God, as was the case with your founders and foundresses, a new meaning is revealed also in the horizontal relations.

In this perspective, the religious makes the option for the poor, not as an exclusive class choice, but as an evangelical option, that is, motivated by the very concern that Christ had for all the poor, which is one of preferential love.

This is why the Church insists that spiritual renewal should always have the primary role, even in the activities of the apostolate (cf. *Perfectae Caritatis*, n. 2). Recall what the decree *Perfectae Caritatis* says: "The members of each institute, therefore, ought to seek God before all else, and solely; they should join contemplation, by which they cleave to God by mind and heart, to apostolic love, by which they endeavour to be associated with the work of redemption and to spread the kingdom of God" (n. 5).

Your presence is an eloquent sign of the richness and of the variety of the charisms by which the Holy Spirit enriches the Church, raising up numerous and varied religious families to respond to the multiple demands of the people of God. There is no spiritual or material need towards which your founders and yourselves are not orientated, according to a wise reading of the signs of the times. Preserve, develop, affirm the choices of the founders! In the urgent needs of the present, your apostolic service should function concretely according to the specific purpose of your institute. It could also adopt new forms which would be compatible with the founder's charism, in line with the most sure and sound tradition, in harmony with the intentions the Church had in approving your institutes.

It would be a somewhat equivocal zeal which would lead you to occupy the apostolic field of another under the pretext of exceptional needs. Today one sometimes encounters a prejudice according to which one should contemptuously ignore the "differences" which constitute and distinguish the religious institutes from one another. Each institute should be careful to maintain its own nature, the special character of its own *raison d'être* which has exercised an attraction, which has stimulated vocations, particular aptitudes, and has given a noteworthy public witness. It is naive and presumptuous to believe that, in the last analysis, each institute should be identical to all the others in practising a general love of God and of neighbour. To think thus would be to neglect an essential aspect of the Mystical Body: the heterogeneity of its constitution, the pluralism of models in which is revealed the vitality of the Spirit who animates it, the transcendent human and divine perfection of Christ, its Head, who can be imitated only by the manifold resources of the human soul animated by grace (cf. *Perfectae Caritatis*, n. 2b).

Regarding the specific theme which has been the object of your study during these days, I think it is useful once again to underline the importance of supernatural charity which is the specific characteristic of Christians.

The social history of the Church has laways been rich in accomplishments. The Church has protected infants, educated the young; she has assisted the sick, the elderly, the refugees, the imprisoned, defending the rights of the most humble categories against every form of oppression and of exploitation.

Yet the justice which she has promoted has always been animated by the love of Christ. The Word became flesh above all to redeem the world from sin, the worst of all injustices. He founded the Church above all to save human beings by making them beneficiaries of his redemptive passion.

In this theological perspective, the secret of a truly prophetic life resides in the existential consistency of the religious woman with the witness which she gives. She is not content with taking up in turn the contestation and the condemnation of injustices. Rather, she offers her own life as a humble and silent message, animated by the purest and certainly effective love.

It pertains to religious, both men and women, to be in the world "what the soul is for the body", as the epistle to Diognetus said of the first Christians (cf. *Lumen Gentium*, n. 38). They must live like pilgrims in the midst of corruption, in expectation of the incorruption of heaven. Their pilgrimage is as it were an incessant proclamation of the Kingdom in process of realisation, because he who has conquered the world has promised it.

In this way, religious profession can achieve a prophetic role, which, in the very works of social service carried to the point of heroism, cannot be compared to activity that remains circumscribed in an inevitably ephemeral present.

The consecrated person should be a banner of hope raised over this world: the hope of a better, purified, renewed world transparent to the light and love of God, as we expect it to be in the world which is to come, but possible and indeed inaugurated today.

In the fulfilment of your apostolic mission, you have for a model the figure of Mary to whom we have decided to dedicate a year at the approach of the third millennium.

In her hymn of praise to God, the *Magnificat*, one finds echoes of the prophetic tradition of the chosen people. This canticle reflects the interior world of the Virgin of Nazareth. It reveals not only the secret of her relationship with God — marked by full confidence and filial gratitude — but also her attitude towards the world of humanity where the humble, the poor and the simple are exalted.

I hope together with you that all your sisters are able to look on Mary in this way. May they discover ever more deeply in her the model of their consecration to God, and at the same time that of their apostolic engagement in the service of their neighbours. While praying that the Holy Spirit will animate your lives as he did Mary's, I wholeheartedly impart to you and to your religious families a special Blessing.

O.R. 8 June 1987

Address to Chapter Members of the Passionists
14 October 1988

I am happy to welcome and greet you all, Capitular Fathers of the Congregation of the Passion of Jesus Christ. In particular, I greet the Superior General, Father Paul Boyle, whom I thank for the words which he has just now addressed to me. You are assembled in Rome for the general chapter; it is a particularly important time for the life of your congregation. I accompany your work with my prayers, that the Lord may enlighten you and that you may respond to the problems and fundamental requirements regarding the institute's identity, as conceived by the Founder and repeatedly approved by the *Church*. This is a task which you face in the light of the teaching of Vatican II, which in the decree *Perfectae Caritatis* offers to all an authoritative instrument for examination, collation, correction and development. The general principles which it recalls for the renewal of religious life exclude *a priori* every possible equivocation inspired by a relativistic mentality, typical of the present culture, often agnostic and historicist. The Church conceives and encourages progress only if it is geared towards a "constant return to the sources of the whole of Christian life and to the primitive inspiration of the institutes" (*Perfectae Caritatis,* 2). The reason is obvious if one reflects that, for the Mystical Body, the most important measure of every human event is neither the "past" nor the "future" but the *present* of the eternal life of Christ, who is above all times as "the Alpha and the Omega, the First and the Last, the Beginning and the End" (*Apoc 22:13*).

I know the seriousness with which, for centuries, you have guarded the patrimony of your institute. The unqualified esteem of the faithful proves this; they have always revered you for your austerity of life and the generosity of your missionary activity. Besides, clear confirmation is offered by the relatively high number of outstanding men who, faithful to the Founder's example, enjoy or are on the way to the honours of the altar. In this regard, I am happy to be able to add two Passionist Fathers, Bernardo Maria di Gesù and Charles of St Andrew, to the catalogue of the Blessed, on next Sunday.

Your congregation is one of the orders of mixed life, which, as the Council has indicated, "from their rule or institution, unite the apostolic life with choral office and monastic observances" (*Perfectae Caritatis*, 9).

According to the charism of the sons of St Paul of the Cross, contemplation is fostered by solitude which is also geographical; this gives every house the character of a "retreat", and guarantees the religious a common life marked by specifically monastic observances, with silence and peace, conducive to "lofty abstraction from all creation", as your holy Founder precisely expressed it.

However, there is more. That which distinguishes your spiritual life, the purpose of solitude, poverty, penance, is that union with God, brought about by an "intense participation in the expiatory and redemptive Passion of Christ". This is so because it is in, and through, the Saviour's crucified humanity that, by achieving complete detachment from creatures, one can reach "the bosom of the Father", immersed in the mystery of his infinite love.

It is this life, "hidden with Christ in God" (*Col 3:3*), that distinguishes the contemplative profession of the Passionist, and, as it were, constitutes the *soul* of his activity in the Church, the inspiring motive of his dealings with the world. Here precisely is the *apostolic dimension* of his charism, also characterised by the mystery of a Passion not only contemplated and lived, but also preached to the world as the "miracle of miracles of God's love" (St Paul of the Cross).

On the occasion of your general chapter, I wish to recall these typical aspects of Passionist spirituality, because they are indispensable premises for every proposal for the congregation's future renewal.

You are all aware how your "identity as contemplatives and apostles of Christ Crucified" is exposed today to the conflict of currents of thought and disruptive customs. It is a question of forces which can disorientate even the most watchful, because they appear to be justified by the very elements which are essential to the nature of the institute, interpreted in a reductive sense, and very often out of the context which forms the synthesis of the way of thinking and acting peculiar to the Founder and the many saints who have graced your congregation.

Therefore, I exhort you not to yield to the "temptations" of our time.

I refer in particular to the difficult synthesis of the two elements, the contemplative and active, since Paul of the Cross founded an institute of contemplative apostles who, from the very richness of a greater concentration on God, drew the power to spread throughout the world.

The mystery of the Passion gives you a name and, like your distinctive religious habit, sets you apart from all the other orders. Therefore, let none of you either take up secular professions or start your own movements of spirituality or become promoters of experiences inconsistent with the specific nature of the vocation professed by your institute; this would be a betrayal of the Founder's original charism.

Solitude, poverty, and *penance* — aimed at union with Christ in God, and forming you into the contemplative solicitous for his own personal sanctification — must enkindle in you the zeal which breaks forth in missionary activity. This activity is not generic but specific, because it is limited to the ministry of the word and proclaims a "wisdom of the Cross" assimilated in the silence of the retreat, in the austerity of the common life, in the deliberate rejection of every profane distraction.

This throws light on the sound tradition of alternating periods of recollection and rest "at the feet of Christ Crucified" with periods of apostolic work carried out *according to very definite forms* of special preaching which owe their irresistible impact to the contemplative reserves accumulated in the quiet of the monastic life.

Certainly, you cannot remain insensitive to the many needs of the Church and to the various requests of new social categories. However, this requires merely adaptation, not the suppression of the traditional ministry of the word, replacing it by forms of activity which would force you to sacrifice the contemplative dimension of your vocation, the only real secret of all missionary work.

To you, perhaps more than to other religious, the Council repeats that "even the best-contrived adaptations to the needs of our time will be of no avail unless they are animated by a spiritual renewal, which must always be assigned primary importance even in the active ministry" (*Perfectae Caritatis,* 2e).

I hope that these reflections will encourage you to a process of renewal capable of revealing the perennial vitality of the institute to a world awaiting intrepid men to proclaim the "wisdom of the Cross" through the witness of their life and word.

With these heartfelt wishes, I impart my Blessing to you and extend it to all the members of the congregation.

O.R.   14 November 1988

INDEX

A
ALBERIONE, FATHER GIACOMO: 293-296.
ALPHONSUS LIGUORI, ST: 287-289.
APOSTOLATE OF RELIGIOUS: 24-25, 26-28, 214-215; care of the sick, 75, 186-188; catechesis, 29, 54; education, 27, 29, 60-62, 75, 126-128, 132-134, 276-277; family apostolate, 88-89, 102, 109, 128-129; traditional apostolates, 35, 75, 143; youth apostolate, 197; requirements for, 144-146.
AUGUSTINE OF HIPPO, ST: 216-220.
AUGUSTINIANS: 216-220.

B
BAPTISM AND RELIGIOUS LIFE: 16, 23, 25-26, 42, 96, 258-259, 285.
BENEDICT, ST: 51, 63-64, 83-87; Rule of, 63-64, 84-87.
BENEDICTINES (MONKS AND NUNS): 84-87.
BISHOPS AND RELIGIOUS: 8, 10-12, 105, 108-109, 109-110, 114, 122-125, 129-132, 195, 198-203, 206, 239-244.
BROTHERS, VOCATION OF: 20, 22-25, 41-45, 59-62, 79-83, 126-128, 136, 186-188, 287-289.
BROTHERS OF THE CHRISTIAN SCHOOLS: 59-62, 106, 126-128.
BROTHERS OF ST JOHN OF GOD: 186-188.

C
CAPUCHINS: 169-172.
CARE OF THE SICK, RELIGIOUS AND,: 75, 186-188.
CARMELITES, ORDER OF DISCALCED: friars, 120-122; nuns, 56-59, 120-122, 165-169.
CATECHESIS AND RELIGIOUS: 29, 54.
CHARISM OF INSTITUTE: 8, 10, 18, 24, 61-62, 70, 83, 105, 129, 164, 192, 195, 296-301.
CHARITY OF ST VINCENT DE PAUL, DAUGHTERS OF: 39-41, 115-116, 118-119.
CHASTITY AND RELIGIOUS: 40, 53, 66-67, 94, 263, 265-266.
CHURCH, LOYALTY OF RELIGIOUS TO: 8, 18, 24-25, 26-29, 54-56, 76-77, 101, 105, 108-109, 130-131, 164, 180-181, 192, 195, 206, 213, 219, 243, 293-296.
CHURCH'S TEACHING ON RELIGIOUS LIFE: 10-12, 36, 41-44, 46, 80-81, 109-110, 112-115, 122-125, 129-132, 142, 169-171, 183, 200, 204, 253.
CLERGY AND RELIGIOUS: 51, 79-80, 105, 114, 130, 151, 197.
COMMUNICATIONS MEDIA AND RELIGIOUS: 114-115, 293-296.
COMMUNITY ELEMENT IN RELIGIOUS LIFE: 23-24, 33-34, 44, 52, 127, 181, 197, 205, 233, 236-237, 246-247, 287-289.
CONFESSIONS, PRIESTS RELIGIOUS AND THE HEARING OF: 182.
CONFIDENCE, NEEDED BY RELIGIOUS: 35, 38.
CONGREGATION OF THE MISSION: 115-119.
CONGREGATION OF THE MOST HOLY REDEEMER: 287-289.
CONGREGATION OF THE PASSION:
CONTEMPLATIVE DIMENSION IN RELIGIOUS LIFE: 108, 296-301.
CONTEMPLATIVE RELIGIOUS: 5-6, 15-17, 21, 28, 33, 49-51, 54, 56-59, 62-65, 68-71, 73-74, 77-78, 99, 108, 137, 158, 162, 166-167, 172-176, 188-189, 193, 205, 215, 282-286.
CONVENTUALS (FRANCISCAN): 211-214.
CONVERSION AND RELIGIOUS: 18, 198-203, 213.

D
DAUGHTERS OF CHARITY OF ST VINCENT DE PAUL: 39-41, 115-116, 118-119.
DAUGHTERS OF MARY HELP OF CHRISTIANS: 132-135.
DE LA SALLE BROTHERS: 59-62, 106, 126-128.
DE LA SALLE, ST JOHN BAPTIST: 59-62, 126-128.
DIFFICULTIES IN RELIGIOUS LIFE: 14, 20, 37, 43, 136, 246.
DOMINIC, ST: 227-234.
DOMINICANS: 227-234.
DRESS, VALUE OF RELIGIOUS: 4, 7-8, 21, 28, 75, 108, 233.

E
EDUCATION, RELIGIOUS AND THE APOSTOLATE OF: 27, 29, 60-62, 75, 126-128, 132-134, 276-277.
ENCLOSURE: 50, 71.
EPISCOPAL VICARS FOR RELIGIOUS: 109-112.
EUCHARIST AND RELIGIOUS, THE: 17, 23, 28, 48-49, 208-211, 216, 279.
EVANGELICAL COUNSELS: 6-8, 53, 66-67, 81, 93-95, 201, 253-271.
EVANGELISATION AND RELIGIOUS: 129, 150-151, 154-156, 229-231.

F
FAITH AND RELIGIOUS: 14, 48, 90.
FAMILY APOSTOLATE AND RELIGIOUS: 88-89, 102, 109, 128-129.
FIDELITY IN RELIGIOUS LIFE: 43, 108, 154-156, 178-179, 192.
FORMATION OF RELIGIOUS: 102, 158, 293-296; ongoing formation, 55-56, 88, 136, 217; human formation, 55-56.
FRANCIS OF ASSISI, ST: 18-19, 24, 169-172, 211-214.
FRANCISCANS: Order of Friars Minor, 18-19; Capuchins, 169-172; Conventuals, 211-214.

H
HABIT, VALUE OF RELIGIOUS: 4, 7-8, 21, 28, 75, 108, 233.
HUMILITY AND RELIGIOUS: 149-151, 279-280.

I
IDENTITY OF RELIGIOUS: 80, 82-83, 246.
IGNATIUS LOYOLA, ST: 138-148, 223-226.
INSTITUTE, CHARISM OF: 10, 18, 24, 26, 61-62, 70, 83, 105, 129, 164, 192, 195, 296-301.

J
JESUITS: 106, 138-148, 220-227.
JOHN BOSCO, ST: 133-134, 275-277.
JOHN OF GOD, ST: 186-187.
JOHN OF GOD, BROTHERS OF ST: 186-187.

L
LOCAL CHURCH: and religious, 10-131; religius life its barometer, 98.
LOUISE DE MARILLAC, ST: 39-40.

M
MAJOR SUPERIORS, UNIONS OF: 123-125, 131.

MARIA DOMENICA MAZZARELLO, ST: 132-135.
MARY, THE BLESSED VIRGIN, AND RELIGIOUS: 13, 17, 19, 22, 25, 31, 35, 46-47, 49, 90-95, 101, 131, 148-151, 165, 182, 184-185, 193, 207-208, 234-235, 274, 296-301.
MODERN SOCIETY AND RELIGIOUS: 218-219.
"MUTUAE RELATIONES": 11, 80, 109-110, 112-115, 122-125, 129-132.

O
OBEDIENCE AND RELIGIOUS: 40, 53, 66-67, 94-95, 267-269.
ORDER OF ST AUGUSTINE: 216-220.
ORDER OF ST BENEDICT: monks and nuns, 84-87.
ORDER OF DISCALCED CARMELITES: friars, 120-122; nuns, 56-59, 120-122, 165-169.
ORDER OF FRIARS MINOR: 18-19; Capuchin, 169-172, Conventual, 211-214.
ORDER OF PREACHERS: 227-234.

P
PASSIONISTS:
PAUL OF THE CROSS, ST:
"PERFECTAE CARITATIS": 36, 41-44, 142, 200, 204.
POOR, RELIGIOUS AND THE: 39-40, 196-197.
POVERTY AND RELIGIOUS: 19, 40, 53, 66-67, 74, 93-94, 153-154, 233, 247, 253, 255-256, 266-267.
PRAYER AND RELIGIOUS: 7, 12, 27, 33, 43, 48-51, 57-58, 63-64, 66, 73-74, 76-78, 81, 100, 119-122, 156, 206, 212, 217-218, 235-236, 241-242, 280.
PRIESTS RELIGIOUS: 79-83; as confessors, 182.

R
REDEMPTORISTS: 287-289.
RELIGIOUS: apostolate, importance of, 24-25, 26-28, 214-215; and bishops, 8, 10-12, 105, 108-109, 109-110, 114, 122-125, 129-132, 195, 198-203, 206, 239-244; and care of the sick, 75, 186-188; and catechesis, 29, 54; and chastity, 40, 53, 66-67, 94, 263, 265-266; loyalty to the Church, 8, 18, 24-25, 26-29, 47, 54-56, 76-77, 101, 105, 108-109, 130-131, 164, 180-181, 192, 195, 206, 213, 219, 243, 293-296; and the local Church, 130-131; and communications media, 114-115, 293-296; contemplative, 5-6, 15-17, 21, 28, 33, 49-51, 54, 56-59, 62-65, 68-71, 73-74, 77-78, 99, 108, 137, 158, 162, 166-167, 172-176, 188-189, 205, 215, 282-286; and conversion, 18, 198-203, 213; and diocesan clergy, 51, 79-80, 105, 114, 130, 151, 197; and education apostolate, 27, 29, 60-62, 75, 126-128, 132-134, 276-277; and the Eucharist, 17, 23, 28, 48-49, 208-211, 216, 279; and evangelical counsels, 6-8, 53, 66-67, 81, 93-95, 201, 253-271; and evangelisation, 129, 150-151, 154-156, 229-231; and faith, 14, 48, 90; and family apostolate, 88-89, 102, 109, 128-129; formation of, 102, 158, 293-296, ongoing f., 55-56, 88, 136, 217, human f., 55-56; and humility, 149-151, 279-280; identity of, 80, 82-83, 246; and obedience, 40, 53, 66-67, 94-95, 267-269; and Our Lady, 13, 17, 19, 22, 25, 31, 35, 46-47, 49, 90-95, 101, 131, 148-151, 165, 182, 184-185, 193, 207-208, 234-235, 274, 296-301; and personal sanctifiction, 20-21, 31, 43-44, 81, 219-220, 232-233, 235, 296-301; and the poor, 39-40, 196-197; and poverty, 19, 40, 53, 66-67, 74, 93-94, 153-154, 233, 247, 253, 255-256, 266-267; and prayer, 7, 12, 27, 33, 43, 48-51, 57-58, 63-64, 66, 73-74, 76-78, 81, 100, 119-122, 156, 206, 212, 217-218, 235-236, 241-242, 280, 287-289; and society today, 218-219; and study, 206-207; and superiors, 157-158; must teach truth, 88, 293-296; and vocations, 5, 33, 55, 159; should be witnesses, 33-34, 99-100, 129, 287-289; "being" rather than "doing", 21, 33, 204-205, 215, 238, 242, 245, 296-301; "being" rather than "having", 281; and youth apostolate, 197.

RELIGIOUS HOUSES: centres of prayer, 12, 78; places of peace, 78, 89.
RELIGIOUS INSTITUTES: collaboration between, 279; communion between, 193; identity of, 70.
RELIGIOUS LIFE: and baptism, 16, 23, 25-26, 42, 96, 258-259, 285; barometer of local Church, 98; Church's teaching on, 10-12, 36, 41-44, 46, 80-81, 109-110, 112-115, 122-125, 129-132, 142, 169-171, 183, 200, 204, 253; community element in, 23-24, 33-34, 44, 52, 127, 181, 197, 205, 233, 236-237, 246-247, 272, 287-289; contemplative dimension in , 108, 296-301; difficulties in, 14, 20, 37, 43, 136, 246; fidelity in, 43, 108, 154-156, 178-179, 192; importance of, 3-4, 6-8, 9-12, 13-15, 46, 47, 65-68, 72-78, 87-89, 103-104, 112-113, 135-136, 160-163, 176-182, 183-184, 190-191, 198-203, 239-244, 247; nature of, 3-4, 6-8, 9-12, 15, 22-25, 27-28, 33-35, 37, 45-47, 52-56, 65-68, 72, 80-83, 87-89, 90-95, 96-97, 164, 184-185, 194-197, 200-201, 204-205, 212, 242-243, 248-252, 252-274, 281, 282, 285; requirements for, 30-31.
REQUIREMENTS FOR RELIGIOUS LIFE: 30-31.
ROSARY, THE: 31, 49.

S

SALESIANS: 275-277.
SALESIAN SISTERS: 132-135.
SEPARATION FROM THE WORLD: 40-41, 68, 74, 82.
SILENCE: 70-71.
SOCIETY OF JESUS: 106, 138-148, 220-227.
SOCIETY OF ST PAUL: 293-296.
STUDY: 206-207.
SUPERIORS: 71-72; superiors general, 6-9, 9-13, 32-35, 36-39, 269, 296-301; religious and, 157-158; union of major, 123-125, 131.

T

TERESA OF AVILA, ST: 119-122, 165-169, 172-176.
THERESE OF LISIEUX, ST: 64, 68-69, 71.
TRADITIONAL APOSTOLATES, IMPORTANCE OF: 35, 75, 143.

U

UNIONS OF MAJOR SUPERIORS: 123-125, 131.

V

VINCENT DE PAUL, ST: 39-40, 115-119; Daughters of Charity of, 39-41, 115-116, 118-119.
VINCENTIANS: 115-119.
VOCATIONS, PROMOTION OF: by prayer, 5, 33, 55; by witness, 5, 35.
VOWS, RELIGIOUS: 6-8, 53, 66-67, 81, 93-95, 201, 253-271.

W

WITNESS OF RELIGIOUS: 33-34, 99-100, 129, 287-289; "being" rather than "doing", 21, 33, 204-205, 215, 238, 242, 245, 296-301; "being" rather than "having", 281.
WORLD, SEPARATION FROM THE: 40-41, 68, 74, 82.

Y

YOUTH APOSTOLATE: 197.